Philippians
Pursuing Spiritual Maturity

The Bible Teacher's Guide

Gregory Brown

BTG
Publishing

I0132677

Endorsements

"The Bible Teacher's Guide … will help any teacher study and get a better background for his/her Bible lessons. In addition, it will give direction and scope to teaching of the Word of God. Praise God for this contemporary introduction to the Word of God."

—Dr. Elmer Towns
Co-founder of Liberty University
Former Dean, Liberty Baptist Theological Seminary

"Expositional, theological, and candidly practical! I highly recommend The Bible Teacher's Guide for anyone seeking to better understand or teach God's Word."

—Dr. Young–Gil Kim
Founding President, Handong Global University

"Helpful to both the layman and the serious student, The Bible Teacher's Guide, by Dr. Greg Brown, is outstanding!"

—Dr. Neal Weaver
President, Louisiana Baptist University

"Whether you are preparing a Bible study, a sermon, or simply wanting to dive deeper into a personal study of God's Word, these will be very helpful tools."

—Eddie Byun
Missions and Teaching Pastor, Venture Christian Church, Los Gatos, California
Author of Justice Awakening

"I am happy that Greg is making his insights into God's truth available to a wider audience through these books. They bear the hallmarks of good Bible teaching: the result of rigorous Bible study and thoroughgoing application to the lives of people."

—Ajith Fernando
Teaching Director, Youth for Christ
Author of A Call to Joy and Pain

"The content of the series is rich. My prayer is that God will use it to help the body of Christ grow strong."

—Dr. Min Chung
Senior Pastor, Covenant Fellowship Church, Urbana, Illinois
Adjunct Professor, Urbana Theological Seminary

"Knowing the right questions to ask and how to go about answering them is fundamental to learning in any subject matter. Greg demonstrates this convincingly."

—Dr. William Moulder
Professor of Biblical Studies, Trinity International University

"Pastor Greg is passionate about the Word of God, rigorous and thorough in his approach to the study of it... I am pleased to recommend The Bible Teacher's Guide to anyone who hungers for the living Word."

—Dr. JunMo Cho
Professor of Linguistics, Handong Global University
Contemporary Christian Music Recording Artist

"I can't imagine any student of Scripture not benefiting by this work."

—Steven J. Cole
Pastor, Flagstaff Christian Fellowship, Flagstaff, Arizona
Author of the Riches from the Word series

Contents

Preface

And entrust what you heard me say in the presence of many others as witnesses to faithful people who will be competent to teach others as well.
2 Timothy 2:2 (NET)

Paul's words to Timothy still apply to us today. The church needs teachers who clearly and fearlessly teach the Word of God. With this in mind, The Bible Teacher's Guide (BTG) series was created. This series includes both expositional and topical studies that help teachers lead small groups, pastors prepare sermons, and individuals increase their knowledge of God's Word.

We based each lesson around the hermeneutical principle that the original authors wrote in a similar manner as we do today—with the intention of being understood. Each paragraph and chapter of Scripture centers around one main thought often called the Big Idea. After finding the Big Idea for each passage studied, readers will discover the Big Question, which will lead the small group through the entire gamut of the text. Alongside the Big Question, notice the added hermeneutical questions such as Observation Questions, Interpretation Questions, and Application Questions. Observation questions point out pivotal aspects of the text. Interpretation questions lead us into understanding what the text means through looking at the context or other Scripture. Application questions lead us to life principles coming out of the text. Not all questions will be used, but they have been given to help guide the teacher in the preparation of his own lesson.

The purpose of this guide is to make the preparation of the teacher easier, as many commentaries and sermons contributed to the development of each lesson. After meditating on the Scripture text and the lesson, the small group leader can follow the suggested teaching outline, if preferred:

(1) Introduce the text and present the big question in the beginning of the study.
(2) Allow several minutes for the members to search out answers from within the text, questions, or ways God spoke to them.

(3) Then discuss the findings and lead the group along through observation, interpretation, and application questions provided in the guide.

The leader may prefer to teach the lesson, in part or in whole, and then give application questions. The leader can also choose to use a "study group" method, where each member prepares beforehand and shares teaching responsibility (see Appendices 1 and 2). Some leaders may find it most effective first to corporately read each main section in a lesson, then to follow with a brief discussion of the topic and an application question.

Again, The Bible Teacher's Guide can be used as a manual to follow in teaching, a resource to use in preparation for teaching, or simply as an expositional devotional to enrich one's own study. I pray that the Lord may bless your study, preparation, and teaching, and that in all of it you will find the fruit of the Holy Spirit abounding in your own life and in the lives of those you instruct.

Introduction

Authorship

Paul authored Philippians during his imprisonment in Rome around AD 60-62. Internal evidence of Paul's authorship includes his name being in the introduction (Phil 1:1) and the writing of the letter in general—"the entire style and wording ring with Pauline tones."[1] Commentator H.A.A. Kennedy sums up the internal evidence saying, "Perhaps no Pauline epistle bears more conclusively the stamp of authenticity. There is an artlessness, a delicacy of feeling, a frank outpouring of the heart which could not be simulated."[2]

External evidence for Pauline authorship consists of:

Those who quote the Letter early—often specifically mentioning it as by Paul—include Ignatius, Clement of Rome, Polycarp, Irenaeus, Clement of Alexandria, and Tertullian. Both Marcion's "canon" and the Muratorian Canon ascribe the book to Paul. [3]

It was the unanimous testimony of the early church that the apostle Paul wrote Philippians.[4]

In addition, Paul wrote Colossians, Philemon, and Ephesians during his imprisonment. These four books, what theologians call the Prison Epistles, "were almost assuredly written and sent at nearly the same time (about A.D. 60)."[5] Most scholars, however, give Philippians a later date of A.D. 61.[6] The reasons for this include "Paul's belief that his case would soon be decided (Phil 2:23-24)."[7] This points to Philippians being written towards the end of Paul's two year imprisonment in Rome. In addition, the time needed for letters, visits, and gifts of money to be exchanged with the Philippians also supports a later date.

Some question whether Paul wrote Philippians during his Roman imprisonment in lieu of his two-year Caesarean imprisonment or a possible Ephesian imprisonment (for which no clear evidence exists). However, "the most natural understanding of the references to the 'palace guard' (1:13) and the 'saints … of Caesar's household' (4:22) is that Paul wrote from Rome, where the emperor lived."[8] Also, the details in Philippians best fit with Paul's Roman imprisonment. For instance, Paul was guarded by Roman soldiers (cf. Acts

28:16, Phil 1:13-14), permitted to receive visitors (cf. Acts 28:30, Phil 4:18), and had opportunities to preach the gospel (cf. Acts 28:31, 1:12-14). This fits perfectly with him being under house arrest in Rome as mentioned in the book of Acts. If he was in Caesarea or Ephesus, this would have been unlikely.

Background

The Philippian church was the first church established in all of Europe. The city of Philippi was part of Macedonia which is modern day Greece. Consider Macdonald's thoughts about this momentous occasion in the history of missions:

> How Christians in the West should rejoice (and even non-Christians, if they knew of the blessed by-products of Christianity they enjoy) that Paul heeded "the Macedonian call" and turned west, not east, in his evangelization of the Roman Empire! Perhaps the continent of Asia would today be sending Christian missionaries to Europe and North America instead of vice versa, had not the gospel taken hold in Europe.[9]

Philippi was named after Alexander the Great's father, Philip of Macedon, who captured the city in 360 BC.[10] It became part of the Roman Empire in 167 BC and existed in relative obscurity for the next two centuries.[11] In 42 BC the Battle of Philippi unfolded, marking one of the greatest events in Roman history.

> The forces of Antony and Octavian defeated those of Brutus and Cassius at the Battle of Philippi, thus ending the Roman Republic and ushering in the Empire. After the battle, Philippi became a Roman colony (cf. Acts 16:12), and many veterans of the Roman army settled there.[12]

Caesar Augustus made Philippi a Roman colony—making it "Rome in miniature."[13] As a Roman colony Philippi had the same rights as cities in Italy. It used Roman law; the residents were exempt from some taxes and had Roman citizenship.[14] This also allowed them freedom from scourging and arrest and gave them the right to appeal to Caesar.[15] Latin was their official language,[16] and their coins bore Latin inscriptions.[17] From their model of government to the clothes they wore, they embodied Roman custom and practices. This brought great civic pride to the Philippians. Throughout the letter, Paul alludes to this Roman pride and loyalty, as he calls for them to similarly live as citizens of heaven on earth (cf. Phil 1:27, 3:20). Philippians 1:27 says this: "Above all, you must live as citizens of heaven, conducting yourselves in a manner worthy of the Good News about Christ" (NLT).

The church of Philippi was founded by Paul on his second missionary journey (Acts 16:12-40). While in Troas, Paul received a vision of a Macedonian man saying, "Come over to Macedonia and help us" (Acts 16:9). Immediately, Paul sailed to Macedonia with Timothy, Luke, and Silas. While in Philippi, Paul first met with women gathered at a river praying (Acts 16:13). Paul preached the gospel to them, and as a result, Lydia, a wealthy seller of purple dyed goods became a believer. Later, the Philippian church probably gathered at her house for worship (cf. Acts 16:40).

Paul encountered opposition in Philippi. While walking through the city a young lady possessed by a spirit of divination continually cried out, "These men are servants of the Most High God, who are proclaiming to you the way of salvation" (Acts 16:17). After many days of this, Paul became so troubled that he cast the demon out. This enraged her masters because they had lost their ability to earn a profit. Therefore, they dragged Paul and Silas to the marketplace to face the magistrates of Rome. Without a trial, they were stripped, beaten, and thrown into prison (Acts16:22-23).

While in prison, Paul and Silas were worshiping the Lord when a great earthquake shook open the doors of their jail cell. Thinking they had escaped, their jailer nearly killed himself before Paul reassured him they had not fled. Then the jailer cried out, "Sirs, what must I do to be saved?" And Paul answered back, "Believe in the Lord Jesus Christ and you will be saved" (Acts 16:31).

The next day the local authorities urged Paul and his companions to leave town—but, Paul refused. When the authorities learned of Paul's Roman citizenship, they were afraid because it was illegal to flog a Roman citizen. But, after another appeal from the magistrates, Paul and his companions visited Lydia's home and then left the city (Acts 16:40).

Sometime after, Paul apparently visited the Philippians twice during his third missionary journey (cf. 2 Cor 8:1-5, Acts 20:6), and throughout his ministry the church regularly supported him (Phil 4:15-16). On his journey to see Paul, Epaphroditus became sick, but God healed him. Paul wrote this epistle, in part, to thank the Philippians for their support and acknowledge Epaphroditus' faithful ministry to him (Phil 2:25-30).

Purpose

What was Paul's purpose in writing the letter? There are several: (1) Paul wrote to inform the Philippians of his imprisonment and how God was using it to further the gospel (1:12). (2) He thanked them for their gracious gift delivered through Epaphroditus (4:10-18). (3) He acknowledged Epaphroditus' faithful service in case they thought he failed (2:30). (4) He encouraged them to be unified (1:27, 2:2), and (5) he warned them of false teachers and carnal believers (3:2, 18-

19). In Philippians we see Paul's most personal and affectionate epistle. Clearly, the Philippians held a special place in his heart.

As he shares these truths, several themes arise from the letter. One of them is joy. The tone of Paul's epistle, though he was in prison, exudes joy. Paul uses forms of the words "joy" and "rejoice" more than twelve times in the book.[18] In the very beginning of the letter, Paul says how he always prays with joy for them (1:4). He commands them several times to rejoice in the Lord (Phil 3:1, 4:4). In Philippians 4:4 he says, "Rejoice in the Lord always. Again I say, rejoice." As we study this epistle, we learn something about having joy regardless of our circumstances.

Another theme is unity. Several times Paul calls for this church to be unified. In Philippians 1:27, he calls for them to stand firm "in one spirit, with one mind, by contending side by side for the faith of the gospel." In Philippians 2:2, he again calls for them to be "united in spirit." The Philippians faced many threats to their unity such as persecution (1:29-30), false teachers (Phil 3:2, 18-19), and discord (4:2). Therefore, Paul encourages them to live in unity by practicing humility and serving one another (Phil 2:1-4). As we study this epistle, we will learn something about humbling ourselves and working for unity in our daily relationships and in the church.

In addition, a major theme of the book is the pursuit of spiritual maturity. Paul prays for them to grow in spiritual maturity in Philippians 1:9-11. He prays for their love to abound in "knowledge and every kind of insight" so they could discern what is best, becoming blameless, and abounding in fruit until the day of Christ. He calls for them to have the mind of Christ in Philippians 2:5 and gives Christ's humiliation—his incarnation and death for the sins of the world—as a model to follow. Then in Philippians 3, he describes his own pursuit of knowing and being like Christ as he counts everything as nothing and makes Christ his one pursuit in life. Studying the epistle to the Philippians inspires spiritual growth.

Finally, Paul focuses on the second coming of Christ. J. A. Motyer said this:

> With six references to the Lord's coming 'day', universal exaltation and near personal return, Philippians is in line with the emphasis of the whole New Testament on the importance of this delightful expectation.[19]

Philippians 3:20 says, "But our citizenship is in heaven—and we also eagerly await a savior from there, the Lord Jesus Christ." Philippians 4:5 says, "Let everyone see your gentleness. The Lord is near!" Our study of Philippians will whet our appetites for the coming of our gracious Lord. Come Lord, Come!

14

Signs of Healthy Church Members

From Paul and Timothy, slaves of Christ Jesus, to all the saints in Christ Jesus who are in Philippi, with the overseers and deacons. Grace and peace to you from God our Father and the Lord Jesus Christ! I thank my God every time I remember you. I always pray with joy in my every prayer for all of you because of your participation in the gospel from the first day until now. For I am sure of this very thing, that the one who began a good work in you will perfect it until the day of Christ Jesus. For it is right for me to think this about all of you, because I have you in my heart, since both in my imprisonment and in the defense and confirmation of the gospel all of you became partners in God's grace together with me. For God is my witness that I long for all of you with the affection of Christ Jesus.
Philippians 1:1-8 (NET)

What does a healthy church and its members look like? Many of us don't know what a right relationship with the church looks like because of bad models or bad experiences. As a military kid, I struggled with having a healthy relationship with the church.

The fact that we were so transient kept me from ever really investing or allowing myself to really be invested in. We found a new church home for a few years, attended, and then we left.

Many of us have similar experiences. But, Paul's relationship with the Philippians shows us a model relationship with a church.

The letter to the Philippians is very unique. It's unique because many of Paul's letters deal with rebuke and correcting sin or false doctrine, as seen in the letters to Corinth and Galatia. In those letters, he began by declaring his apostleship. He declared his right to correct the issues going on in these churches. But in the letter to the Philippians, he introduces himself as a slave (or servant) of Christ (v. 1). Paul writes to them as a friend updating them on his current circumstances and encouraging them in their faith. In fact, one of the themes of this letter is joy—his joy in God and his joy over the Philippians.

Paul, at the time he wrote the letter, was imprisoned in Rome awaiting his sentence. He was chained to a Roman guard and was under house arrest (cf. Acts 28:16). It would seem like a time of great sorrow—the potential end of dreams and aspirations—but not for Paul. It was a time of great joy as he considered this wonderful church and God's faithfulness.

In this letter, specifically verses 3-8, we will see a picture of what healthy church members look like. In fact, he uses this church as a model for other churches. Consider what he says to the Corinthians:

> Now we make known to you, brothers and sisters, the grace of God given to the churches of Macedonia, that during a severe ordeal of suffering, their abundant joy and their extreme poverty have overflowed in the wealth of their generosity.
> 2 Corinthians 8:1-2

As we study this passage, we should ask ourselves, "Is my church spiritually healthy?" "Am I a spiritually healthy church member?" And if not, "In what ways can I help improve this?" In this study, we will consider seven signs of healthy church members.

Big Question: What signs of healthy church members can be discerned from Paul's relationship with the Philippian church and how can we apply these to our lives?

Healthy Church Members Think of One Another Often

> I thank my God every time I remember you.
> Philippians 1:3

We cannot but stand in awe at the thoughts of a man in prison awaiting the possibility of death (cf. Philip 1:20). Yet, while in this horrible circumstance, his thoughts continually came before the Lord in praise for the faithfulness of this church.

While many deserted Paul during his time in prison (cf. Phil 1:17), the Philippian church cared for him, prayed for him, and supported his ministry. They were a faithful church.

Again, we must consider the typical reaction of people going through a difficult time. We often are prone to becoming self-centered—thinking that the world revolves around us. We become consumed with our problems and our circumstances, but this was not true of Paul.

Despite imprisonment, Paul constantly thought about this church and thanked God for them. How about us? Do you often think about the members of your congregation and thank God for them? This is a sign of spiritual health.

Christ's Example

Did we not see this with Christ? Listen to what Hebrews 12:2 said about Christ's thoughts as he endured the cross: "...keeping our eyes fixed on Jesus, the pioneer and perfecter of our faith. For the joy set out for him he endured the cross, disregarding its shame, and has taken his seat at the right hand of the throne of God."

What was the "joy set out" for Christ? It was his church. Like Paul, Jesus, in his hour of distress, focused his thoughts on those for whom he was suffering. While on the cross, he thought about believers—those who would spend eternity with him—and it gave him joy. They were the "joy set out" for him.

Saints, as we consider what healthy church members look like, we must ask ourselves, "Do we continually think of one another?" Are thoughts of the members of our church always coming to our mind even in the midst of a busy week or a trial? Do these thoughts cause us to thank God?

Application Question: What type of thoughts should we have and to what should they lead us?

Hebrews 10:24 says this: "And let us take thought of how to spur one another on to love and good works." The writer of Hebrews said that church members should "take thought of" how they can spur one another toward love and good deeds. During the week, church members should continually think about how they can help each other love God more and love one another more—how they can help each other use their spiritual gifts for the kingdom. This is a sign of being spiritually healthy—thinking about how to help each other grow.

When someone prospers in the church, we should rejoice with them. When someone is sick, we should pray for them. When somebody mourns, we should weep with them. We should constantly think about how to stir up one another to love God and others.

Practically, when we think often of one another, it leads to acts of service. These simple acts of service might look like writing an encouraging letter, as Paul did, or taking someone to lunch to get to know them or to pray for them.

Application Question: In what ways is God calling you to consider the members of your congregation so you can stir them toward love and good deeds?

Bitter Thoughts toward God's Church

In the same way that pleasant thoughts of the church are a sign of spiritual health, unpleasant thoughts are a sign of spiritual sickness. Woe to us when our thoughts of Christ's church are unkind, jealous, angry, or bitter! Woe to us when we have negative emotions towards those for whom Christ died! James 3:14-16 says this:

> But if you have bitter jealousy and selfishness in your hearts, do not boast and tell lies against the truth. Such wisdom does not come from above but is earthly, natural, demonic. For where there is jealousy and selfishness, there is disorder and every evil practice.

Many church members harbor these types of thoughts and emotions. Perhaps their church experienced a split, the pastor had a moral failure, or the members were political. Therefore, their thoughts of church turned unpleasant. But, we must remember that the Philippian church wasn't perfect either. People grumbled and complained in the church (Phil 2:13-14). False teachers were in the church (Phil 3:2), and two women were fighting in the church (4:2). In fact, when Christ joyfully thought about us on the cross, he was aware of all our failures—we are far from perfect.

If Christ on the cross had joy thinking about his church, if Paul in prison had encouraging thoughts about the Philippians, even though they were imperfect, how much more should we have pleasant thoughts about our church throughout the week?

Application Question: If we harbor bitterness and anger towards God's church, what should we do?

1. We should forgive those who harmed and failed us in the church. Paul taught we should forgive just as Christ forgave us (Col 3:13).

2. We should pray for them. Christ said: "Bless those who curse you, pray for those who mistreat you" (Luke 6:28).

3. We should serve them as an act of love. Consider Romans 12:20-21:

   Rather, if your enemy is hungry, feed him; if he is thirsty, give him a drink; for in doing this you will be heaping burning coals on his head. Do not be overcome by evil, but overcome evil with good.

As we love them practically through forgiving, praying, and serving, we will find that our hearts will change towards them. God's grace will change our hearts toward his church.

Application Question: How are your thoughts towards the church? Are they full of bitterness, joy, or apathy? How is God calling you to work on your heart?

Healthy Church Members Pray for One Another Often

> I always pray with joy in my every prayer for all of you
> Philippians 1:4

Here we see another aspect of Paul's relationship with the Philippians, and thus a characteristic of healthy church members. He constantly prayed for the church. He said he always prayed for the church with joy.

Intercessory prayer underscored many of Paul's relationships with churches. Consider what he said in Romans 1:9-10: "For God, whom I serve in my spirit by preaching the gospel of his Son, is my witness that I continually remember you and I always ask in my prayers, if perhaps now at last I may succeed in visiting you according to the will of God."

What's most challenging about this is that he had never visited the Roman church (cf. Rom 1:13). Despite that, he said God witnessed how he constantly prayed for them at all times. For Paul, intercessory prayer for the church was not something done on occasion but constantly. He came before God and called the churches and members by name. Intercession for churches is a re-occurring theme in his epistles.

In fact, in many of his letters, he told them exactly what he prayed. In Ephesus, he prayed that they would have the spirit of wisdom and revelation to know God more (1:17). He prayed for the church to be strengthened by the Spirit in the inner man (3:16). He also prayed that they would know the depth, the height, and the width of Christ's love for them (3:17-19). For the Colossians, he prayed that they would be filled with the knowledge of God's will, that they would walk worthy of the Lord, and also bear fruit in every good work (1:9-10). Later in this letter to the Philippians, he prayed that their love for one another would grow in knowledge and wisdom so they could discern what was best (1:9-10).

Certainly, we should take lessons from Paul not only on our need to pray but also on how to pray for the church. We never see Paul praying for people's needs, wants, or even healing in the epistles. He always prayed for the church to grow in love, to be filled with the knowledge of God's will, to know God more, etc. These are the primary types of prayers we should bring before the Lord for our churches as well. It's not that the temporal doesn't matter; it's just that the spiritual is more important because it's eternal. We should remember one another every day in prayer, even as Paul did for the churches.

Constant intercession for the church shows a healthy spiritual life. But, lack of intercession flows out of an unhealthy spiritual life. When a Christian is unhealthy, his prayers will primarily be selfish—concerned with one's own needs.

Example of Christ

19

If Paul's example were not enough, we must also consider Christ's. Right before he went to the cross he prayed, "Father, sanctify them by your truth, your word is truth" (John 17:17, paraphrase). Help the disciples and those who will believe in me grow through hearing and studying the Word of God; let it be like food for them. He prays, "Father, make them one as we are one" (v. 20-22, paraphrase). Help them to be a unified church. He also prayed, "Father, keep them safe from the evil one" (17:15). Protect your saints from every attack of the devil.

Not only did Christ pray before going to the cross, he now prays in heaven for the church. Hebrews 7:25 says, "So he is able to save completely those who come to God through him, because he always lives to intercede for them." When we continually intercede for the church, we are connected to our head, Christ.

Saints, do you remember the church in your prayers daily? Do you bring struggling members of the church before the Father to receive his grace?

Example of Godly Pastors

I've studied the disciplines of other godly pastors and found that they often practice very similar disciplines as Paul and Christ. Many times they seek to cover every member in the church by name throughout the week or month.

They might list all the church members, divide them by seven, and pray for each throughout the week. Or they divide that list by thirty and pray for each member throughout the month. This is a good discipline that we should consider adopting.

Prayer for the Universal Church and Local Churches

In addition, we should not only pray for our local church, but for the universal church and other specific congregations, even as Paul did. When Scripture talks about the church being the body (Eph 4:4), many times we think first of our local church, but that is incorrect. The reality is our local church is not the body—it is only part of the body. The church universal is the body, and we should continuously pray for it, since we are connected to it and dependent upon it. In Ephesians 6:18, Paul actually commands us to pray this way. He says, "With every prayer and petition, pray at all times in the Spirit, and to this end be alert, with all perseverance and requests for all the saints." We should be alert and "at all times" keep on praying for "all the saints."

How is your prayer life? How often do you pray for your local church? How often do you intercede for the church universal? Christ did, so did Paul, and so should we.

20

Saints, we must understand how important this is—prayer is the power of the church. When the church becomes prayerless, it begins to die and becomes fruitless. This is also true of our spiritual lives. Healthy church members pray often for the church.

Application Question: How would you rate your prayer life 1-10? What tips or practices have you found effective in cultivating your prayer life?

Healthy Church Members Have Gospel Fellowship

> because of your participation in the gospel from the first day until now. For I am sure of this very thing, that the one who began a good work in you will perfect it until the day of Christ Jesus.
> Philippians 1:5-6

Next, Paul tells the church why he was so thankful and prayerful for them. He cites their participation or "partnership in the gospel" (NIV 1984). "Partnership" in Greek is the word "koinonia," which also translates as "fellowship." It simply means "to have in common with."

Most of our friendships are based on koinoinia. We partner with people because they share similar cultural experiences, similar hobbies, or similar dreams. In the same way, healthy churches and church members share a similar partnership—a partnership of the gospel.

Interpretation Question: What does gospel fellowship or "partnership in the gospel" mean?

1. Gospel partnership means people have been saved by the same gospel—the same good news.

2. Gospel partnership means people partner with one another to spread the gospel.

Paul probably focused on the latter, which is also a sign of a healthy congregation. When each member shares a common passion and ministry of spreading the gospel, it creates a tremendous fellowship. The Philippians partnered with Paul's ministry by supporting him financially and meeting his practical needs. In fact, they sent Epaphroditus to care for him while in prison (Phil 2:25), and their partnership with Paul in gospel ministry created a special bond between them. And this is true for healthy churches and church members as well.

However, let us hear this: Most members of the church know nothing about gospel fellowship. They come to church based on the fact that they share a common ethnicity or socio-economic status. They are all black, white, yellow, rich, poor, etc. That is not gospel fellowship.

You can tell it's not gospel fellowship by changing the music, the carpet, or how you take the offering in most churches. A split might happen if you do this. However, when the fellowship or the "common thing" truly centers on the gospel, there is unity.

Gospel fellowship is one of the greatest intimacies we ever experience. At times, you may meet Christians and only fellowship with them for fifteen minutes and yet find deeper fellowship than with family members. This is because of the common bond of desiring and working to see all nations know Christ. Again, many Christians know nothing of this. It is a special bond shared by those who work and sacrifice to see others know Christ.

Consider what Christ said about this in Mark 10:29-30:

> Jesus said, "I tell you the truth, there is no one who has left home or brothers or sisters or mother or father or children or fields for my sake and for the sake of the gospel who will not receive in this age a hundred times as much—homes, brothers, sisters, mothers, children, fields, all with persecutions—and in the age to come, eternal life.

Christ described the reward of sacrificing for the gospel as receiving brothers, sisters, mothers, and children. When he said this, he was talking about God's reward of intimate, familial relationships for those who sacrificially serve the kingdom. However, many Christians never experience this reward—the gospel fellowship that Paul and the Philippians shared.

Have you experienced gospel fellowship? Are you experiencing it with your church?

Application Question: How can we develop a greater gospel fellowship in our lives and in our churches?

1. We develop gospel fellowship by gathering together to pray for the lost.

In 1 Timothy 2:1-4, Paul tells Timothy that the church should pray for everyone because God desires that all be saved.

> First of all, then, I urge that requests, prayers, intercessions, and thanks be offered on behalf of all people, even for kings and all who are in authority, that we may lead a peaceful and quiet life in all godliness and dignity. Such prayer for all is good and welcomed before God our Savior, since he wants all people to be saved and to come to a knowledge of the truth.

22

This implies the church should gather to pray for "all people to be saved." Do you partner with your church to pray for the lost? This creates gospel fellowship.

2. We develop gospel fellowship by serving together, as we build God's kingdom through discipleship, evangelism, and missions.

This could be as simple as inviting people to church, evangelizing, serving, supporting missions, etc.

Do you invite people to church? Are you practicing personal evangelism with friends and church members? Are you supporting the work of missions? Are you partnering with your church to reach your city and the world for Christ? If not, your gospel fellowship will be weak or nonexistent. Healthy church members experience gospel fellowship.

Application Question: How would you characterize the fellowship of most churches? In what ways is God challenging you to foster gospel fellowship in your life and your church?

Healthy Church Members Have a Growing Confidence in God

> For I am sure of this very thing, that the one who began a good work in you will perfect it until the day of Christ Jesus.
> Philippians 1:6

Interpretation Question: What does Paul mean by being "sure" that God would complete the "good work" he began in the Philippians till the day of Christ?

"Sure" can also be translated "confident" as in the NIV 1984. Confidence is simply another word for trust or faith. Paul had great faith in God that he would complete the work that he began in the Philippians until the day of Christ.

What work was Paul talking about? What work did he believe God would complete in the life of the Philippians? Romans 8:28-29 tells us. It says,

> And we know that all things work together for good for those who love God, who are called according to his purpose, because those whom he foreknew he also predestined to be conformed to the image of his Son, that his Son would be the firstborn among many brothers and sisters.

23

In Romans 8:28-29, Paul taught that God foreknew, meaning he chose, and predestined believers to be conformed to the image of his Son. In fact, he said that God works everything out to the good so these special people will conform to Christ's image.

This means if a truly born-again person backslides, somehow God uses that backsliding for the purpose of making him like Christ. It means for those truly born again, even when they stumble, they stumble in God's direction. Even trials help a believer to look like Christ. It is a tremendous promise that believers should take great comfort in while going through trials and tribulations.

We are often quick to quote this verse, "all things work together for good for those who love God," but we must remember that "good" means looking like Christ, being holy like him. Yes, we often quote it, but the question is "Do we really have confidence in it?"

Faith in God for our Walk

Let's consider this truth first about ourselves. If we really have confidence that God is going to complete the work he began in our own lives, it should affect how we go through trials.

Application Question: How can I know if I lack faith in God to complete his work in me?

1. Be careful if you're an anxious person.

The anxious often become frantic or overwhelmed in their trials. This is because they lack confidence that the trial is ordained, the trial is chosen, and God is working in the trial to make them look like Christ. Consider these verses:

> If an alarm sounds in a city, do people not fear? If disaster overtakes a city, is the Lord not responsible?
> Amos 3:6

> I am the one who forms light and creates darkness; the one who brings about peace and creates calamity. I am the Lord, who accomplishes all these things.
> Isaiah 45:7

Do you believe that God is in control and that he works every situation for your good? Or are you a worrier and an anxious person? Worry shows a lack of faith in God.

2. Be careful if you're prone to anger or depression over your failures.

Being impatient with God or yourself also shows a lack of trust in God. These Christians often become angry at God and sometimes very angry at themselves when they fail. They get very frustrated when they fail and struggle to get back up after stumbling.

We must consider that our trials are meant to make us know God more and to have greater trust or confidence in him. In our trials and failures, God desires to draw us closer to him through his Word, prayer, and the saints. He even uses our failures to help us hate our sin so we can turn away from it and learn how to get rid of it (cf. Matt 5:30).

The situation that causes us to doubt God and fall into depression, God intends it as a breeding ground for greater faith. Let your faith in God grow, as you draw near him.

Faith in God for Others

Application Question: How can I know if I lack faith in God to complete his work in others?

We first looked at what it means to grow in faith in our own spiritual lives, but Paul in this text spoke about believing God to work in the lives of others. He was confident in God despite the Philippians' complaints (2:14), false teaching (3:2), and discord (4:2). Paul believed God is faithful.

What does this look like? How can we know if we trust God to complete his work in others?

We can tell if we have "confidence in God" to complete his work in others by how we treat them, especially in conflict or when they fail us. Listen to what Paul teaches in 2 Timothy 2:24-26 (NIV 1984):

> And the Lord's servant must not quarrel; instead, he must be kind to everyone, able to teach, not resentful. Those who oppose him he must gently instruct, in *the hope that God* will grant them repentance leading them to a knowledge of the truth, and that they will come to their senses and escape from the trap of the devil, who has taken them captive to do his will.

Paul tells Timothy the Lord's servant should not quarrel with people, but he should have a reputation of kindness, not resentment. Why? Paul says this person hopes or trusts in God to grant them repentance.

The Lord's servant is gentle and gracious, even when in a disagreement, because he trusts in God. He has proper theology. He knows it is God who changes the hearts, not him.

He knows yelling at the person will not change him, because only God grants repentance and changes hearts. The servant of the Lord still teaches and challenges, but he does it in love, with gentleness, because he realizes only God transforms lives. Scripture says we plant the seed and water it, but God makes it grow (cf. 1 Cor 3:6).

How do you treat people during a conflict? Do you trust God is going to complete the work he began in them? Certainly, this doesn't remove the need for rebuke or discipline. It just changes the manner because of our faith in God.

Are you an arguer? Are you resentful and unforgiving? If so your faith in God is small. Your confidence lies more in yourself or others, and therefore, you stay constantly frustrated.

We see an example of how Paul handled people in the church who disagreed with him in Philippians 3:15. It says, "Therefore let those of us who are 'perfect' embrace this point of view. If you think otherwise, God will reveal to you the error of your ways."

He understood that they might disagree with what he taught, but he essentially said this to them: "Stay open, God will make this clear to you." I have confidence that God will reveal these things to you.

When you look at the church, you will find much disorder—fighting over doctrine, impatience, unforgiveness, and church splits. Part of this chaos springs from a lack of trust in God to complete the work he began in others.

Confidence in God often means waiting for him to make his will clear to people in his own timing. This doctrine will heal many marriages and many churches. It will heal the hearts of many people. We must learn to trust God to complete what he began in his followers.

God, like any good teacher, doesn't teach us everything at once. If he did, we would become frustrated and overwhelmed. So, he patiently works on each area of our lives to conform us into the image of the Son. We must trust him—both in our lives and in others.

Application Question: How do you typically respond when you fail or others fail you? How can we as believers develop greater confidence in God's perfect work for each believer's life?

Healthy Church Members Love One Another

> For it is right for me to think this about all of you, because I have you in my heart, since both in my imprisonment and in the defense and confirmation of the gospel all of you became partners in God's grace together with me. For God is my witness that I long for all of you with the affection of Christ Jesus.
> Philippians 1:7-8

Another characteristic of healthy church members is love for one another. Paul had a genuine love for this congregation. He said that he had them in his "heart" in verse 7 and that he longed for them with the affection of Christ in verse 8. He loved these believers.

In addition, the Philippians loved him. They sent Epaphroditus to care for Paul's needs while he was in prison (Phil 2:25), and they supported him financially when no other church would (Phil 4:15). Paul loved this congregation, and they loved him.

In one sense, this should be true of every believer since Scripture teaches that love is a proof of salvation. First John 3:14 says, "We know that we have crossed over from death to life because we love our fellow Christians. The one who does not love remains in death."

Christ also taught that the world would identify believers by this love. In John 13:35, he said, "Everyone will know by this that you are my disciples—if you have love for one another."

Application Question: What does biblical love look like? How should we demonstrate it in the church?

1. Love is practical.

While Paul was in prison, the Philippians provided for his needs through Epaphroditus. Philippians 2:25 says, "But for now I have considered it necessary to send Epaphroditus to you. For he is my brother, coworker and fellow soldier, and your messenger and minister to me in my need."

If Paul was sick, Epaphroditus probably got him medicine. If he needed materials to study or write, he probably provided it. No doubt, when he was discouraged, he listened. The Philippians met Paul's practical needs, and we should do this for one another.

In addition, we see Paul's concern for the Philippians as he writes a letter to encourage them in the faith. First John 3:18 reiterates the importance of the practical nature of love. It says, "Little children, let us not love with word or with tongue but in deed and truth."

2. Love is forgiving.

Peter said this about love: "Above all keep your love for one another fervent, because love covers a multitude of sins" (1 Peter 4:8).

Love covers a multitude of sins; love is forgiving. To support this, Warren Wiersbe shared a story of a husband who was interviewed on a radio station about his wife. Let's consider the conversation:

"Tell us some of the blunders your wife has made," a radio quizmaster asked a contestant.

"I can't remember any," the man replied.

"Oh, surely you can remember something!" the announcer said.

"No, I really can't," said the contestant. "I love my wife very much, and I just don't remember things like that."[20]

This is very biblical. First Corinthians 13:5 (NIV 1984) says that "love keeps no record of wrongs." Sadly, many members in the church are historians. They keep a long record of wrongs which dates back years. Whenever they discuss them, it's like they're fresh in their hearts—all the bitterness comes back. However, healthy church members love one another and practice forgiving one another.

Who is God calling you to forgive?

3. Love is sacrificial.

Jesus said this: "I give you a new commandment—to love one another. Just as I have loved you, you also are to love one another" (John 13:34).

Christ taught his disciples to love as he loved. How did he love us? Christ died for us. Therefore, sacrificing for others should characterize our lives. Certainly, we see this in Epaphroditus' relationship with Paul. Epaphroditus left his home, job, and family to serve Paul who was in prison. While there, he gets sick and almost dies. His love was sacrificial.

In addition, Paul's imprisonment demonstrated his sacrifice for the Philippians and other Gentiles. In Ephesians 3:1, he said, "For this reason I, Paul, the prisoner of Christ Jesus for the sake of you Gentiles." He suffered for the Gentiles. His love for the Philippians was sacrificial. We also see this sacrifice in the early church. In Acts 2:45, the early church sold all they owned to provide for the poor in the church. No doubt, all who saw them identified them as Christ's followers (cf. John 13:34). Healthy church members love sacrificially.

Application Question: How is God challenging you to love the church more like Christ? How can we grow in this radical, Christlike love?

Healthy Church Members Share God's Grace with One Another

For it is right for me to think this about all of you, because I have you in my heart, since both in my imprisonment and in the defense and confirmation of the gospel all of you became partners in God's grace together with me.

Philippians 1:7

Next, Paul says it was right for him to have such deep-seated thoughts, love, and affection for this church. It was appropriate because whether he was in prison, defending the Word of God, or preaching the Word of God, they shared in God's grace with him.

Interpretation Question: What does Paul mean by the Philippians sharing in God's grace with him?

To share in God's grace simply means they supported him as a ministry from God. When Paul had needs, the Philippian church supported and encouraged him. In fact in chapter 4, he talked about how no other church shared with him financially but them (Phil 4:14). They were there for him; they allowed themselves to be conduits of God's grace to Paul.

Consider how Paul boasted about the Philippians when addressing the Corinthian church. Second Corinthians 8:1-2 says this:

> Now we make known to you, brothers and sisters, the grace of God given to the churches of Macedonia, that during a severe ordeal of suffering, their abundant joy and their extreme poverty have overflowed in the wealth of their generosity.

He said that even though the Philippians, who were part of the Macedonian churches, were struggling themselves, God's grace was manifest through them. In their great poverty, they gave exceedingly to support the struggling church in Jerusalem. Paul saw this giving as a grace of God. The Philippians allowed God to work through them.

This grace is not only seen in using our finances but specifically in using our spiritual gifts to build up others. Consider what Paul says in Romans 12:5-8:

> so we who are many are one body in Christ, and individually we are members who belong to one another. And we have different gifts according to the grace given to us. If the gift is prophecy, that individual must use it in proportion to his faith. If it is service, he must serve; if it is teaching, he must teach; if it is exhortation, he must exhort; if it is contributing, he must do so with sincerity; if it is leadership, he must do so with diligence; if it is showing mercy, he must do so with cheerfulness.

We share God's grace by using our spiritual gifts to bless others. They are gifts of his grace. Some have the gift of mercy—meaning they can listen to people and feel their pain and empathize. Some have the gift of exhortation, the ability to challenge and encourage people. Many will not grow in their spiritual lives unless challenged. This is how the body of Christ grows. Paul said this in Ephesians 4:16: "From him the whole body grows, fitted and held together through every supporting ligament. As each one does its part, the body grows in love." Churches grow as each person uses God's grace to build one another up.

In a sense, God's grace is not just about giving of one's finances or using one's spiritual gifts. It is using all of the abilities God gave us to advance his kingdom. Are you sharing the grace God gave you to build up his church? Are you allowing God to work through you to build up other Christians? This is a characteristic of spiritual health.

Are you using God's grace? Or are you a lone ranger Christian, not serving or getting involved in the life of the church? It is possible for God's grace to be without effect in us—meaning not used. Paul said this about the grace God gave him. "But by the grace of God I am what I am, and his grace to me has not been in vain. In fact, I worked harder than all of them—yet not I, but the grace of God with me" (1 Cor 15:10).

In Paul's life God's grace was not without effect. This means he used God's grace. He worked hard with it to build up God's church. It must be the same for us. Sadly, very few in the church faithfully use God's grace, which handicaps the church.

If the church is a body, then when one part is not working, it hinders the ministry of God's church. Most churches are handicapped because the members do not exercise their gifts. It has been said that only 20% of the church does all the work. What about the other 80%? Can you imagine how effective churches would be if they were operating at 100% capacity?

What grace has God given you? In what ways is God calling you to get involved in your church? Some don't have much time, but they come to church to greet people at the door. Some have a God-given ability to make money. He gave it so they could advance the kingdom through showing hospitality, giving, and living sacrificially.

A believer might be asking these questions, "How can I know what my spiritual gift is? How can I find it?"

Spiritual gifts are given to build up the church (1 Cor 12:7). One finds them by serving and getting involved with the body of Christ. In the midst of teaching, listening, serving, helping, leading, etc., you will find that God has given you grace in a certain area or areas. It will edify others and it will edify you (1 Cor 14:4).

In what way have you received grace? Healthy church members use God's grace to build God's church.

Application Question: What are your spiritual gifts? How do you feel God has called you to use it in building God's church?

Healthy Church Members Long to Be with the Church

> For God is my witness that I long for all of you with the affection of Christ Jesus.
> Philippians 1:8

Finally, Paul declared how he longed for the Philippians with the affections of Christ. "Affection" is an interesting word in the Greek. It is a medical word used for the bowels or intestines (cf. Acts 1:18). This word started to be used for compassion or affection since we often feel our greatest emotions in our stomach. When a person is nervous, he feels it in his stomach. When a person really likes someone, he often feels it right in his gut.

Essentially, Paul said that he felt the same affection Christ felt for them and that he desired to meet with them. Paul missed these saints while away in prison and desired to meet with them.

It's the same for other healthy Christians. Because they are intimate with Christ, they feel his affection for the saints, and they continually want to meet with them.

Consider what Paul said in other passages about longing for the church:

> But when we were separated from you, brothers and sisters, for a short time (in presence, not in affection) we became all the more fervent in our great desire to see you in person. For we wanted to come to you (I, Paul, in fact tried again and again) but Satan thwarted us.
> 1 Thessalonians 2:17-18

> I am thankful to God, whom I have served with a clear conscience as my ancestors did, when I remember you in my prayers as I do constantly night and day. As I remember your tears, I long to see you, so that I may be filled with joy.
> 2 Timothy 1:3-4

> and I always ask in my prayers, if perhaps now at last I may succeed in visiting you according to the will of God. For I long to see you, so that I may impart to you some spiritual gift to strengthen you
> Romans 1:10-11

Paul longed to meet with the Philippians, with the Thessalonians, with Timothy, and even with the Romans whom he had never met. This is a sign of spiritual health in a Christian.

Listen, Saints, if you don't long to meet with the church then something is wrong with your spiritual life. If you are growing in your relationship with Christ, then you will naturally grow in your love and longing for the church as well. Paul said I long for you with the loins of Christ—the very inner parts of Christ were yearning through Paul to be with this church.

I often hear Christians say, "Oh, I am a Christian, but I don't need to go to church to practice my faith." Yes, maybe you don't need to, but you will want to if you are a true Christian and a healthy Christian at that. Love for Christians is a characteristic of genuine salvation, and when you really love someone, you always desire to meet with them. First John 3:14 says, "We know that we have crossed over from death to life because we love our fellow Christians. The one who does not love remains in death." A lack of desire to meet with the church may prove a lack of love and therefore true salvation.

When one is saved, God gives him a love for the church. Romans 5:5 says, "the love of God has been poured out in our hearts through the Holy Spirit who was given to us." He gives believers the ability to love God and one another. And it is natural when you love someone to want to meet them and to long for them.

Since Christ died for the church and he lives in us, it will be natural to continually long for the one he died for. It will be natural to yearn with the affections of Christ.

Do you long for the church? Do you long to meet with brothers and sisters throughout the week for fellowship and prayer? Or does your "longing" for work, success, and wealth overtake Christ's passion within you? Are you a healthy Christian?

Healthy Christians want to be with one another, and they meet as often as possible. Hebrews 10:25 says, "…not abandoning our own meetings, as some are in the habit of doing, but encouraging each other, and even more so because you see the day drawing near."

The early church who lived in the wake of Christ's coming met every day from house to house breaking bread (Acts 2:46). Because they longed for one another, they met as much as possible. This natural desire should be growing in us "even more so" as we see the day approaching (Heb 10:25).

Do you long to meet with believers throughout the week? Do you want to live life with the people of God?

Interpretation Question: What are some of the reasons Paul longed to meet with believers?

Why did Paul long for them? Why should we long to meet with our brothers and sisters in Christ? Here are a couple of healthy reasons:

1. Accountability

Listen again to 1 Thessalonians 3:5: "So when I could bear it no longer, I sent to find out about your faith, for fear that the tempter somehow tempted you and our toil had proven useless."

We should desire to meet with believers to see how they are doing spiritually. We should meet with believers to find out the temperature in their spiritual life. We should ask them how their relationship with God is, their devotional life, their battle with temptation, etc. Paul wanted to know, so he sent Timothy to find out (1 Thess 3:2).

2. To Study the Bible

Romans 1:11 says, "For I long to see you, so that I may impart to you some spiritual gift to strengthen you." Most commentators believe this spiritual gift was his teaching of the book of Romans and not a charismatic gift of some sort. He wanted to help them grow by teaching them the Word of God (cf. 1 Peter 2:2).

3. Mutual Encouragement

In Romans 1:11-12, we see another reason to meet together. Paul said, "For I long to see you, so that I may impart to you some spiritual gift to strengthen you, that is, that we may be mutually comforted by one another's faith, both yours and mine."

We should long to meet with others not just to give but also so we can receive—to be mutually encouraged by others' faith. Similarly, Paul said this to Timothy: "As I remember your tears, I long to see you, so that I may be filled with joy" (2 Tim 1:4).

I'm sure much of the depression in the church is because many do not have healthy fellowship with others. Paul longed not only to give, not only to check up on them, but also to receive and be encouraged. Oh, there is joy in meeting with the people of God! There is joy in the midst of God's people!

What does your Christian fellowship look like? Are you longing? Do you long to see believers to impart a spiritual gift? Do you long to see them to make sure they have not been tempted by the devil? Do you long to see them for mutual encouragement?

Application Question: How is your longing to meet with the saints? How is God calling you to grow in this endeavor? Why is it so important?

Conclusion

What are signs of spiritually healthy church members?

1. Healthy Church Members Think of One Another Often
2. Healthy Church Members Pray for One Another Often
3. Healthy Church Members Have Gospel Fellowship
4. Healthy Church Members Have a Growing Confidence in God
5. Healthy Church Members Love One Another
6. Healthy Church Members Share God's Grace with One Another
7. Healthy Church Members Long to Be with the Church

Application Question: How is God challenging you to grow in your relationship with his church?

Marks of Spiritual Maturity

And I pray this, that your love may abound even more and more in knowledge and every kind of insight so that you can decide what is best, and thus be sincere and blameless for the day of Christ, filled with the fruit of righteousness that comes through Jesus Christ to the glory and praise of God.
Philippians 1:9-11 (NET)

What are marks of a person who is growing in spiritual maturity? How do I know if I am growing spiritually?

Spiritual life has often been compared to walking upstream. If you are not progressing forward, then you are going backwards. The waves of the world are too powerful; the ungodly TV shows, the ungodly music, the depraved culture of this world are always seeking to push a believer backwards. Therefore, we must always seek to progress in our spiritual lives; otherwise, we will be spiritually declining.

Paul wrote this letter to the church of Philippi. Here in this text, he was praying for them to continue to progress spiritually. He was not praying because they lacked maturity. As seen throughout the letter, the Philippians were a very special church that he enjoyed tremendously. They were the only church in Paul's early ministry that supported him financially (Phil 4:15). He spoke of his pleasant thoughts and memories of her and how he loved this church with the loins of Christ (1:1-8). In many ways, the Philippians were a model church.

However, this church was not perfect, and no church, on this side of glory, will be. It needed to continue to progress. Therefore, in Philippians 1:9-11, Paul shares his prayers for her—prayers consumed with the church's spiritual growth.

As we look at Paul's prayer, it should encourage us in our own prayer lives—it should encourage us in how to pray and what to pray. Many times our prayers are very obscure. We say, "Bless sister Martha." "Bless our church." "Bless our country." However, it only makes sense that if we are bringing a petition before the One who has all power that our petitions would be specific.

In addition, Paul's prayer should challenge us in the area of our spiritual growth. As we study this passage, we must ask ourselves, "Are we progressing spiritually as individuals and as a congregation?" We are always either growing or going backwards. Our spiritual life is never standing still.

Big Question: What specific petitions does Paul pray for the Philippian church? What do these petitions teach us about a mature Christian?

A Mature Christian Is Marked by Abounding Love

> And I pray this, that your love may abound even more and more
> Philippians 1:9

The first mark of a mature Christian is continually abounding in love. Christ said all of the laws were summed up in love. Matthew 22:37-40 says this:

> Jesus said to him, "'Love the Lord your God with all your heart, with all your soul, and with all your mind. This is the first and greatest commandment."

He also taught that love would be the mark of every true follower of Christ. He said this: "Everyone will know by this that you are my disciples—if you have love for one another" (John 13:35).

If we are growing in Christ, we will see ourselves both loving God more and loving others more. When people see us, they should see someone who is enamored more and more with God and people. Christians are identified by this. Consider what David said in Psalm 16:2-3 (NIV 1984): "I said to the LORD, 'You are my Lord; apart from you I have no good thing.' As for the saints who are in the land, they are the glorious ones in whom is all my delight."

David said the Lord was his focus in life and that all his delight was in the saints. This is something that should be seen in each one of us. We should love God and love people more.

In addition, one of the marks of a mature church is its continual growth in love. People come into these congregations and are overwhelmed with a sense of love. In contrast, a characteristic of an immature church is that when people visit, they are alienated and left out. They don't feel welcomed or loved.

What are further characteristics of this love?

This is an important question because most people don't know how to define love. What is love? Is love primarily a feeling? Is love a bunch of butterflies in one's stomach? I often hear people trying to describe their intimate relationships with, "I love him, but I don't know if am 'in love' with him." What does that mean?

In the Greek, Paul used the word, agape—God's love. What are characteristics of agape love?

36

Interpretation Question: What is agape love? What are its characteristics?

1. Love is resident in every believer.

Again, Philippians 1:9 says, "And I pray this, that your love may abound even more and more in knowledge and every kind of insight."

One of the things we must notice about this love is that the Philippians already possessed it. He prays that the love they already possess would abound more and more. As mentioned previously, agape—God's love—is a characteristic of every person who is truly born again. One commentator says this about the Philippians' love:

> At Philippi, love showed itself to be of the very essence of the new nature given to the believer. No sooner had Lydia become a Christian than she pressed Paul and his company to become her house-guests. No sooner had the jailor become a Christian than, though he had earlier fastened the apostle's feet in the stocks, he began to bathe his wounds. When the hostility of the people made Paul leave Philippi, the church, by contrast, identified with the persecuted apostle (verses 5–7) and sent him help more than once (4:16). Love was their new nature in Christ.[21]

Similarly, look at what Paul said to the Thessalonians about their love:

> Now on the topic of brotherly love you have no need for anyone to write you, for you yourselves are taught by God to love one another. And indeed you are practicing it toward all the brothers and sisters in all of Macedonia. But we urge you, brothers and sisters, to do so more and more.
> 1 Thessalonians 4:9-10

Paul said of the Thessalonians that God had taught them to love each other and that they already loved all the brothers throughout Macedonia. They did not only love people in their local church but even those in Philippi, as that was part of Macedonia. Love is resident in every believer because God has given it to them, and he is constantly teaching believers to love more and more. In fact, John said this: "We know that we have crossed over from death to life because we love our fellow Christians. The one who does not love remains in death" (1 John 3:14).

Every person who is truly born again loves the family of God. They love one another. John also said this: "Dear friends, let us love one another, because love is from God, and everyone who loves has been fathered by God and knows God. The person who does not love does not know God, because God is love" (1 John 4:7-8).

Agape love was immediately poured out into believers when they got saved. Romans 5:5 says this: "And hope does not disappoint, because the love of God has been poured out in our hearts through the Holy Spirit who was given to us."

2. Agape love is decisive—an act of the will.

As mentioned previously, often love is thought of as primarily a feeling. When someone says they love a person, that typically means he or she has strong feelings towards that person. However, love may or may not include strong feelings. Love is primarily an act of the will. Listen again to what Christ said in John 13:34: "I give you a new commandment—to love one another. Just as I have loved you, you also are to love one another."

This might not make sense to someone who only thinks of love as a feeling. How can you command your feelings? We've all heard this said before, "I can't choose who I fall in love with." However, Scripture would not affirm this. Love is an act of the will. That is why God can command us to not only love fellow believers but even our enemies. Look at what Christ said in Matthew 5:44-45:

> But I say to you, love your enemy and pray for those who persecute you, so that you may be like your Father in heaven, since he causes the sun to rise on the evil and the good, and sends rain on the righteous and the unrighteous.

How can someone "love" his enemies? It is only possible because love is an act of the will—an act of obedience to God. We can love because God has commanded us to do so. In fact, Scripture even declares that biblical love is obedient. Christ said this:

> If you love me, you will obey my commandments.
> John 14:15

> The person who has my commandments and obeys them is the one who loves me. The one who loves me will be loved by my Father, and I will love him and will reveal myself to him.
> John 14:21

When Jesus talked about love, he said that love and obedience to God were synonymous. Whoever loves Christ will obey his commands. Whoever does not love Christ will not obey his commands.

38

Love is decisive. It is an act of the will. I choose to love God. I choose to love my neighbors by serving them. I choose to love my enemies by praying for them and blessing them. I may not feel like doing this, but as an act of obedience to God—an act of the will—I choose to love them.

That is why I don't understand when Christian couples say, "We just fell out of love, so we decided to get a divorce." That doesn't make sense. If the foundation of our relationships is based on feelings then our relationships will always be unstable. Feelings come and go based on circumstances such as what you ate for lunch. Feelings are affected by being sick. But, love truly is an act of the will. I love you Lord, so I will obey you. I love my roommate so I will pray for him. I love my church members so I will serve them.

Paul is praying for this church to grow in loving one another. The fact that "love" is an act of the will makes every person more accountable. If it was an elusive feeling that we couldn't control, how could God judge us based on the fact that we don't love him and we don't love our neighbor. But, the fact that love is a choice—an act of the will—means that we all are responsible to love one another and God as Scripture commands.

Application Question: In what ways has God called you to demonstrate love towards someone when you didn't feel like loving him or her?

3.   Agape love is dynamic—it should be growing.

As already mentioned, another characteristic of agape love is that it should be constantly growing. Paul prays that the love of these believers would abound—that it would overflow. One of the characteristics of believers who are maturing and growing in Christ is that their love for God and their love for one another is growing.

Let us be afraid when our love is stagnant. It is possible to simply attend church every Sunday and exist in the same community without our love increasing. We constantly see one another. We see one another's children grow up, and we go to the same small group, but our love for one another is not growing. Lord, forgive us for having a stagnant love.

Living in a church community is the perfect place for this love to grow and to be fostered. When someone is sick, we have a chance to not only pray for them but to find ways to serve them in their sickness. We have a chance to stretch our love for one another in the midst of the difficulties of life. Many times it is during trials that our love for one another is forced to stretch and grow.

Also, let us hear that not only are trials the perfect time for our love to grow but specifically while in conflict. Many people see conflict as the antithesis of love, but this is not true. Conflict can often be the catalyst for loving more. The roommate that gets on our nerves, the co-worker or employer that is

39

impossible to deal with—those are people and situations that can stretch our love. They are opportunities for us to grow in love for someone.

Listen to what Peter said about the Christian's responsibility to love: "You have purified your souls by obeying the truth in order to show sincere mutual love. So love one another earnestly from a pure heart" (1 Peter 1:22).

When he calls for believers to love one another earnestly, it can also be translated "fervently." It was a word used of a muscle being stretched to the furthest limit. Many times that is exactly what God allows in our lives so that our love can grow. In conflict, he stretches it and forces it to grow.

It's just like going to the gym. When a person works out, the muscles are stretched and fatigued by carrying a certain load. By carrying that load one is telling the muscles, "You must grow stronger in order to carry this load!" In response the muscles grow bigger, develop more strength, and more endurance.

It's the same with us. It is hard to grow in love for people that we are not often around or that we know only at a surface level. Many times, by going through difficulties together, our love is stretched so that it can grow. This is also true in our relationship with God. He often increases our love for him through stretching our love in the midst of trials or difficulties.

Paul's prayer for the Philippian church that already loved God and loved one another was that their love would abound.

Are you increasing in your love for God? Are you increasing in your love for the brothers and sisters in your church? Are you partnering with them in difficulties? Are you lifting them up in prayer? Are you willing to humble yourself in the midst of conflict to love them more?

Spiritually mature Christians are not stagnant—they have not peaked in their love. They are seeking for it to grow. They are seeking for it to abound both towards God and towards others. In fact, what marks them as mature is the fact that they are still growing more and more in love with God every day and they are growing more and more in love with their neighbor every day.

Application Question: What ways has God stretched your love in order for you to both love God and others more? Or in what ways has your heart been hurt resulting in a struggle to love?

4. Agape love should be increasing in knowledge.

And I pray this, that your love may abound even more and more in knowledge and every kind of insight.
Philippians 1:9

Paul prays for the Philippians' love to grow more in knowledge and insight. He is praying for their love to be intelligent. Often we hear comments like "love is blind." Love is not blind—love is intelligent and wise.

When you are truly in love with somebody or something, the natural reaction is for you to increase in "knowledge" of that person or thing. If a person really loves the NBA, then they will spend a tremendous amount of time reading up on their favorite team or player. If a person really loves another person, they commonly will get married and spend the rest of their lives getting to know that person intimately.

Here is a tip for single people. When you go on a date with a person and this person doesn't ask you questions and only talks about him or herself, that is a problem. That means they really don't care about you. When someone really loves someone or something, the natural inclination is to increase in knowledge of that person or thing. Because there is much more that could be said about growing in knowledge, we will cover this as a second characteristic of a maturing Christian.

5. Agape love is judicious.

He prays for the love to not only grow in knowledge but every kind of insight. "Insight" can be translated "discernment." Love always is discerning so it can choose what is best. As with the previous point, I have chosen to expand this in a later section as a mark of spiritual maturity.

Application Question: What are some common ways that the world defines love? How does that compare to biblical love? In what ways is God challenging you to grow in love for him and others?

A Mature Christian Is Marked by Growing Knowledge

> And I pray this, that your love may abound even more and more in knowledge and every kind of insight.
> Philippians 1:9

Interpretation Question: What type(s) of knowledge is Paul praying for this church to grow in?

What type of knowledge must we be growing in as believers? I think we can tell by the context. In verse 10 he says, "so that you can decide what is best." What type of knowledge is needed in order for us to discern what is best?

1. A mature Christian is growing in the knowledge of Scripture.

41

One of the reasons that many people can't discern what is best when they are trying to find a job or pick a mate for the future is because they don't know the Word of God. David said this: "Your word is a lamp to walk by, and a light to illumine my path" (Psalm 119:105). When the lights are on, it is easier to have discernment and make the best decisions.

One can't know what is best if he/she doesn't know the Word of God. It is a necessary component of a mature Christian's life. They are constantly abounding in the knowledge of the Word of God.

We never peak in understanding the Word of God. The Word of God is "simple enough that a child can understand it but deep enough that a scholar can drown in it." A mature Christian is not stagnant in his knowledge of the Bible. He is always seeking to abound in it, seeking to understand it more, seeking to teach it more, and seeking to obey it more.

Just as we can never have enough love, we can never have enough knowledge of Scripture. This is a characteristic of mature Christians. As they know God's Word better, they are better able to discern what is best in all areas of life (cf. 1 Cor 2:15).

2. A mature Christian is growing in the knowledge of God.

We see Paul pray for this all the time in his letters. Consider what he said in Ephesians and Colossians:

> I pray that the God of our Lord Jesus Christ, the Father of glory, may give you spiritual wisdom and revelation in your growing knowledge of him.
> Ephesians 1:17

> For this reason we also, from the day we heard about you, have not ceased praying for you and asking God to fill you with the knowledge of his will in all spiritual wisdom and understanding.
> Colossians 1:9

Now this knowledge is not primarily academic, it is experiential. The Greek and Hebrew word for "know" typically speak of a deep, intimate, and experiential knowledge. In the Old Testament, it was used of sexual relations. Adam "knew" his wife (Gen 4:1, KJV). A mature Christian is growing in an intimate knowledge of God.

We see this in the narratives and writings of the mature believers in the Bible. Moses who spoke to God face to face, prayed for God to show him his glory (Ex 33:18). He prayed to see God in an even more intimate way.

David said this to God: "As a deer longs for streams of water, so I long for you, O God! I thirst for God, for the living God. I say, 'When will I be able to go and appear in God's presence?'" (Psalm 42:1-2).

Paul said this about Christ: "My aim is to know him, to experience the power of his resurrection, to share in his sufferings, and to be like him in his death, and so, somehow, to attain to the resurrection from the dead" (Philippians 3:10-11).

David was desperate to know God and so was Paul. Paul wanted to suffer and die like Christ. He wasn't just looking for academic knowledge; he wanted to continually experience Christ. He wanted the power and sufferings of Christ in his life. This is a characteristic of mature believers. They are constantly seeking to know God more, and this knowledge allows them to discern what is best.

Proverbs 9:10 says, "The beginning of wisdom is to fear the Lord, and acknowledging the Holy One is understanding." This seems to be written in a form of Hebrew parallelism. To fear God is to acknowledge the Holy One, and to have wisdom is to have understanding. The more we know God, the more we will be able to discern what is best and to make wise decisions. Mature Christians are growing in the knowledge of God.

3. A mature Christian is growing in the knowledge of others.

In order to discern what is best for my daughter, not only do I need to know what Scripture says and need to know God more, but I also need to know the way God made my daughter. Is she gifted in athletics? Is she very talented in music? Proverbs 22:6 says this: "Train a child in the way that he should go, and when he is old he will not turn from it."

It can also be translated this way: "Initiate a child in accordance with his way" (Pulpit Commentary). This means that in order to best train my daughter, I not only need to teach her Scripture, but I also need to help her discern the way God made her—the way she is wired. I am not here to conform her into my image. She doesn't have to play basketball, join the military, or write books (all things I wouldn't mind her doing). God may have made her different than me. I think one of the reasons so many children rebel at some point in life is because they were molded into their parents' way, the world's way, or the church's way instead of the way God made them.

God already has a plan for my daughter. My wife and I need to help in the process of discerning God's plan. If I really love and want what's best for her, I need to help her discern the way she is wired.

It's the same with my wife. First Peter 3:7 says I need to dwell with my wife "according to knowledge" (KJV). I need to know her and understand her. That is the only way I can serve her best and also help her discern what is best.

This is why any good counselor is not only going to teach a person truth but also ask important questions in order to help guide him along "his way."

Similarly, mature church members are constantly trying to get to know one another more. They are seeking to know one another so they can better serve and encourage others in the way God uniquely created them.

How is God calling you to get to know others in your church, school, or work place better? Maybe, he is calling you to ask someone out to lunch, dinner, or coffee? Maybe, he is calling you to ask someone questions and just listen.

Are you growing in the knowledge of the Word of God? Are you growing in the knowledge of God—growing in intimacy with him? Are you growing in the knowledge of others?

Application Question: How would you rate your growth in "knowledge" in these three categories: knowing God's Word, knowing God, and knowing others? What strategies do you believe God is calling you to implement to increase your knowledge? Be specific.

A Mature Christian Is Marked by Spiritual Discernment

> And I pray this, that your love may abound even more and more in knowledge and every kind of insight so that you can decide what is best, and thus be sincere and blameless for the day of Christ
> Philippians 1:9-10

The next mark of a mature Christian is spiritual discernment. This is emphasized twice in verses 9 and 10. He prays for the church's love to grow in knowledge and "every kind of insight." As mentioned, "every kind of insight" in verse 9 can also be translated discernment or judgment (NASB, KJV). Discernment is again mentioned in verse 10. Hendricks adds this about the addition of the phrase "every kind of insight."

> A person who possesses love but lacks discernment may reveal a great deal of eagerness and enthusiasm. He may donate to all kinds of causes. His motives may be worthy and his intentions honorable, yet he may be doing more harm than good. Also, such an individual may at times be misled doctrinally.[22]

The word "decide" in verse 10 can be translated "approve" or "examine." It was used of a metallurgist testing metals or coins to determine their purity or genuineness.[23] In Luke 12:56, it is translated "interpret or analyze." Look at what it says: "You hypocrites! You know how to interpret the appearance of the earth and the sky, but how can you not know how to interpret the present time?"

Christ rebuked the Pharisees because they could discern the weather by looking at the signs, but they couldn't determine the present time with the messiah standing right in front of them.

Maybe Paul was emphasizing discernment because of the false teaching that was happening in the church. It seems that Judaizers were in the church calling the Christians back to circumcision and the law (Philippians 3:2). There also was division happening in the church (Philippians 4:2), and the Philippians needed a wise love to know how to handle these situations. They needed discernment which is a sign of spiritual maturity.

We often see this lack of maturity in a child's inability to discern. Toddlers may know what a car is but they typically can't tell the difference between a Toyota and a Lamborghini. To them they are both just a "Car!" When my daughter Saiyah was younger, she really liked tea. I don't understand why, but she did. However, with Saiyah everything was "tea." "Saiyah, do you want some milk?" She would look at you and say, "Tea!" We would say, "Saiyah, do you want some cheese?" She would respond, "Tea!" For her it was all the same. Everything she ate was tea.

However, as she got older she learned to discern the differences. "No, this is a T-bone steak. This is better than tea." Discernment is a mark of growing in maturity.

It's the same with our spiritual lives. Paul says one of the reasons that God gave pastors and teachers to the church was to help the congregation grow into maturity so they would no longer be like children tossed to and fro with every form of doctrine (Ephesians 4:14). A spiritual child can't always tell what is most healthy for them. They often will accept teaching that does not line up with Scripture, and therefore, they are often prey for cults or self-help Christianity. The spiritually immature often can't discern what is best.

But, those who are mature can not only discern between good and bad but also between what is good and what is best. The spiritually mature are marked by testing everything and choosing what is best—choosing what is best for others and choosing what is best for their spiritual lives.

When a young Christian will listen to just about any music, watch just about any TV show, hang out with just about any people, the spiritually mature instead practices discernment in order to do what is best for his spiritual life and others. This is what marks the spiritually mature and that's what Paul prayed for this church. He prayed that their love would grow in knowledge so they could choose what is excellent.

Paul will say the same thing later on in the book. Listen to what he says in Philippians 4:8-9:

Finally, brothers and sisters, whatever is true, whatever is worthy of respect, whatever is just, whatever is pure, whatever is lovely, whatever is commendable, if something is excellent or praiseworthy, think about these things. And what you learned and received and heard and saw in me, do these things. And the God of peace will be with you.

Did you see what he said? He commands them to think on what is excellent and praiseworthy. He also commands them to practice what they have heard or seen in Paul and then the God of peace would be with them. Mature Christians practice this discernment in their entertainment, their relationships, their church activities, etc., so they can always think on what is "excellent." The result of this is the manifest presence of God being in their lives. The spiritually mature have God's anointing on their lives because they choose what is best in order to know God and do his will. This is what marked Moses, David, Paul, and other great saints—choosing what is best and excellent.

Do you practice discernment in your hobbies, your career ambitions, your friendships, and even your meditations in order to live in the presence of God? Are you a mature Christian? Or do you watch things, listen to things, go to certain places, and hang out with certain people that would not be what is best for your life or others?

Mature Christians are discerners who test everything to hold onto what is good and best for their spiritual life and others. They put everything into the fire—to see if it is excellent.

Interpretation Question: How can we practice this type of discernment in order to choose what is best?

1. Mature Christians test everything by the Word of God.

Hebrews 5:13-14 says this:

For everyone who lives on milk is inexperienced in the message of righteousness, because he is an infant. But solid food is for the mature, whose perceptions are trained by practice to discern both good and evil.

The writer of Hebrews says the mature can distinguish between good and evil because of their "practice" of the "message of righteousness." They are constantly using the Word of God. They don't just hear it on Sundays and in small group, but they are using it daily to share it with others, to study it, and to pray through it. And, because of this, they develop the ability to distinguish.

The Christian that can go long periods of time without having a daily quiet time is going to have a very hard time distinguishing not only between good and evil but the good and the best. It has often been said the enemy of the best is often the good. Young Christians often have many good things in their lives, but these good things keep them from what is best.

Are you constantly using the Word of God in order to develop spiritual discernment?

What else is needed to develop spiritual discernment?

2. Mature Christians test everything by discerning what edifies.

First Corinthians 10:23-24 says, "'Everything is lawful,' but not everything is beneficial. 'Everything is lawful,' but not everything builds others up. Do not seek your own good, but the good of the other person"

Mature Christians ask, "Will this build me up?" "Will this build others up?" If not, then maybe I should not do it. Immature Christians typically just ask, "Is this sin?" or "Is this OK for me to do?" Just because it is OK or not morally wrong doesn't mean that it is best. We should ask, "Does it edify?"

3. Mature Christians test everything by discerning what is evil.

Paul said in 1 Thessalonians 5:21-22, "But examine all things; hold fast to what is good. Stay away from every form of evil."

The other necessity of developing spiritual discernment is a willingness to avoid every kind of evil. Some versions say, "Abstain from all appearance of evil." Many Christians don't like that verse. It is too limiting. "Abstain from all appearance of evil." If it is promoting sexual immorality, if it is teaching different values on marriage or one's body image, don't listen to it. Don't watch it. Just avoid it.

Many Christians are unwilling to do that, and therefore, they remain in a state of immaturity. Satan continues to have a door into their lives.

Mature Christians test everything through the Word of God, and they are willing to abstain from all appearance of evil. They are pursuing "the best in priorities—the best in habits—the best in pleasures—the best in pursuits—the best course of action for themselves and for their families."[24]

Application Question: What are some areas in your life in which you are prone to accept or practice things that are not best?

A Mature Christian Is Marked by Spiritual Integrity

so that you can decide what is best, and thus be sincere and blameless for the day of Christ

Philippians 1:10

Interpretation Question: What does it mean to be sincere and blameless?

Next, Paul prays for the Philippians to be sincere and blameless which refers first to the inner attitudes and then to the outward behavior. In general, he is praying for spiritual integrity. Integrity really is the practice of honesty and morality no matter the situation—even when nobody is looking. Let's look at how he calls for integrity first by looking at the word "sincere."

Sincere

The word "sincere" carries the idea of testing something by sunlight.[25] Our English word "sincere" comes from the Latin word "sin cere," "without wax." In ancient Rome those who made pottery often covered cracks with wax to deceive those who purchased them. However, one could discern if the pot was "sin cere" by lifting the pot to the sun and allowing the light to shine through it.

When Paul was praying for the Christians to be sincere, he was not praying for perfection. He knows they will not be perfect until Christ comes. He was praying for them to be free of hypocrisy—to not cover the flaws in their life with wax. One of the problems in the church today is wax—pretense. We put on the wax of church attendance. We put on the wax of "everything is OK," and therefore, we often never share our issues with anybody. We would rather act like everything is perfect than admit our flaws before one another and even God. There is a lot of hypocrisy in the church.

One of the consequences of sin in the Garden of Eden was that man began to hide from both God and man. Adam and Eve ate of the tree and then hid from one another and from God. There was no transparency. That is how the world is. They hide their insecurities and pain behind nice cars, nice clothes, nice jobs, etc.

The counseling industry has become large primarily because people need a place to share the issues they are hiding and not telling anybody. That is what the church is supposed to do. It's a place where we confess our sins before God and one another in order to help each other heal and grow. James 5:16 says, "So confess your sins to one another and pray for one another so that you may be healed. The prayer of a righteous person has great effectiveness."

James called for the church to confess their sins to one another and pray for one another so they could be healed. Even the Lord's Prayer implies this. It says, "Forgive us our debts." This implies a community of believers confessing their sins before one another and before God. When this happens, there is healing. God heals individuals, churches, and nations.

How do we live sincere lives?

48

It is not by being perfect. It is by being willing to confess our sins to others and before God. It is by saying, "I am not perfect. I need mercy and encouragement from the community to help me grow in Christ. And God, I need your forgiveness and grace because I continually fall into sin."

This is the mark of mature Christians. They are humble and open about their continual struggles with sin. Remember, Paul in Romans 7 said, "The things I would do, I don't do. The things I wouldn't do, I do" (paraphrase). In First Timothy 1:15, he said he was the "chief of sinners" (KJV).

When we act like we are perfect, we turn into Pharisees. We may have the wax of daily devotions and the wax of faithful church attendance, but inside we are full of dead men's bones. We are full of pride and anger. We are judgmental and unforgiving. Judgmentalism is a characteristic of someone who is not sincere with themselves, others, or God. They look at their church attendance and outwardly righteous behavior and look down on anybody else that isn't like them.

Paul was praying for this church to be free of hypocrisy. When Christ gave the Parable of the Prodigal Son, the purpose was not to condemn the son who came home but to condemn the older brother. In the beginning of Luke 15, the Pharisees were mocking Christ because he was a friend of sinners. They were the older brothers who judged others and yet could not see their evil attitudes. They mocked and condemned those who sinned outwardly, but it was their sin of pride and self-righteousness that was keeping them out of the presence of God and would ultimately condemn them to hell. They were not sincere. They were full of hypocrisy.

Are you free of hypocrisy?

Application Question: Who do you confess your struggles to in the church? Who do you ask for prayer so that you may be healed?

Blameless

The next aspect of spiritual integrity is being blameless. What does it mean to be blameless? The word blameless means "without stumbling, or offense," and has both the idea of not falling into sinful conduct and of not causing others to fall into sin.[26] This was the same characteristic that Paul gave as a requirement for those selected as elders and deacons in 1 Timothy 3. The leaders needed to be blameless, or it could be translated "above reproach" (1 Tim 3:2). This means that there must not be any areas of clear rebellion in their lives or any areas that could cause others to stumble. They are seeking to live a life that is blameless.

Being blameless does not only have to do with clear areas of sin, it also has to do with areas of freedom that could potentially cause a weaker or less mature brother to sin. Paul said this in Romans 14:21: "It is good not to eat meat or drink wine or to do anything that causes your brother to stumble."

In talking about eating meat and drinking wine, he was talking about areas that were not sin. Scripture in no place forbids eating meat or drinking alcohol; however, Paul says he would not do it if it caused a weaker brother to stumble. This demonstrates the fact that Paul was spiritually mature and seeking to live a blameless life—one that was above approach.

This is commonly a problem with young Christians. Their youth often leads them to only ask, "What are my rights? What am I allowed to do according to the Scripture?" But, that is not the only question a mature Christian will be asking. One should also ask, "Would this freedom cause anybody else to stumble?" Sure there are many things that I could probably do that would not lead me into sin. I am a pretty disciplined person. However, I know that some things I might choose to partake in might actually destroy another believer.

This is what marks the mature in Christ. They are seeking to be blameless. They don't want to stumble into sin or cause others to.

Are you seeking to live a life that is sincere and blameless before God and others? Are you willing to give up your freedoms and rights in order to be blameless before God and others?

Application Question: In what ways can we, as individual believers and the church, practice being more sincere and blameless in our Christian walk?

A Mature Christian Is Marked by Good Works

> filled with the fruit of righteousness that comes through Jesus Christ to the glory and praise of God.
> Philippians 1:11

The next mark of a mature Christian is being filled with the fruit of righteousness. The word "filled" speaks of something completed in the past and having continuing results.[27] Paul pictures these Christians as having born fruits throughout their life and one day standing at the judging seat of Christ surrounded by these fruits (v. 10). This is a mark of mature Christians.

In fact, it is the one of the reasons that God created us. Ephesians 2:10 says, "For we are his workmanship, having been created in Christ Jesus for good works that God prepared beforehand so we may do them."

We were created for good works. The word "workmanship" comes from the Greek word "poiema." We are God's poem—his artistry. Each one of us has been given different spiritual gifts and different experiences so that we can minister for God and bear fruit in a unique way.

Mature Christians are bearing fruits that God prepared in advanced for them. We get a picture of the process of God preparing works for us in advance as we look at Jeremiah. He said to Jeremiah that before he was even in the womb, he knew him and called him to be a prophet to the nations (Jeremiah 1:5). That was God's call on Jeremiah's life and yet he still had to choose to be obedient and submit to God's will.

Fruit always bears the mark of the tree it came from. An apple tree bears apples and an orange tree bears oranges. In the same way, mature Christians demonstrate the fruit of Christ. They demonstrate his character, and people can tell that they are his disciples (John 13:35).

However, immature Christians are not filled with fruits of righteousness. Because they are true Christians, they will bear some fruits. But in many ways, they will resemble the world instead of God. First Corinthians 3:1-3 says this:

> So, brothers and sisters, I could not speak to you as spiritual people, but instead as people of the flesh, as infants in Christ. I fed you milk, not solid food, for you were not yet ready. In fact, you are still not ready, for you are still influenced by the flesh. For since there is still jealousy and dissension among you, are you not influenced by the flesh and behaving like unregenerate people?

These Christians were not yet mature, and you could tell by their fruits. They couldn't handle the deep teachings of the Word yet; they still needed spiritual milk. They were prone to jealousy and quarreling. They were worldly.

Many Christians are like this. Sometimes it's hard to discern if they are really Christians because of the worldly fruits in their lives. Immature Christians are like children—as mentioned before, they lack discernment. This leads to having the wrong friendships and the wrong dating relationships. They are prone to discord—they are always in a fight with somebody. Because they are not choosing what is best, it leads them further away from God.

From personal experience, I spent a large part of my Christian life living as a worldly Christian. Cursing, a fruit of the world, still marked my life until I was freshman in college. I had ungodly language and ungodly relationships. However, even though I resembled the world in many ways, God still used me by his grace. I often brought people to church and led people to Christ, but I was compromised and therefore missed out on God's best. I missed out on the abundant fruits that God wanted to bear in me.

With cursing specifically, during my freshman year while reading James 1:26, God really convicted me and set me free from that sin. It says, "If someone thinks he is religious yet does not bridle his tongue, and so deceives his heart, his religion is futile." God essentially said that my religion was worthless and potentially not real. This really convicted me and from that day, I never struggled with that specific sin again. I knew I had to grow up and mature.

This was God's plan for the Philippians, and it is his plan for every believer. God wants believers to grow up, to bear fruit, and to walk in his specific calling for their lives. However, many Christians are like Esau; they forfeit the Father's inheritance to enjoy a temporary meal.

Interpretation Question: What are some fruits of righteousness?

1.   Godly attitudes are a fruit of righteousness.

Galatians 5:22-23 says, "But the fruit of the Spirit is love, joy, peace, patience, kindness, goodness, faithfulness, gentleness, and self-control. Against such things there is no law."
Are you growing in these godly attitudes? Are you growing in patience, joy, peace, gentleness, and self-control?

2.   Praise is a fruit of righteousness.

Hebrews 13:15 says, "Through him then let us continually offer up a sacrifice of praise to God, that is, the fruit of our lips, acknowledging his name."
Be careful of being a complainer instead of a worshiper. That is a fruit of the world. Paul describes unbelievers as having this fruit in Romans 1:21. He says, "For although they knew God, they did not glorify him as God or give him thanks."
Are you growing in your worship? Are you praising him throughout the day? Or are you a complainer and arguer?

3.   Discipleship is a fruit of righteousness.

Paul said this in Romans 1:13:

I do not want you to be unaware, brothers and sisters, that I often intended to come to you (and was prevented until now), so that I may have some fruit even among you, just as I already have among the rest of the Gentiles.

He seems to primarily be referring to the Gentiles coming to Christ and growing in him—discipleship. Are you growing in the areas of evangelism and discipleship?

Interpretation Question: How do we produce these fruits?

Mature Christians produce these fruit by an abiding relationship with Christ. Again, look at what Paul says: "filled with the fruit of righteousness that comes through Jesus Christ to the glory and praise of God" (Philippians 1:11).

Believers produce these fruits "through Jesus Christ"—through an abiding relationship with him. If we are not abiding in him, we cannot produce fruits. It is by living a life in his presence, abiding in his Word, praying, and fellowshipping with his people that these fruits will naturally blossom in our lives. Look at what Christ said in John 15:4-5:

> Remain in me, and I will remain in you. Just as the branch cannot bear fruit by itself, unless it remains in the vine, so neither can you unless you remain in me. "I am the vine; you are the branches. The one who remains in me—and I in him—bears much fruit, because apart from me you can accomplish nothing.

Are you abiding in the vine? This marks a mature believer. They can't miss a morning without starting their day with Christ and abiding in his presence. This enables them to produce fruit.

When Christ returns, Paul wants the Philippians to be like fruit trees at harvest, their branches hung low, laden with the good deeds that Christ has worked in and through them.[28] This marks mature believers and a healthy church. God is using them greatly because they are abiding in his Son. They are like trees planted by the river, their leaves never fade. "They will be called oaks of righteousness, trees planted by the Lord to reveal his splendor" (Isaiah 61:3).

Application Question: Recently, what type of fruits has God been bearing in your life? What type of fruits do you feel like you are missing or desire more of? How is God calling you to pursue them?

A Mature Christian Is Marked by Glorifying God

> filled with the fruit of righteousness that comes through Jesus Christ to the glory and praise of God.
> Philippians 1:11

The mature Christian's life will glorify God while on the earth and ultimately throughout eternity. Again, the context of verse 10 is the day of Christ. This refers to the day when Christ will return and ultimately judge and reward believers for their good works. Second Corinthians 5:10 says, "For we must all appear before the judgment seat of Christ, so that each one may be paid back according to what he has done while in the body, whether good or evil."

When these believers are rewarded in heaven for their good works, their rewards will ultimately bring glory to God throughout eternity. It will demonstrate that these works have been done through him and by him for his glory (Philippians 2:12-13).

These Christians will ultimately bring glory to God in heaven throughout eternity, but they will also bring glory to God through their works on earth. Their lives will constantly point people to God. Listen to these Scriptures:

> My Father is honored by this, that you bear much fruit and show that you are my disciples.
> John 15:8

> In the same way, let your light shine before people, so that they can see your good deeds and give honor to your Father in heaven.
> Matthew 5:16

People will glorify God because of their prayers, counsel, works of service, etc.

We saw this in the life of Christ. His works drew people into worship. Look at the people's response after he healed a blind man: "And immediately he regained his sight and followed Jesus, praising God. When all the people saw it, they too gave praise to God" (Luke 18:42). This should also happen in the lives of believers. People worship God because of their faithful lives.

First Corinthians 10:31 says, "So whether you eat or drink, or whatever you do, do everything for the glory of God." This should be the daily aim of every believer.

However, where the mature believer's life glorifies God, the immature believer's life detracts from glorifying God. Like the Pharisees, even their good works are done in order to receive praise or honor.

Are you living a life for the glory of God or for your glory? Are you seeking to live in such a way that people are drawn into God's presence? Is that the ultimate aim of your life? Or does your life detract from God's glory?

Application Question: How can we consciously live for the glory of God in our daily endeavors? How can we be careful of the pharisaical spirit which seeks to bring honor to ourselves instead of God?

Conclusion

What does a mature Christian look like?

1. A Mature Christian Is Marked by Abounding Love
2. A Mature Christian Is Marked by Growing Knowledge

3. A Mature Christian Is Marked by Spiritual Discernment
4. A Mature Christian Is Marked by Spiritual Integrity
5. A Mature Christian Is Marked by Good Works
6. A Mature Christian Is Marked by Glorifying God

Application Question: In what ways is God calling you to pursue spiritual maturity?

Becoming a Mature Witness for Christ

I want you to know, brothers and sisters, that my situation has actually turned out to advance the gospel: The whole imperial guard and everyone else knows that I am in prison for the sake of Christ, and most of the brothers and sisters, having confidence in the Lord because of my imprisonment, now more than ever dare to speak the word fearlessly. Some, to be sure, are preaching Christ from envy and rivalry, but others from goodwill. The latter do so from love because they know that I am placed here for the defense of the gospel. The former proclaim Christ from selfish ambition, not sincerely, because they think they can cause trouble for me in my imprisonment. What is the result? Only that in every way, whether in pretense or in truth, Christ is being proclaimed, and in this I rejoice. Yes, and I will continue to rejoice
Philippians 1:12-18 (NET)

What are characteristics of a mature witness for Christ—a mature evangelist?

As we look at Philippians 1:12-18, we see Paul's description of the gospel being spread throughout Rome while he was imprisoned there. Paul had earlier stated his desire to preach in Rome (Romans 1:11-12). It was the most influential city in the world, and by reaching Rome, he would affect the entire world. However, he probably never thought he would reach Rome through imprisonment. At this point in Paul's ministry, he had already been imprisoned for two years in Caesarea for preaching the gospel, and he was to be in prison for two more years in Rome. He was under house arrest with a Roman guard chained to him twenty-four hours a day. Yet, while there he says, "that my situation has actually turned out to advance the gospel" (v. 12). The word "advance" has the meaning of a pioneer advance. It was a military term used of an army advance; the army would go before everybody to clear the way into new territory.[29] While in prison, God used Paul to break new territory for the gospel, and others were following. Here we see the ministry of a mature witness—a mature evangelist—who all of us can learn from.

It must be remembered that every believer is called to be a gospel pioneer as well. We are all missionaries in whatever context God has placed us—whether that be as a student, a teacher, a business man, or some other profession. Where ever God has placed us, he placed us there to be a witness. Matthew 28:18-19 says,

> Then Jesus came up and said to them, "All authority in heaven and on earth has been given to me. Therefore go and make disciples of all nations, baptizing them in the name of the Father and the Son and the Holy Spirit,

We are all called to make disciples. We are all called to be pioneers—mature witnesses—who spread the gospel to places where people have never heard it. However, if we are honest, many of us would admit to struggling with witnessing. We fear being rejected. We fear being incompetent in our gospel presentation. We fear pushing people away and dishonoring our Lord. As we look at Paul's description of the gospel ministry in Rome, the hope is that we will be inspired to become gospel pioneers as well—mature witnesses for Christ.

God is looking for gospel pioneers to break new ground in schools, businesses, and nations around the world. Will you allow God to use you to break new ground for the gospel so others can follow?

Big Question: What characteristics of a mature witness do we see in Paul's description of the gospel-ministry happening in Rome?

A Mature Witness Shares the Gospel in Every Circumstance

> The whole imperial guard and everyone else knows that I am in prison for the sake of Christ.
> Philippians 1:13

The first characteristic of a mature witness is that he shares the gospel in every circumstance. Here we see Paul, who has already been in prison for two years in Caesarea, imprisoned in Rome and still sharing the gospel. Look at the superlatives he uses in Philippians 1:13. It says that it has become clear throughout the "whole imperial guard" and to "everyone else" that his chains are in Christ. Everybody was hearing the gospel through Paul during his imprisonment. We learn more about his situation in Acts 28:16, 30-31. It says,

> When we entered Rome, Paul was allowed to live by himself, with the soldier who was guarding him...Paul lived there two whole years in his own rented quarters and welcomed all who came to him, proclaiming

the kingdom of God and teaching about the Lord Jesus Christ with complete boldness and without restriction.

Paul was under house arrest—guarded by a soldier all day. While there, people came to see him all the time. Obviously, having an apostle of Paul's stature in Rome became very well known. People from all throughout the Empire started to come to Paul, and he would share the gospel and preach to them.

The palace guards chained to Paul would switch every four hours. "Imperial guard" in the Greek is actually the word "praetorian." The praetorian were high ranking military officers—hand selected to protect the emperor and keep the general peace. They received double the pay of a regular soldier with a generous retirement. There were anywhere from 9,000 to 16,000 praetorian. These soldiers were well known and became very powerful in the government. They became known as "king makers," as they would in later years use their power to select emperors.[30] There has been renewed interest in these well-known soldiers with the release of the movie Gladiator (2000) and 300 (2007). As these high-ranking soldiers were chained next to Paul, they listened to his testimony, heard his prayers, and consequently the gospel started to spread among them and throughout Caesar's palace (Philippians 4:22).

Paul's situation was not ideal. He didn't have freedom—he couldn't go and visit the city. He never had privacy, even when using the bathroom. However, this never affected his willingness to share the gospel. Again, Acts 28:31 says he boldly, without hindrance, preached the kingdom of God and taught about the Lord Jesus Christ. This potentially could have worsened his situation. However, even the prospect of retribution or consequences, didn't hinder his witness.

That is the type of Christians we must become as well. We must share the gospel in every circumstance. "We must never let circumstances get us down—never let our situation hinder our testimony and witness for Christ, no matter what they are...

- persecution
- accident
- failure
- financial loss
- rejection
- bankruptcy
- sin

- abuse
- divorce
- poverty
- imprisonment
- age
- loss of a loved one"[31]

Often it is these types of circumstances that actually quiet our witness. When talked about, criticized, persecuted, or while going through difficult circumstances, we often become self-consumed instead of gospel-consumed. We often become quiet instead of becoming even more outspoken for Christ.

This is what we see with Paul and that is what we have seen throughout much of church history in the midst of persecution. Second century Church Father Tertullian said, "The blood of the saints is the seed of the church." When persecution against the church has increased, Christians have often been more inspired to preach and spread God's Word. On the other side, when the church has lived in comfort—free from persecution—it has often become apathetic and stagnant in sharing the gospel.

Similar to Paul's situation, we can learn a great deal from the story of John Bunyan who wrote the book *The Pilgrim's Progress*, which historically is one of the most popular books outside of the Bible. This is what John MacArthur shared about John Bunyan:

> John Bunyan's preaching was so popular and powerful, and so unacceptable to leaders in the seventeenth-century Church of England, that he was jailed in order to silence him. Refusing to be silent, he began to preach in the jail courtyard. He not only had a large audience of prisoners, but also hundreds of the citizens of Bedford and the surrounding area would come to the prison daily and stand outside to hear him expound Scripture. He was silenced verbally by being placed deep inside the jail and forbidden to preach at all. Yet in that silence, he spoke loudest of all and to more people than he could have imagined. It was during that time that he wrote *The Pilgrim's Progress*, the great Christian classic that has ministered the gospel to tens of millions throughout the world. For several centuries, it was the most widely read and translated book in the world after the Bible. Bunyan's opponents were able to stop his preaching for a few years, but they were not able to stop his ministry. Instead, they provided opportunity for it to be extended from deep within a jail in the small town of Bedford to the ends of the earth.[32]

As we consider Paul and John Bunyan in prison still sharing the gospel, I can't but think of a story Rick Warren, author of the *Purpose Driven Life*, shared about his dying father. While his father was on his death bed, he suddenly became disturbed and tried to get out of bed. The family tried to calm him down and asked him what he wanted. He replied, "I've got to save one more soul for Jesus! One more soul for Jesus!" Rick said his father probably repeated that phrase 100 times within the next hour.[33] Even while on his death bed, he wanted to share the gospel.

How do your circumstances affect your witness? Are you still seeking to advance the gospel no matter your present circumstances? This is a picture of a mature Christian witness—a gospel pioneer.

Application Question: What experience do you have with evangelism? Describe your struggles and also the grace you have received in the area of evangelism?

A Mature Witness Is Courageous and Fearless

> and most of the brothers and sisters, having confidence in the Lord because of my imprisonment, now more than ever dare to speak the word fearlessly.
> Philippians 1:14

Similar to the last point, another characteristic of a mature witness is that he is courageous and fearless in sharing the gospel. As mentioned previously, Acts 28:31 shares how Paul preached the Word boldly to all who came. It says that Paul was "proclaiming the kingdom of God and teaching about the Lord Jesus Christ with complete boldness and without restriction."

Not only was he preaching boldly, other Christians started to preach boldly because of him. Philippians 1:14 actually says "most of the brothers and sisters" were encouraged "to speak the word fearlessly."

With Christians being persecuted in Rome, many of the saints ceased to share their faith for fear of persecution and its potential effects on their jobs and family. However, when these Christians saw Paul's bold witness while in prison and facing death, they began to boldly and fearlessly share the gospel as well. No longer were they afraid of losing their jobs—no longer were they afraid of what people thought or of people being offended. They became fearless.

Application Question: How can we become more bold and fearless in proclaiming the gospel?

1. Boldness is a result of prayer.

Boldness in sharing our faith is a result of personal prayer and the prayers of others. Paul himself commonly asked for prayer to speak boldly. In Ephesians 6:19-20, he said this:

> Pray for me also, that I may be given the message when I begin to speak—that I may confidently make known the mystery of the gospel, for which I am an ambassador in chains. Pray that I may be able to speak boldly as I ought to speak.

Ephesians is a prison epistle along with Philippians—something he wrote while in Rome. He essentially petitioned for others to pray for his boldness twice. He asked for prayer to preach the word "confidently" and "boldly." It was not Paul's natural strength which made him a bold witness. It was his recognition of weakness which caused him to depend upon God and the prayers of others. He needed their prayers to preach boldly every day, even though he knew his preaching could make his situation worse. He needed prayer to be bold while sitting next to a soldier with a large sword in his hand. Just like Paul, we need prayers too.

We must petition the Lord for boldness to witness, and we should ask others to pray for our boldness as well. We must do this if we are going to be fearless in whatever situation God places us.

We also see this need for prayer in the book of Acts when the apostles were warned to not share the gospel any more. The apostles responded with corporate prayer and casting their cares before the Lord. Acts 4:23-24 and verse 31 says this:

> When they were released, Peter and John went to their fellow believers and reported everything the high priests and the elders had said to them. When they heard this, they raised their voices to God with one mind and said, "Master of all, you who made the heaven, the earth, the sea, and everything that is in them..." When they had prayed, the place where they were assembled together was shaken, and they were all filled with the Holy Spirit and began to speak the word of God courageously.

The church was empowered to speak the Word of God boldly through prayer. Maybe, we lack boldness in our witness because we lack prayer. Maybe, we lack boldness because we are not weak enough to ask others for prayer.

What else enables us to have boldness in our witness for Christ?

2. Boldness is a result of watching and partnering with other bold witnesses.

Paul says that "most of the brothers and sisters" were encouraged to share the gospel because of his example. Proverbs says, "The one who associates with the wise grows wise, but a companion of fools suffers harm" (Proverbs 13:20). One of the wisest things we can do with our life is witness for Christ.

This boldness is increased by being around wise Christians who are serious about God and serious about the gospel. Our relationships always affect our witness for Christ. They can affect it positively by helping us become bolder or negatively by silencing us.

Paul said this in Philippians while he was in prison. He called the people to follow his example which no doubt included his faithfulness in sharing the gospel even while being persecuted. Look at what he said: "Be imitators of me, brothers and sisters, and watch carefully those who are living this way, just as you have us as an example" (Philippians 3:17).

We should all have people we are watching and/or who are mentoring us to help us grow in the faith and to help us share the faith. This includes studying faithful witnesses like Paul in Scripture and also the faithful throughout the history of the church. I have read the stories of many contemporary pastors who were deeply impressed and encouraged by the witness of Hudson Taylor, Jim Elliot, Martin Luther, and other great saints. Their lives and examples challenge us and encourage us to become bolder in our witness for Christ.

Application Question: Who has inspired you the most to grow in your spiritual life and to become a mature witness for Christ?

A Mature Witness Encourages Others to Share Their Faith

and most of the brothers and sisters, having confidence in the Lord because of my imprisonment, now more than ever dare to speak the word fearlessly.
Philippians 1:14

As mentioned previously, the Christians in Rome were encouraged to speak the Word of God fearlessly because of Paul's chains. Paul said the things that happened to him worked out for the advancement of the gospel, and Christians becoming encouraged to spread the gospel was one of the ways God worked it out (v. 12).

Again the word "advancement" Paul used is a military term for an army going ahead to prepare the way to enter into new territory. Paul's imprisonment in Rome was used to make a military advancement into the kingdom of darkness. There, he not only preached the gospel but made a way for others to preach it. He cleared the path like a pioneer. We can be sure he did this not only by his example in prison but also by challenging the church to share their faith. We see this with Philemon whom he wrote to while also imprisoned in Rome. In the letter, he said, "I pray that you may be active in sharing your faith, so that you will have a full understanding of every good thing we have in Christ" (Philemon 1:6, NIV 1984).

He prays that Philemon would be active in sharing his faith so that he could fully know the blessings we have in Christ. As you can imagine, this would have been very challenging coming from a man who was in prison for sharing the faith. While Paul was in Rome, he called the church to stand up and be pioneers—he called them to be mature witnesses.

Paul did this not only so the lost could hear the gospel, but because he realized sharing was important for Christians to grow. With Philemon, Paul said that if he shared his faith, the result would be coming to a "full understanding of every good thing we have in Christ." Paul realized that if Philemon shared the gospel that God would give more understanding of himself—more grace.

Christians who faithfully share God's Word—God can entrust with more. Those who do not, God cannot entrust with more. God will not give them more because they are not trustworthy. They will become like the Dead Sea which is dead because it has no ocean, sea, or tributaries to pour into.

Many Christians are like this. They read every Christian book they get their hands on and listen to all the famous preachers' sermons, but they will not share the gospel. When this happens, instead of growing, they actually start to decrease in faith. Christ said this:

> And he said to them, "Take care about what you hear. The measure you use will be the measure you receive, and more will be added to you. For whoever has will be given more, but whoever does not have, even what he has will be taken from him."
> Mark 4:24-25

Many Christians do not share and actually experience a taking away instead of receiving more blessings from Christ. It is crucial for us to share our faith not only for others to hear but also for our faith to grow.

Therefore, Paul and Christ both encouraged Christians to be faithful in sharing what they received. Pioneers of the gospel—mature witnesses—encourage others to share their faith. They do this by their faithful example and also by their teaching. We can have no doubt that the church was emboldened to preach not only because of Paul's example but because he encouraged them to do so, as he did with Philemon.

Let us understand that we must encourage other Christians to witness as well. This is crucial for those we disciple. They cannot know every good thing, every blessing they have in Christ, if they do not share their faith. With the measure we use what God has given, he gives back. Some are abounding in the knowledge of Scripture, abounding in peace, abounding in grace because they faithfully share God's Word. However, others do not, and therefore, they become spiritually stagnant.

Are you sharing your faith so you can know every good thing we have in Christ? Are you encouraging others to faithfully share their faith? It is crucial for their spiritual growth.

Application Question: In what ways have you experienced spiritual growth by consistently sharing your faith and serving? In what ways have you experienced spiritual stagnation for not sharing and not serving?

A Mature Witness Should Expect Attack and Respond to It in a Godly Manner

> Some, to be sure, are preaching Christ from envy and rivalry, but others from goodwill... The former proclaim Christ from selfish ambition, not sincerely, because they think they can cause trouble for me in my imprisonment. What is the result? Only that in every way, whether in pretense or in truth, Christ is being proclaimed, and in this I rejoice. Yes, and I will continue to rejoice,
> Philippians 1:15, 17-18

The next characteristic of a mature witness that we can discern from Paul's account of his ministry in Rome is that a mature witness should expect attacks and respond to it in a godly manner. It should be noticed that Paul was not describing attacks from those in the world or even from false teachers. The attacks Paul shared about were from other peers in the gospel. They had an orthodox faith—they taught Christ. However, they taught Christ out of envy and rivalry.

When Paul was imprisoned in Rome, many congregations and ministers started to make pilgrimages to hear him preach and teach at his rented home which may have caused a spirit of rivalry in other minsters. The word "envy" has the connotation of jealousy—they wanted the prominence and favor that God gave Paul's ministry, and they also wanted to see him fail. They were hoping to stir up trouble for Paul as they preached to their churches.

Maybe they were saying his imprisonment meant that he was not really an apostle or a godly man or that he was in sin. We saw this mentality with Job's friends. They had an early form of the "prosperity gospel." The fact that Job was sick and lost his wealth meant to them that he had sinned in some way. They believed this because for them, it was never God's will to allow trials in the life of someone who was righteous. Possibly, it was this form of false doctrine that was used to attack Paul and his ministry in prison.

Let us understand that if we are going to be faithful witnesses for Christ, this will stir up animosity towards us. Second Timothy 3:12 says, "Now in fact all who want to live godly lives in Christ Jesus will be persecuted." Sometimes this attack will come from the very people that we love most. It will at times come from people you expect to support you. It will come from the people you pray for and often minister to.

65

I remember when I went through my ordination process, one pastor said to me that if I was going to remain in pastoral ministry, I needed to develop the "hide of an alligator." I must develop thick skin. To serve faithfully in ministry, to step up and preach the Word of God, means to be an open target for criticism, even at times by those I love.

In the book of Corinthians, Paul was attacked by some false prophets who had turned many in the church against him. Look at some of the criticism Paul received: "because some say, 'His letters are weighty and forceful, but his physical presence is weak and his speech is of no account'" (2 Corinthians 10:10).

They criticized his writing, his looks, and his speaking. Nothing was off limits, and these were people who he loved and served. If we are going to be faithful witnesses for Christ, we should expect attack.

In fact, if we are not receiving attack, whether through persecution, criticism, or even spiritual warfare, I would be concerned. Satan has no reason to attack somebody who is content on the side-lines not working for God. But those who are faithful should expect attack to come, even at times from those they invest in most.

If we are serving God—speaking his Word—and by God's grace we suffer criticism and attack, let it not weigh too heavily upon us. Yes, let us consider the criticism and evaluate it, for it might be God speaking to us. But, we also must realize that attacks from the enemy are common to those who speak for God. Let those who are faithfully serving the Lord and being attacked be encouraged—for this happened to the prophets and faithful men and women of God before us. Christ said this:

> "Blessed are you when people insult you and persecute you and say all kinds of evil things about you falsely on account of me. Rejoice and be glad because your reward is great in heaven, for they persecuted the prophets before you in the same way."
> Matthew 5:11-12

This happened to the prophets before you, and it also happens to other faithful witnesses around the world today (cf. 1 Peter 5:9). Let us therefore be encouraged.

Observation Question: How did Paul respond to these attacks from the brethren, and what can we learn from his response?

Not only should we learn to expect attacks as we consider what Paul endured, but we also should learn how to respond to attacks. When it came to false teachers attacking God and the church, Paul was fierce. He was like a lion. Look at what he said to the Galatians:

66

"But even if we (or an angel from heaven) should preach a gospel contrary to the one we preached to you, let him be condemned to hell! As we have said before, and now I say again, if any one is preaching to you a gospel contrary to what you received, let him be condemned to hell!
Galatians 1:8-9

Paul said, "Let him who preaches another gospel be condemned—eternally condemned!" Listen to what he says in Galatians 5:12: "I wish those agitators would go so far as to castrate themselves!"

Paul said he wished that those who preached circumcision would just completely castrate themselves. When it came to the gospel, protecting the church, and honoring God, Paul was like a lion. However, when it came to personal offense, Paul was like a lamb. He said this to the Philippians: "But what does it matter?" (v. 18, NIV 1984). "What does it matter? Who cares if they mock me—make up lies about me? Who cares if they mock my appearance and talk bad about my sermons? All that matters is that Christ is preached"—that was his primary concern because that concern would affect eternity.

How do you respond when people criticize you—when people treat you wrong, possibly out of envy and a desire to see you fail? How do you respond? Are you quick to fight and get angry? Or are you like Paul—willing to overlook the wrong? Are you like Christ—willing to turn the other cheek and at times even practice silence?

I'll be honest as a pastor who also suffers criticism—sometimes just, others unjust, or simply unwise. It is a great place to practice sanctification. I commonly think of Paul and Christ, and I take comfort. I practice biting my tongue even when I feel my rights have been violated. "What does it really matter? As long as the gospel is being preached, what does it matter?" A mature witness should expect attack and also respond in a godly manner.

Application Question: In what ways have you seen or experienced attacks for being a faithful witness for Christ? How can we practice a wise response to attacks? What does a wise response look like?

A Mature Witness Has the Right Motives

The latter do so from love because they know that I am placed here for the defense of the gospel.
Philippians 1:16

Application Question: What are possible wrong motives one might have in sharing the gospel or serving in ministry?

67

Another characteristic of a mature witness is having the right motives. Why do we share the gospel with others? Why do we serve in children's ministry, youth ministry, or worship ministry? What are our motives?

In this scenario, we see both those who served out of envy and rivalry and those who served out of love. Let us realize that a lot of ministry is done out of wrong motives. The disciples commonly argued about who was the greatest. A competitive spirit was still in them from their life in the world. Many churches are competitive. I talked with one pastor who previously started a church plant in a city. When he started this church, a local pastor called his father and said that he was really bothered that his son started a church in the same city because now they were going to be competitors.

A competitive spirit is not uncommon among ministers. "Which seminary did you go to?" "How big is your church?" Often when there is a publicized fall by a well-known pastor or a divide in a church, people are quick to point fingers and criticize, instead of mourning for those hurting and over the dishonoring of God. Like the disciples, a competitive spirit is still upon us from the world.

In considering this, there are many wrong reasons to do ministry. Some do it to compete with others; some do it for glory, prestige, and exaltation. We saw this with the Pharisees who loved to be greeted by others. They wore long robes so people would know they were ministers (Luke 24:46). That was the problem with Paul's critics; they preached, but they did it for the wrong reason.

It should also be noted, as we consider those who did it for the wrong reasons that many times God probably blessed their ministry. They preached the gospel and people got saved, and yet their hearts were not right with God. We see this throughout the Bible. Jonah hated the people he preached to in Nineveh and was angry at God, and yet, the Lord still brought a great revival. The false prophet Balaam prayed a blessing upon Israel and through the Holy Spirit gave a prophecy about the messiah, and yet he still worshiped another god.

Application Question: Why does God use and often bless those serving in ministry even though they have wrong hearts?

The primary reason God many times prospers their ministry is because God is committed to honoring his Word. Paul said the gospel is the power of God unto salvation to the Jew first and also to the Greek (Romans 1:16). In Isaiah 55, God says he watches over his Word. It is like water and dew, and it will never return void.

The rain and snow fall from the sky and do not return, but instead water the earth and make it produce and yield crops, and provide seed for the planter and food for those who must eat. In the same way, the promise that I make does not return to me, having accomplished nothing. No, it is realized as I desire and is fulfilled as I intend.
Isaiah 55:10-11

Many times the ministries of those who are corrupt and ungodly will excel, and the primary reason is because God is faithful to his Word. He will not let it return void. That was no doubt true of the people attacking Paul.

However, the best ministers—mature witnesses—serve out of a selfless, loving heart. Listen to what Paul said about the majority of the believers who were emboldened to witness and share the gospel: "The latter do so from love because they know that I am placed here for the defense of the gospel" (Philippians 1:16).

Similarly, when Paul talked about his motivation for sharing the Word of God with others, he said this in 2 Corinthians 5:14: "For the love of Christ controls us, since we have concluded this, that Christ died for all; therefore all have died."

He said that he was compelled by love. He proclaimed the Word of God, suffered, and wrote letters to encourage churches all because he loved God and loved people.

What is the real reason we don't evangelize? It is not because of fear—it is because of a lack of love. I don't love others as I should, and therefore, I don't witness as I should.

Paul said that love compelled him. The Christians throughout the Roman Empire who were sharing the gospel felt compelled by love—love for God, love for others, and love for Paul. Love compelled them to preach and proclaim the gospel.

Love is the only true motivation to do gospel ministry, and it is the only motivation that will be rewarded by God. Paul said this about his ministry:

If I speak in the tongues of men and of angels, but I do not have love, I am a noisy gong or a clanging cymbal. And if I have prophecy, and know all mysteries and all knowledge, and if I have all faith so that I can remove mountains, but do not have love, I am nothing. If I give away everything I own, and if I give over my body in order to boast, but do not have love, I receive no benefit.
1 Corinthians 13:1-3

He said that nothing he did for others or God mattered if it didn't come from love. Mature witnesses serve others out of love. Love means that it is not about me. It is not about what I get in return. Love can be criticized and hated, and it won't matter because love is only concerned with the object it loves. Love is not selfish—it is not concerned with self-interest. It is consumed with the glory of God and the good of others.

Why don't we witness? It is because we don't love properly.

Application Question: How can we grow in love in order to become mature witnesses of Christ?

1. Love increases by prayer.

First Thessalonians 3:12 says, "And may the Lord cause you to increase and abound in love for one another and for all, just as we do for you."

Paul prayed for the love of the Thessalonians to increase. Love is increased by prayer. We should pray for our love to increase and also for our church's love to increase.

2. Love increases by an act of the will

John 13:34 says, "I give you a new commandment—to love one another. Just as I have loved you, you also are to love one another."

Love is not necessarily a feeling but primarily an act of the will. We grow in love by choosing to act in love towards people and God. Jesus said if you love me, obey my commands (John 14:15). We love God by obeying him. We love others by serving them. Consider what John said: "Little children, let us not love with word or with tongue but in deed and truth" (1 John 3:18).

We grow in love by acting in love. Love is not primarily an emotion but an act of the will that may include emotions. We grow in love by choosing to serve, share, listen, forgive, etc. Love grows as we choose to act in love towards others.

Application Question: In what ways is God calling you to love others in order to be a better witness?

A Mature Witness Is Gospel-Centered

What is the result? Only that in every way, whether in pretense or in truth, Christ is being proclaimed, and in this I rejoice. Yes, and I will continue to rejoice
Philippians 1:18

Application Question: What are some common things that take away your joy or give you joy? What does that say about what your life is centered on?

The next thing we see with Paul is that he declares that, even in the face of prison and the attack of other Christians, he could rejoice because of the gospel's advancement. In fact, he repeats the word "rejoice" twice in verse 18 to emphasize his joy in the gospel.

I believe one of the things this teaches about Paul is that his life was gospel-centered. His life was centered and focused on the gospel. You can tell what your "center" or "focus" is by what gives or takes away your joy. People who constantly lose their joy when criticized or their joy increases when praised show what their center is. It is probably self. Their joy or lack of it is based on how they are treated.

But for Paul, his joy was primarily affected by the advancement of the gospel. It didn't matter that he was in prison. It didn't matter that he lost his freedom. It didn't matter that he was away from his family. It didn't matter that he could potentially lose his life. In fact, in speaking about the Jews in the letter to the Romans, he wished that he could be cursed and cut off from Christ if only his brothers could know Christ (9:3). His life was not about himself; it was about the gospel advancing. His life was gospel-centered. This made him an effective and mature witness for Christ—it made him a pioneer.

People who are the most effective witnesses are gospel-centered. That is where they get their joy. They get joy from seeing the gospel shared and accepted by others. They get a tremendous joy from supporting the work of missions financially and praying for the work of missions. Their joy is not tied to what they own or do not own but to the kingdom of God advancing. This is a gospel-centered person.

Where is your joy centered? What is your heart tied to?

Application Question: Why are so many of us not gospel-centered? Why is our joy not primarily in the gospel and its advancement?

The reason many of us are not gospel-centered is because we have a heart problem—a heart defect that affects our focus and our joy in the work of the gospel. Solomon said this: "Guard your heart with all vigilance, for from it are the sources of life" (Proverbs 4:23). Because of this reality, Jesus commanded us to not store up riches on this earth in order to protect our hearts—in order to make our hearts kingdom-centered. He said this:

> Do not accumulate for yourselves treasures on earth, where moth and rust destroy and where thieves break in and steal. But accumulate for yourselves treasures in heaven, where moth and rust do not destroy, and thieves do not break in and steal. For where your treasure is, there your heart will be also.
> Matthew 6:19-21

One of the reasons many of us are not gospel-centered is because our hearts, and therefore, our joy is tied to the things of this earth. It is tied to our phones, our computers, our cars, our clothes, and many other materials. It is tied to our promotion and our advancement instead of kingdom advancement, and therefore, we are not mature and effective in witnessing for Christ. Paul's heart was centered on seeing people in heaven. Consider what he later says to the Thessalonians: "For who is our hope or joy or crown to boast of before our Lord Jesus at his coming? Is it not of course you? For you are our glory and joy" (1 Thessalonians 2:19-20).

This was Paul's joy. His joy was seeing the Thessalonians in heaven. His heart was tied to the gospel. He lived a gospel-centered life, not primarily concerned with the temporary things of this earth but the things of heaven. Christ commands us to have a similar heart and passion. Look at what he said in Luke 16:9: "And I tell you, make friends for yourselves by how you use worldly wealth, so that when it runs out you will be welcomed into the eternal homes."

Christ said to use our wealth on earth to make friends in heaven. Christ says we should be motivated by this picture of people in heaven welcoming us and thanking us because we gave to the work of missions, and they came to know Christ because of it. Christ essentially said, "Make that your ambition—live a gospel-centered life."

In fact one time Christ had a very crude response for two disciples who put off the call of the gospel for something else. Look at Christ's interaction in Luke 9:59-62:

> Jesus said to another, "Follow me." But he replied, "Lord, first let me go and bury my father." But Jesus said to him, "Let the dead bury their own dead, but as for you, go and proclaim the kingdom of God." Yet another said, "I will follow you, Lord, but first let me say goodbye to my family." Jesus said to him, "No one who puts his hand to the plow and looks back is fit for the kingdom of God."

Christ essentially said this call must be first before all things; neither job nor duty to one's family can come before the call to preach the gospel. If it does, we are not fit for his kingdom. His disciples must be gospel-centered.

This is true for us as individuals, but it is also true corporately. It is very easy for churches to lose their focus on the gospel. Sometimes their focus can become worship, helping the poor, or some other social cause. All those things are important, but they are not more important than the gospel. Churches must be gospel-centered. Commentator Kent Hughes said this about the fall of many denominations into liberalism:

> The history of some of the mainline Protestant denominations in our country serves to make the point. There were generations that

72

believed the gospel and held that there were certain accompanying social and political entailments. Then came a generation that assumed the gospel but identified with the entailments. The next generation denied the gospel but made the entailments everything. This is a caricature that is simplistic and reductionist. Nevertheless, in broad swaths it describes Protestant liberalism in America.

When the gospel is no longer the main thing, when it becomes assumed, the next generation may be lost. As evangelicals we must take note. All kinds of issues cry for our attention—abortion, pornography, media bias, economic justice, racial discrimination, classism, sexism, to name a few. And we need to be alert and involved in certain of them. But if any of them become the main thing so that the gospel is marginalized, beware![34]

What are our lives centered around? What are our churches centered around? Is it centered around our success? Is it centered around our comfort and safety? Or is it centered on the gospel and seeing multitudes of people from every language, tribe, and tongue worshiping God together? Lord, help us and our churches to live gospel-centered lives for only that really matters.

Application Question: How can you develop a more gospel-centered life? In what ways is God calling you to make your focus evangelism and missions?

Conclusion

What are characteristics of a mature witness for Christ? What are characteristics of a gospel pioneer—someone who advances the gospel into new territory so others may follow? We see these characteristics in Paul and his gospel ministry in Rome.

1. A Mature Witness Shares the Gospel in Every Circumstance
2. A Mature Witness Is Courageous and Fearless
3. A Mature Witness Encourages Others to Share Their Faith
4. A Mature Witness Should Expect Attack and Respond to It in a Godly Manner
5. A Mature Witness Has the Right Motives
6. A Mature Witness Is Gospel-Centered

How to Really Live for Christ

for I know that this will turn out for my deliverance through your prayers and the help of the Spirit of Jesus Christ. My confident hope is that I will in no way be ashamed but that with complete boldness, even now as always, Christ will be exalted in my body, whether I live or die. For to me, living is Christ and dying is gain. Now if I am to go on living in the body, this will mean productive work for me, yet I don't know which I prefer: I feel torn between the two, because I have a desire to depart and be with Christ, which is better by far, but it is more vital for your sake that I remain in the body. And since I am sure of this, I know that I will remain and continue with all of you for the sake of your progress and joy in the faith, so that what you can be proud of may increase because of me in Christ Jesus, when I come back to you.
Philippians 1:19-26 (NET)

What does it mean to really live for Christ? How do we know if we are truly living for him?

In the book of Philippians, Paul was imprisoned in Rome, awaiting a potential death sentence for his gospel ministry. In this specific text, he says one of the most quoted passages in the Bible. He says, "For to me, living is Christ and dying is gain" (v. 21). This verse is the major theme of this passage. What does it mean to say, "Living is Christ."

I remember when I was a basketball player in high school and college, I owned a t-shirt that said, "Life is basketball and the rest is details." The idea behind the phrase on the shirt was that basketball was the primary focus of life and everything else really didn't matter. At that point in my life, I could relate to that shirt and that is why I bought it. For me basketball was one of the greatest priorities in my life. Sadly, that also was a reflection of my relationship with God. For a large portion of my Christian life, God was really just a part of my life; he was not everything. I think that is the idea behind Paul's phrase, "For to me, living is Christ and dying is gain." Paul was saying that Christ was everything to him.

For many Christians, they know this verse by heart, but they don't know it by practice. Like myself as a young Christian, Christ is not their life. Life is school. Life is family. Life is career, or life is some hobby or entertainment.

One author said, "Life is what we are alive to."[35] It is what really gets us excited. For many, their passions lie outside of their relationship with Christ.

What does it mean to really live for Christ? Jesus said this was the very reason that he came to the earth. He came that we might have life and have it abundantly (John 10:10). He came so we could truly be alive to God—that he would be our passion and joy. Paul had found this life, and he constantly proclaimed it. In Galatians 2:20 he said, "I have been crucified with Christ, and it is no longer I who live, but Christ lives in me. So the life I now live in the body, I live because of the faithfulness of the Son of God, who loved me and gave himself for me."

Paul saw himself as no longer alive—he left his past life behind, and now Christ was his life and Christ alone. His life began when he was blinded on his way to Damascus, and he became a follower of Christ. Later in Philippians 3, he recounts all the former things he took pride in—his Jewish upbringing, following the law, and being a Pharisee, and yet, he says he counted it all dung—all nothing for the sake of gaining Christ (v. 7-8). Christ was the beginning of his life and getting to know him more was the continuation of his life. And, one day dying would be gain because that would mean dwelling in the unhindered presence of Christ.

Is Christ your life? Is he your daily passion? Is he your hope for the future? In Philippians, we get the opportunity to watch and study a mature Christian—Paul. He is somebody we should be modeling. In 1 Corinthians 11:1, Paul says, "Be imitators of me, just as I also am of Christ." We can be sure that what we see here in Paul is not just descriptive of his emotions and experiences while in prison, but it is also prescriptive. It is a challenge to us to grow into spiritual maturity. Paul says this later in Philippians: "Be imitators of me, brothers and sisters, and watch carefully those who are living this way, just as you have us as an example" (Philippians 3:17). He taught them to follow his example, and that example was a life truly lived for Christ and Christ alone.

What is your life? What is it that you're really living for? Is it success, wealth, comfort, or family? If so, you will not be able to say to die is gain—to die would really be the loss of all you are truly living for. In this text we will see five principles about how to really live for Christ.

Big Question: What does Philippians 1:19-26 show us about how Paul lived for Christ? How can we apply these principles to our lives so we can also really live for Christ?

To Really Live for Christ, We Must Trust and Submit to God's Plan

> for I know that this will turn out for my deliverance through your prayers
> and the help of the Spirit of Jesus Christ.
> Philippians 1:19

In this passage Paul says that, because of the prayers of the saints and the help given by the Spirit of Christ, what had happened to him would turn out for his deliverance. What does he mean by what has happened? Paul is here referring to his imprisonment for preaching the gospel and the criticism by the Christian detractors. Despite all that, he believed everything would work out for his deliverance.

What does Paul mean by deliverance?

Interpretation Question: What does Paul mean by his confidence in eventually being delivered?

1. Paul's deliverance could mean that he was confident that he would be released from prison.

    Some commentators have taken this view point. He does say in verse 25 that he knew that he would "remain" with the Philippians. He was convinced that it was not God's will for him to die but to be set free and to continue his ministry to others. Paul could be referring to this. However, the fact that Paul demonstrates some uncertainty in verse 21 of his final outcome makes many believe he can't be referring to deliverance from prison. Paul says in verse 20 that his hope is that Christ will be glorified in his body by life or by death. Therefore, deliverance probably does not refer to being released from prison.

2. Paul's deliverance probably means that God would work everything out for his sanctification.

    The word deliverance can also be translated "salvation" (KJV). There is a salvation in the past tense when we accepted Christ and began to follow him, but there is also a progressive sense of salvation. Philippians 2:12-13 says, "So then, my dear friends, just as you have always obeyed, not only in my presence but even more in my absence, continue working out your salvation with awe and reverence, for the one bringing forth in you both the desire and the effort—for the sake of his good pleasure—is God."

    This aspect of salvation is our being made into the image of Christ. God did not just save us to enter heaven but also to be made into the image of his Son. And, God uses everything—good things and bad things—to make us into his image. This is the promise in Romans 8:28-29:

And we know that all things work together for good for those who love God, who are called according to his purpose, because those whom he foreknew he also predestined to be conformed to the image of his Son, that his Son would be the firstborn among many brothers and sisters.

What is the good thing that God promises for every believer? It is to be made in the image of Christ. That was the deliverance Paul was confident in. He was confident that he would look like Christ, and specifically that Christ would be glorified in him whether by life or death (v. 20).

See, it wasn't that Paul knew whether he would live or die. He didn't seem to know for sure that he would be released, though he was convinced of it. However, he did know that it was God's will to glorify Christ in his life through the process. He trusted God's will.

What does this tell us about Paul and what it means to live for Christ?

For Paul, it meant to trust God's plan and his purpose. He may not have fully understood why God allowed him to be placed in prison. He may not have understood why the very people he was trying to build up were criticizing him, but he did know it would all work towards his deliverance—his sanctification. Paul trusted in God's sovereign plan. In fact, he was consumed with God's sovereign plan.

We see this with many men of God in Scripture especially when confronted with suffering. Jesus Christ prayed, "If you are willing, take this cup away from me. Yet not my will but yours be done" (Luke 22:42). He said, "If there is any other way to save the world other than being separated from you, then do it, but your will be done. I entrust my life to you---trusting your will is best." He also declared that his life was to do the will of the Father (John 6:38). Christ was consumed with the will of God.

I love the story of David after being kicked out of his own kingdom by his son Absalom. David and his mighty men were walking away from the kingdom as exiles, and a man named Shimei began to curse David and throw stones at him (2 Samuel 16). David's mighty men became angry and asked, "Why are you allowing him to curse you, let us take off his head." But David replied, "Leave him alone so that he can curse, for the Lord has spoken to him. Perhaps the Lord will notice my affliction and this day grant me good in place of his curse" (2 Samuel 16:11-12). David trusted in God's plan for his life and that God was working everything for his good.

It is the very promise we have as believers in Romans 8:28: "And we know that all things work together for good for those who love God, who are called according to his purpose." We know God is working all things—good and bad—for our good. This was Paul's confidence. Everything was working out for his deliverance. "Living is Christ" means to trust God's will for our lives.

See, many only trust God's will when it is his will to bless us, but what about when he is making us like his Son through suffering? What if he is making us like his Son through persevering through trials (2 Thessalonians 3:5)?

Are you trusting God's plan for your life? Lord, if your plan means sickness or disability like it was with Jacob; Lord, if your plan means loss of my wealth and health as Job; Lord, if your plan means being persecuted or martyred as many of the prophets before me, Lord, your will be done. Lord, just allow me to be faithful in doing your plan.

Many Christians are like Abraham when he first came to faith. "Go to the land I've called you to dwell in, and I will make you into a great nation." Abraham gets to the land in Genesis 12, but there is a famine in the land, so he immediately packs up and moves to Egypt. It was incomprehensible to him that it was God's plan for him to suffer. "God, you called me to this? How can this be your will?"

However, later in Abraham's spiritual life, he matured. His life wasn't about his comfort or his will anymore—it was about God's plan. When God commanded him to offer his son as a sacrifice, he didn't ask questions. He had learned how to trust God with his life and also that of his family. To live was to follow God. If it was God's plan to take the son of promise away, he trusted that God would work even that out for his deliverance.

Are you living for and trusting God's plan? Or are you only trusting and submitting to his plan when it matches up with yours? "Living is Christ" means to trust and obey God's plan. Lord, whatever your will is.

Application Question: In what ways has God been challenging or teaching you to trust his plan for your life and not your own plans? How can we learn to faithfully trust and obey God's plan for our life even when it leads to trials and suffering?

To Really Live for Christ, We Must Depend on the Body of Christ

> for I know that this will turn out for my deliverance through your prayers and the help of the Spirit of Jesus Christ
> Philippians 1:19

Paul's confidence in this deliverance came from the prayers of the Philippians and the help given by the Spirit of Jesus Christ. Paul realized that in order for him to be faithful to God, he needed the prayers of the saints. He could not be bold in his witness, he could not die faithfully, nor could he be released without the prayers of the saints and the help of the Holy Spirit.

79

That is part of what it means to live for Christ—it means to not only be dependent upon God but also dependent upon his body. This is where much of Christ's help and resources come from. There are many Christians who live detached from Christ because they are not depending on his body. They lack the wisdom that comes from Christ. They lack the strength that comes from Christ, and they lack his comfort because they are independent, instead of dependent upon Christ's body.

In fact, when Paul says the prayers and the help given by the Spirit of Jesus Christ, it can also be translated "'your prayers and the consequent supply …"[36] Paul realized that the supply of the Holy Spirit—the boldness, the strength, and the patience come in part as a response to the prayers of the saints. It is impossible to live for Christ and not be dependent upon his people—the body of Christ.

It must be noted that many in the church claim to live for Christ without being dependent upon his body. This was the very problem that Paul confronted in 1 Corinthians 12:21-22. Look at what he said: "The eye cannot say to the hand, 'I do not need you,' nor in turn can the head say to the foot, 'I do not need you.' On the contrary, those members that seem to be weaker are essential."

We cannot say that we don't need one another because we do, and this need is often augmented in difficult times. When a person is blind, the rest of the senses in the body become stronger; the hearing and the touch become more acute in order to navigate the various aspects of life. This was true of Paul in prison. The Philippians not only sent Epaphras to care for and support him financially, but most importantly, they supported him through constant prayer.

In fact, we see Paul petitioning many churches for prayer while he was prison. He wrote to the Ephesians asking for prayer that he may preach the Word of God fearlessly (Ephesians 6:19). He wrote to the Colossians asking for prayer for both open doors and for clarity in speaking the Word of God (Colossians 4:2). In addition, the majority of Paul's letters ask for prayer. In this we learn the secret to much of Paul's great strength and usefulness for the kingdom. His great strength and usefulness came from his great weaknesses. He saw his inability and God's ability, and he knew God's ability often came through the saints.

We even saw this in Christ while he was on the earth. If there was anybody who could be independent, it was the Son of God. However, in his worst hour right before going to the cross, he called his disciples and said, "My soul is deeply grieved, even to the point of death. Remain here and stay alert" (Mark 14:34). When Christ was weak, he called a prayer meeting with the other disciples. He was dependent upon those God had given him. He came to the earth to demonstrate what man should really look like. He was dependent on the people of God and the supply of the Holy Spirit that came through them as they prayed.

Are you truly "alive" when you are with Christ's body? "To live is Christ" means being dependent and confident in his body. If we are not dependent, then we are missing much of the "abundant life" that is in Christ.

Application Question: In what ways has God taught you to rely on the body of Christ? In what ways have you experienced the supply of the Spirit through the body of Christ? How is God calling you to be a channel of his supply to others?

To Really Live for Christ, We Must Exalt Christ in Everything We Do

> My confident hope is that I will in no way be ashamed but that with complete boldness, even now as always, Christ will be exalted in my body, whether I live or die.
> Philippians 1:20

Interpretation Question: What does Paul mean by Christ being exalted in his body, whether by life or by death?

Here we see another aspect of what "living is Christ" means. It means to exalt Christ in everything we do. The phrase "confident hope," or "eagerly expect" in the NIV 1984, is really one word in Greek, and it has the idea of "watching something with the head turned away from other objects".[37] Paul's attention was wholly occupied with one thing to the exclusion of others. While in prison, unsure of what his sentence might be, he had one expectation more than anything else. What was it? He expected that Christ would be exalted in his body. His one focus was glorifying Christ. That's what living for Christ meant to Paul. It meant to glorify him in everything. In fact, he taught this in 1 Corinthians 10:31: "So whether you eat or drink, or whatever you do, do everything for the glory of God." Even in the mundane things of life—our eating and drinking—they should all be done in such a way that Christ is glorified. That should be our aim and that was Paul's earnest expectation as he went through this trial.

This phrase can literally be translated that "Christ will be enlarged in my body."[38] Other versions translate the word "magnify." Now certainly, Christ can get no bigger than he already is. Paul's hope was that his body would be like a telescope to all those around him. When we look at the stars, we realize that they are truly humongous objects in the universe. However, when looking at them from earth, they are so small that most of us walk around at night and barely notice them. However, if we looked through a telescope, the same small stars become a lot larger.

This is how most people's view of Christ is. Christ is the biggest and most important thing in the universe, and yet people, including us, commonly walk around without a thought of him. It is for this reason that living for Christ is so important because the world and many Christians miss out on seeing Christ and truly knowing his magnificence. One of the ways that people see Christ and know how big and great he is by looking at the lives of those who are truly living for him. Their life is not about comfort; it is not about wealth or prestige; it is all about magnifying Christ's name and helping people come to know him more. That should be our passion and our desire in life—to make him known.

We see this daily in lesser things. Someone goes to a movie they really like and they leave that movie magnifying the movie's name. They post on Facebook and tell all their friends how good it was. People also do this when they go to a restaurant that they really enjoyed—they tell the world about how great it was. That's what a Christian looks like who is really alive to Christ. It's their passion; it's their purpose.

Charles Ellicott translated Paul words this way: "My body will be the theatre in which Christ's glory is displayed."[39] This is a challenge for us each day. The reality is that Christ's worthiness and beauty is judged by our lives. We either demonstrate the glory and beauty of Christ or we demean him. The world judges Christ by his followers.

Paul said this about believers: "For we are a sweet aroma of Christ to God among those who are being saved and among those who are perishing" (2 Corinthians 2:15). We give off the smell of Christ. We magnify him by our lives. He also said to the Corinthians that they were a letter from Christ written for all to read (2 Corinthians 3:3).

Are we magnifying him? Are we demonstrating his goodness and grace?

Let us hear that, when we go through trials, our life speaks the loudest. When a person goes through a trial everybody watches, and it shows what our "life" really is. If comfort is our life or if getting our way is our life, we yell, complain, and get angry at anybody that affects what we want. But when Christ is our life, the aroma of Christ is constantly spread—the words of Scripture are constantly displayed on the tablet of our lives. Our lives say such things as: "Blessed are the peacemakers, for they will be called the children of God" (Matthew 5:9). Our lives say, "It is more blessed to give than to receive" (Acts 20:35). It says, "Trust in the Lord with all your heart, and do not rely on your own understanding" (Proverbs 3:5). It says, "Rather, if your enemy is hungry, feed him; if he is thirsty, give him a drink; for in doing this you will be heaping burning coals on his head. Do not be overcome by evil, but overcome evil with good" (Romans 12:20-21).

Certainly, we see this with Christ and his life on the earth—his desire was to glorify God. Not only was he consumed with doing God's will, but he also only said God's words (John 12:49). The works that he did were the Father's (John 10:37). He came to give glory to the Father.

What does your life shout when you go through trials? What does it speak to everybody who watches? Does it declare, "My way—my comfort—my dreams!" Or does it speak, "Christ—the gospel—the glory of God!"

Every day we must aim to allow our bodies to be theatres through which Christ is glorified whether through life or death. LORD, let this be true of us! Amen.

Application Question: How can we magnify Christ in the trials of life and in the mundane things of life? How is God calling you to glorify Christ more?

To Really Live for Christ, We Must Properly View Eternity

> For to me, living is Christ and dying is gain... I feel torn between the two, because I have a desire to depart and be with Christ, which is better by far
> Philippians 1:21, 23

Next, we see this battle in Paul's mind about what he should choose—life or death. To depart and be with Christ was better by far, and therefore, to die was gain.

In this verse we learn a great deal about what it truly means to live for Christ. How a person views the end of something always affects how they live. If a person views themselves as being a doctor in the future, it will affect the type of classes they take and how hard they study. They realize they must be at the top of the class in order to be competitive and to get into med schools. Our view of the end always affects how we live now.

This is also true about how we view death and therefore eternity. Many Christians don't view death as gain because they don't realize that what is waiting for them on the other side is so much better than life here. When Christ calls them to store up riches in heaven instead of on this earth (Matt 6:19) that doesn't motivate them much because they think their job, career, car, house, and X-box are really what life is all about. Your view of the end affects how you live now. In 1 Corinthians 15:32, Paul said, "If the dead are not raised, let us eat and drink, for tomorrow we die?" If there is no resurrection and no heaven to look forward to, why not live life for pleasure like everybody else? But if there is a resurrection and eternity, then it should constantly affect how we live. This is why Paul viewed death as gain and also why he chose to daily live for Christ. In fact, we can learn a lot more about his view of eternity by his use of the word "depart" to describe death. The Greek word for "depart" is a very rich word picture which teaches us a great deal about how we should view death and eternity.

Interpretation Question: What can we learn about eternity from Paul's use of the word "depart" in referring to death?

1. To depart is a camping metaphor.

As Paul was a tent maker, dying to him was a picture of taking up his tent and going home. He saw life as a temporary dwelling until he went to his permanent abode. This is the same picture he used in 2 Corinthians 5:1-2:

> For we know that if our earthly house, the tent we live in, is dismantled, we have a building from God, a house not built by human hands, that is eternal in the heavens. For in this earthly house we groan, because we desire to put on our heavenly dwelling.

Paul groaned to go to his permanent home. If we realized how temporary this life really was, then we wouldn't spend so much time investing in it; instead, we would focus on the eternal. When I stay at a hotel, I don't spend a lot of time or money making the hotel room more comfortable. I don't buy a better microwave or buy a better bed. Why? It's because I realize it is temporary. This is true of our lives on the earth as well.

Many spend their entire lives focusing on the tent, instead of preparing and investing in their eternal dwelling. Paul describes these people as just escaping the fire at the judgment seat of Christ in 1 Corinthians 3:15. When God tests their works—they will be found to be lacking. They will enter heaven, but none of their works are rewarded because they were all temporary. They spent their life building their tent instead of their eternal home (Matt 6:19-21).

2. To depart is a sailing metaphor.

It means to pick up your anchor and set sail. He saw life as sitting at the dock. A sailor lives for the journey—the adventure. They love being at sea. It is while at sea that they are really alive. If we think this life is exciting, wait until the next. That is when life really begins. Sadly, our view of heaven has been dulled by Hollywood and the movie industry. We think heaven is sitting on a cloud—playing a harp. However, we see Christ describing himself as awarding believers with cities and properties to manage in the coming kingdom for their faithfulness on earth (Luke 19:12-27). We won't be bored—we'll be serving our King.

The book of Revelation helps give us a clearer picture of heaven. In Revelation 20 we are seen ruling with Christ on the earth. Revelation 21 shows heaven as a city. From that we can assume all the characteristics of any city. There will be commerce, art, entertainment, business, leisure, and food. In Revelation 22:2, I love how it describes the tree of life bearing twelve kinds of fruit, one for each month. A regular tree bears fruit once a year and one kind of fruit. Heaven is beautiful, rich, and diverse. To depart is to start our adventure.

The person whose life is Christ is not living for this world but living for the next. To die is gain. To depart is to begin the real adventure.

3.   To depart is a political metaphor.

It means to set a prisoner free. Here on this earth we are bound to the flesh—our sin nature. I struggle with pride, insecurity, lust, anger, and many other sins. But in heaven, I will be like Christ. I will no longer carry around this old nature in my body; my body will be totally free from sin. One of the greatest things about death is that we will finally be free. We will be fully free to worship, to serve, to love, and to enjoy our God and others.

A person who is living for Christ is yearning with the rest of creation to be set free from the decay on this earth. Romans 8:22-23 says,

> For we know that the whole creation groans and suffers together until now. Not only this, but we ourselves also, who have the firstfruits of the Spirit, groan inwardly as we eagerly await our adoption, the redemption of our bodies.

4.   To depart is a farming metaphor.

It means to release a yoke. Paul saw himself serving Christ on this earth, laboring to see the kingdom come and to help Christians grow in maturity. But in heaven, he awaited a release from labor. It is not that we will not serve in heaven because we will, but the burden and the weight of service will no longer be there. Revelation 14:13 says this:

> Then I heard a voice from heaven say, "Write this: 'Blessed are the dead, those who die in the Lord from this moment on!'" "Yes," says the Spirit, "so they can rest from their hard work, because their deeds will follow them."

In heaven we will rest from our labor and our deeds will follow us. We will be rewarded for our deeds, and the benefits will continue throughout eternity. To live for Christ means to labor here on earth—to sweat, to discipline ourselves, to bear pain and lack of sleep for Christ, but at death it means to release the yoke. Come, Lord! Come! Maranatha!

What is your view of eternity? You can tell by how you live. If you haven't given much thought to heaven and eternity, it will show in your life. It will show by what truly makes you "alive." If we don't view death as gain, we will live this life just like the world, consumed with promotion, retirement, and the temporary things of this life instead of eternity. Paul saw departing as something better.

It should also be noted that if you don't view death and eternity properly, it will also affect how you view the passing of others. This doesn't mean that we don't mourn—we do. However, our mourning should not be like the world, for we mourn in hope (1 Thess 4:13). Like Christ at Lazarus's funeral, he cried because of his death and because of the pain of others (John 11:35), but he also knew that he was about to resurrect him. We mourn but not like the world. We mourn with hope in the resurrection, especially when our friends or relatives are believers. And when they are not, we trust in God's sovereignty and goodness.

What does the way you live your life say about your view of the end? "Living is Christ" means to die is gain.

Application Question: What metaphor of departing/death stood out to you most and why? How does Paul's view of death and eternity challenge how you live your life and how you view the passing away of others?

To Really Live for Christ, We Must Focus on Discipleship

Now if I am to go on living in the body, this will mean productive work for me... And since I am sure of this, I know that I will remain and continue with all of you for the sake of your progress and joy in the faith, so that what you can be proud of may increase because of me in Christ Jesus, when I come back to you.
Philippians 1:22, 25-26

Interpretation Question: How did Paul become convinced that it was God's will for him to remain (v. 25)?

When Paul considered the richness of going to be with Christ and how it was far better than living, he still felt compelled to stay and be with the Philippians and other churches for their spiritual progress.

When Paul says he is convinced of this and knows that he will remain, it doesn't necessarily mean he received a word from God that he would live. As we've watched him wrestle through the benefits of staying and leaving, it's possible that it was just "biblical reasoning." Paul was convinced that God would have him stay and be set free from prison because it would be more profitable for the Philippians (and others), and also because Paul, himself, wanted to stay for the same reason.

Observation Question: Why does Paul want to stay for the believers at Philippi?

Specifically, he says he wants to stay for their "progress." The word progress is a military term that speaks of a "pioneer advance." "It is a Greek military term referring to the army engineers who go before the troops to open the way into new territory."[40] Paul wanted this church to advance in areas spiritually that they had never been before. He wanted them to grow ultimately so that others would follow along the same path.

This should be our purpose as well as we live for Christ. While Christ was on the earth, he discipled others. To really live for him means to do the same. Consider what Paul said to Timothy: "And entrust what you heard me say in the presence of many others as witnesses to faithful people who will be competent to teach others as well" (2 Timothy 2:2).

In this verse we see four generations of Christians: Paul teaching Timothy, Timothy teaching other men, and other men teaching others. That is what it means to live for Christ. It means to be a disciple that disciples others, so one day they can do the same.

Being a disciple-maker doesn't necessarily mean you have to meet with somebody every day, read a book with him, and talk through the implications of the book. It simply means living life with others—meeting with them to listen, share, pray, and apply the Word of God together.

Are you willing to be available to others—to live with them, to encourage them, to share life experiences with them, and to help them spiritually progress? That is what "living is Christ" means. Like Christ, Paul spent his life discipling others and helping them progress in the faith.

Not only does Paul say he would stay for their progress in their faith but their joy in the faith. He wanted them to have joy in the Lord. This church was being persecuted (1:27), it had false teachers (3:2), and it had division (4:2). The Christian life is hard and there are constant threats to the believer's joy both from outside and inside. But part of growing in God is learning to delight in and rejoice in him more, no matter the circumstance. Paul himself declared in Philippians 4:11 that he had learned how to be content in every circumstance, and he even commanded this church to "Rejoice in the Lord always. Again I say, rejoice" (Phil 4:4).

Not only should we take from Paul's example our need to disciple others but also to be discipled. Someone said we all should have both a Paul and a Timothy in our lives. We need someone who is pouring into us, and we need others to pour into. Who is your Paul? Who is your Timothy?

In order to really live for Christ, we must focus on discipleship. Christ discipled others and so must we, as we follow him.

Application Question: What is your experience in discipling others or being discipled? How can we grow in the area of discipleship? What are some practical principles?

Conclusion

Paul said, "Living is Christ!" What can we learn from his example about really living for Christ?

1. To Really Live for Christ, We Must Trust and Submit to God's Plan
2. To Really Live for Christ, We Must Depend on the Body of Christ
3. To Really Live for Christ, We Must Exalt Christ in Everything We Do
4. To Really Live for Christ, We Must Properly View Eternity
5. To Really Live for Christ, We Must Focus on Discipleship

How to Live Worthy of the Gospel

Only conduct yourselves in a manner worthy of the gospel of Christ so that—whether I come and see you or whether I remain absent—I should hear that you are standing firm in one spirit, with one mind, by contending side by side for the faith of the gospel, and by not being intimidated in any way by your opponents. This is a sign of their destruction, but of your salvation—a sign which is from God. For it has been granted to you not only to believe in Christ but also to suffer for him, since you are encountering the same conflict that you saw me face and now hear that I am facing.
Philippians 1:27-30 (NET)

How can we live a life worthy of the gospel? How can we live a life that demonstrates its immense value?

In this text, Paul reminds the Philippian church of their responsibility to walk in a worthy manner. He says: "Only conduct yourselves in a manner worthy of the gospel of Christ" (Philippians 1:27).

He said as recipients of the gospel—the good news of Christ's life, death, burial, and resurrection for the sins of the world (1 Cor 15:2-4)—we have a responsibility to it. We are responsible to walk "worthy" of it.

John MacArthur said this about the Greek word for "worthy":

Axios (worthy) has the root meaning of balancing the scales—what is on one side of the scale should be equal in weight to what is on the other side. By extension, the word came to be applied to anything that was expected to correspond to something else.[41]

Similarly, the root of the English word "worthy" is "worth"—the value of something, how much something costs, or, in this context, how much something really matters. We should walk in a way that demonstrates the extreme value, the extreme worth of the gospel in our lives. The implication of this exhortation is that some in the Philippian church were not walking worthily. In this context, Christians were being persecuted for the gospel. They were being tempted to compromise their beliefs and their lifestyle, and some had probably even fallen away.

Likewise, we also are always being tempted to walk in an unworthy manner by the world, our flesh, and the devil. However, we must always demonstrate the extreme worth of the gospel—the fact that Christ saved us from this world, sin, Satan, and death.

How do we walk in a manner worthy of the gospel? In this text Paul describes what it means to walk worthy of this gospel so that we can live in a manner that honors Christ and his sacrifice for us.

Big Question: What does it mean for a Christian to walk worthy of the gospel of Christ as seen in Philippians 1:27-30 and how can we practically live out this reality?

Christians Walk Worthy of the Gospel by Living as Citizens of Heaven

> Only conduct yourselves in a manner worthy of the gospel of Christ
> Philippians 1:27

In order to walk worthy of the gospel, we must remember our citizenship is in heaven. John MacArthur's comments about the word "conduct" are helpful. He said:

> Politeuomai (conduct) is the main verb in verses 27–30, which in the Greek is a single sentence. It comes from the root word polis (city), which in earlier times usually referred to the city-states to which inhabitants gave their primary allegiance. The verb carries the basic meaning of being a citizen. But, by implication, it means being a good citizen, one whose conduct brings honor to the political body to whom one belongs.[42]

The New Living Translation translates verse 27 this way: "Above all, you must live as citizens of heaven, conducting yourselves in a manner worthy of the Good News about Christ."

One of the ways that we walk worthy of the gospel is by making our aim and focus to reflect our citizenship in heaven. This would have resonated with the Philippian church. Philippi had earned the distinction of a Roman colony. It was considered a "little Rome." When Rome was in power, it established many colonies outside of the city in order to protect Rome from barbarian invasions. In fact, it would grant veteran soldiers citizenship if they went out to settle these colonies. After years of faithful service, these colonies established by Rome eventually became Roman colonies—with all the rights and privileges of Rome.[43]

These colonies took great pride in their citizenship. They spoke the Latin language, wore Roman clothes, and their magistrates bore Roman titles. It didn't matter how far the colony was from Rome; they lived as Romans. We see something of how important Roman citizenship was in Acts 22. Paul was in Jerusalem and his presence in the temple caused a great uproar. Therefore, he was taken into custody by the Roman guard. As they were about to flog him, Paul said, "Is it legal for you to lash a man who is a Roman citizen without a proper trial?" (v. 25). When the soldiers heard this, they were shocked, and no one would flog or question him. Great privileges and esteem came with being a citizen of Rome. Therefore, when Paul used the word "conduct," it would have challenged the Philippians, as they were reminded of their greatly esteemed Roman citizenship. Paul was reminding them that their heavenly citizenship was even greater than Rome's, and it came with greater privileges.

Likewise, we should take great honor in our heavenly citizenship. It was purchased at great price through our savior's blood, and this reality should never leave our minds. As citizens of heaven we must have a new language, different clothing, and different attitudes. Paul essentially says, "Whatever happens in life, whatever you go through, always remember your citizenship. Always live as citizens of heaven."

How do we daily reflect this citizenship?

Application Question: How do we live as citizens of heaven with new language, clothing, and character?

1. As citizens of heaven, we must change our thinking.

   Romans 12:2 says,

   Do not be conformed to this present world, but be transformed by the renewing of your mind, so that you may test and approve what is the will of God—what is good and well-pleasing and perfect.

   Paul says that one of the ways we stop conforming to the ways of this world is by changing our views. We must change our thinking on what it means to be a success in life. In Luke 22:26 Christ describes greatness as being the "youngest" or the one who serves. In the Jewish culture the youngest served everybody, and therefore age was desired so one would no longer have to serve. However, Christ confronted their understanding of greatness—their understanding of success. He said greatness in the kingdom of heaven is the opposite of the world. Greatness is in being last—it is in serving everybody. Christ said this was true greatness. Let your understanding and pursuit of success reflect your heavenly citizenship, not your earthly citizenship.

91

We must change our thinking on what it means to be a man or a woman. Often the world perverts things. Men walk around thinking they must conquer as many women as possible. Women walk around thinking that they must be perfect—"perfect skin" and "perfect bodies." They must be "sexy" drawing the attraction and applause of men. This thinking does not reflect the ethos of heaven. God said, "Man looks at the outside but I look at the heart" (1 Sam 16:7). Solomon's mom said, "Charm is deceitful and beauty is fleeting, but a woman who fears the Lord will be praised" (Prov 31:30). Peter said this to Christian women:

> Let your beauty not be external—the braiding of hair and wearing of gold jewelry or fine clothes— but the inner person of the heart, the lasting beauty of a gentle and tranquil spirit, which is precious in God's sight.
> 1 Peter 3:3-4

Citizens of heaven are focused on the inward because this is the aspect that pleases God, not the outward.

We must change our thinking by constantly studying and thinking on the Word of God. The Word of God teaches us what a citizen of heaven should live and think like. Are you constantly transforming your thinking according to the Word of God? This is how a citizen of heaven should think.

2. Citizens of heaven must get rid of wrong character traits.

Consider what Paul said to the Colossians:

> You also lived your lives in this way at one time, when you used to live among them. But now, put off all such things as anger, rage, malice, slander, abusive language from your mouth. Do not lie to one another since you have put off the old man with its practices
> Colossians 3:7-9

Being a citizen of heaven means continually taking off wrong thought patterns, wrong attitudes, and wrong actions in order to conform to our new citizenship. James said this: "Pure and undefiled religion before God the Father is this: to care for orphans and widows in their misfortune and to keep oneself unstained by the world" (James 1:27).

As citizens of heaven we must keep ourselves from the pollution of the world. We must daily get rid of character traits unfitting of our new citizenship.

3. Citizens of heaven must continual put on the right character traits.

Paul exhorted Timothy to not only flee evil desires but to pursue righteousness—to run after it. Listen to what he said in 2 Timothy 2:22: "But keep away from youthful passions, and pursue righteousness, faithfulness, love, and peace, in company with others who call on the Lord from a pure heart."

Being a citizen of heaven does not mean that you are perfect, but it should mean that you are in pursuit of perfection. It means that it's your daily desire to look like Christ. You are pursuing righteousness, faith, love, and peace with those who call on the Lord out of a pure heart.

Can people tell that you are different? Can they tell that you talk differently, think differently, and have different goals in life? We must walk worthy of the gospel. The gospel has made us citizens of heaven, and we must live in a manner that represents that. We should constantly be changing our thinking and getting rid of wrong attitudes and sin in our life. We must pursue godly character as a citizen of heaven.

Christ purchased our heavenly citizenship, and it would be dishonoring to him and his gospel to live with disregard for it.

Application Question: What are some other ways in which citizens of heaven should think and act differently than the world? What characteristics of the world is God calling you to get rid of?

Christians Walk Worthy of the Gospel by Standing Firm

> Only conduct yourselves in a manner worthy of the gospel of Christ so that—whether I come and see you or whether I remain absent—I should hear that you are standing firm in one spirit
> Philippians 1:27

Interpretation Question: What does Paul mean by standing firm?

Paul says that one of the things that Christians should do in order to walk worthy of the gospel is to stand firm. But, what does it mean to stand firm?

Standing firm is war terminology. It is a picture of an army advancing against the gates of a kingdom and the soldiers standing firm fighting at the gates—not giving up any ground. This is the reality of the Christian life. Christians are always under attack both individually and as a community.

In the context of Philippians, the church was receiving persecution, much like Paul was. Paul, at this time, was in prison for preaching the gospel. Some Christians might have been tempted to fall away from the faith—to go back to their former life styles—instead of continuing to follow Christ amidst persecution. However, Paul called for them to "stand firm."

This is not only true with persecution, but it is also true with the influence of the world system. The world system is always trying to conform

Christians into its very image (Rom 12:2). It confronts Christians in the classroom, the work place, the media—through TV and music—in order to make Christians give up their ground.

Today we see the church being confronted with many issues. It is confronted on the issue of marriage. Scripture teaches that marriage is between a man and a woman, but many Christians have given up this belief in order to conform and show compassion for the world and their beliefs. Some have given up their beliefs because they realize this view could cost them opportunities. It could cost them a promotion or a friendship. Therefore, many Christians have chosen to not stand firm. The church is confronted with issues like abortion—the value of life. It is confronted constantly on exclusivity of the gospel. Christians are told that the gospel is too narrow—too bigoted. They are challenged to accept many ways to God—to be pluralistic.

Paul challenges this church and us to stand firm—to stand our ground in following God. Don't retreat. Don't turn away from God. Don't turn away from the truths of Scripture. Don't turn away from the exclusivity of the gospel.

But we should also realize our attacks are not just from the world, but they are also from Satan specifically. This is what Paul taught in Ephesians 6:11-12:

> Clothe yourselves with the full armor of God so that you may be able to stand against the schemes of the devil. For our struggle is not against flesh and blood, but against the rulers, against the powers, against the world rulers of this darkness, against the spiritual forces of evil in the heavens.

Certainly, Satan's attacks come against the church through the world, but they also come in many other ways. Sometimes his attacks come emotionally through spiritual depression. They come physically through sickness, sleeplessness, and weariness. They come through harassment and sometimes persecution. These attacks come to push a Christian away from the faith. Remember what Christ said to Peter when Satan asked to sift him like wheat. He said, "I have prayed for you, Simon, that your faith may not fail" (Luke 22:32).

Christ prays for Peter's faith because that was the very thing Satan was after. He wanted Peter's faith. He wanted Peter to doubt God. He wanted Peter to ultimately turn away from Christ, and it is the same with us. Satan's attacks come to make us leave the precious holy ground of our relationship with God. Many Christians have left the church. They no longer believe the Bible. They have accepted the liberalism of the world and turned fully away from God. This is the purpose of the enemy's attacks, and therefore, Christians must stand their ground.

94

Interpretation Question: How can Christians stand their ground against the enemy?

1. Christians stand their ground by being unified.

Philippians 1:27, in the NIV 1984, says, "I will know that you stand firm in one spirit, contending as one man for the faith of the gospel."

When Paul says "one spirit" and "one man," it is clear he is calling this church to be unified. One of the ways that Satan turns people away from the faith is by division. He brings conflict and discord in a church in order to conquer it. We cannot fight this battle if we are walking in discord with our brother or sister. Like any good military general, Satan's plan is "to divide and conquer."

The Philippian church, though in many ways was a model church, it also had problems. In Philippians 4:2 two women were fighting. Since Paul mentions this in the letter, it must have been a serious situation that was probably causing the church to separate into factions. In chapter 3 some false teachers were teaching circumcision in the church. The enemy was very much involved in this church trying to divide it. However, while under attack, they needed to stay unified—walking in one spirit and as one man.

Paul said this in Ephesians 4:26-27: "Be angry and do not sin; do not let the sun go down on the cause of your anger. Do not give the devil an opportunity."

Paul realized that anger and unforgiveness in the church simply opened a door for the evil one to bring destruction. "Opportunity" can be translated "foothold," which is war terminology. Anger and unforgiveness give Satan a strategic piece of property that he can attack from and potentially bring total devastation through. Christians stand their ground by being unified.

2. Christians stand their ground by being empowered by the Spirit of God.

Many commentators believe that when Paul says "one spirit," he is actually referring to the Holy Spirit as in Ephesians 4:4—"There is one body, one Spirit." In fact, the NIV 2011 version capitalizes the word "Spirit." As you may know, in the New Testament the word "spirit" can either refer to the human spirit, spirits such as angels and demons, or the Holy Spirit. We have to look at the context to tell how the word is being used.

One of the reasons many believe this could be referring to the Holy Spirit is because of similar language Paul used elsewhere. Consider what Paul says in Philippians 4:1: "So then, my brothers and sisters, dear friends whom I long to see, my joy and crown, stand in the Lord in this way, my dear friends!" He calls them to stand firm "in the Lord." This could be synonymous with Philippians 1:27. Another support could be how Paul calls the Ephesian church to stand firm against spiritual warfare, not in their own power, but by putting on the full armor of God. He says, "Clothe yourselves with the full armor of God so that you may be able to stand against the schemes of the devil" (Ephesians 6:11).

If the Philippians were going to stand their ground against the attacks of the evil one, it had to be in the Spirit's power. We need supernatural power to not be conformed to this world. We need supernatural power if we are going to stay unified in the church. We need supernatural power to stand against the growing animosity and persecution coming from the world.

We gain this power by being filled with the Spirit of God on a daily basis as we live in worship, prayer, the Word of God, and fellowship with the saints (Ephesians 5:18). We, as branches, must abide in the Vine, Jesus Christ, to have his power flow through us (John 15:5).

If you are a person that is not daily being filled with the Spirit of God by prayer, time in God's Word, and fellowship with the church, you are a Christian that will not stand. You will find anger, jealousy, lust, and selfish ambition ruling over you. You will find yourself slowly being drawn away from God and living more like the world. You can only fight this battle through the power of the Spirit of God.

If we as a church are going to stand our ground, we must fully depend upon God. This is why the early church was a praying church. When persecuted, they would throw prayer meetings as in Acts 4:23-42. After the apostles were threatened to no longer preach the Word of God, they called up the members of the church to pray, and God empowered them by the Spirit. Acts says this:

> When they had prayed, the place where they were assembled together was shaken, and they were all filled with the Holy Spirit and began to speak the word of God courageously. The group of those who believed were of one heart and mind, and no one said that any of his possessions was his own, but everything was held in common.
> Acts 4:31-32

This was the very thing that Paul challenged the Philippian church to do—to contend as "one man." When the early church prayed, the text says they were filled with the Spirit (v. 31), and they had "one heart and mind" (v. 32). They needed the Spirit of God to stand as one against the attacks of the world, the devil, and the flesh, and we need the Spirit as well.

To be honest, as I look at the persecution the church is going through even in Western society, with homosexual marriage and the like, I cannot but feel it is a serious time to pray and fast. It is a time for the church to stand firm in the Spirit of God, because if we don't, we will not be able to stand. There will be a great exodus and a great falling away. In this hour we must stand firm in the Holy Spirit. We must be a praying church, an abiding church—otherwise we cannot hope to stand. The time where complacent Christianity could survive is no more; we must be full of the Spirit, or we will not stand at all.

Furthermore, as we look at the church today in comparison to the early church, we can easily tell why the church is no longer advancing. While the early church was dependent upon prayer and the Holy Spirit, we are dependent on programs, entertainment, and business principles instead of the power of the Spirit of God. Paul said the weapons of our warfare are not carnal but mighty in God for casting down strongholds (2 Corinthians 10:4). Our weapons are not secular—they do not come from secular wisdom. Our weapons are the weapons of God himself.

If we are going to stand as a church in this increasingly dark age, we must be unified in truth, and we must be filled with the Spirit of God. We need his power to stand.

Application Question: Do you agree that much of the contemporary church relies on secular wisdom and tactics instead of the power of God to stand and therefore is giving up much ground to the enemy? If so, in what ways do we see this happening? How can the church again begin to be filled with the Spirit and the power of God in order to stand?

Christians Walk Worthy of the Gospel by Working as a Team

> Only conduct yourselves in a manner worthy of the gospel of Christ so that—whether I come and see you or whether I remain absent—I should hear that you are standing firm in one spirit, with one mind, by contending side by side for the faith of the gospel
> Philippians 1:27

The phrase "contending side by side" can also be translated "striving together." It comes from the Greek word "sunathleo" from which we get the word "athlete."[44] Paul commonly used athletic illustrations in his preaching and teaching (cf. 1 Corinthian 9:24, Ephesians 6:12, 1 Timothy 4:7, 2 Timothy 2:5), and here he calls for them to work together as an athletic team for the faith of the gospel.

Interpretation Question: What does "faith of the gospel" refer to?

"The faith of the gospel" is somewhat ambiguous. It could refer to faith as in trusting the gospel. It could refer to faith as in the doctrines in the gospel— the death, burial and resurrection of Christ. Or it could refer to the "faith" as in everything the Bible teaches like in Jude 1:3. Jude says, "Dear friends, although

I have been eager to write to you about our common salvation, I now feel compelled instead to write to encourage you to contend earnestly for the faith that was once for all entrusted to the saints." There is sense in which we as a church need to contend for all these aspects of the gospel because they are all under attack.

In the early church there were many attacks on the faith, just as there are today. In the church of Colosse a cult was attacking the deity of Christ. That is why Paul taught that "all things were created through him and for him" (Col 1:16) and that Christ was the very "image of the invisible God" (v. 15). In the Corinthian church some were teaching that there was no resurrection at all (1 Cor 15). In the Galatian church some were teaching salvation by works (Gal 1:6-9). Cults were attacking the foundation of the gospel.

It's the same today. We have the attacks of salvation by works—some teach salvation comes by faith plus works. We have attacks on the exclusivity of the gospel—some teach that Christ is just one way to salvation or that all will ultimately be saved. Some have attacked the very need for salvation by saying there ultimately is no judgment at all—there is no such thing as hell. Many attack the foundation of the gospel primarily by attacking the reliability of the Word of God. They declare it not true, that it can't be trusted, and it is full errors. This was the very first attack of Satan on Adam and Eve. He said, "Did God really say that man could not eat of any tree in the garden?" He wanted them to doubt the Word of God. In the same way, liberalism is attacking the foundation of the gospel in churches throughout the world. If the enemy can get us to doubt the Word of God, then soon we will doubt the gospel itself.

The enemy also attacks the gospel by bringing persecution. If you share that you are a Christian or your belief in the teachings of the faith, you will be attacked—left out when it comes time for promotion and mocked by friends. Satan works hard through shame and fear of retaliation to keep believers from sharing their faith. As in the early church, there is still a need to contend for the faith of the gospel. Are you willing to contend for it? Are you willing to work together as a team to do so?

Application Question: How can we contend for the faith of the gospel like an athletic team?

1. Christians contend for the faith like a team by developing chemistry as each person does his part.

No team can excel unless each person fulfills his role. This includes praying, giving, encouraging one another, and using our spiritual gifts. Every person must do his part in order for a team to be successful.

One of the reasons the gospel doesn't spread is because much of the church is not willing to work together. When Christ sent the disciples out to share the gospel, he sent them out in twos in Mark 6. When the Holy Spirit called Barnabas and Paul to missions, he didn't call them to go separately. He called them to go as a team in Acts 13. The gospel advances as we work together— each person doing his part.

We see this need for team work clearly in the life of Paul. While Paul was in prison, he constantly asked for prayer for open doors and for the Word of God to be spoken clearly and boldly through him. Look at what he said to the Colossians:

> Be devoted to prayer, keeping alert in it with thanksgiving. At the same time pray for us too, that God may open a door for the message so that we may proclaim the mystery of Christ, for which I am in chains. Pray that I may make it known as I should.
> Colossians 4:2-4

Paul knew that if the gospel was going to advance, it would only happen with a team effort. He could not do it on his own. He needed the support of the church. Jesus said this in his prayer before going to the cross: "...that they may be completely one, so that the world will know that you sent me, and you have loved them just as you have loved me" (John 17:23).

The church must be brought to complete unity in order for the work of the gospel to prosper. This is not just referring to the local church but churches throughout the world working together. Instead of competing, they must pray together, put their resources together, and support one another so that the world will know that God sent the Son.

2. Christians contend for the faith like a team by playing holy defense as they protect the gospel.

One of the ways that Christians contend for the faith of the gospel is by guarding it. Look at what Paul said to Timothy:

> Hold to the standard of sound words that you heard from me and do so with the faith and love that are in Christ Jesus. Protect that good thing entrusted to you, through the Holy Spirit who lives within us.
> 2 Timothy 1:13-14

How did Paul protect the faith—the teachings of the gospel? (1) He did it by teaching it to others. He passed down the pattern of sound teaching to Timothy, and he commanded Timothy to do the same (2 Tim 2:2). We are only a generation away from losing the deposit that was handed down to us from our parents and our teachers.

We saw this in the book of Judges right after Israel took over the land of Canaan. A generation arose that did not know God or what he had done for Israel (2:10). There arose a generation that no longer knew God's Word or obeyed his commands. Israel then went into one of the most corrupt seasons of its history. The deposit had not been guarded. It had not been faithfully passed down.

We not only protect the faith of the gospel by teaching it but also (2) by confronting false doctrine. It's not something we like to do, but it's something that must be done if we are going to keep the faith from decay. Listen to what Paul told Titus the job of an elder was: "He must hold firmly to the faithful message as it has been taught, so that he will be able to give exhortation in such healthy teaching and correct those who speak against it" (Titus 1:9).

Many of the New Testament epistles are written for this very purpose. Paul confronted those corrupting the gospel in Galatia, Corinth, and Colosse. John in his epistle confronted the attack on the gospel by the Gnostics. The writer of Hebrews confronted the attacks on the gospel by people who taught the law. In confronting these false doctrines the apostles sometimes were very harsh. Paul said anybody who taught a new gospel should be accursed— eternally condemned (Galatians 1:8-9). The apostles handed false teachers over to Satan by kicking them out of the church (1 Timothy 1:20). They warned the sheep by naming names (1 Tim 1:20, Phil 3:2, 2 John 1:9). All this may be a bit uncomfortable, but at times it is necessary. The gospel must be guarded like a team playing defense.

3. Christians contend for the faith like a team by playing holy offense as they spread the gospel.

Listen to what Paul told Timothy: "You, however, be self-controlled in all things, endure hardship, do an evangelist's work, fulfill your ministry" (2 Timothy 4:5).

No team can win games with only defense; there is a need to play offense. Sometimes I think the church is only playing defense, only trying to not give up ground and because of this, we are losing. There is a need to be offensive. As Timothy, we often need reminders to do the work of an evangelist as well. We must share the faith with others. We must be strategic with missions locally, and we must be strategic with missions abroad. As a team we must work together to spread the gospel.

Application Question: What are some attitudes that will hinder the team work of Christians?

• Christians must be careful of selfish ambition.

Anybody that has played in sports knows that one thing that makes a team ineffective is selfish individuals who are seeking all the glory. In basketball we call this person a "ball-hog." Individualism destroys teamwork. This is also true of individuals who want to be first in the church. They want to be seen. They always want to get their way, and they get mad when others don't listen to or honor them. John described a person like that in his third epistle. He said,

> I wrote something to the church, but Diotrephes, who loves to be first among them, does not acknowledge us. Therefore, if I come, I will call attention to the deeds he is doing—the bringing of unjustified charges against us with evil words! And not being content with that, he not only refuses to welcome the brothers himself, but hinders the people who want to do so and throws them out of the church!
> 3 John 1:9-10

There was a man in the church who loved to be first. He was causing division and gossiping against the apostolic leadership. He was selfish. He wanted his way, and it was hurting the team and therefore the mission of the church. I have seen people leave a church because they weren't selected to be an elder or a deacon. Successful teams have individuals that don't care who gets the glory. They don't need to be seen as long as the team is successful.

Are you comfortable with never being acknowledged for your contributions?

- Christians must be careful of laziness.

One aspect that always destroys a team is when some members are lazy. It destroys the synergy of a team when one person is not doing his part. Paul said this: "Do not lag in zeal, be enthusiastic in spirit, serve the Lord" (Romans 12:11).

Zeal is contagious. One person on fire can get a whole team on fire. In the same way, one person who is lazy, lethargic, and lacking energy can zap the zeal of the team. We must keep ourselves zealous for the work of God in order to faithfully contend for the gospel.

Are you still zealous for God's work?

- Christians must be careful of complaining.

Words are very powerful. Solomon said the power of life and death is in the tongue (Proverbs 18:21). Words can either build up or destroy. This is especially true on a team. A team that is always giving positive affirmation can work wonders.

I remember being an assistant coach for a women's college basketball team, and we practiced something called "props." After every practice and game, we got in a circle and each member of the team said something positive about another and then we would clap. Also, in practice or a game if some of the players were not playing, they were required to clap and give praise to those playing. The encouragement became contagious, and if it wasn't initially genuine, it became genuine. I loved coaching that team. However, I have also been around teams where bitterness and complaining took over and destroyed the community. Look at what the writer of Hebrews said: "See to it that no one comes short of the grace of God, that no one be like a bitter root springing up and causing trouble, and through him many become defiled" (Hebrews 12:15).

With Israel, the complainers stirred up a rebellion against Moses and God. Complaining can destroy a good work. It seems this complaining spirit had entered the Philippian church because in 2:14, Paul said, "do everything without grumbling or arguing."

Are you a complainer or a bitter person? The remedy for complaining is to choose to always give thanks in everything (1 Thess 5:18) and also to let no corrupt communication come out of your mouth but only what edifies others (Eph 4:29). Are you constantly building others up with your words?

Application Questions: How have you seen these types of attitudes negatively affect a church, a workplace, or a family? How is God challenging you to get rid of certain attitudes and to develop others in order to better contend as a team for the gospel?

Christians Walk Worthy of the Gospel by Being Confident in the Face of Opposition

and by not being intimidated in any way by your opponents. This is a sign of their destruction, but of your salvation—a sign which is from God. For it has been granted to you not only to believe in Christ but also to suffer for him, since you are encountering the same conflict that you saw me face and now hear that I am facing.
Philippians 1:28-30

One of the ways that we walk worthy of the gospel is by living confidently in the face of opposition without fear. The word Paul used for "intimidated" was a word used of horses being startled and beginning a stampede.[45] As mentioned previously, it is clear that the Philippians were receiving persecution for their faith, as were other Christians throughout the Roman Empire. Paul calls them to not panic, be shocked, or flee from the opposition.

Paul taught his disciple Timothy that everyone who wants to live a godly life in Christ Jesus will be persecuted (2 Tim 3:15). Jesus similarly said this to all who would follow him: "If anyone wants to become my follower, he must deny himself, take up his cross, and follow me" (Mark 8:34). We could quote Scripture after Scripture that teaches that persecution will be the lot of believers in this life.

At this period of time Nero was on the throne in Rome setting Christians on fire to light his garden or placing animal flesh on them before sending dogs after them. Today, statistics say around 400 Christians die for the faith every day. However, in some nations, specifically western nations, the persecution is not that overt. This persecution may show up in being considered strange, not being promoted, being hated or ridiculed because of our values. This should not startle Christians at all. Peter said this: "Dear friends, do not be astonished that a trial by fire is occurring among you, as though something strange were happening to you" (1 Peter 4:12).

A Christian that is surprised or frightened at this might be tempted to compromise his values and beliefs to conform to the world. He might be inclined to get mad at God or fall away from him altogether. The gospel message that is often taught in churches today is that following God will make everything better. Following Christ will make you wealthy and healthy. By overtly teaching this or implying it, we leave Christians unprepared for the reality of following Christ. And like the soil on shallow ground, we raise up Christians with shallow commitment to Christ. Therefore, when persecution comes, they fall away. Jesus said:

> The seed sown on rocky ground is the person who hears the word and immediately receives it with joy. But he has no root in himself and does not endure; when trouble or persecution comes because of the word, immediately he falls away.
> Matthew 13:20-21

I personally believe the "prosperity gospel" is severely weakening the church and as persecution comes we are going to see a stampede of Christians falling away from the faith. Paul said don't be frightened or shocked at those who oppose you for your faith and commitment to Christ. We walk worthy of the gospel by living confidently in the face of persecution.

Observation Question: What are the reasons that Paul gives for being confident in the face of opposition?

> and by not being intimidated in any way by your opponents. This is a sign of their destruction, but of your salvation—a sign which is from God. For it has been granted to you not only to believe in Christ but

103

also to suffer for him, since you are encountering the same conflict that you saw me face and now hear that I am facing.
Philippians 1:28-30

1.   Christians should be confident in the face of opposition because it is a witness to the world.

Philippians 1:28 says, "This is a sign of their destruction, but of your salvation—a sign which is from God."

By watching the response of Christians during persecution—their boldness, their willingness to suffer for Christ without fear—many unbelievers will be convinced of their coming destruction and the salvation of believers. One ancient observer said this about Christian martyrs: "They die so well." When Christians are bold for Christ, it is a challenging witness to the world. Moreover, when Christians compromise their faith in the face of opposition or simply worldliness, it pushes people away from Christ. No doubt the world thinks, "If it's not worth suffering for, it must not be real." They think, "If she claims to be a Christian and yet lives just like everybody else, the gospel must not be true." When Christians are confident in the face of persecution, it is a witness to the world.

2.   Christians should be confident in the face of opposition because it is a blessing.

Paul says, "For it has been granted to you not only to believe in Christ but also to suffer for him" (v. 29). "The word 'granted' can literally be translated 'graced.' It means 'to give freely or graciously as a favor.'"[46] Paul taught that persecution was a work of God's grace.

Interpretation Question: Why should persecution be considered a work of grace?

•   Persecution is a work of grace because it confirms our salvation.

Not only does it confirm our salvation to those who persecute us, but it confirms it to us as well. Jesus taught that persecution for righteousness was the stamp—the gold seal—on those who were part of the kingdom of heaven. Consider what he said in the Beatitudes: "Blessed are those who are persecuted for righteousness, for the kingdom of heaven belongs to them" (Matthew 5:10).

Christ said that those who are persecuted for righteousness, and those alone, are part of the kingdom of heaven. It's a proof of salvation. The Beatitudes give the characteristics of those who are part of the kingdom of heaven, and persecution is the gold seal. If we are without any form of persecution, then we may not be part of the kingdom of heaven. God uses persecution for righteousness to confirm our salvation.

- Persecution is a work of grace because it will be richly rewarded by God.

Jesus gave this promise to those who were persecuted for righteousness right after the last Beatitude. He said,

> Blessed are you when people insult you and persecute you and say all kinds of evil things about you falsely on account of me. Rejoice and be glad because your reward is great in heaven, for they persecuted the prophets before you in the same way.
> Matthew 5:11-12

God will richly reward all those who are persecuted for righteousness. In the book of James, God promises that those who faithfully endure trials will receive the crown of life (James 1:12). In Revelation 2:10, Christ promises the same to those who are about to be imprisoned for their faith. All that is suffered for the name of Christ and for the sake of righteousness will not be forgotten by God—it will be abundantly rewarded.

- Persecution is a work of grace because it leads to the development of godly virtues.

Romans 5:3-4 says, "Not only this, but we also rejoice in sufferings, knowing that suffering produces endurance, and endurance, character, and character, hope."

It says endurance—the bearing up under of difficult things—creates character. Dealing with difficult people helps us develop patience. It stretches our love. It helps us depend on God more. Character leads us to hope. Sufferings in life help us hope more in God and not be so focused on the temporary things in this world. Certainly, we see this with believers who have been laid up in the hospital for months with a terminal disease. All of a sudden they can't wait to go to heaven. Their hope is fully resting on being with God. Not only persecution for the faith but also trials in general are a grace from God. They lead us to develop godly virtues and to hope in God. Let us consider John Calvin's wise and challenging words about persecution:

> Oh, if this conviction were fixed in our minds, that persecutions are to be reckoned among God's benefits, what progress would be made in the doctrine of godliness! And yet, what is more certain

than that it is the highest honour of the Divine grace, that we suffer for His name either reproach, or imprisonment, or miseries, or tortures, or even death, for in that case He decorates us with His insignia. But more will be found who will order God and His gifts to be gone, rather than embrace the cross readily when it is offered to them. Woe, then, to our stupidity![47]

We should not be intimidated by persecution because it is a gift of God's grace. For what other reasons does Paul say we should not be intimidated?

3. Christians should be confident in the face of opposition because other believers are also suffering throughout the world.

Philippians 1:29-30 says this: "For it has been granted to you not only to believe in Christ but also to suffer for him, since you are encountering the same conflict that you saw me face and now hear that I am facing."

While Paul was in Philippi in Acts 16, he was stripped, beaten, and thrown into prison for his ministry. The Philippians had witnessed his struggles for the faith, and they partnered with him while he was imprisoned in Rome. Paul encourages them with the fact that their struggles were also his.

Similarly, Peter encouraged the Christians scattered and suffering in Rome. He said,

Be sober and alert. Your enemy the devil, like a roaring lion, is on the prowl looking for someone to devour. Resist him, strong in your faith, because you know that your brothers and sisters throughout the world are enduring the same kinds of suffering
1 Peter 5:8-9

One of the most common attacks of the enemy is to make us feel isolated—to make us feel like nobody else is going through the same sufferings as us. But Scripture says the trials and difficulties we go through are common to man (1 Cor 10:13). And therefore, we should be encouraged and emboldened, especially in the face of opposition. Other godly people are suffering the same things all throughout the world. We don't have to feel alone or isolated.

It is common for people to think that God made a mistake or is angry when they are going through suffering or persecution for the faith. However, persecution for the faith is actually a gift of God's favor. We shouldn't run or retreat from it (cf. James 1:4) but allow it to complete its sanctifying work in our lives. It is a proof of our salvation, and it brings great reward in heaven. Let us rejoice in it if God so graciously allows us to suffer for his name (cf. Matt 5:12).

Application Question: Do you feel that persecution for Christians is increasing? If so, in what ways? In what ways have you received persecution for the faith?

Conclusion

How do we walk worthy of the gospel of Christ?

1. Christians Walk Worthy of the Gospel by Living as Citizens of Heaven
2. Christians Walk Worthy of the Gospel by Standing Firm
3. Christians Walk Worthy of the Gospel by Working as a Team
4. Christians Walk Worthy of the Gospel by Being Confident in the Face of Opposition

How to Maintain Unity in the Church

> Therefore, if there is any encouragement in Christ, any comfort provided by love, any fellowship in the Spirit, any affection or mercy, complete my joy and be of the same mind, by having the same love, being united in spirit, and having one purpose. Instead of being motivated by selfish ambition or vanity, each of you should, in humility, be moved to treat one another as more important than yourself. Each of you should be concerned not only about your own interests, but about the interests of others as well.
> Philippians 2:1-4 (NET)

How can the church walk in unity?

In this passage Paul calls for the church of Philippi to be unified. Even though in many ways they were a model church, they were not a perfect church. They had many threats to their unity. In chapter 1, it is clear that they were being persecuted from outside for their faith. Paul said that God had granted them to not only believe in Christ but to suffer for him as well (v.29). In chapter 3, we see that there were false teachers teaching circumcision (v. 2). In chapter 4, two women were fighting in the church possibly causing it to divide into factions (v.2). Though a model church, the Philippians had many threats to their unity. William Barclay perceptively observed this:

> the one danger which threatened the Philippian church was that of disunity. There is a sense in which that is the danger of every healthy church. It is when people are really in earnest, when their beliefs really matter to them, that they are apt to get up against each other. The greater their enthusiasm, the greater the danger that they may collide. It is against that danger Paul wished to safeguard his friends.[48]

Passions which are good things can often lead to discord. Paul calls for this church to make his joy completed by being like-minded, having the same love, being one in spirit and purpose (2:2). Essentially, he called them to be unified, to be one.

The Philippians' struggle with unity was not unique; there were problems with unity from the inception of the church. In Acts 6:1 one of the

109

issues was cultural. The church was caring for Greek widows and Hebrew widows, but while distributing the food, the Greek widows were being left out. Amongst the Roman Christians, there were divisions over preference (Romans 14). Some preferred to worship on Sunday, and others practiced the Sabbath day. Some ate only vegetables, and others ate everything. These differences created division. The Corinthian church was divided over the personalities and teaching gifts of their greatest teachers (1:12-13). Similarly, each church today has the potential of disunity over such things as ethnic culture, church culture, doctrinal differences, personality differences, and personal preferences. Disunity is something the church must be aware of and wisely labor against.

Moreover, it must be noted that unity does not mean conformity. The world wants us to be all the same. We should all have the same body type, the same skin, the same education, the same type of clothes, etc. However, in the church (and the world for that matter) God made everybody different with different roles, and these differences make the body of Christ beautiful. The eye needs the hand, and the hand needs the feet. We give honor to the hidden parts like the heart and liver (1 Cor 12:23). Unity does not mean that everybody is the same but that we honor our differences and work together despite our differences.

Are there any conflicts in your life with family, peers, co-workers, or church members? How can we learn to walk in unity, especially in the body of Christ? In this text we will consider several ways to maintain unity in the body of Christ.

Big Question: How can the church and its members walk in the unity God called us to according to Philippians 2:1-4?

To Be Unified, Christians Must Focus on the Right Resources

> Therefore, if there is any encouragement in Christ, any comfort provided by love, any fellowship in the Spirit, any affection or mercy Philippians 2:1

Some might be tempted to think that it is impossible to have unity. They might declare, "We are too different! We have different backgrounds, different styles of worship, and we enjoy different things. We also express ourselves differently. How in the world can we be unified?"

Paul seems to be answering this question as he reminds the church of the resources they have for unity. He describes four resources which are both commonalities of each Christian and empowerments for unity. He says,

110

"Therefore, if there is any encouragement in Christ, any comfort provided by love, any fellowship in the Spirit, any affection or mercy" (Phil 2:1).

This really is not a question but a confirmation. Paul gives the conditional "if" because he knows they have experienced these things. They had encouragement from being united with Christ, comfort from Christ's love, and fellowship with the Spirit, etc.

Most of our close relationships are based on commonalities—what we share in common. With relatives, it may be the blood we share in common. With friends, it may be a common ethnicity or hobby. These commonalities help us be unified. However, what we share in common as Christians is even greater than any commonality we could share with the world.

But God has not just given us these as commonalities but also as empowerments. The grace to be unified has been given by God, and we must appropriate and access it. Since God has given us all these resources—all these supernatural empowerments—we should be a unified church.

Interpretation Question: What are the resources God has given the church for unity?

"Therefore, if there is any encouragement in Christ, any comfort provided by love, any fellowship in the Spirit, any affection or mercy" (Philippians 2:1).

1. God has given us encouragement in Christ.

One of the commonalities we have as believers is encouragement from our relationship with Christ. The word "encouragement" means to come alongside someone, to give assistance by offering comfort, counsel, or exhortation.[49] It means to come alongside to help. "It combines encouragement with alleviation of grief."[50] Christ used a similar word in referring to the Holy Spirit and his ministry to us. The Holy Spirit is the "paraclete"—our counselor, our advocate, our helper (John 15:26). The word represents exactly what we see in the Parable of the Good Samaritan (Luke 10). The Samaritan comes alongside the person hurting, anoints his wounds, puts him in a hotel, and pays for his stay. He does whatever is needed to help. Christ does the same with us.

This is one of the reasons we can be unified. We can be unified because we have in common the same friend, the same comforter, the same encourager. For each of us, Christ comes alongside to walk us through the pains and the struggles of life. Where ever you go, Christ goes with you. He said this to his disciples and to us through them, "And remember, I am with you always, to the end of the age" (Matt 28:20).

We have the same person to come to in order to find grace and mercy in time of need. Listen to what the writer of Hebrews said about Christ.

111

For we do not have a high priest incapable of sympathizing with our weaknesses, but one who has been tempted in every way just as we are, yet without sin. Therefore let us confidently approach the throne of grace to receive mercy and find grace whenever we need help.
Hebrews 4:15-16

We have a Savior that can sympathize with our weakness and minister to us the exact mercy and grace we need. He understands being alone. In the hour of his greatest need, his family and friends left him. He knows depression. He said, "I'm weary unto death." He knows being betrayed. He knows being hungry. He knows being tired. He knows being tempted by the devil, and yet, he is without sin.

Surely, we each have great encouragement in Christ. This commonality is a motivation for us to be unified. But again, this is not just a commonality; it is also an empowerment for unity.

Christ could still love his disciples who failed him. He could love those who mocked and accused him. He could forgive them. And he can encourage us to do the same when we suffer. We can be unified because we have someone who has been through it all before us, and he comes alongside us to help us.

Yes, we can be unified because we have the help of Christ. You can love your roommate, your parent, and your church because of the help and encouragement of Christ. He comes alongside you to do so.

What else has God given us for unity?

2.   God has given us comfort from his love.

Another commonality and empowerment for unity that God has given us is "comfort" from his love. Each believer became a recipient of God's love at spiritual birth.

For this is the way God loved the world: He gave his one and only Son, so that everyone who believes in him will not perish but have eternal life.
John 3:16

But God demonstrates his own love for us, in that while we were still sinners, Christ died for us.
Romans 5:8

While we were still sinners, Christ died for us. We have all become recipients of this great love; we have received comfort in our sin and failures through God's love for us. This is a tremendous consolation that the world does not know. We have received God's love which comforts and enables us to be unified.

John said this: "There is no fear in love, but perfect love drives out fear, because fear has to do with punishment. The one who fears punishment has not been perfected in love" (1 John 4:18). Fear and anxiety are often the driving forces behind conflict. We fear being rejected. We fear not being loved. We fear people talking about us. We fear losing things important to us, and this encourages us to think bad thoughts about others and sometimes to even fight with them. Many of us stay awake at night rehearsing conflict and cultivating anxieties. However, Paul says we can be unified because we have comfort from Christ's love, and this comfort should enable us to be unified. Love drives away those fears. With the Ephesians, Paul actually prays for them to have power to grasp this love. He prays:

> that Christ may dwell in your hearts through faith, so that, because you have been rooted and grounded in love, you may be able to comprehend with all the saints what is the breadth and length and height and depth, and thus to know the love of Christ that surpasses knowledge, so that you may be filled up to all the fullness of God. Ephesians 3:17-19

To be filled to the fullness of God means to be empowered by God (cf. Eph 5:18). That is the result of grasping the greatness of Christ's love. Christ's perfect love casts out fears and anxieties that keep us from unity. Fear of rejection and fear of being hurt not only cause us to fight but keep us from seeking to restore relationships. These fears are not God's will for the believer, so he sends us his supernatural love to comfort us and enable us to live in unity with one another (cf. Rom 5:5).

3. God has given us fellowship with the Spirit.

Another commonality and empowerment to be unified that God gave us is the Holy Spirit. When we were saved, God did a miraculous work in us through the Holy Spirit. We were baptized with the Holy Spirit into the body of Christ. First Corinthians 12:13 says, "For in one Spirit we were all baptized into one body. Whether Jews or Greeks or slaves or free, we were all made to drink of the one Spirit."

Now this baptism happened at the very moment every Christian was saved. They became part of the body of Christ and eternally attached to Christ and to believers. One person becomes the hands, and another becomes the feet. God did a supernatural work through the Holy Spirit that will never be undone. Throughout eternity we will be the body of Christ, attached to Jesus and dependent upon one another. It's a phenomenal concept.

However, even though the Holy Spirit made us one in Christ and gave us spiritual gifts that we must use for one another's edification, we must still labor to keep this unity in the Spirit. Paul said this: "making every effort to keep the unity of the Spirit in the bond of peace" (Ephesians 4:3).

The Spirit of God already made us one and works in us to work together and depend upon one another; however, we must labor to keep the unity he forged. The Spirit made us one, and we must work to maintain it.

This labor for unity is also done through the Spirit. Listen to the fruits that he bears in our lives to help us be unified: "But the fruit of the Spirit is love, joy, peace, patience, kindness, goodness, faithfulness, gentleness, and self-control. Against such things there is no law" (Galatians 5:22-23).

Can you not hear Paul challenging this church and us? Some might say, "We are divided because this person is unreasonable!" But Paul says, "Yes, I know, but the Holy Spirit has given both of you patience." One says, "We can't be unified because we are so different!" But Paul says, "Yes, but God has given you love."

Everything we need to be unified has been given to us by the triune God. Christ has come alongside us to help and encourage us. He comforts us with love in times of discouragement and fear. He has given us the power of the Holy Spirit to help us be unified. There is no excuse for us to be divided. However, Paul says, "Wait! There is more."

What else has God given us so we can be unified?

4. God has given us affection and mercy.

Paul says God has given us "affection" and "mercy" in order to be unified. The word "affection" is translated "bowels" in the KJV. It is a physical word related to one's stomach. It means the ability to feel somebody's pain or hurt with them through trials. Paul used this word earlier in Philippians 1:8. He said that he longed for the Philippians with the very "affections" (or bowels) of Christ. He felt the same pain and yearning for the Philippians that Christ felt.

This is very important because when we are in discord we often only feel our own pain. We can't hear the cries of the other person because we are too upset about being disrespected and dishonored, but the bowels of Christ feels the pain of others. This affection leads us into mercy, also translated compassion. It leads us to serve the very needs of those who hurt us.

We can be unified because Christ gave us his own affection and mercy. When Christ looked at the crowds and saw them like sheep without a shepherd, he had compassion on them and went to minister to them (Matt 9:36).

Excuses may abound about why we cannot be unified. We have different backgrounds, different cultures, etc. But the triune God speaks to us and says,

114

I have empowered you. My Son comes alongside you to help and bring you encouragement. I have given you my love to comfort you in pain and to empower you to love the unlovely. I have made you one through the Holy Spirit and given you his fruits to help you be unified in trials. Finally, where others only feel their pain, I have given you tenderness—sensitivity to the pain of others—and desire to respond with compassion like my Son did with you.

Does Paul's rhetorical argument make sense? Certainly, it does. He challenges the Philippians and us to look at the resources God has given us to be unified. These are both commonalities and empowerments for unity.

Application Question: In what ways have you experienced the resources of God in your life, and how have you, by his grace, found them helpful in working for unity?

To Be Unified, Christians Must Develop the Right Attitudes

complete my joy and be of the same mind, by having the same love, being united in spirit, and having one purpose
Philippians 2:2

Disunity always begins in the heart—the mind, will, and emotions—before it manifests outwardly. Therefore, if we are going to be a unified people, we must work on the inner man; for it is from the inner man that all divisions come. James 4:1 says this: "Where do the conflicts and where do the quarrels among you come from? Is it not from this, from your passions that battle inside you?"

The reason I have conflict is because I have a heart problem. It's an inner man issue.

Observation Question: What attitudes must believers cultivate in order to be unified?

1. Believers must have the same mind.

Paul says that believers must have the "same mind." It literally means "to think the same thing."[51]

Interpretation Question: What does Paul mean by being like-minded in order to be unified?

115

It seems that this question is answered by looking further along in the context. In Philippians 2:5 Paul says that every person should have the same "attitude" or "mind" as Christ. When Christians develop the mind of Christ, it will be easy to be unified. The mind of Christ is further clarified in Philippians 2:7 where it says that Christ took the very nature of a "slave" or "servant." He didn't come to earth to be served, he came to serve. That is the type of mindset each believer must develop in order to be unified in the church.

In fact, one of the major reasons that we fight and argue in the church is because people treat us like servants. We feel disrespected. We feel like others are not respecting our position. Church members don't mind serving on occasion, but don't ever treat them like servants.

However, Christ took the "form" of a servant. He wasn't simply a king that was serving—he was a king that was a servant. His attitude was consumed with others over himself. That is the mindset that must be developed if we are going practice unity in the church. We must care more about others than about ourselves. We must be more about other's happiness. Paul expands this thought in the following verse. He says this: "Instead of being motivated by selfish ambition or vanity, each of you should, in humility, be moved to treat one another as more important than yourself" (Philippians 2:3).

This is the servant mind that each one of us must adopt. Unity cannot be achieved if only one person has this mindset. Each of us must decide to be servants in order to be unified. "No, not my way, let's do it your way." It's the mindset of a servant. Lord, help us develop this.

2.   Believers must have the same loving attitude.

The next attitude Paul says we must develop in order to be unified is a loving attitude. He says make my joy fulfilled by having the same love. What type of love? The type of love that Paul is talking about here is "agape." He uses the Greek word for God's love in this text. It is not a selfish love or a love of the emotions that is many times seen in world. "I love you until you hurt me. I love you because you love me. I love you because I feel this way, but when I don't feel this way I don't love you anymore." That type of love will never result in unity. It is like the wind—it is here today and gone tomorrow. It cannot be relied on.

Interpretation Question: What does this agape love look like which unifies the church?

•   Agape love is an act of the will.

"I choose to love even when you are unlovable. I have committed to love you no matter how much you harm me or do wrong to me." Many would

116

call this an irrational love or a crazy love. But it is actually the type of love found in God. Look at how Scripture describes God's love:

> But God demonstrates his own love for us, in that while we were still sinners, Christ died for us… For if while we were enemies we were reconciled to God through the death of his Son, how much more, since we have been reconciled, will we be saved by his life?
> Romans 5:8, 10

God loved us while we were sinners and enemies of his, and yet, he still gave his life for us. That is the type of love that brings unity. In fact, some have defined love as this: "Love is when you give not caring what you get in return." That is the type of love God gives us. We fail and dishonor him, and yet he still loves us. He gives the unjust "rain and sunshine" even as he does the righteous (Matt 5:45). This common grace is a reflection of agape love.

Because agape is a love of the will, it can be "commanded." We can be commanded to love our enemies, to bless them, and to do them good. We can be commanded to feed our enemy when he is hungry, and when he is thirsty to give him drink (Romans 12:20).

Is your love an act of the will in obedience to God? Or is your love up and down based on how you feel emotionally?

- Agape love is a sacrificial love.

Christ gave up his life for us and taught that we should do the same thing for others. People who would truly die for one another are not going to be divided by temporary petty issues. Agape is a sacrificial love that is willing to give up its privileges.

"We have come to know love by this: that Jesus laid down his life for us; thus we ought to lay down our lives for our fellow Christians" (1 John 3:16).

- Agape love is practical.

John said this: "Little children, let us not love with word or with tongue but in deed and truth" (1 John 3:18). Agape love is not simply saying you love the church; it is being overwhelmed with a desire to serve the church and meet one another's needs. Romans 12:10 and 13 says this: "Be devoted to one another with mutual love, showing eagerness in honoring one another… Contribute to the needs of the saints, pursue hospitality."

Is your love sacrificial—willing to give up your rights for others? Is your love practical? Is it given to acts of service among the church?

117

This is the same love that we must have if we are going to be unified. We must choose to love each other sacrificially and practically, regardless of how we are treated. This is the type of love that unifies.

If your love is the selfish love of the world, you will love your church as long as they don't fail or disappoint you. But when they do, you will hold a grudge and complain causing more dissension or you will simply leave. We must all have agape love in order to maintain unity.

I don't mean to imply that this is easy; it is not. But it is possible because the ability to love like this was given to believers in their salvation. Romans 5:5 says, "And hope does not disappoint, because the love of God has been poured out in our hearts through the Holy Spirit who was given to us." The love of God has been lavishly poured out in our hearts. God has given the church ability to love like him. Let us then in faith choose to love each other the way God loves us.

3. Believers must be united in spirit.

The word "united" literally means "one-souled"[52]; therefore, to be united in spirit means to care for one another as though we were caring for ourselves. This means to follow the golden rule, to love your neighbor as yourself (Mark 12:31). When we are united in spirit and love one another as ourselves, then we will become a united church.

We see something of what it means to be "one-souled"—"united in spirit"—by reading Romans 12:15-16. It says, "Rejoice with those who rejoice, weep with those who weep. Live in harmony with one another."

We should rejoice when others are successful or happy. We should mourn when others mourn. Paul actually describes this as living "in harmony with one another." He essentially describes this as being "united in spirit."

Too often members of the church live independently of one another. Church is just to fulfill their desire to worship on Sundays and that is it. However, in order to be "united in spirit," we must live life together. We must get to know one another and be connected to one another.

I remember during my junior year of high school, we got a new basketball coach. And one of the things he initially implemented was our strategically getting to know one another better. He said he wanted us eating together, going to the movies together, etc., so we could essentially become one in spirit. He said chemistry on the basketball court did not happen only by practicing and playing together. It came by living life together. This was the type of culture that he fostered in order for us to be successful, and this culture should be similarly fostered in the church. The early church met every day breaking bread from house to house (Acts 2:46). They were united in spirit— one souled—and we must be as well.

How are you fostering unity in spirit with your church? How are you developing intimate relationships? How are you getting to know one another in such a way that you think the same and feel the same—where you weep and rejoice together? When we are "one-souled," we will care about people so much that we will make every effort to be unified with them (Eph 4:3).

A good example of becoming one-souled is a marriage. When a couple gets married, they move in with one another, eat together, and share entertainment together, among other things. Then all of a sudden, weird things start happening like finishing one another's sentences or being able to sense when the other person is upset or something is wrong. They start to become united in spirit—one-souled. As this process continues to deepen, the conflicts typically lessen in a marriage union. However, when they are less united, more conflicts happen.

This is God's will for his people as well that they would live as "one body" (Ephesians 4:4). The phrase "one body" is actually very similar to the one God uses for marriage—"one flesh" (Genesis 2:24). We must be united in soul to maintain the unity.

4. Believers must have one purpose.

Finally, Paul says believers must have the same purpose. What purpose is Paul referring to?

Many commentators believe Paul is referring to the gospel being the church's primary focus. Paul mentioned the gospel five times in chapter 1, and in the last one he said this:[53]

> Only conduct yourselves in a manner worthy of the gospel of Christ so that—whether I come and see you or whether I remain absent—I should hear that you are standing firm in one spirit, with one mind, by contending side by side for the faith of the gospel
> Philippians 1:27

A support for the possibility that Paul is referring to the gospel being their purpose is the fact that chapter 2 is connected to chapter 1. When Paul says, "Therefore, if there is any encouragement in Christ, any comfort provided by love, any fellowship in the Spirit, any affection or mercy" (Phil 2:1), the "therefore," points back to Paul's emphasis in Philippians 1:27—walking in a manner worthy of the gospel.

When the church is unified around something as big as the gospel, then our petty differences, by necessity, fall to the wayside. What will unify a people with different cultures, different careers, different ages, etc.? It has to be something bigger than all those things. It is the gospel—the life, death, burial, and resurrection of Christ for the world. Competing purposes will only divide.

If your purpose is your kingdom and your will be done, then you will fight with everybody who gets in your way. If your purpose is your comfort, then if the music changes in the church, the seats change, or the order of service changes, you will fight against everybody and against everything that makes you uncomfortable. But when your purpose is the gospel, you will gather with people very different from you, even doctrinally, to seek to advance the same cause.

Is your purpose the gospel—seeing people know Christ and living out the faith of the gospel? This is the purpose that will unify us.

What attitudes must we have in order to be unified? We must have the mind of Christ—serving others. We must have the love of Christ—loving sacrificially and practically. We must live as the body of Christ—being unified in spirit—living as though we are one. Finally, we must have the same purpose of Christ—to spread the gospel.

Application Question: Which attitude necessary for unity challenged you the most? In what ways is God calling you to work on a specific attitude in order to increase the unity of your church?

To Be Unified, Christians Must Develop the Right Practices

> Instead of being motivated by selfish ambition or vanity, each of you should, in humility, be moved to treat one another as more important than yourself. Each of you should be concerned not only about your own interests, but about the interests of others as well.
> Philippians 2:3-4

Next Paul goes from our inward motives to outward actions. We must develop certain practices in order to maintain unity in the church.

Observation Question: What type of practices must we develop if we are going to maintain unity in the church?

1. Believers must practice forsaking selfish ambition or vanity.

Paul gives us a very difficult challenge. He says, "Instead of being motivated by selfish ambition or vanity, each of you should" (v. 3). The phrase "selfish ambition" pictures "a person who persistently seeks personal advantage and gain, regardless of the effect on others."[54] They will use anything to get what they want including: "flattery, deceit, false accusation, contentiousness, and any other tactic that seems advantageous."[55] The word was often used of

120

politicians.[56] It has the connotation of building oneself up by bringing others down. In politics the desire to win is so great that they will often do anything to get what they want including tearing down the other candidates' family, past, etc.

"Vanity" can literally be translated "empty glory" or "empty conceit." There are some differences between selfish ambition and vanity. John MacArthur said this:

> Whereas selfish ambition pursues personal goals, empty conceit seeks personal glory and acclaim. The former pertains to personal accomplishments; the latter to an overinflated self-image. Understandably, a person with such conceit considers himself always to be right and expects others to agree with him. The only unity he seeks or values is centered on himself.[57]

One causes division because of goals they are pursuing; the other causes division in order to receive or protect glory. Selfish ambition and vanity often go together. We saw this in the Pharisees who loved to be greeted by others and to sit in the best places. They desired to both be honored and maintain their position. Therefore, the Pharisees were in conflict with both John the Baptist and Jesus because they were threats to their position and glory.

This is often how the world is. Life is all about selfish ambition and vain glory—getting the best grades, the best degree, the best job, the nicest car, and receiving praise because of these things. Therefore, the world will often do anything to get or protect these things. The world system is driven by selfish gain. People will cheat to get what they want. They will cut others down. They will fight, steal, or do any number of dishonest things to achieve their desires.

It is not surprising that Paul lists selfish ambition and vain glory as attitudes we must forsake to have unity since these attitudes originally brought disorder in the world. It was Satan's desire to be like the Most High that brought division in the heavenlies. He had an inflated view of himself. Satan then tempted Adam and Eve with the same desire to be like God causing a division between God and man. Selfish ambition and vanity are really the root of all sin. It is the desire to get our will done over God's and have our glory over his. It is the cause of all division.

James said, "For where there is jealousy and selfishness, there is disorder and every evil practice" (James 3:16). Where jealousy and selfish ambition are, you will find disorder and every evil practice. He then described how this was affecting the early church. Look at what he said:

> Where do the conflicts and where do the quarrels among you come from? Is it not from this, from your passions that battle inside you? You

121

desire and you do not have; you murder and envy and you cannot obtain; you quarrel and fight. You do not have because you do not ask.
James 4:1-2

These Christians were warring because they were living like the world. They were seeking their own desires and glory instead of the desires and glory of God. Somebody had even died amongst these scattered congregations because of their selfish ambition. Similarly, selfish ambition and vain glory led the Pharisees to kill Jesus. They did not want to lose their place and authority in Israel.

Paul simply said, "Do nothing out of selfish ambition or vanity" (paraphrase). Do nothing to exalt yourself and your goals. This was not something seen in Christ. He gave up everything to come to the earth and to serve those he ruled over. Christ wasn't living for his glory; he lived for the glory and the will of the Father and for others. He often would do miracles and say, "Shh... now don't tell anybody" (Matt 8:4). Sometimes he would try to avoid the crowds (Mark 1:35-38). He wasn't a glory seeker, and he wasn't fighting for his glory like others. He came to do the Father's will and give glory to the Father. This type of attitude will deliver us from much division. We must forsake selfish ambition and vanity.

Ambition and desire for glory in itself are not wrong, but our ambition must be to honor God and receive glory from him. Christ didn't even rebuke the disciples for desiring to be great; he just tells them how to do it by being last, for the last will be first in heaven (Mark 9:35).

Application Question: How do we practice doing nothing out of selfish ambition or vanity?

- We should survey and question our motives.

Christ challenged the disciples to look at their motives when they did works of righteousness. Don't do it to be seen by men like the Pharisees (Matt 6). Therefore, we must always survey our motives, especially when in conflict and struggling with anger.

We should ask ourselves questions when feeling tempted to react with anger or to fight with others. "What is really motivating this? Is it my desire to be respected? Is it my desire to see my will done? Or is it my desire to do God's clearly revealed will? Is it my desire to help others?" We should ask ourselves these types of questions.

- We should ask God to test our motives.

This is what David did. Consider what he prayed: "Examine me, and probe my thoughts! Test me, and know my concerns! See if there is any idolatrous tendency in me, and lead me in the reliable ancient path" (Psalm 139:23-24).

2. Believers must practice the humility of a servant.

Paul said, "in humility, be moved to treat one another as more important than yourself" (v. 3). The word "humility" can also be translated "lowliness of mind." In secular Greek literature this word "was used exclusively in a derisive way, most commonly of a slave. It described what was considered base, common, unfit, and having little value."[58]

Again, Paul gives us this slave or servant metaphor in order to teach us how to have unity. We must practice the humility of the servant. We must not see ourselves better than others but less than others.

This is very countercultural. We live in a culture that is all about "self-esteem." We must all know how special we are, how good we are. If you are depressed, the world would say, go to the mirror and say to yourself over and over again, "I am special. I am significant." This is the very opposite of what Paul says and also opposite of how he lived. Consider some of Paul's comments about himself.

> For I am the least of the apostles, unworthy to be called an apostle, because I persecuted the church of God. But by the grace of God I am what I am, and his grace to me has not been in vain. In fact, I worked harder than all of them—yet not I, but the grace of God with me.
> 1 Corinthians 15:9-10

Was Paul really the least of the apostles? We probably hear about Paul more in the Bible than any other apostle. He wrote almost half of the New Testament. Paul, is that really a fair assessment of yourself? What else did Paul say?

> This saying is trustworthy and deserves full acceptance: "Christ Jesus came into the world to save sinners"—and I am the worst of them!
> 1 Timothy 1:15

Why did Paul talk about himself in this way? He called himself the worst sinner; the KJV translates it the chief of sinners. Why did Paul have such "low self-esteem"—the least apostle and the chief sinner? Why was his esteem so low? It was because he esteemed everybody else higher than himself.

If this were not enough, Paul also said that he made himself a servant or slave of everyone. "For since I am free from all I can make myself a slave to all, in order to gain even more people" (1 Corinthians 9:19).

Here we see the reason we are so divided. We think too highly of ourselves (vanity). Satan has developed a system that is all about self-esteem—building ourselves up—, and therefore, it is a system full of division. However, the kingdom of God is all about coming down—becoming low like Christ—to serve others. Christ lowered himself in order to unify the earth. It should be the same for us. The kingdom of heaven should be full of peace-makers.

Application Question: How do we develop humility in order to view others better than ourselves?

- We practice humility by living in the presence of God.

A person that lives in the presence of God will by necessity continuously see their sin (Isaiah 6:4). They will by necessity see how far they fall short. They will also by necessity become a servant of all. That is why Paul saw himself as least of the apostles, chief of sinners, and slave of all. A person only looking at others or himself will develop an exaggerated view of himself that will cause division.

- We practice humility by an act of the will—by choosing to put others before ourselves and consider their interest.

What other practice must believers develop in order to have unity?

3. Believers must take care of their own personal interests in order to have unity.

"Each of you should be concerned not only about your own interests, but about the interests of others as well" (Philippians 2:4).

It must be noted that Paul does not teach us to eliminate our interests all together. He says that we should not only look to our own interests. Throughout the history of the church some have taken a view that Christians must forsake all interests and adopt a form of asceticism. Like many monks, they forsook all forms of pleasure and treated their bodies harshly in order to pursue God and serve others. We see that asceticism had crept into the Colossian church. Colossians 2:20-23 says this:

If you have died with Christ to the elemental spirits of the world, why do you submit to them as though you lived in the world? "Do not handle! Do not taste! Do not touch!" These are all destined to perish with use, founded as they are on human commands and teachings. Even though they have the appearance of wisdom with their self-imposed worship and humility achieved by an unsparing treatment of the body—a wisdom with no true value—they in reality result in fleshly indulgence.

People in the church were teaching "Don't eat this!" and "Don't touch that!" They were treating their bodies harshly in order to restrain their urges. In 1 Timothy 4:3 we see that this teaching sometimes even included abstaining from marriage. Scripture does not teach that we are to forsake all of our interests; however, it does teach that our interests must be submitted to the Lordship of Christ. John MacArthur said this:

Christians who do not take reasonable care of their bodies cannot live or minister effectively. Nor are they required to forsake all personal interests in other regards. Paul's point here relates primarily, though certainly not exclusively, to personal interests in serving the Lord.

At times Christ left his disciples and the crowds to go up on the mountain so he could pray and be with God. The crowds were looking for him, but in order to properly minister to the crowds, he had to take care of his spiritual needs by being with God (Mark 1:35-37). At times, he took the disciples away so they could have rest and food. There is a proper balance of taking care of ourselves in order to better serve God and others.

This is very important for anybody in a serving ministry. It is very easy to become overworked, overburdened, and eventually burn out. There are always more needs and more people struggling, and if you don't take reasonable care of yourself, you cannot properly serve them. Certainly, in this time of church history the pendulum has swung where most people are caring for themselves and their interests over others. The church is about its health, wealth, and prosperity, and therefore, it is not a great servant. However, we must see the balance in Scripture, lest we swing again to the opposite side—asceticism.

4. Believers must look out for the interests of others in order to have unity.

"Each of you should be concerned not only about your own interests, but about the interests of others as well" (Philippians 2:4).

Not only must we take care of our personal interests, but ultimately we must exalt the interests of others. This is the nature of the servant. We should notice the word "concerned," or it can be translated "look," as in the NIV 1984. "Look" means to observe something. But, as in this context, it often carries the additional ideas of giving close attention and special consideration.[59] I think many Christians would be servants if others just told them their needs. However, the best servants are not just waiting to be asked; they are observant. They are looking out to discern others' needs and how to best meet them.

They notice needs in the children's ministry. They notice a need for the walls to be cleaned. They notice how people are doing. But, they just don't notice; they want to meet those needs. I think many times the very reason we have discord is because we are not observant enough. We haven't observed how to best serve or edify others and have only observed how to best serve and edify ourselves.

Consider what Hebrews says about how the church should function: "And let us take thought of how to spur one another on to love and good works" (Hebrews 10:24).

Churches that are unified are always looking out—considering how they can best "spur one another on to love and good works." This attentive look delivers them from much discord. If I observed my wife more and discerned her needs, we would be delivered from much conflict. It's the same for us as a church community. This is what Paul exhorted this congregation to do.

If believers are going to be unified, they must have the right practice. They must forsake selfish ambition and vanity. They must practice the humility of a servant. They must take care of their own interests in obedience to God, and finally they must look out for the interests of others. These are essentials for unity.

Application Question: At which of these practices are you the weakest? In what ways is God calling you to grow in these in order to stir the church more towards unity?

Conclusion

How can we as a church be unified? How is unity possible if we are so different—different backgrounds, cultures, gifts, etc.?

1. To Be Unified, Christians Must Focus on the Right Resources. We have Christ who comes alongside us to help, comfort from Christ's love, fellowship with the Spirit, and Christ's tenderness and compassion.
2. To Be Unified, Christians Must Develop the Right Attitudes. We must have the same mind—the mind of a servant. We must have the same

love—agape. We must be unified in soul and unified behind the purpose of the gospel.

3. To Be Unified, Christians Must Develop the Right Practices. We must forsake selfish ambition and vain conceit. We must in humility esteem others better than ourselves. We must take care of ourselves. Finally, we must look out for the interests of others.

128

Unity through the Mind of Christ

You should have the same attitude toward one another that Christ Jesus had, who though he existed in the form of God did not regard equality with God as something to be grasped, but emptied himself by taking on the form of a slave, by looking like other men, and by sharing in human nature. He humbled himself, by becoming obedient to the point of death—even death on a cross! As a result God highly exalted him and gave him the name that is above every name, so that at the name of Jesus every knee will bow—in heaven and on earth and under the earth—and every tongue confess that Jesus Christ is Lord to the glory of God the Father.
Philippians 2:5-11 (NET)

Sometimes it has been asked, "What is the greatest miracle that Christ ever performed?" Was it turning water into wine or the feeding the five thousand? Maybe it was calming the storms or his resurrection? But the greatest miracle was the incarnation itself—Christ coming down and becoming a man.

The incarnation is the miracle that no one can fully comprehend. How can the omnipotent God—the all-powerful God—become a vulnerable baby? How could someone hold God in his hand? Yet, Christ was so vulnerable as a baby that Satan quickly tried to wipe him out by killing all the baby boys in Israel. The all-powerful God became the all-weak infant.

How can the independent God become the dependent child who needs his mother's milk and touch to survive?

But not only is this a tremendous concept to grasp, the all-knowing God—the omniscient God who knows all things—became a child who knew nothing and grew in wisdom and stature (Luke 2:25). How can someone all-knowing grow in wisdom?

The greatest miracle that ever happened on this earth was not changing water into wine, multiplying bread, or even resurrecting. The greatest miracle of all time was the incarnation—Christ coming into this world as a man.

But yet, as we marvel at the incarnation and the birth of Christ, it is not just a concept that theologians should marvel at and ponder deeply. Paul says that the incarnation in some way is a model that should be demonstrated in each of our lives. Our thoughts of this grand event should change us.

129

Consider what he said: "You should have the same attitude toward one another that Christ Jesus had" (Philippians 2:5). Other versions say, "Let this mind be in you that was once in Christ Jesus." Before he teaches us about Christ's incarnation, he challenges us to develop his mindset.

Paul writes this in the context of a call to the Philippian church to be unified. He says, "complete my joy and be of the same mind, by having the same love, being united in spirit, and having one purpose" (2:2). This congregation was being threatened by disunity in several ways. There were false teachers in the church (Phil 3:2), people complaining and grumbling (Phil 2:14), and two women fighting (Phil 4:2). Paul taught them that the secret to unity was through studying and applying Christ's humiliation—his coming to the earth as a man to die for the sins of the world. This makes sense, as it was Christ's incarnation and death that brought reconciliation between God and man and between men as well. Therefore, we must model Christ and his actions in order to bring unity as well. We must model his actions in order to be the peacemakers Christ called us to be (Matt 5:9).

In studying the incarnation of Christ, we learn secrets to unity. We are commanded to ponder it and allow the character and attitude of Christ to be ours. It is the remedy for every conflict.

Big Question: What character traits or attitudes of Christ can be discerned from Philippians 2:5-11 that are necessary for the church to have unity.

In Order to Be Unified, Christians Must Practice Giving Up Their Rights

> You should have the same attitude toward one another that Christ Jesus had, who though he *existed in the form of God* did not regard equality with God as something to be grasped but *emptied himself* by taking on the form of a slave, by looking like other men, and by sharing in human nature.
> Philippians 2:5-7

Paul declares that Jesus is God in the phrase "Who, though he existed in the form of God." We see this specifically in the two words Paul used, "existed" and "form." William Barclay says this about the word "existed," which can also be translated "being":

> The word which the King James Version translates "being" is from the Greek verb [huparchein] which is not the common Greek word for "being." This word describes that which a man is in his very essence and which cannot be changed. It describes that part of a man which,

in any circumstances, remains the same. So Paul begins by saying that Jesus was essentially and unalterably God.[60]

Similarly, the word "form" means the "outward manifestation of an inward reality"[61] and "the essential form which never alters."[62] This all means that Christ preexisted before the incarnation as fully God and equal to God in his deity, and in the incarnation, he continued in that status. John 1:1 says, "In the beginning was the Word, and the Word was with God, and the Word was fully God."

Yet, though Christ was God he did not consider equality with God something "to be grasped." The phrase "to be grasped" means something "to be held onto" or "to cling to." He instead became nothing.

The phrase "emptied himself" is the word "kenosis" in the Greek. It is sometimes translated "made himself nothing" (NIV 1984). What does it mean for Christ to empty himself or make himself nothing? This has caused a tremendous debate throughout history. Some scholars said that Christ stopped being God when he became man. However, we know that cannot be true since the words Paul used in the very same passage negate that. In addition, if Christ was not God, then his sacrifice could not sufficiently pay for the sins of the world. It also conflicts with many of the teachings of Christ where he clearly claimed to be God. He said, "The person who has seen me has seen the Father!" (John 14:9). A more accurate understanding of "emptied himself" and what happened in the incarnation is that Christ voluntarily limited his divine rights as God while on the earth in human form. We see this in several ways.

Interpretation Question: In what ways did Christ in his incarnation limit his divinity?

1. In the incarnation, Christ limited his divine attributes such as his omniscience.

Christ said this about his second coming: "But as for that day and hour no one knows it—not even the angels in heaven—except the Father alone" (Matthew 24:36). The omniscient one put aside the full use of his omniscience.

2. In the incarnation, Christ limited his divine right of independent freedom.

He said this: "I tell you the solemn truth, the Son can do nothing on his own initiative, but only what he sees the Father doing. For whatever the Father does, the Son does likewise" (John 5:19). In his humanity, he could do nothing independently.

In fact, Hebrews 5:8-9 says this: "Although he was a son, he learned obedience through the things he suffered. And by being perfected in this way, he became the source of eternal salvation to all who obey him."

As a man, Christ learned obedience to the Father in a way he never did as God the Son. Isaiah 50:4 says this: "The sovereign Lord has given me the capacity to be his spokesman, so that I know how to help the weary. He wakes me up every morning; he makes me alert so I can listen attentively as disciples do."

The Son in his incarnation gave up his independent right as God. He relied totally upon the Father and did nothing apart from him. Like a man, each morning he got up to hear the Father's will and direction. In his incarnation, he was guided like a man dependent solely upon God.

3. In the incarnation, Christ limited his glory.

He put aside the manifestation of his glory and instead hid it in flesh. In heaven he was glorified daily by the angels and the righteous men made perfect, yet as a man he received scorn and shame. He gave up his glory for the life of being a man. In fact, in John 17:5, he prays, "And now, O Father, glorify thou me with thine own self with the glory which I had with thee before the world was."

But we see this emptying in many other ways.

4. In the incarnation, Christ gave up moment by moment intimacy with God.

We see this on the cross. There he was totally separated from God as he cried, "My God, my God, why have you forsaken me" (Matt 27:46).

5. In the incarnation, he gave up the wealth of heaven to become poor.

Second Corinthians 8:9 says, "For you know the grace of our Lord Jesus Christ, that although he was rich, he became poor for your sakes, so that you by his poverty could become rich."

In the incarnation, Christ limited his God-head. He laid aside many of his divine rights in order to become a man and serve others, and it was in his incarnation that he brought unity on the earth. He became a man and died so people could be restored to God and to one another. This mind must also be in us.

Interpretation Question: What other ways do we see this attitude of being willing to give up one's rights as necessary for unity in Scripture? How can this be applied practically when in discord?

We see the need to give up rights in a conflict in several Scriptures. In 1 Corinthians 6, people in the church were suing one another. Look at what Paul said to them: "The fact that you have lawsuits among yourselves demonstrates that you have already been defeated. Why not rather be wronged? Why not rather be cheated?" (6:7).

Paul says, "Why not just give up your rights for justice in order to have peace?" Often in our relationships, instead of giving up our rights for the sake of others, we hold grudges and get in fights. Paul implies that keeping unity is sometimes as easy as giving up our rights. We need to just allow ourselves to be wronged and forgive those who wronged us.

He teaches something similar in Romans 14 to a church that was divided over secondary issues like food and days to worship. He essentially says, "You want the answer to fix the disunity in your church? Give up your rights!" He said, "It is good not to eat meat or drink wine or to do anything that causes your brother to stumble" (Romans 14:21).

The incarnation speaks to us about giving up our rights for the benefit of others in order to reconcile relationships. Christ put aside many of his rights on earth, and we must do the same. This type of mindset will heal churches, and it will heal marriages and relationships. In order for us to be peacemakers like Christ, we must often give up our rights.

Application Question: In what ways has God called you to give up your rights to better serve people or work for unity?

In Order to Be Unified, Christians Must Practice Servanthood

> but emptied himself by taking on the form of a slave, by looking like other men, and by sharing in human nature.
> Philippians 2:7

One of the things that must be learned from the incarnation of Christ is that we must become servants. The word "form" means "the outward expression of the inward nature."[63] The Son of God did not become a "slave," which can also be translated "servant," when he came to the earth; it was an expression of who he always was as God. It was an outward expression of his inward nature. This teaches us that the abiding nature of God is that of a servant. It is a phenomenal concept to consider. Look at what Christ said about his second coming:

> Get dressed for service and keep your lamps burning; be like people waiting for their master to come back from the wedding celebration, so

that when he comes and knocks they can immediately open the door for him. Blessed are those slaves whom their master finds alert when he returns! I tell you the truth, he will dress himself to serve, have them take their place at the table, and will come and wait on them!
Luke 12:35-37

Christ said that when he returns to the earth, though the Master, he will serve all his faithful servants. He will have them recline at the table and wait on them. This is a concept that is mind blowing. When Christ came to the earth as a servant, he was representing the very nature of God. This must be our nature as well, if we are going to be a church that is unified. We must serve others.

The Greek word "doulos," translated "slave," tells us a little more about Christ in the incarnation. A "doulos" was a bondservant—the poorest of the poor. A bondservant usually didn't even own his own clothes. One commentator said this:

> Jesus did own His own clothes, but He owned no land or house, no gold or jewels. He owned no business, no boat, and no horse. He had to borrow a donkey when He rode into Jerusalem on Palm Sunday, borrow a room for the Last Supper, and even was buried in a borrowed tomb. [64]

Christ came to earth to be a servant. This is what he said to his disciples: "For even the Son of Man did not come to be served but to serve, and to give his life as a ransom for many" (Mark 10:45).

One of the greatest pictures of this was when the disciples were arguing about who would be greatest in the kingdom in John 13, and Christ took off his robe, got on his knees, and performed the duties of a servant as he washed their feet. He then said, "If you understand these things, you will be blessed if you do them" (v. 17).

The very reason many of us are in conflict is because we don't want to be servants, and we certainly don't want to be treated like servants. It is the desire to be served and esteemed that often leads to discord. However, this was not the mind of Christ, and it shouldn't be ours either. He was willing to become low and take the form of the lowliest servant, even though he deserved glory.

Application Question: What does being a servant look like? How do we develop this mindset?

1. A servant considers others better than himself.

Listen to what Paul said in the previous verses: "Instead of being motivated by selfish ambition or vanity, each of you should, in humility, be moved to treat one another as more important than yourself" (Philippians 2:3).

This is what a servant does. He doesn't ask, "What will make me the most happy?" or "What is best for me?" He asks, "What is best for those I serve?"

Paul said this about himself: "For since I am free from all I can make myself a slave to all, in order to gain even more people" (1 Corinthians 9:19).

Servanthood is not only the doorway to unity in the church but it's also the doorway to uniting people with God. It is the doorway to the gospel. Paul served others in order to win them to God. Christ did the same. He met people in their weakness and served them. We must also become slaves of others if we are going to effectively preach the gospel.

2. Servants serve without a need for applause.

Christ described the mindset of a servant in a parable he gave in Luke 17. It says,

> "Would any one of you say to your slave who comes in from the field after plowing or shepherding sheep, 'Come at once and sit down for a meal'? Won't the master instead say to him, 'Get my dinner ready, and make yourself ready to serve me while I eat and drink. Then you may eat and drink'? He won't thank the slave because he did what he was told, will he? So you too, when you have done everything you were commanded to do, should say, 'We are slaves undeserving of special praise; we have only done what was our duty.'"
> Luke 17:7-10

Christ asks a rhetorical question. He says when servants do what they are told to by their master, should they expect to be thanked? From this, he teaches: "you too, when you have done everything you were commanded to do, should say, 'We are slaves undeserving of special praise; we have only done what was our duty.'"

True servants don't need to be thanked or rewarded. Serving is reward enough. How often do we harbor grudges or evil thoughts because we don't feel appreciated? Servants serve to bless others, not to be blessed by others. A characteristic of a servant is that they serve without a need for applause.

Application Question: What are some other characteristics of a true servant? In what ways is God challenging you to grow in your servanthood?

In Order to Be Unified, Christians Must Practice Humility

135

> but emptied himself by taking on the form of a slave, by looking like other men, and by sharing in human nature. He *humbled* himself, by becoming obedient to the point of death—even death on a cross!
> Philippians 2:7-8

One of the attitudes that we must practice and develop from looking at the incarnation is humility. It is our pride that creates most of our fights and disagreements. We feel as though we deserve this or someone owes us. Essentially, both Falls in heaven and on earth were created by pride. Satan and man wanted to be like God.

But the one who brought peace to the earth and good will towards men was humble. He was willing to become low. Not only did he humble himself to become a human and a bondservant, but he humbled himself to death, even death on a cross.

When Paul says "even death on a cross," he was demonstrating the gravity of Christ's humility. For the Jews, being on the cross was equivalent to being cursed by God. This potentially was the worst way for a Jewish man to die. Deuteronomy 21:22-23 says,

> If a person commits a sin punishable by death and is executed, and you hang the corpse on a tree, his body must not remain all night on the tree; instead you must make certain you bury him that same day, for the one who is left exposed on a tree is cursed by God. You must not defile your land which the Lord your God is giving you as an inheritance.

Whoever hung on a tree overnight was cursed by God. This meant they were cut off from the promises and blessing of God. They were outside of God's grace. This was the most shameful death for a Jew because it brought God's curse.

But, nevertheless, Christ humbled himself to die the worst death possible in order to become a curse for us (Gal 3:13). On the cross Christ was cut off from the blessing of God. He cried out to him, "My God, My God why have you forsaken me?" On the cross he bore the shame of the world and the full wrath of God for our sins.

Paul is actually trying to show a continual pathway of humility demonstrated in Christ's incarnation. Christ humbled himself by becoming a man. He further humbled himself by becoming the poorest of the poor—a bond-slave. He humbled himself ultimately by dying on the cross—the most shameful death possible.

Let this mind be in you that was once in Christ Jesus. If Christ was humble enough to lower himself to the greatest possible extent, how can we boast in anything other than him?

How can we boast about our skills, our job, or our educational background when the God who has everything is humble? Every gift that we have comes from God. He is the source of all good things---our intellect, our athletic ability, our discipline, and anything else. All are gifts of his grace. How can we boast in ourselves or look down on others if it is all grace?

Humility is an attitude we must develop as Christians, and it is this attitude that will help us work for unity. We must be willing to humble ourselves to the greatest possible extent for "God opposes the proud, but he gives grace to the humble" (James 4:6).

The word "opposes" literally means he fights against them, but he gives grace to the humble.

Application Question: How can we tell if we are struggling with pride?

Pride will manifest itself through our words. "For his mouth speaks from what fills his heart" (Luke 6:45). Pride often shows up in boasting—talking about our works or achievement. It also will show up in insecurity. We become insecure or ashamed if we are not as good as we think we should be. Insecurity and shame are just pride unfulfilled. "I don't look this way." "I'm not good at this." It is just another form of pride.

Pride will not only show up in how we talk about ourselves, but it will show up in how we view and treat others. The Pharisee said of himself, "God, I thank you that I am not like other people: extortionists, unrighteous people, adulterers—or even like this tax collector" (Luke 18:11). He built himself up by tearing down somebody else.

Application Question: How can we practice humility, especially when in conflict? In what ways is God calling you to grow in humility?

In Order to Be Unified, Christians Must Practice Absolute Obedience

He humbled himself, by becoming obedient to the point of death—even death on a cross!
Philippians 2:8

But not only do we see humility in this verse but also obedience. Again, Paul means to show how far Christ was willing to go in order to bring unity between God and humanity and between humans in general. He was willing to be obedient even unto death. Why did Christ come to earth? "For this is the way God loved the world: He gave his one and only Son, so that everyone who believes in him will not perish but have eternal life" (John 3:16).

Christ came to the world because of the Father, but he also died because of the Father. Listen to what he prayed right before the cross: "Father, if you are willing, take this cup away from me. Yet not my will but yours be done" (Luke 22:42).

As we seek to have the mind of Christ, we must develop his absolute obedience. His obedience made him willing to not only give up his glory but even die. This especially applies to seeking unity in the church. If we practice absolute obedience to God's commands as well, this will help the church live in harmony. Listen to some of God's commands in considering unity:

> If possible, so far as it depends on you, live peaceably with all people. Do not avenge yourselves, dear friends, but give place to God's wrath, for it is written, "Vengeance is mine, I will repay," says the Lord. Rather, if your enemy is hungry, feed him; if he is thirsty, give him a drink; for in doing this you will be heaping burning coals on his head. Do not be overcome by evil, but overcome evil with good.
> Romans 12:18-21

> bearing with one another and forgiving one another, if someone happens to have a complaint against anyone else. Just as the Lord has forgiven you, so you also forgive others.
> Colossians 3:13

We are commanded to do as much as depends on us to live at peace with others. Like Christ, we often must obey to the greatest extent in order to bring unity. We should ask ourselves in every conflict, "Is there anything else I can do in order to have peace?" "Can I humble myself more?" "Can I further give up my rights?" "Can I serve more?"

We are also commanded to forgive as Christ forgave. Many say things like, "I have forgiven them, but I don't want to talk to them. I don't ever want to see them again." We are commanded to "forgive as the Lord forgave us." This means continuing to love them and seeking to grow in intimacy with them, if at all possible and wise.

Christ was able to achieve unity by obeying God even unto death. His peacemakers help in bringing unity by practicing absolute obedience to God as well. Are we practicing obedience to the furthest extent?

Application Question: Are there any ways you are not practicing absolute obedience in your life, especially regarding unity? If so, what is keeping you from completely obeying God?

In Order to Be Unified, Christians Must Practice an Eternal Perspective

> As a result God highly exalted him and gave him the name that is above every name, so that at the name of Jesus every knee will bow —in heaven and on earth and under the earth— and every tongue confess that Jesus Christ is Lord to the glory of God the Father.
> Philippians 2:9-11

We see that because Christ did not hold onto the rights of his deity and became a man, because he served others, because he humbled himself and was obedient even to death, God exalted him.

In fact his exaltation includes privileges he didn't have even before the incarnation. Hebrews 2:17 says, "Therefore he had to be made like his brothers and sisters in every respect, so that he could become a merciful and faithful high priest in things relating to God, to make atonement for the sins of the people." Christ had to become man so he could become our high priest in heaven and be a propitiation for our sins. Christ has been exalted because of his humiliation.

He has been given a new name and that name is "Lord" in verse 11. One day all people unsaved and born again will call Christ "Lord" and bow down to him. The only difference is that some people will be saved by this confession, while others will do it as they are under eternal judgment. But nevertheless, all will call Christ "Lord."

We no doubt learn a secret here. Though it may be hard to let go of our rights, though it may be hard to practice sacrifice and to put others before us, it is the pathway to eternal glory.

God will glorify saints just as he glorified Christ for having this mindset. Christ said this: "For everyone who exalts himself will be humbled, but the one who humbles himself will be exalted" (Luke 14:11). He will bless believers eternally for humbling themselves to work for unity. The way down is the way up.

Satan sought glory without a cross and without humility and was brought down. Man also sought glory without the cross and was humbled, but those who seek it through humiliation and servanthood shall be exalted.

While on the earth, Christ always had an eternal perspective. He said this to Pilate before the cross: "My kingdom is not from this world. If my kingdom were from this world, my servants would be fighting to keep me from being handed over to the Jewish authorities. But as it is, my kingdom is not from here" (John 18:36).

Christ realized that his time on the earth was not his time to be exalted. His kingdom was in heaven. He understood that one day the Son of Man would come in the clouds to establish his kingdom on the earth (Mark 13:36). He also taught that the meek would inherit the earth (Matt 5:5). Many are currently fighting for their piece of the earth, but at Christ's coming, it will be taken from them and given to the meek—the humble.

Christ had an eternal perspective. This enabled him to humble himself, become a man, become a servant, and become obedient unto death. He knew this was the pathway to being exalted and ultimately to bringing glory to God. Look at what Paul said: "and every tongue confess that Jesus Christ is Lord to the glory of God the Father" (v.11). Christ's exaltation has brought glory to the Father. He prayed this right before the cross: "Father, the time has come. Glorify your Son, so that your Son may glorify you" (John 17:1).

And ultimately it will be this way for every saint who has an eternal perspective. They will be rewarded for not having the grasping hand, being a servant to others, and practicing a lifestyle of humility and obedience to the glory of God. Their riches are in heaven and not on this earth. The person whose heart and mind are earthly will continually fight for the things of this world—causing discord with others. But the person whose mind is heavenly will fight for unity. His eternal mindset will enable him to give up his rights and serve all.

Application Question: In what ways is an eternal mindset helpful in seeking unity? How can we develop an eternal mindset in order to be peacemakers?

Conclusion

The greatest miracle in the world happened 2,000 years ago; the eternal God became a perishable man. The omnipotent God became a fragile child. The omniscient God became one that grew in stature and wisdom. Yet, this is not just for us to marvel at; it is ultimately meant to change our lives. Let this mind be in us that was once in Christ Jesus.

The Philippian church was being threatened by discord and disunity, and it was the humiliation of Christ that was the remedy. Christ humbled himself by becoming a man and dying on the cross to unify people with God and with one another. We must model his attitudes—his mindset—in order to be peacemakers as well.

What are the attitudes we must develop in order to have unity in the church?

1. In Order to Be Unified, Christians Must Practice Giving Up Their Rights
2. In Order to Be Unified, Christians Must Practice Servanthood
3. In Order to Be Unified, Christians Must Practice Humility
4. In Order to Be Unified, Christians Must Practice Absolute Obedience

5. In Order to Be Unified, Christians Must Practice an Eternal Perspective

Work Out Your Salvation: The Process of Sanctification

> So then, my dear friends, just as you have always obeyed, not only in my presence but even more in my absence, continue working out your salvation with awe and reverence, for the one bringing forth in you both the desire and the effort—for the sake of his good pleasure—is God.
> Philippians 2:12-13 (NET)

What is the process of spiritual growth—sanctification? Paul speaks to this congregation and challenges them to work out their salvation with fear and trembling. Now it must be noticed that Paul does not say "working for" your salvation but "working out" your salvation. Scripture everywhere teaches that we are saved not by our works but by grace through faith in Christ. Ephesians 2:8-9 says, "For by grace you are saved through faith, and this is not from yourselves, it is the gift of God; it is not from works, so that no one can boast."

We are not saved by our works. In fact, Paul argues that even our faith is a gift from God, and therefore, there is no room for man's boasting. Salvation is a work of God. However, salvation is not simply a work that happens when we are born again. It is a work that continues till we are made into the full image of Christ. It will end at death or at the rapture, whichever happens first. Romans 8:29-30 says,

> because those whom he foreknew he also predestined to be conformed to the image of his Son, that his Son would be the firstborn among many brothers and sisters. And those he predestined, he also called; and those he called, he also justified; and those he justified, he also glorified.

Paul here describes the process of salvation. It begins before time when God foreknew some in a saving relationship. The word "foreknew" does not mean to know some facts about a person but to know in an intimate saving relationship. Christ said in the last days many would say, "Lord, Lord," but he would reply, "I never knew you. Go away from me, you lawbreakers!" (Matt 7:23). Similarly, God said to Jeremiah, "Before I formed you in your mother's womb I chose you [or knew you]" (Jeremiah 1:5). He knew Jeremiah in a saving

143

relationship. He selected him not based on any merit of his own but based on grace—unmerited favor.

The next part of salvation is predestination. What is predestination? In this text it is God choosing those he knew in a saving relationship to be conformed to the image of his Son—to look like Christ. At some point, God effectually calls them as they hear the gospel and respond in faith. He then justifies them—declaring them righteous, then he will glorify them which is the completion of salvation. One day all believers will fully resemble Christ.

This is what Paul is talking about when he says "working out your salvation." He is saying to work out this process of being made into the image of Christ. We often call this "sanctification"—the daily process of growing into the very image of Christ.

What is this process? How can we daily pursue growth into the image of Christ?

Throughout history many have held different views on this process. Some have said that this process happens solely by a work of God without the participation of man. What we must do is "Let go and let God." We must rely on grace and give up working and striving to be holy. Sometimes these preachers will preach simply, "Grace! Grace! Grace!" to the exclusion of any discipline of our own. However, Paul said, "train yourself to be godly" or "exercise yourself to godliness" (1 Tim 4:7).

On the opposite side, others will preach "Work! Work! Work! Discipline yourself!" to the exclusion of reliance on God at all. These types of ministries often become legalistic, relying totally on works of the flesh. Listen to what Paul said to the Galatians: "Are you so foolish? Although you began with the Spirit, are you now trying to finish by human effort?" (Galatians 3:3).

What is the proper way to progress in holiness—to work out our salvation? Here in Philippians 2:12-13 Paul teaches a paradox. We must work and God works. We must work alongside God in the process of our sanctification. Paul says God brings forth in us "both the desire and the effort—for the sake of his good pleasure." He gives us the very desires to grow in Christ and he works in us to do it. This is why, when we get to heaven, there will be no room for boasting. Why? Because God did it all. However, both realities are true. We must work and God is working. Listen to what Paul said about this reality in his own life:

> For I am the least of the apostles, unworthy to be called an apostle, because I persecuted the church of God. But by the grace of God I am what I am, and his grace to me has not been in vain. In fact, I worked harder than all of them—yet not I, but the grace of God with me.
> 1 Corinthians 15:9-10

Paul said he worked harder than everybody else but not him, the grace of God within him. He said that God's grace was not without effect in him. The reality is that God's grace works in each one of us to grow spiritually, but for some it is without effect. Some instead resist the work of the Holy Spirit (cf. Acts 7:51). We must work with God in the process of sanctification—responding to his conviction, allowing him to empower us to accomplish his will for our lives.

It should be noted that when Paul calls this church to work out its salvation, he is probably specifically referring to the problems going on in the church. At the end of chapter 1 and the beginning of chapter 2, he challenges them to be one in spirit—to be unified (1:27, 2:2). In chapter 4, some divisions were threatening the church's unity (v.2). Paul calls for them to be unified by developing the mind of Christ (2:5) and working out their salvation together (2:12).

As we study this text, we will learn steps to work out our salvation—our sanctification.

Big Question: What is necessary for a believer and a congregation to work out their salvation—their sanctification?

In Order to Be Sanctified, We Must Focus on Our Model—Jesus Christ

> So then, my dear friends, just as you have always obeyed, not only in my presence but even more in my absence, continue working out your salvation with awe and reverence,
> Philippians 2:12

What is the first step in the process of sanctification? It is focusing on our model—Jesus Christ. The phrase "So then" in Philippians 2:12 means "because of this" and points the reader back to Paul's previous comments. In Philippians 2:6-11, Paul gave Jesus Christ's incarnation, death, and exaltation as a model for the church to follow in developing unity. Christ did not grasp onto his rights as God but became a man. In his incarnation he did not come as a wealthy king but a poor servant. His descent continued as he was obedient unto death—even death on a cross.

Paul says if we are going to work out our salvation—our sanctification—we must follow the model of Christ. He is the person we must seek to study and to emulate. The writer of Hebrews said this:

> keeping our eyes fixed on Jesus, the pioneer and perfecter of our faith. For the joy set out for him he endured the cross, disregarding its shame, and has taken his seat at the right hand of the throne of God.

145

Think of him who endured such opposition against himself by sinners, so that you may not grow weary in your souls and give up.
Hebrews 12:2-3

The author says that we must fix our eyes on Jesus. The word "fixed" means to focus on something to the exclusion of everything else. It essentially means to be single-minded. A person who has a fixed look on Christ is seeking to know and please Christ in everything he does. He wants to do God's will in his career, marriage, hobbies, entertainment, etc. Paul said, "So whether you eat or drink, or whatever you do, do everything for the glory of God" (1 Cor 10:31). We must have an unwavering focus on Christ in order to grow in our sanctification. Surely, we focus on him through time in the Word, prayer, serving, etc.

We must know our model in order to be sanctified. I cannot but think of Peter trying to walk on water in Matthew 14:22-33. As long as his focus was fixed on Christ, he could walk on the water. However, when he started to focus on the wind and the waves, he began to sink. It is the same with us. We cannot grow in Christ if we are focused on anything other than him. Sometimes the trick of Satan is to get us focused on our sin, failures, or even the devil himself to stop our spiritual growth. However, the more we focus on our struggles the more we fail. Similarly, the more someone focuses on demons, conspiracy theories, or the world, the more they become consumed with them. This is the opposite of how to be sanctified. We are not to focus on sin or the world. We are to focus on Christ in order to be sanctified.

Christ said this: "I am the vine; you are the branches. The one who remains in me— and I in him—bears much fruit, because apart from me you can accomplish nothing" (John 15:5). If we make our home in Christ, if we make him our focus, then all good fruits will grow out of that relationship. Love, joy, peace, self-control all come from an abiding relationship—an abiding focus on Christ.

Listen to what Paul said in Philippians 3:10-12:

My aim is to know him, to experience the power of his resurrection, to share in his sufferings, and to be like him in his death, and so, somehow, to attain to the resurrection from the dead. Not that I have already attained this—that is, I have not already been perfected—but I strive to lay hold of that for which Christ Jesus also laid hold of me.

Paul said he wanted to know Christ. He wanted to know his power and have fellowship with his sufferings. For Paul, following Christ did not mean skipping the cross to go to glory—it meant being like Christ even in suffering. Paul said he pressed or ran after this since it was the reason that Christ took hold of him. Christ took hold of him for a relationship and for Paul to be made

146

into Christ's very image. Therefore, Paul challenged the Philippians to pursue the same path he took—an endless pursuit of Christ as his goal (Phil 3:15-17). In order to be sanctified, like Paul, we must focus on Christ. He must be our ambition and focus.

Application Question: How do we keep a fixed eye on Christ in order to grow into his image?

In Order to Be Sanctified, We Must Know the Love of God

> So then, my dear friends, just as you have always obeyed, not only in my presence but even more in my absence, continue working out your salvation with awe and reverence,
> Philippians 2:12

The next step in the process of sanctification is to know the love of God. Paul says, "dear friends." This can also be translated "beloved." The implication of Paul calling them "beloved," as he commands them to work out their salvation, is that they needed to hear and understand that God loved them.

Love is a tremendous motivation for spiritual growth. Paul said this: "For the love of Christ controls us [or compels us]..." (2 Cor 5:14). What motivated the great apostle to suffer, serve, and preach the gospel? Love—the love of Christ compelled him. In fact, he thought it was so important for the church to understand this love that he prayed for them to grasp it. Ephesians 3:17b-19 says this:

> that Christ may dwell in your hearts through faith, so that, because you have been rooted and grounded in love, you may be able to comprehend with all the saints what is the breadth and length and height and depth, and thus to know the love of Christ that surpasses knowledge, so that you may be filled up to all the fullness of God.

He prayed for them to know Christ's love so that they may be "be filled up to all the fullness of God." To be "filled" means to be controlled and empowered by God (cf. Eph 5:18). Similarly, if the Philippians could know how much God loved them, it would propel them in their spiritual growth—into working out their salvation.

I believe it is for this reason that Satan constantly works against believers knowing the love of God. With Eve, he said, "Is it true that you cannot eat of every tree in the garden?" He wanted her to think God was a tyrant—that he was keeping the best from her. By doubting the love of God, she would be encouraged to sin. It was the same with Job. Satan, by bringing trials, was trying to get Job to curse God. Even his own wife said, "Why don't you just curse God

147

and die?" Satan wanted Job to doubt the love of God because that would encourage him to sin and curse God. However, Job's reply to his trials was, "Even if he slays me, I will hope in him" (Job 13:15).

In order for us to be sanctified, we must know the love of God. For when we know the love of God—the depth, the height, and the width of it—it will compel us to grow in our spiritual lives.

Application Question: How do we grow in knowing God's love?

1. We grow to know God's love through the love of others.

When Paul says "beloved friends," he was not only speaking of God's love but his own (v. 12). He loved the saints at Philippi (cf. Phil 1:8). Many times the way God will demonstrate his love to us is through others (cf. 2 Cor 5:20). Therefore, in order to know the love of God, we must be intimate with his saints. Many times they are the channel by which God lavishes his love on us.

2. We grow to know God's love through prayer.

Paul prayed for the Ephesian church to grasp the love of Christ (Eph 3:17-19). We must pray this for ourselves and for others as well.

3. We grow to know God's love through loving others.

Paul said this: "For God is my witness that I long for all of you with the affection of Christ Jesus" (Phil 1:8). Paul could feel Christ's love radiating through him as he loved the Philippians. Many times we have to make ourselves vulnerable by getting involved in people's lives and messes to know the love of God. While serving others, he pours out his love in us to bless others, and through this experience we come to know God's love for us more.

I specifically have experienced this when loving people who have hurt me. By forgiving and serving them, God gave me a supernatural love that I couldn't explain and didn't make sense to me. I just knew I was experiencing God's love for them.

4. We grow to know God's love through spending time with God and obeying him.

Christ said this: "If anyone loves me, he will obey my word, and my Father will love him, and we will come to him and take up residence with him" (John 14:23). Jesus promised that he would make his home in people who were obedient to him. This happens at salvation, but it happens as we continue to

148

obey him. He makes his home in us, as we become more intimate with him (cf. Eph 3:16-17).

In order for us to be sanctified, we must know his love. Love is one of the greatest motivations in this world—whether that be love for a sport, a person, or some goal. It motivates us. Knowing how much God loves us is a tremendous motivation to be sanctified. "God's kindness leads you to repentance" (Rom 2:4). One of the reasons many Christians are stagnant is because they don't really know Christ's love. Lord, help us to grasp and know your great love!

Application Question: What are some of the ways that you have experienced God's love? How has this love or lack of recognizing it affected you?

In Order to Be Sanctified, We Must Grow in Obedience to God

> So then, my dear friends, just as you have always obeyed, not only in my presence but even more in my absence, continue working out your salvation with awe and reverence,
> Philippians 2:12

Here Paul gives the next necessary step in the process of sanctification—we must grow in obedience to God. He says that they had always obeyed, but they must do it "even more" in his absence. They needed to be more obedient to God to work out their salvation.

Obedience to God is not only a necessary practice in sanctification but it is a proof of salvation. A person who professes Christ but does not practice daily obedience to God is deceived about his salvation. Jesus said this: "Not everyone who says to me, 'Lord, Lord,' will enter into the kingdom of heaven— only the one who does the will of my Father in heaven" (Matthew 7:21).

Profession alone is not enough. Jesus said that in order to enter the kingdom of God one must be born again (John 3:3). A person that is born again has a new nature—a nature that desires to practice righteousness. Those who are truly part of the kingdom of God hunger and thirst for righteousness as Christ taught in the beatitudes (Matt 5:6). John said this in his epistle: "By this the children of God and the children of the devil are revealed: Everyone who does not practice righteousness—the one who does not love his fellow Christian—is not of God" (1 John 3:10).

The practice of daily righteousness is a proof of salvation, and this is what Paul said about the Philippians. He said they "always obeyed." This doesn't mean that they were perfect. Paul even said in his epistle that they were not (cf. Phil 4:2). Therefore, he meant that even when they failed, they repented

149

and continued to practice obedience. However, in order to work out their salvation, they had to obey God "even more" (v. 12).

Interpretation Question: In what ways is obedience necessary to continue to progress in our sanctification?

1. Obedience to God's Word leads to God's blessing on our lives and progression in our sanctification.

James 1:25 says, "But the one who peers into the perfect law of liberty and fixes his attention there, and does not become a forgetful listener but one who lives it out—he will be blessed in what he does."
The man who obeys God's words will be blessed by God. This doesn't necessarily mean wealth and health, though it doesn't necessarily exclude those things. It primarily refers to spiritual blessings. God gives them more of the Word of God, more peace, more fruits of the Holy Spirit, etc.
Christ said this:

And he said to them, "Take care about what you hear. The measure you use will be the measure you receive, and more will be added to you. For whoever has will be given more, but whoever does not have, even what he has will be taken from him."
Mark 4:24-25

Whoever faithfully obeys—using what God teaches them—will be given more. They will grow in Christ. Obedience is necessary for growth. This leads us to the next point.

2. Obedience to God's Word protects us from stagnation and going backwards in our sanctification.

Listen again to what Christ said:

And he said to them, "Take care about what you hear. The measure you use will be the measure you receive, and more will be added to you. For whoever has will be given more, but whoever does not have, even what he has will be taken from him."
Mark 4:24-25

When we are unfaithful to God's Word, God begins to take away what we have. He takes away the knowledge that we have already attained of him. We become forgetful Christians like the Israelites. The Israelites saw the miracles of God in Egypt. They saw the parting of the Red Sea and manna

150

come from heaven, but they still constantly failed God and didn't believe in him. This was a natural result of lack of obedience—they could not appropriate the knowledge they had.

Many Christians are like the Israelites. They have sat under many sermons, seen the blessings and miracles of God but because their hearing wasn't mixed with faith—obedience—they continued in the infant stage without progression. They stay in the wilderness—a time of stagnation and discipline in their spiritual life.

In order for the Israelites to leave the wilderness and go into the promised land, they had to practice obedience. This was a necessary component. Whoever has will be given more but he who does not have even what they have will be taken away.

What areas have you been unfaithful in that God is again calling you to obedience? Is it Scripture reading and prayer? Is it serving? Is it getting out of an ungodly relationship? Is it changing your language or entertainment? He who has will be given more, but he who does not have even what he has will be taken away.

Application Question: What areas of obedience is God calling you to practice "more" in order to progress in your sanctification?

In Order to Be Sanctified, We Must Practice Continuous Discipline

> So then, my dear friends, just as you have always obeyed, not only in my presence but even more in my absence, continue working out your salvation with awe and reverence,
> Philippians 2:12

The phrase "continue working out" is written as a command with a continuing emphasis. "The idea is, 'Keep on working out to completion, to ultimate fulfillment.'"[65] This implies the need for discipline in our spiritual lives. Yes, God gives us grace, but we must be disciplined in order to grow. We must "keep on working it out." We see this taught throughout the Scriptures. Paul told Timothy, "train yourself for godliness" (1 Tim 4:7).

I had a professor in seminary that said, "I have never met a godly person that wasn't a morning person." What he meant was that he had never met somebody truly godly who hadn't developed discipline in their lives. This is the kind of discipline seen in Christ who got up early before everyone else and went to the mountain to pray. Mark 1:35 says this about Christ: "Then Jesus got up early in the morning when it was still very dark, departed, and went out to a deserted place, and there he spent time in prayer."

An implication of "keep on working out your salvation to completion" is that we must have continuous discipline in order to be holy.

Application Question: What types of disciplines must we practice in order to grow in sanctification?

1. Sanctification happens through rigorous study of the Word of God.

Jesus prayed this right before going to the cross: "Sanctify them in the truth; your word is truth" (John 17:17 ESV).

In order for us to grow in Christ, we must be people of the Word of God. We must be devoted to the study, memorization, and teaching of it. Peter said this: "And yearn like newborn infants for pure, spiritual milk, so that by it you may grow up to salvation" (1 Peter 2:2).

The verb "may grow" here is passive—it literally means "it may grow you."[66] When a person is rigorously studying the Word of God, it makes him grow. Scripture says the Word of God is active and alive (Heb 4:12). It equips the man of God for all righteousness (2 Tim 3:17). If you are consistently getting into the Word of God and obeying it, it will make you grow. It will make you look more like Christ. This is a discipline that all believers must develop in their lives so that they may grow up into their salvation.

2. Sanctification happens through rigorous prayer.

Jesus said this to the disciples right before he went to the cross, "Stay awake and pray that you will not fall into temptation. The spirit is willing, but the flesh is weak'" (Mark 14:38).

Jesus had previously told Peter and the other disciples that they would deny him; however, Christ also taught them how not to fall to the temptation— how not to sin. They needed to be disciplined in prayer. This prayer was not a quick arrow prayer but a disciplined time in prayer. He called them to pray for an hour so they would not stumble. He put a time limit on it. This amount of prayer would make them strong enough not to deny him.

How many of us stumble into frustration, depression, anger, pride, or lust because we are not disciplined in our prayer lives? If we are not going to succumb to temptation, we must find time to pray, a space to pray, and people to pray with. It should be noted that when Christ was preparing for his own temptation, he not only prayed but called a prayer meeting. He said to his disciples, "So, couldn't you stay awake with me for one hour" (Matt 26:40)? We must not only have individual times of prayer but also corporate times of prayer. It will build us up and make us strong to stand against temptation.

3. Sanctification happens through godly fellowship.

152

Proverbs 27:17 says, "As iron sharpens iron, so a person sharpens his friend." Being around godly brothers and sisters who are serious about Christ will help us grow. Developing accountability relationships where we confess sin to one another and pray for one another will bring healing and victory in our lives. James said this: "So confess your sins to one another and pray for one another so that you may be healed. The prayer of a righteous person has great effectiveness" (James 5:16).

Who are your accountability brothers and sisters? Many Christians have fellowship but their fellowship is centered around TV shows, shopping, sports, etc. Let our Christian fellowship be centered around spiritual growth and knowing God more.

In fact, this may be the primary method of spiritual discipline Paul had in mind when addressing the Philippians. Each of the pronouns in Philippians 2:12-13 are plural. The Philippians were to become more like Christ together. They needed one another, and we need one another as well. There are no lone rangers in the Christian life. The eye cannot say to the hand, "I don't need you." If I will become like Christ, I need the body and the body needs me. Sanctification happens in the context of Christian fellowship. Thus Christians who do not go to church and are not involved in the life of the church are going to struggle with their spiritual progress.

How is the Lord calling you to develop godly fellowship?

4. Sanctification happens through mentorship.

Along with the idea of growth through Christian fellowship is mentorship. Paul was mentoring the Philippians as he challenged them to work out their salvation. Proverbs 13:20 says this: "The one who associates with the wise grows wise, but a companion of fools suffers harm."

The more you get around people who are wiser than you and know God more than you, the wiser you will become. We see this model throughout the Scripture. We see Moses and Joshua, Elijah and Elisha, Jesus and his disciples, Paul and Timothy, Peter and Mark. It was through mentorship relationships that these people grew up into their salvation and fulfilled God's calling on their lives.

Someone compared mentorship to walking in the airport. While in an airport, you see people walking to their destination, but you also see others walking to their destination on escalators. The people on escalators get there faster than people who are walking by foot only. Similarly, mentorship is God's process to help us grow. We never get too old for mentorship because there is always somebody who knows more than us and who has walked with the Lord longer.

How do we develop these mentoring relationships?

153

Sometimes the mentor approaches us. Elijah approached Elisha. Jesus approached the disciples. However, sometimes the potential mentee should approach the mentor. In Luke 9:57 and 61, we see two people approach Christ and say, "I will follow you wherever you go." We must seek out mentoring relationships, and we should not be discouraged when we are turned down. I've asked several people to mentor me throughout the years and at times, I have been turned down—sometimes simply because they were already too busy. Mentoring helps us grow.

With this said, we must understand that we not only grow by being mentored but by mentoring others. Teachers always learn more than their pupils. This is often true in mentoring relationships as well. We should not see mentoring as a burden, but as a way for us to grow as well.

5. Sanctification happens through serving.

Paul said this to Philemon: "I pray that you may be active in sharing your faith, so that you will have a full understanding of every good thing we have in Christ" (Philemon 1:6, NIV 1984).

Paul told Philemon to be active in sharing his faith because through sharing he would come to a full understanding of every good thing believers have in Christ. He would come to know God and his blessings more through sharing his faith—serving. If a person is not serving then he, by necessity, will be going backwards and will never come to a full understanding of Christ.

If we are going to grow in Christ we must be disciplined. These disciplines include but are not limited to studying the Word of God, prayer, fellowship, mentorship, and serving. Other disciplines include worship, celebration, solitude, simplicity, secrecy, fasting, etc.

Application Question: What disciplines have you found most helpful in your spiritual life? Are there any ways God is calling you to be more disciplined?

In Order to Be Sanctified, We Must Develop Perseverance

So then, my dear friends, just as you have always obeyed, not only in my presence but even more in my absence, continue working out your salvation with awe and reverence,
Philippians 2:12

Again "continue working out" has the idea of "Keep on working out to completion, to ultimate fulfillment."[67] This means that sanctification doesn't happen overnight. It is a process that must be worked out till it is fully completed which ultimately won't happen until we get to heaven. The implication of this is that we must persevere until it is complete.

154

Application Question: Why is perseverance in working out our salvation important?

1. Perseverance in working out our salvation is important because of temptations toward complacent, apathetic Christianity.

In this process of following Christ there will be temptations to give up the pursuit and just become spiritually comfortable and lethargic. The church is full of those who have not "persevered" in the discipline of "working out their salvation." We see this with one church in particular in the New Testament—the church of Laodicea. Christ said this to the church:

> To the angel of the church in Laodicea write the following: "This is the solemn pronouncement of the Amen, the faithful and true witness, the originator of God's creation: 'I know your deeds, that you are neither cold nor hot. I wish you were either cold or hot! So because you are lukewarm, and neither hot nor cold, I am going to vomit you out of my mouth! Because you say, "I am rich and have acquired great wealth, and need nothing," but do not realize that you are wretched, pitiful, poor, blind, and naked,
> Revelation 3:14-17

This church was of no use to God—they were lukewarm. They thought to themselves that they needed "nothing." They were content and apathetic in their spiritual life, and therefore, they brought great displeasure to God. The church is full of Christians like this. Practically, they are of no use—fit only to be disciplined by God. This is a temptation for all Christians. We must persevere in our work of being sanctified. We must fight against lethargy.

Paul said this: "Do not lag in zeal, be enthusiastic in spirit, serve the Lord" (Romans 12:11). We all have this responsibility to persevere in our pursuit of holiness and fight against apathetic, lukewarm Christianity.

2. Perseverance in working out our salvation is important because of temptations to fall away from God all together.

Paul confronts this reality commonly in his teachings. In Colossians, he said this:

> but now he has reconciled you by his physical body through death to present you holy, without blemish, and blameless before him— if indeed you remain in the faith, established and firm, without shifting from the hope of the gospel that you heard. This gospel has also been

preached in all creation under heaven, and I, Paul, have become its servant.
Colossians 1:22-23

Paul writes to this church that was being attacked by a Gnostic cult who denied the deity of Christ and thus the gospel and said that they must continue in the faith—in the gospel. The church is constantly confronted with threats that cause many to fall away. Some fall away because of discord or moral failure in the church. Some fall away because of liberal—secular thinking—that challenges the exclusivity of the gospel. Some fall away into cults, and others fall away because of persecution the church encounters. Christ talks about some of these realities in Matthew 24. He says,

"Then they will hand you over to be persecuted and will kill you. You will be hated by all the nations because of my name. Then many will be led into sin, and they will betray one another and hate one another. And many false prophets will appear and deceive many, and because lawlessness will increase so much, the love of many will grow cold. But the person who endures to the end will be saved.
Matthew 24:9-13

Christ talked about how persecution, false teachers, and increased sin and wickedness in the end times will cause many to not persevere in the faith. They will simply fall away. He says that those who persevere are the ones who are really saved. Perseverance is a proof of genuine salvation (cf. 1 John 2:19). There are many threats to us continuing this process of "working out our salvation," but we must persevere.

3. Perseverance in working out our salvation is necessary because it is the ground where character is developed.

Listen to what Paul said:

Not only this, but we also rejoice in sufferings, knowing that suffering produces endurance, and endurance, character, and character, hope.
Romans 5:3-4

So we must not grow weary in doing good, for in due time we will reap, if we do not give up.
Galatians 6:9

Paul said we rejoice in suffering because it creates perseverance and perseverance creates character. He said don't give up in doing good because

156

in due time you will reap a harvest. Yes, I know you're working hard in studying the Word of God, praying, and serving, yet you don't feel like you're growing. Don't give up and don't grow weary for the fruit will come. I know it seems like you are going through trial after trial but don't give up because that is where patience and joy, regardless of circumstances, are grown. We must persevere in working out our salvation until it's complete. Perseverance in trials, perseverance in doing good and serving others is where character is developed.

Are you a Christian that commonly gives up? You start a small group but don't finish it. You start serving a ministry but quit. You start certain spiritual disciplines but don't complete them. You quit a relationship when it gets hard. You leave a church when there is a conflict or a problem. Listen, perseverance is necessary. It's necessary for spiritual growth. James said this: "And let endurance have its perfect effect, so that you will be perfect and complete, not deficient in anything" (James 1:4).

Perseverance is important in working out our salvation because of tendencies toward apathetic Christianity which plague the church, threats to falling totally away from the faith, and because it is only through perseverance—bearing up under a heavy weight—that we develop character. Are you persevering?

Application Question: In what ways has God been challenging you to not give up—to persevere—in order to grow spiritually? How can we find encouragement when we want to give up?

In Order to Be Sanctified, We Must Develop a Healthy Fear

> So then, my dear friends, just as you have always obeyed, not only in my presence but even more in my absence, continue working out your salvation with awe and reverence,
> Philippians 2:12

Paul says that another aspect of sanctification is developing a healthy fear. The word "awe" means fright or terror. "Reverence" refers to a shaking—it is where we get the English word tremor.[68] There is a fear, a reverential awe needed in the believer's life in order to continue to work out his salvation.

Interpretation Question: What type of healthy fear is Paul talking about?

1. In order to work out our salvation, we must revere God.

This means we must see and know the awesomeness of God. When one truly realizes the awesomeness of God, he will not give up intimacy with him for other things. Many pursue school, work, family, or hobbies over God.

157

The problem these people have is that they don't eally stand in awe of God; they don't have a reverent fear and trembling of him. Consider what David said about God: "Taste and see that the Lord is good! How blessed is the one who takes shelter in him" (Psalm 34:8).

David said, "Taste and see how good he is. See how awesome our God is." When we really know how wonderful he is, how can we choose the bitterness of sin over him? How can we choose the created over the Creator? Taste and see how good he is. When one really knows how good he is—when one truly reverences God—it will be a motivation towards holiness. In fact, look at the context in which David wrote this:

> The angel of the LORD encamps around those who fear him, and he delivers them. Taste and see that the LORD is good; blessed is the man who takes refuge in him. Fear the LORD, you his saints, for those who fear him lack nothing. The lions may grow weak and hungry, but those who seek the LORD lack no good thing. Come, my children, listen to me; I will teach you the fear of the LORD
> Psalm 34:7-11 (NIV 1984)

He says there is protection and deliverance for those who revere God (v. 7). He says those who fear him will lack nothing—there are provisions for those who fear him (v. 9). He speaks to those younger than him and says, "Listen, I will teach you the fear of the Lord" (v. 11). The benefits are too good. You must revere God. Give up your games, hobbies, and small ambitions. Make the reverence of the Lord your greatest pursuit. The benefits are glorious.

Do you revere God? Is God truly awesome to you? We must have a reverence of God in order to pursue him and our sanctification.

2.   In order to work out our salvation, we must fear God's discipline.

The writer of Hebrews said this: "For the Lord disciplines the one he loves and chastises every son he accepts" (Hebrews 12:6). He says every child of God is disciplined. God will not allow us to ignore him. He will not allow us to ignore his Word, and he will not allow us to live in sin. When we try, we will be disciplined. It may start off with a gentle rebuke through study of Scripture and/or the preaching of a sermon, but if we do not respond, it will turn into a whipping. Jonah ignored God, and God brought a terrible storm in his life that almost killed him and others associated with him. We must have a healthy fear of God's discipline.

Consider what Paul said to the Corinthians who were disciplined by God for disrespecting the Lord's Supper:

That is why many of you are weak and sick, and quite a few are dead. But if we examined ourselves, we would not be judged. But when we are judged by the Lord, we are disciplined so that we may not be condemned with the world.
1 Corinthians 11:30-32

They were weak, sick, and some even died because of God's discipline. He then says, "if we examined ourselves, we would not be judged." He challenges them to survey their lives and their heart motives in order to avoid God's discipline. Proverbs 9:10 says, "The beginning of wisdom is to fear the Lord, and acknowledging the Holy One is understanding"—it is the beginning of living a wise life—a holy life. If we are going to grow in Christ, we must fear God's discipline.

What other fear should believers have?

3.   In order to work out our salvation, we must revere God's Word.

Consider what God said through Isaiah: "These are the ones I look on with favor: those who are humble and contrite in spirit, and who tremble at my word.'" (Isaiah 66:2, NIV 2011). God esteems—he thinks highly of the one who trembles and shakes at God's Word. Sadly, many Christians ignore it; they sleep during the preaching of it. They ignore God's commands in it and choose to sin instead. God says he looks with esteem on the one who trembles at his Word.

This is necessary for us to grow in our sanctification. If we don't reverence the Word of God, we won't read it, study it, or memorize it. We will allow the Bible to collect dust on our shelf. If we don't fear God's Word, we will disobey it and dishonor it in our life.

Do you reverence it? If you reverence it, you will pursue understanding of it. If you reverence it, you will obey it because you realize God speaks through it. It is not a pastor or a parent speaking; it is God speaking, and he is worthy to be revered.

If we are going to be sanctified, we must reverence God, fear his discipline, and revere his Word. Christians should minister with a holy fear and trembling of the one they serve. Consider how Paul described his ministry to the Corinthian church: "And I was with you in weakness and in fear and with much trembling" (1 Corinthians 2:3). Paul was a man who lived in a reverential fear of God. One could tell by the way he spoke and served. He served with a constant view of a majestic God—a God who is a "devouring fire" (Hebrews 12:29).

159

Application Question: Do you feel like you have a healthy fear of God and his Word? Why or why not? How do we grow in the fear of God? How do we know if we have an unhealthy fear of God?

In Order to Be Sanctified, We Must Allow God to Work in Us

> for the one bringing forth in you both the desire and the effort—for the sake of his good pleasure—is God.
> Philippians 2:13

After speaking about the believer's role in working out his salvation, Paul speaks about God's role. As he focused on the necessity of our labor in sanctification, you can imagine how some felt discouraged over their sins, failures, and lack of discipline. Here Paul comforts them with, "for the one bringing forth in you both the desire and the effort—for the sake of his good pleasure—is God." This is similar to Paul's encouragement for Timothy in 2 Timothy 1:6-7. He said,

> Because of this I remind you to rekindle God's gift that you possess through the laying on of my hands. For God did not give us a Spirit of fear but of power and love and self-control.

He says, "rekindle God's gift"—make it strong and maximize it—and then he says "for God has given us power, love, and self-control through the Holy Spirit." He has given us everything needed through his indwelling Spirit to be holy and maximize our gifts. He is working in us; therefore, we must work as well.

Observation Question: How does God work in us?

1. God works in us to desire his will.

Jesus said this about the work of the Holy Spirit in the world: "And when he comes, he will convict the world concerning sin and righteousness and judgment" (John 16:8 ESV). Even though Christ was speaking to the world, this certainly happens to believers as the Spirit produces a desire in them to do God's will. This happens in various ways.

Interpretation Question: In what ways does God bring forth his desires in us?

*   God brings forth his desires in us by convicting us of sin.

160

Some have called this a holy discontent. By the Holy Spirit's convicting work in our heart, he enables us to hate and despise our sin. He does this through God's Word, fellowship with godly saints, and through discipline. Consider how Isaiah responded when he saw God: "I said, 'Too bad for me! I am destroyed, for my lips are contaminated by sin, and I live among people whose lips are contaminated by sin. My eyes have seen the king, the Lord who commands armies'" (Isaiah 6:5).

Seeing God revealed to Isaiah how sinful he and his people were. Similarly, Paul said this: "Wretched man that I am! Who will rescue me from this body of death?" (Romans 7:24). The Holy Spirit convicts us of sin—enabling us to hate it and to desire to get rid of it. He gives us a holy discontent.

- God brings forth his desires in us by convicting us of righteousness.

God gives us holy aspirations—desires to be more like him or to fulfill his will. We see both Paul's holy discontent and his holy aspirations in Philippians 3:12-14:

> Not that I have already attained this—that is, I have not already been perfected—but I strive to lay hold of that for which Christ Jesus also laid hold of me. Brothers and sisters, I do not consider myself to have attained this. Instead I am single-minded: Forgetting the things that are behind and reaching out for the things that are ahead, with this goal in mind, I strive toward the prize of the upward call of God in Christ Jesus.

Paul desired to press to be more like Christ daily—he had holy aspirations.

- God brings forth his desires in us by convicting us of judgment.

God brings forth his desires in us as the Holy Spirit reminds us of the coming judgment—the second coming of Christ. We as believers will not be condemned for our sins, but we will be rewarded or lose rewards based on our works. Second Corinthians 5:9-11 says,

> So then whether we are alive or away, we make it our ambition to please him. For we must all appear before the judgment seat of Christ, so that each one may be paid back according to what he has done while in the body, whether good or evil. Therefore, because we know the fear of the Lord, we try to persuade people, but we are well known to God, and I hope we are well known to your consciences too.

Paul said that he and the other apostles were motivated by the judgment seat of Christ. There they would either have reward or loss of reward. They wanted reward not out of selfish ambition but in order to please God and out of fear of his judgment (v. 9, 11). First Corinthians 3:15 talks about those who will be saved by fire (KJV)—meaning they will receive no reward in heaven. The Holy Spirit convicts us of this judgment.

- God brings forth his desires in us by the manifestation of peace or removal of peace.

Colossians 3:15 says, "Let the peace of Christ be in control in your heart (for you were in fact called as one body to this peace), and be thankful."
The word "control" is an athletic word used of an umpire in an athletic contest. It can also be translated "decide." The umpire says that this person is safe or that this person won the race. Many times as we are seeking God's will about a future decision or what path we should take, he works in us to do his will by the presence of peace or by the absence of peace.
With Pilate's wife, God's grace was manifest by tormenting dreams the night before Christ's crucifixion. She told Pilate to have nothing to do with that righteous man (Matt 27:19). God took away her peace to help her discern God's will. One person said this about God's peace: "Darkness about going is light about staying." Many times in discerning God's will, a consistent lack of peace is enough revelation to not make a decision or to not go forward. He works in us to will by peace.

- God brings forth his desires in us by the manifestation of his sovereign will.

Another way God works on our wills is simply through the manifestation of God's sovereignty—directing our hearts by various means. For instance, Proverbs 21:1 says, "The king's heart is in the hand of the Lord like channels of water; he turns it wherever he wants."
We saw this with Pharaoh as God hardened his heart (Ex 9:12). But God also sovereignly works in our hearts through directing circumstances, events, demons, waiting seasons, and everything else in order to guide us into his will. God could use a donkey on the side of the road to change our desires to his purposes (cf. Num 22, Balaam and the donkey).
How else does God work in us according to Philippians 2:13?

2. God works in us by giving us the power or effort to work.

The Greek word for "effort" in verse 13 is "energio." It is where we get the English word "energy."[69] God energizes us—empowers us—to do his will.

162

Paul said this about his ministry: "We proclaim him by instructing and teaching all people with all wisdom so that we may present every person mature in Christ. Toward this goal I also labor, struggling according to his power that powerfully works in me" (Colossians 1:28-29).

Paul said he labored, literally "labored to exhaustion," and the reason he could do that is because the power of God worked in him so strongly. In fact, Paul prayed for the power of God to be operating in the Ephesian church. In Ephesians 3:16, he says, "I pray that according to the wealth of his glory he may grant you to be strengthened with power through his Spirit in the inner person."

How does God's power begin to operate in our lives? Jesus simply said this: "I am the vine; you are the branches. The one who remains in me—and I in him—bears much fruit, because apart from me you can accomplish nothing" (John 15:5). We must abide in Christ so that his power can fully manifest in our lives to accomplish his work—to be sanctified.

Application Question: How is God calling you to rely more on him in your sanctification? How do we keep that delicate balance of our work and God's work?

Conclusion

How do believers work out their salvation—their sanctification?

1. In Order to Be Sanctified, We Must Focus on Our Model—Jesus Christ
2. In Order to Be Sanctified, We Must Know the Love of God
3. In Order to Be Sanctified, We Must Grow in Obedience to God
4. In Order to Be Sanctified, We Must Practice Continuous Discipline
5. In Order to Be Sanctified, We Must Develop Perseverance
6. In Order to Be Sanctified, We Must Develop a Healthy Fear
7. In Order to Be Sanctified, We Must Allow God to Work in Us

Beware of Complaining and Arguing

Do everything without complaining or arguing, so that you may become blameless and pure, children of God without fault in a crooked and depraved generation, in which you shine like stars in the universe as you hold out the word of life—in order that I may boast on the day of Christ that I did not run or labor for nothing. But even if I am being poured out like a drink offering on the sacrifice and service coming from your faith, I am glad and rejoice with all of you. So you too should be glad and rejoice with me.
Philippians 2:14-18 (NIV 1984)

Why should Christians do everything without complaining or arguing?

Paul in the previous text called for the Philippian church to "work out their salvation with fear and trembling" (v.12, NIV 1984). Here he calls for them to continue the work of conforming to the image of Christ through doing everything without complaining and arguing (cf. Phil 2:6-11). This was especially important because situations in the church were threatening to stagnate or even destroy their spiritual life. They were experiencing persecution for the faith (1:28). False teachers were present in the church (3:2), and there was a division between two women in the congregation (4:2). Many threats to the spiritual growth of this congregation existed, and he calls for them to work out their salvation to completion by not "complaining or arguing" (v. 14).

This is very important for us to hear. We live in a world and society that is prone to complaining. In companies, the employees complain about their bosses and one another. In homes, husbands complain about their wives. Wives complain about their husbands. Children complain about their siblings and their parents. In churches, the members of the congregation complain about one another and the pastor. The pastor complains about the congregants. We live in a world full of complaining and arguing.

This tendency began at the Fall. Before sin entered the world, Adam and Eve never complained about anything. They didn't complain about God putting a tree in the garden that they were forbidden to eat. They didn't complain about not having any clothes on. Nor did they complain about the command to only eat vegetables. One of Satan's first temptations was to get Adam and Eve discontent with God's plan for them. He says, "Is it true that you cannot eat of

165

every tree in the garden?" He tries to make God's plan for them feel restrictive and domineering. He then tries to make them feel that God is trying to keep them from the best. He said, "God knows that when you eat of this tree you will be like God." Satan's overall temptation was to get them to not trust God and to become discontent with what they already had.

Isn't that the state of the world today? We are discontent about everything. We are discontent about our job, our home, our TV, our phone, our family, our church, etc. For some people it is hard to find anything that they are content with. In fact, right when Adam sinned we see the tendency of man's new sin nature to complain. He says to God, "The woman you gave me, gave me the food and I did eat." When God asked him if he had eaten from the Tree of the Knowledge, he didn't respond with, "Yes." He responded by blaming God and the woman for his failure. The woman then blamed the serpent.

What we now see in the world is a tendency to complain. As a veteran of the U.S. military, I can say that the military is probably the place where I have experienced the most complaining. While I was on active duty and now as a reservist, it seems to be part of the culture. We all complained about the military, and this complaining bonded us together. We had a common animosity. I would say the church is at times not too far behind the military. We complain about the worship, the sermon, the seating, the lighting, the offering, the leadership, the members, and anything else we can complain about. Paul realized this tendency was in the Philippians, and Christians overall, and therefore, he challenged them to do "everything without complaining and arguing." He didn't say "some things" but "everything."

Is this realistic? Why should we do "everything" without complaining? In this text Paul teaches us why we should do everything without complaining. His hope was to motivate Christians to live in a manner that would properly reflect our relationship both to God and the world.

Big Question: Why should Christians do "everything without complaining or arguing" according to Philippians 2:14-18?

Christians Should Not Complain and Argue in Order to Obey God

> Do everything without complaining or arguing
> Philippians 2:14 (NIV 1984)

Again, Paul says that Christians should do everything without complaining and arguing. "Complaining" can also be translated "grumbling." "'Grumbling' (goggusmon) is an onomatopoeic word that sounds like what it means similar to words such as: buzz, boom, meow, or murmur."[70] It "describes the low,

166

threatening, discontented muttering of a mob who distrust their leaders and are on the verge of an uprising."[71] It is a verbal expression of one's dissatisfaction with circumstances.

The word "arguing" in the Greek is the word "dialogismos" which is where we get the English word "dialogue".[72] It describes both one's inner reasoning as we argue in our minds and one's outer reasoning with our mouths. When we are discontent, we argue both in our minds and with our mouths— with ourselves, other people, and with God. Paul says this is one of the things we must get rid of as we work out our salvation.

The classic story on complaining and arguing is seen in Israel's wilderness wanderings. When God delivered them from slavery in Egypt and they went into the wilderness, they complained about a lack of water (Ex 15) and a lack of food (Ex 16). In Numbers 11 they complained about their trials in the wilderness, and how they wanted meat. And throughout their time in the wilderness, they complained against Moses and God. Because of their complaining, God judged them and many died. Paul said this about Israel's experience in 1 Corinthians 10:9-11 (NIV 1984):

> We should not test the Lord, as some of them did—and were killed by snakes. And do not grumble, as some of them did—and were killed by the destroying angel. These things happened to them as examples and were written down as warnings for us, on whom the fulfillment of the ages has come.

Paul said God killed them because of their grumbling through a destroying angel. In Numbers 11 God brought a fire and a severe plague in the camp that wiped out many of them. I don't think many of us have truly meditated on Israel's wilderness experiences. Think about this, they wandered in the wilderness without water for three days, and when they found some, it was bitter (Ex 15:22-23). For us, we are accustomed to having a drink anytime we want, just as the Israelites were in Egypt. It would be very hard for us to not complain when lacking fluids. Then God gave them manna from heaven for food, but the problem was that was all they ate for days at a time. What if they didn't like the taste or the texture of it? Wouldn't it be normal to complain and even acceptable? Plus, even if they liked the taste or the texture, they still ate the same food every day. Who wouldn't complain? "Come on, God, isn't your anger and punishment a little unreasonable—to kill them? Father, that just seems like a little too much." And, also let us consider the fact that they wanted some meat (Num 11:4). I complain all the time while living here in Korea because many meals have no meat or very little meat. To me a meal without meat is not a meal. It is a snack. I want a meal. I figure that if I was in the wilderness with them, I would have complained alongside them.

167

One of the things we learn from Israel's wilderness wanderings is that complaining is incompatible with our salvation. They were saved from slavery in Egypt and God deemed it unreasonable for them to complain after such a large display of grace. However, we have received much more grace. We have been delivered from slavery to sin, the world, and the devil. We have been given eternal life and the status of children of God. How much more is our complaining a sin in the sight of God? Therefore, God calls us to work out the completion of our salvation without complaining and arguing.

We must understand that complaining is not a little sin; it is a big sin. The writer of Hebrews said this about bitterness, which again was possibly an allusion to the wilderness wanderings of Israel: "See to it that no one misses the grace of God and that no bitter root grows up to cause trouble and defile many" (Hebrews 12:15, NIV 1984). Bitterness and complaining is contagious. Not only does it blind us to all the ways God has graced us, but it also spreads to others. It spreads throughout a family, an organization, and a church—limiting and sometimes destroying spiritual growth.

Let us remember the time Israel was at the border of the promised land, and how they sent ten spies to survey the land. Two of them came back with a positive report of God's faithfulness and how good the land was; while eight of them complained about the giants and the impossibility of taking the land. They then complained about God and Moses and convinced the Israelites not to go into the land (Numbers 13-14). "This task is too great!" they said. This root of bitterness coming from only eight Israelites defiled the whole nation and led to God's judgment. The Israelites were judged by God and called to wander in the wilderness for forty years while everybody over twenty died for their rebellion.

Many people in the church are in a wandering experience in their spiritual life. They are not progressing; they are not going anywhere. And the reason is because there is a bitter root destroying their harvest and inviting the chastisement of God on their lives. It also might be bringing God's chastisement on others' lives as well. Maybe this bitterness is an anger against somebody that harmed them. Maybe it's simply discontentment with their circumstances or lack of trust in God's goodness. Whatever it may be, it must be known that this complaining spirit is a very dangerous sin that brings God's discipline.

Personally, the gravity of this makes me very strict as a parent. My baby daughter is at an age where she likes to throw tantrums and fall on the ground when she doesn't get her way or simply because she doesn't like her circumstances. Because of God's anger about this in Scripture, this is very serious to me. Some parents think tantrums are cute, but it is a very dangerous sin that if not remedied will carry on into adulthood and invite the chastening of God. By training my daughter, I realize that this could save her life—the Israelites died because of their complaining spirit. If I allow her to continue this practice, she will not only complain about us—her parents—she will complain

168

about her teachers, her boss, her husband, and ultimately God, potentially leading to severe discipline.

Some Christians, because of a tendency to complain, are constantly under God's discipline. God, like a loving parent, is seeking to turn them away from their petty tantrums and their distrust of him. Complaining is like telling God he doesn't know what's best and that he doesn't care. It is an affront to God. Therefore, Christians must forsake complaining and arguing because it is forbidden by God.

Interpretation Question: How can we get rid of this complaining disposition?

1. We get rid of a complaining disposition by learning to trust God more.

Solomon said this: "Trust in the LORD with all your heart and lean not on your own understanding" (Prov 3:5, NIV 1984). The reason we complain and argue essentially is because we don't trust God with our circumstances. We don't trust that he is working all things out for our good (Rom 8:28). Some of us like Adam and Eve doubt God's essential nature—his goodness (Psalm 135:3). The Lord is good and everything that is good comes from him (James 1:17). He is how we define good, and therefore, to complain is to challenge his nature—his goodness. When we trust that we have an all wise God working all things out for our good, then this trust will deliver us from complaining—complaining about God and others.

2. We get rid of a complaining disposition by acknowledging God's sovereignty in all situations.

Ephesians 1:11 says God works "all things" according to the counsel of his will. Scripture teaches that God is in control of everything. Proverbs 21:1 (NIV 1984) says, "The king's heart is in the hand of the LORD; he directs it like a watercourse wherever he pleases." God controls the heart of man like a person moving around water in his hand. He is sovereign.

We should recognize that the sovereignty of God is a difficult and controversial doctrine and for that reason many don't like it. However, let it be known that this doctrine is crucial for us to "do everything without complaining and arguing," and therefore, it is an essential doctrine for our holiness. It is also an essential doctrine for prayer. If God isn't in control of everything, why pray? It is the backbone of a deep prayer life. If we don't see God is in control of everything, then we will not pray as we ought.

In order to not complain we must not only trust in God's goodness but also acknowledge God's sovereignty. Only a person who is fully trustworthy and good is worthy to be sovereign over the affairs of all things. I may not understand why tragedies happen in the world, but I can have peace because my God is all together good, trustworthy, and sovereign over all situations.

3. We get rid of a complaining disposition by learning contentment with God's provisions.

First Timothy 6:6-8 (NIV 1984) says, "But godliness with contentment is great gain. For we brought nothing into the world, and we can take nothing out of it. But if we have food and clothing, we will be content with that."

He says if we have food and clothing we should be content. The word "clothing" just means covering so it could refer to clothes and shelter. We live in a society that teaches us to not be content. Every commercial says, "You need this!" "You need that!" Therefore, we live in a society not content with anything. We get a new phone that we are all excited about until the newer version comes out. Then we are back to being discontent. This society works off discontentment.

One of the disciplines we must develop is to be content with whatever God has provided even if it is only basic food and covering. This is a discipline Paul challenges Christians to grow in (1 Tim 6:6-8). This is exactly what God promises to provide us with in Scripture. He promises to meet our needs—to give us our daily bread. He doesn't promise riches, wealth, and health on this earth in contrast with the "prosperity gospel." Christ told his disciples that God would meet their needs for clothing and food as they sought first the kingdom of heaven (Matt 6:33). We see Paul himself had learned this reality in Philippians 4:11-13. He said he had learned to be content in every circumstance whether in prosperity or lack because of God's strength working in him.

How do we learn contentment? We learn it by finding our fullness and satisfaction in God. We should ask ourselves these questions, "Is God really enough? Is he really all I need? Will I be satisfied with just him? Do I really need all the clothes, the shoes, the entertainment, the electronics, etc.? Can I be content with just him?" The writers of Hebrews says this: "Keep your lives free from the love of money and be content with what you have, because God has said, "Never will I leave you; never will I forsake you" (Hebrews 13:5, NIV 1984).

How can we be free from the love of things which is a common cause of discontentment? We can be free by believing God will never leave us nor forsake us. We can be content with what we have because we have God. Christians should be radically different than the rest of the world because they already have everything. They have everything in their relationship with God.

When you are not content with God and his provisions, it is then that you will be tempted to fall into all types of sin including complaining and arguing. Like Adam and Eve, you will spend your time looking at the one thing you don't have or don't like instead of the many blessings given to you by God. Trusting

170

God, acknowledging his sovereignty in all things, and practicing contentment will help us to not complain and grumble.

Application Question: What are some areas that you are often tempted to argue and complain about? How would you rate yourself 1-10 on complaining and arguing?

Christians Should Not Complain and Argue in Order to Grow in Godliness

> ...so that you may become blameless and pure, children of God without fault
> Philippians 2:15a (NIV 1984)

Paul gives further reasons for us to not argue and complain. In the next phrase, he gives the purpose clause "so that." Paul says do not argue and complain "so that" or "in order that" you may become blameless and pure, children of God without fault.

What does Paul mean by becoming children of God? We are already children of God when we accept Christ as our Lord and Savior and are born again. He simply means that we will manifest that we are children of God. What we are in position, we must become in practice. Children by nature bear the characteristics of their parents, and they are identified by these characteristics. People look at my daughter and immediately say, "She looks just like Greg." She has many of my features. In the same way, we should both by nature and practice look like our Father in heaven. Paul said this, "Be imitators of God, therefore, as dearly loved children" (Eph 5:1, NIV 1984). We, therefore, demonstrate the character of the Father when we live without complaining and arguing—we grow in godliness.

Observation Question: How do children of God grow in godliness according to Philippians 2:15?

Paul seems to be giving descriptors of children of God who are growing in godliness by not complaining and arguing. We will look at the descriptors Paul gives.

1. Christians grow in godliness by becoming blameless.

The word "blameless" does not mean perfection, but it does mean that a person is practicing holiness. It means that no charge can be sustained against a person. It is very similar to what we saw in the life of Daniel. Daniel 6:4-5 (NIV 1984) says this:

> At this, the administrators and the satraps tried to find grounds for charges against Daniel in his conduct of government affairs, but they were unable to do so. They could find no corruption in him, because he was trustworthy and neither corrupt nor negligent. Finally these men said, "We will never find any basis for charges against this man Daniel unless it has something to do with the law of his God."

While in Babylon, Daniel demonstrated that he was a child of God. The administrators had nothing to accuse him of other than his faith in God—the character of his Father. It should be the same with us.

We see this blamelessness in Paul as well. He said he would not eat meat nor drink wine if it caused another to stumble (Rom 14:21). He was willing to give up even things that were not sin in order to not cause others to stumble. This is a blameless life—a person seeking to live above accusation not only with sinful things but even with things that are his or her right.

Again, this has particular reference to not complaining and arguing. A person who is a complainer or an arguer will often be worthy of blame or accusation. They cause conflict and division and promote murmuring. This should not be the character of a child of God.

2. Christians grow in godliness by developing purity.

The word "pure" means unmixed. "The term was used to describe pure wine that was unmixed with water and pure metal that was not alloyed. The believer's life is to be absolutely pure, unmixed with sin and evil."[73] Paul said in Romans 16:9 (NIV 1984), "I want you to be wise about what is good, and innocent [pure] about what is evil." Not only must we seek to be free of wrongful actions but we must seek to have right hearts before God. We must keep them from becoming mixed. Jesus said this in Matthew 15:18-19 (NIV 1984):

> But the things that come out of the mouth come from the heart, and these make a man 'unclean.' For out of the heart come evil thoughts, murder, adultery, sexual immorality, theft, false testimony, slander.

God always looks at the heart, and therefore, we must practice being pure in our hearts and our minds. Again, this especially has reference to doing all things without complaining and arguing. Some of us may not complain outwardly, but we are bitter inwardly. God is always looking at the heart to see if it is pure—unmixed with sin and evil.

3. Christians grow in godliness by being without fault.

"Without fault" can be translated "without blemish, spot or defect." "This is a word that is taken from the Old Testament sacrifices made to God."[74] The concept behind this is that the believer is to live and walk as a sacrifice to God by keeping himself from divisive behavior such as complaining and arguing. Romans 12:1 (NIV 1984) similarly teaches that believers must seek to live as acceptable sacrifices to God. It says, "Therefore, I urge you, brothers, in view of God's mercy, to offer your bodies as living sacrifices, holy and pleasing to God—this is your spiritual act of worship." James 1:27 (NIV 1984) says, "Religion that God our Father accepts as pure and faultless is this: to look after orphans and widows in their distress and to keep oneself from being polluted by the world."

The implication that Paul gives is that complaining and arguing is a practice that blemishes our offerings before God and makes them unacceptable. In describing public worship in 1 Timothy 2:8 (NIV 1984), he said that he desired "men everywhere to lift up holy hands in prayer, without anger or disputing." When men led the congregation in prayer, it had to be done "without anger and disputing." Anger and disputing would corrupt the offering. Jesus said this in Matthew 5:23-24 (NIV 1984):

> "Therefore, if you are offering your gift at the altar and there remember that your brother has something against you, leave your gift there in front of the altar. First go and be reconciled to your brother; then come and offer your gift.

If you have an offering to give God (prayer, worship, tithe, etc.) but you realize somebody has something against you, Jesus said first go make that right. Again, the implication is that the offering will not be accepted by God if we are living in discord with others. In order to grow in godliness, we must make sure our offerings are without blemish by being free of complaining and arguing. We must seek to be acceptable to the Lord in all we give him, and by doing this, we manifest ourselves as children of God—we grow in godliness.

Christians must seek to be without blame—having no fault in them that others can point to. They must seek to be pure in their motives and actions. Finally, they must seek to be without fault and blemish as acceptable sacrifices to God. And, all these things are done so that they can grow spiritually—manifesting themselves as "children of God." Complaining and arguing hinders spiritual growth.

Application Question: In what ways is God calling you specifically to grow in godliness by being blameless, pure, and without fault? What practical steps is he calling you to take?

Christians Should Not Complain and Argue in Order to Be Witnesses to Unbelievers

> without fault in a crooked and depraved generation, in which you shine
> like stars in the universe as you hold out the word of life
> Philippians 2:15b-16 (NIV 1984)

The next reason Paul gives for not complaining and arguing is our witness to unbelievers. He pictures the world as a dark place and believers as stars in the universe. The word "crooked" is an interesting word in the Greek. John MacArthur said this about the word:

> Crooked is from skolios, referring to what is bent, curved, or twisted. The medical condition scoliosis involves an abnormal curvature and misalignment of the spine. The term was used metaphorically of anything that deviates from a standard or norm, and in Scripture, it is often used of things that are morally or spiritually corrupt.

This world is twisted—it deviates away from God's original plan. Paul also says the world is "depraved" meaning "corrupt and wicked." This world is a dark place primarily because they refuse to acknowledge God. Romans 1:28 (NIV 1984) says this:

> Furthermore, since they did not think it worthwhile to retain the knowledge of God, he gave them over to a depraved mind, to do what ought not to be done. They have become filled with every kind of wickedness, evil, greed and depravity.

The world is a dark place filled with every kind of evil because they choose to not acknowledge God. This leads them not only into complaining but into all kinds of perverse sin: idolatry, sexual immorality, homosexuality, disobedience to authorities, murder, and the approval of all these things (cf. Romans 1:28-32).

However, because believers have a relationship with God, they should shine as stars. The word "stars" can also be translated "lights" as in the ESV. We don't shine because we are light in ourselves, but because we reflect the light of God. In practice, we are more like the moon than stars, as it radiates the sun's light off its surface. Throughout history people have always recognized that there was something special about the moon. On its own it is just a big pile of rock and dust, but when it is in just the right spot, the sun shines on it and the moon radiates. All of a sudden in the radiance of the moon, people stand in awe, take pictures to remember the moment, and some even fall in love. In one sense, the moon is no different than us. There is nothing special about us on our own. We are just a big ball of dust, but in the light of Christ, magical things happen—people's lives are changed, people find strength and encouragement, and people are led to Christ. That is the type of light Christians are to manifest in this crooked and depraved world. They should manifest the light of Christ as they dwell daily in his presence (John 15:5).

As long as we are dwelling in the light of God, we reflect his light and his glory. Paul implies three particular ways that we are lights: (1) by not complaining and arguing (2) by growing in godliness—being blameless, pure, and without fault as previously discussed, (3) and by holding out the word of life. "Holding out the word of life" is probably better translated "holding forth" the word of life which seems to refer to evangelism—the preaching of the gospel. However, the primary way we shine as lights to the world in the context is by not complaining and arguing which leads to all the other characteristics.

As Christians live a lifestyle of light, they draw people to Christ. People should look at believers and see a stark difference. This light will either push them away or draw them closer so they can learn about Christ—the reason for this light (cf. John 3:19-21). Again, the primary way we live as lights is by not complaining. When we practice complaining and arguing, we look more like a child of this world.

Scripture actually describes the world as not being "thankful." Paul said this in Romans 1:21 (NIV 1984): "For although they knew God, they neither glorified him as God nor gave thanks to him, but their thinking became futile and their foolish hearts were darkened." Paul describes the world as those who knew God but refused to glorify or give thanks to him. By denying the knowledge of God, the world has become a thankless place. They refuse to acknowledge the Giver of all good gifts, and therefore, their hearts become dark.

When Christians are in a work place, a family, or a ministry and they choose to be thankful instead of complainers, they demonstrate that they are children of God and lights in the world. They stand out. Their lifestyle becomes a witness to the world and therefore draws others to Christ.

However, it should be heard that when Christians choose to complain and be thankless like the world, they dim the light of the gospel. They instead look just like the world which is characterized by not glorifying and giving thanks to God.

While Job was suffering and he declared, "The Lord giveth and he taketh away. Blessed be the name of the Lord," he shined like a star in the world (Job 1:21, NIV 1984). It pointed those watching him toward faith in God. When Paul was in prison singing worship songs to the Lord in Acts 16, he shined like a star in that prison, and when the jailor accepted Christ, no doubt Paul's unique, joyful disposition was part of the reason (Acts 16:25-31).

175

Does how you respond to uncomfortable situations draw people to Christ or does it push people away? Christ said we either gather or scatter (Matt 12:30). There is no in between. One of the reasons we must choose to not complain and argue is for the world—so that they may know Christ.

Application Question: Is unthankfulness a valid descriptor of the world? Why should thankfulness characterize believers?

Christians Should Not Complain and Argue in Order to Honor Our Leaders

> in order that I may boast on the day of Christ that I did not run or labor for nothing
> Philippians 2:16 (NIV 1984)

Surprisingly, the next reason Paul gives for not complaining and arguing is in order to honor the apostle and his ministry to them. He says "in order that I may boast on the day of Christ that I did not run or labor for nothing." The day of Christ means the second coming of Christ and specifically the day that Christ will reward believers for their works (2 Cor 5:10). It is a picture of Paul's future happiness at his disciples' faithfully following Christ. We see him reiterate the prospect of this future joy both to the Philippians and also to the Thessalonians. Look at what he says:

> Therefore, my brothers, you whom I love and long for, my joy and crown, that is how you should stand firm in the Lord, dear friends!
> Philippians 4:1 (NIV 1984)

> For what is our hope, our joy, or the crown in which we will glory in the presence of our Lord Jesus when he comes? Is it not you?
> 1 Thessalonians 2:19 (NIV 1984)

The word Paul uses for "crown" in both of these texts is not a royal crown for ruling but a wreath given to the winner of an athletic contest. Paul says essentially that his "victory" on the day of Christ—his greatest "reward"—will be seeing that his disciples were faithful. Paul asked them to give him that joy as they worked out their salvation without complaining and arguing.

To some this may seem selfish, but Scripture teaches that those who teach us, especially our elders, will one day give an account for us before God. It also teaches that we should obey them so their work will be a joy and not a pain. The writer of Hebrews says this:

176

Obey your leaders and submit to their authority. They keep watch over you as men who must give an account. Obey them so that their work will be a joy, not a burden, for that would be of no advantage to you.
Hebrews 13:17 (NIV 1984)

In this text, the writer's primary incentive given for the Hebrew believers' obedience was their leader's "joy." For many pastors and leaders their work is not a joy, in part, because of the constant complaining and arguing of the members of the congregation. The nation of Israel constantly pointed their finger at Moses and complained about his leadership. Even his own family complained against him. Moses became so burdened by the people's complaints one time, he simply asked God to let him die. Consider what he said:

Moses heard the people of every family wailing, each at the entrance to his tent. The LORD became exceedingly angry, and Moses was troubled. He asked the LORD, "Why have you brought this trouble on your servant? What have I done to displease you that you put the burden of all these people on me? Did I conceive all these people? Did I give them birth? Why do you tell me to carry them in my arms, as a nurse carries an infant, to the land you promised on oath to their forefathers? Where can I get meat for all these people? They keep wailing to me, 'Give us meat to eat!' I cannot carry all these people by myself; the burden is too heavy for me. If this is how you are going to treat me, put me to death right now—if I have found favor in your eyes—and do not let me face my own ruin."
Numbers 11:10-15 (NIV 1984)

The people were receiving manna from heaven, but they decided that they wanted more variety in their diet. They were tired of bread and wanted meat. Therefore, they complained against Moses and against God. Moses finally responded, "Lord, are these my children? Why do I have to care for them? Why me?" One of the reasons we shouldn't complain is because of our leaders, not only for their joy on the day of Christ but for their joy now.

Scripture commands us to be considerate of our leaders and to bless them. Galatians 6:6 (NIV 1984) says, "Anyone who receives instruction in the word must share all good things with his instructor." We should honor those who feed us and care for us even though they are not perfect. They sin and make mistakes just like everybody else. I think it is their imperfections that should make us honor them even more. They need grace. Paul implies that one of the reasons we should not complain and argue is for our pastors' joy—so they may boast on the day of Christ.

I can relate to this both as a member of the church and now as a pastor. As member of the church, I look forward to one day meeting with my

177

former Sunday school teachers and pastors who imparted into my life, even just to say, "Thank you." I also want to encourage them by saying, "I was the apathetic student in your Sunday school class, but one day I got serious about God. Thank you for your labor. Thank you for your prayers." With that, my other great joy will be those I have labored for and served as a pastor in ministry. Like Paul, I will rejoice to see how they progressed in their spiritual lives. They will be my crown of rejoicing in heaven.

Application Question: Which spiritual leaders have made the greatest impact in your life?

Christians Should Not Complain and Argue in Order to Be Joyful in Every Circumstance

> But even if I am being poured out like a drink offering on the sacrifice and service coming from your faith, I am glad and rejoice with all of you. So you too should be glad and rejoice with me.
> Philippians 2:17-18 (NIV 1984)

Finally, the last reason Paul gives for not complaining and arguing is in order for us to have joy. Paul says "even if I am being poured out like a drink offering on the sacrifice and service of your faith." The drink offering was the final part of an offering (Lev 23:18, 37). A person would offer a burnt sacrifice to the Lord and then pour some wine on top of the offering as a sweet smelling savor to the Lord. It was the final act of the offering. Paul here was referring to both his and the Philippians' suffering for the Lord as a sacrifice (Phil 1:27), and he may be alluding to the possibility of his future death as the drink offering. He essentially says, "Even if this is my final offering to the Lord as I face potential death, I rejoice with you and you should rejoice as well." He commands them to not complain and argue so that they can have joy in their mutual offering to the Lord.

This is the reality: complaining and arguing not only affects others negatively, but it also affects us. It ruins our own joy. Most Christians are up and down in their spiritual life based on the events that happen. Therefore, their joy is not constant. One cannot have joy if he is constantly complaining and arguing. Paul says that even if the worst thing happens, his potential death, the Philippians should still rejoice.

Paul will command them to rejoice three more times in the letter (Phil 3:2, 4:4). He says in Philippians 4:4 (NIV 1984), "Rejoice in the Lord always. I will say it again: Rejoice!" He wants them to have joy in spite of their suffering and in spite of the difficulties happening in the church (Phil 4:2). But in order to do that, they must stop complaining. It is the same for us, God wants us to learn

178

to have joy even in the worst circumstances, and one of the ways we do this is by choosing not to complain and argue.

Do you realize that complaining steals our God-given joy? Joy is a fruit of the Holy Spirit (Gal 5:22); however, it can be lost when we choose to complain and argue. We grieve the Holy Spirit and forfeit the grace that God wants to give us. Paul said this:

> Do not let any unwholesome talk come out of your mouths, but only what is helpful for building others up according to their needs, that it may benefit those who listen. And do not grieve the Holy Spirit of God, with whom you were sealed for the day of redemption.
> Ephesians 4:29-30 (NIV 1984)

The implication is that we grieve the Holy Spirit when we let anything unwholesome come out of our mouths—cursing, lying, complaining, and arguing. When we grieve the Spirit, we lose the supernatural joy and peace that we should have in our circumstances. Paul says one of the reasons we must not complain or argue is so that we can have joy. Nehemiah said, "The joy of the Lord is our strength" (8:10, NIV 1984). Therefore, to complain and argue can actually weaken and cripple us for God's work.

Application Question: Is it really possible to have joy in every circumstance? If so, how do we develop this? Does being joyful mean never mourning or being sad?

Conclusion

Arguing and complaining is a characteristic of the world. We live in a world that has rejected God and therefore abides in a state of unthankfulness. Many homes and work environments have a culture of grumbling and complaining. However, for Christians this should not be true. God has called us not only to not complain and argue but to be thankful. First Thessalonians 5:18 (NIV 1984) says, "give thanks in all circumstances, for this is God's will for you in Christ Jesus." God's will is for us to be thankful in every situation.

Why should Christians do "everything" without grumbling and complaining?

1. Christians Should Not Complain and Argue in Order to Obey God
2. Christians Should Not Complain and Argue in Order to Grow in Godliness
3. Christians Should Not Complain and Argue in Order to Be Witnesses to Unbelievers

4. Christians Should Not Complain and Argue in Order to Honor Our Leaders
5. Christians Should Not Complain and Argue in Order to Be Joyful in Every Circumstance

Becoming Servants Worthy of Honor

Now I hope in the Lord Jesus to send Timothy to you soon, so that I too may be encouraged by hearing news about you. For there is no one here like him who will readily demonstrate his deep concern for you. Others are busy with their own concerns, not those of Jesus Christ. But you know his qualifications, that like a son working with his father, he served with me in advancing the gospel. So I hope to send him as soon as I know more about my situation, though I am confident in the Lord that I too will be coming to see you soon. But for now I have considered it necessary to send Epaphroditus to you. For he is my brother, coworker and fellow soldier, and your messenger and minister to me in my need. Indeed, he greatly missed all of you and was distressed because you heard that he had been ill. In fact he became so ill that he nearly died. But God showed mercy to him—and not to him only, but also to me—so that I would not have grief on top of grief. Therefore I am all the more eager to send him, so that when you see him again you can rejoice and I can be free from anxiety. So welcome him in the Lord with great joy, and honor people like him, since it was because of the work of Christ that he almost died. He risked his life so that he could make up for your inability to serve me.
Philippians 2:19-30 (NET)

What are characteristics of honorable servants—servants worth honoring and imitating? How do we become servants worth honoring?

In this text, Paul bestows a special honor on two men for their faithful service to God. Paul says this about Timothy and then Epaphroditus:

For there is no one here like him who will readily demonstrate his deep concern for you Others are busy with their own concerns, not those of Jesus Christ.
Philippians 2:20-21

Therefore I am all the more eager to send him, so that when you see him again you can rejoice and I can be free from anxiety. So welcome him in the Lord with great joy, and honor people like him.

Philippians 2:28-29

Paul said of Timothy that he had no one else like him; everyone else looked out for their own interests. Concerning Epaphroditus, he said that the Philippians should honor men like him because he almost died for the work of Christ. There were many Christians around Paul who professed to follow and serve Christ, but Paul knew that Christians with the makeup of Timothy and Epaphroditus were uncommon. They deserved special honor and so he honors them in this letter to the Philippians. He also implicitly gives them as a model of the mind of Christ and godly servants (cf. Phil 2:5-7).

Up to this point in Philippians, Paul has been challenging the church to be "united in spirit" (or "one in spirit") (2:2), to, in humility, consider others better than themselves (v. 3) and to not only care for their own interests but the interests of others (v. 4). Essentially, Paul was calling this congregation to be servants. This was especially important because of the division in the church, as two women were fighting in Philippians 4:2. In order to flesh out this command to be "united" and to serve one another, Paul calls the church to have the mind of Christ and gives Christ's incarnation to demonstrate Christ's mind (v. 6-11). Christ gave up his rights as God to become a man and not just a man but a servant (v. 7). He humbled himself and became obedient even unto death.

He now mentions two other model servants who the Philippians would be very well acquainted with. He mentions Timothy and Epaphroditus. Timothy's name meant "honoring God" or "one who brings honor to God." He was raised in a Christian home. His mother was a Jewish Christian woman; his father was Greek and probably a pagan (cf. Acts 16:1, 2 Tim 1:5). He learned the Scriptures from his mother and grandmother as a child (2 Tim 1:5, 2 Tim 3:14-15). Some believe that Timothy was led to Christ by Paul on his first missionary journey (Acts 14:6, 7) since he always calls him "his true son in the faith" (1 Tim 1:2). Whether that happened or not, by Paul's second missionary journey, Timothy had matured in the faith and was well spoken of by everybody, and therefore, Paul decided to take him as his protégé in the ministry (Acts 16:1-3). Timothy would have been with Paul at the founding of the church in Philippi (cf. Acts 16:12). We also know that Timothy was later sent to Ephesus to care for the church there. It was for this reason that Paul wrote the letters of 1 and 2 Timothy. He struggled with fear, maybe fear of incompetence in the ministry (2 Tim 1:7), and he was prone to sickness (1 Tim 5:23).

We don't know much about Epaphroditus. His name means "favored by Aphrodite," who was the Greek goddess of love. His name later came to mean "lovely" or "loving."[75] It seems that this man came from a pagan background and was possibly saved when Paul founded the church in Philippi. He was sent by the Philippian church to care for and minister to Paul's needs. As a prisoner in Rome, Paul would have needed food, clothing, and medical care since the prison system in Rome didn't provide those things.[76]

182

Therefore, the Philippian church, who was deeply concerned about Paul, needed to enlist a strong man, one who could journey 800 miles to Rome and care for him. This man needed to be brave because if Paul was found guilty of being an enemy of Rome, that would have implicated him and potentially led to his death.

Some may ask the question, "Why does Paul give further examples of the mind of Christ?" (Phil 2:5). The Philippians had already been given Christ as a model and also Paul, as he talked about being poured out as a drink offering (2:17-18). Here in the examples of Timothy and Epaphroditus, they could see pictures of ordinary people who served Christ and others as servants. Timothy struggled with fear and anxiety; he was constantly sick. He was not what many would call a "prominent man." He was a man who spent his life being second—serving Paul. Epaphroditus, from what we can tell, wasn't a preacher or an apostle. He wasn't a miracle worker or a great figure, but he was a man willing to take great risks in serving Christ (2:30).

What are characteristics of honorable servants? How can we become servants worth honoring as seen in Timothy and Epaphroditus? Here, Paul honors them for their service. As we look at this text, we see characteristics of honorable servants who are worth imitating.

Big Question: What characteristics of honorable servants are seen in the example of Timothy and Epaphroditus?

Honorable Servants Are Willing to Be Discipled

> Now I hope in the Lord Jesus to send Timothy to you soon, so that I too may be encouraged by hearing news about you. For there is no one here like him who will readily demonstrate his deep concern for you... But you know his qualifications, that like a son working with his father, he served with me in advancing the gospel.
> Philippians 2:19-20, 22

While Paul was in prison, he became very concerned about the Philippians. We see his concern throughout the letter. Paul mentions how they were suffering for the faith (1:28), how there were false teachers in the church (3:2), and finally how there were two women fighting and causing discord (4:2). Paul was so worried about the Philippians (even though he was the one in prison) that he planned to send Timothy to check on them. He says he hopes "in the Lord Jesus to send Timothy to you" (2:19), which simply meant that Paul was making plans, but he realized it was ultimately up to God's will.

He wanted to send Timothy to the Philippians, instead of someone else, because he was like the apostle himself. Philippians 2:20 can also be translated, "For I have no one else of kindred spirit who will genuinely be concerned for your welfare" (NASB). "Kindred spirit" or "like" can be translated "equal-souled" or "one-souled."[77] Timothy had been discipled by Paul for many years and now he was just "like" Paul. When Paul says, "But you know his qualifications," it can also be translated, "But you know Timothy's proven worth" (v. 22 ESV). The word "proven" means "proof after testing. Used of a person, it described proven character or tested value."[78] He was like a "son working with father" to advance the gospel (v. 22). He had faithfully served Paul and now was just like Paul.

Jesus said, "A disciple is not greater than his teacher, but everyone when fully trained will be like his teacher" (Luke 6:40). Timothy thought, cared, and had the same training as Paul, and when Timothy was sent to check on this church, it was like sending Paul—they were "one-souled."

This is one of the things that made Timothy such a special servant—he was willing to be trained. In Acts 16, he left his family, his career aspirations, and everything else to follow and serve Paul. When Paul says, "I hope in the Lord Jesus to send Timothy to you soon," it demonstrated Timothy's submission to Paul. He was willing to serve Paul and be second. He was willing to submit to Paul and his leadership, as Paul followed Christ.

This is an all but lost discipline in today's church. Joshua followed Moses; Elisha followed Elijah. The disciples followed Christ. Mark followed Barnabas and Peter. For each of these people who were willing to be second and to serve, they each were one day fully equipped just as their teacher. Joshua eventually replaced Moses. Elisha was given a double-portion of Elijah's anointing. The apostles turned the world upside down after Christ's resurrection. Mark eventually wrote the Gospel of Mark. These people sat under their teachers till one day they became one-souled. They had become just like them.

This is what made Timothy a servant worth honoring and imitating. A lot of zealous disciples want to skip the season of training in order to do great things. However, training is an essential requirement of being used by God. It develops skill and humility in the servant. And it also can lead to an impartation of special gifts. Paul said this about Timothy: "Because of this I remind you to rekindle God's gift that you possess through the laying on of my hands" (2 Timothy 1:6). Timothy received a gift from the laying on of Paul's hands. Commentators are not sure exactly what this means. At Timothy's ordination did Paul pray over Timothy and impart a special gifting to him? Or, while Paul was praying, did he simply recognize the gifting on Timothy's life? It seems that while Timothy followed Paul, there was some type of impartation. Timothy started to develop Paul's grace in the exposition of the Word of God; he started to develop Paul's grace in overseeing churches. An impartation through Paul's relationship with Timothy made him a more effective servant of Christ.

This is the very reason that many Christians are not effective servants. They are not willing to submit themselves to anyone's authority and discipline. They are not willing to humble themselves to learn from others. They are not willing to follow anyone. They want to keep their independence. Warren Wiersbe shares the story of a young Christian who was not willing to wait and grow under the leadership of another:

> A popular local nightclub performer visited a pastor and announced that he had been saved and wanted to serve the Lord. "What should I do next?" he asked.
> "Well, I'd suggest you unite with a good church and start growing," the pastor replied. "Is your wife a Christian?"
> "No, she isn't," the musician replied. "I hope to win her. But, do I have to wait? I mean, I'd like to do something for God right now."
> "No, you don't have to wait to witness for the Lord," explained the pastor. "Get busy in a church, and use your talents for Christ."
> "But you don't know who I am!" the man protested. "I'm a big performer—everybody knows me. I want to start my own organization, make records, and appear before big crowds!"
> "If you go too far too fast," warned the pastor, "you may hurt yourself and your testimony. And the place to start winning people is right at home. God will open up places of service for you as He sees you are ready. Meanwhile, study the Bible and give yourself a chance to grow." The man did not take the pastor's counsel. Instead, he set up a big organization and started out on his own. His "success" lasted less than a year. Not only did he lose his testimony because he was not strong enough to carry the heavy burdens, but his constant traveling alienated him from his wife and family. He drifted into a "fringe group" and disappeared from public ministry, a broken and bankrupt man.
> "His branches went out farther than his roots went deep," the pastor said. "When that happens, you eventually topple."[79]

That is exactly what we do not see in Timothy. He was willing to wait and serve as second until one day he was "one-souled" with Paul. He thought like him, had developed many of the same gifts as him, and now was competent to serve on his own when sent to Philippi. Timothy was willing to be trained and equipped through discipleship in order to more successfully serve God.

It should be added that many honorable servants may never be discipled in the same way as Joshua, Elisha, the apostles, or Timothy. The primary element of discipleship is training. Sometimes God chooses different ways to train and equip his servants. This may happen through many teachers instead of one prominent one. It may happen in part through lots of reading and studying the writings of godly people. Paul discipled many through his writings (cf. 1 and 2 Timothy, Philemon, and Titus). Training may happen formally through Bible school or seminary. It may happen through patiently enduring various trials (James 1:2-4, 2 Cor 1:3-6). Either way, the principle is still the

185

same; honorable servants are willing and humble enough to be discipled and trained.

Application Question: What makes it hard for people to be "second" by coming into a discipleship relationship under someone? Have you ever experienced a relationship like this? In what ways is God calling you to be further trained?

Honorable Servants Are Consumed with the Concerns of Christ and Others

> For there is no one here like him who will readily demonstrate his deep concern for you. Others are busy with their own concerns, not those of Jesus Christ.
> Philippians 2:20-21

One of the things that makes Timothy a servant worth honoring—a servant worth imitating—is his genuine concern for others. He demonstrated the mind of Christ as he put the interest of others before his own (cf. Phil 2:2-5). Paul said, "For there is no one here like him who will readily demonstrate his deep concern for you." The word "concern" can also be translated "worry" or "anxiety."[80] It's the same word Paul used in Philippians 4:6 when he said, "Do not be anxious about anything." Christ used it in Matthew 6:25-28 when he said, "I tell you, do not worry about your life, what you will eat or drink, or about your body, what you will wear." When spoken about negatively, it refers to somebody's selfish concerns about themselves and their futures. When spoken of positively as in this context, it refers to somebody's deep selfless concern about others.

Paul himself shared that one of his greatest trials was his constant "anxious concern for all the churches" (2 Cor 11:28). This is what made Paul constantly pray for the churches and write letter after letter to them. This is what made him travel mile upon mile visiting them. Therefore, since Timothy was "one-souled" with Paul, he bore this same pain. In fact, in many of his letters Timothy was with him in the writing of the letters (Phil 1:1, 1 Thess 1:1, 2 Thess 1:1, Philemon 1:1). He carried an anxiety—a deep concern for all the churches.

Timothy's deep concern for all the churches shined even greater in comparison to the Christians throughout the Roman Empire. Paul said this about them: "Others are busy with their own concerns, not those of Jesus Christ." We have already seen that many in Rome were preaching the gospel out of selfish ambition and rivalry with Paul (Phil 1:17). But, Paul now says, "others are busy with their own concerns, not those of Jesus Christ"—he can't find anyone willing to put the interest of the Philippians, and thus Christ's, before their own.

186

This is a sad admission, but the truth is Christians today often are not very different from those in Rome. While professing Christ, most are living for their own desires, goals, and self-advancement. This is very different from Christ's model which Paul taught only a few verses earlier (Phil 2:5-11). Christ, instead of holding on to his privileges as God, came down and took on not only humanity but the form of a servant—the lowest of the low, the poorest of the poor. Instead of seeking his own advancement, he descended in order to serve more people. However, the majority of the church is consumed with their own agenda and therefore has no time to care for the interests of others or Christ.

Often when a person wants some of our time—to talk to us about his or her problems or seek our advice—we commonly see them as a distraction to our goals and even unnecessary burdens. We find ourselves looking at our watches because our real purpose is not this person's "concerns" or "interests" but our own. This is something our Lord must deliver us from.

In both Timothy and Epaphroditus, we see people who not only cared about others but also were available to serve them. This is what an honorable servant—a servant worth imitating—looks like. Listen to what Dietrich Bonhoeffer said:

> We must be ready to allow ourselves to be interrupted by God. God will be constantly crossing our paths and canceling our plans by sending us people with claims and petitions. We may pass them by, preoccupied with our more important tasks, as the priest passed by the man who had fallen among thieves, perhaps—reading the Bible. When we do that, we pass by the visible sign of the Cross raised [in] our path to show us that, not our way, but God's way must be done. It is a strange fact that Christians frequently consider their work so important and urgent that they will allow nothing to disturb them. They think they are doing God a service in this, but actually they are disdaining God's "Crooked yet straight path." They do not want a life that is crossed and balked. But it is part of the discipline of humility that we must not spare our hand where it can perform a service and that we do not assume that our schedule is our own to manage, but allow it to be arranged by God.[81]

Similarly, Paul said, "Carry one another's burdens, and in this way you will fulfill the law of Christ" (Galatians 6:2). What does it mean to fulfill the law of Christ? It simply means when we carry other's burdens, we are fulfilling our duty as followers of Jesus. We must empty ourselves of selfishness and fill ourselves with the desires of God and the interests of others. Paul said, "Instead of being motivated by selfish ambition or vanity, each of you should, in humility,

187

be moved to treat one another as more important than yourself" (Phil 2:3). Honorable servants are consumed with the interests of Christ and others.

Application Question: In what ways is God challenging you to carry the burden of others? Why is this often so difficult for us to do?

Honorable Servants Are Balanced

> But for now I have considered it necessary to send Epaphroditus to you. For he is my brother, coworker and fellow soldier, and your messenger and minister to me in my need.
> Philippians 2:25

Next, Paul begins to heap praise on Epaphroditus who is being sent back to the Philippian church. The reason Paul spends so much time praising Epaphroditus' ministry is probably because some at Philippi might have questioned why he returned. Did he fail at caring for Paul? Was he afraid of the potential persecution that might accompany serving Paul? Therefore, Paul assures the congregation of how faithful Epaphroditus was and calls for them to honor him for his great work.

In Philippians 2:25 Paul gives Epaphroditus five different titles to demonstrate his faithfulness. Three of these titles focus on his relationship to Paul and the next two focus on his relationship with the Philippians. He calls him his brother, coworker, fellow soldier, their messenger, and minister. Young's Literal Translation actually translates the latter as "servant." The Philippians sent Epaphroditus as a minister to serve Paul's needs.

What can we learn from the five different titles that Paul gives Epaphroditus? Warren Wiersbe notes in his commentary that Epaphroditus was a balanced Christian.[82] We see this in each of his titles.

Interpretation Question: What do the five titles that Paul gave Epaphroditus demonstrate about him, and how do they represent being a balanced Christian?

1. The title "brother" demonstrates his intimacy with Paul. Epaphroditus loved Paul and served him as if he were his own natural brother. It also represented Epaphroditus' and Paul's relationship to God. Jesus said, "Here are my mother and my brothers! For whoever does the will of God is my brother and sister and mother" (Mk 3:34-35). Paul and Epaphroditus were brothers in their obedience and submission to God. This gave them a tremendous intimacy because they both lived to please and serve the Lord.

188

2. The title "coworker" demonstrates how they partnered in spreading the gospel and helped people come to know Christ. Paul also called himself a "coworker" with God in 1 Corinthians 3:9. They both were serving together while building God's church.

3. The title "fellow soldier" demonstrates how they faithfully defended the gospel together, and it also represents their sufferings for Christ (cf. Phil 1:27). Paul said to Timothy, "Take your share of suffering as a good soldier of Christ Jesus" (2 Tim 2:3). Every good soldier is willing to suffer and even die for his cause. Epaphroditus traveled 800 miles to care for Paul and almost died in the process. Paul eventually did die in his service for Christ (cf. 2 Tim 4:6-7). They were fellow soldiers.

4. The title "messenger" demonstrates how he faithfully carried the message of the Philippian church to Paul. The word can also be translated "apostle" which means "sent one." He was not an apostle in the same way Paul was. An apostle had seen the resurrected Christ and worked miracles in order to persuade people to follow Christ. Though not an apostle like Paul, he faithfully represented the church at Philippi by caring for Paul's needs. He was their messenger.

5. The title "minister" demonstrates how he faithfully served Paul and put his needs before his own. He left his family, career, and church to serve Paul. He was a faithful servant of Christ.

   William Barclay points out that this word would have great meaning to the Greek minds of the Philippian church. The word was used only of great men. The title was bestowed only upon great benefactors, men who loved their city, culture, arts, or sports so much that they gave huge sums of money to support these functions. The person was looked upon as a great servant or minister given over to his cause. Paul is here bestowing the great title of minister upon Epaphroditus. Epaphroditus was an extraordinary minister of God who ministered to Paul's needs.[83]

By using this term Paul was setting Epaphroditus apart as a great man in the kingdom of God. Though he may not have been a pastor, a preacher, or an evangelist, he was a tremendous benefactor for the kingdom. His ministry was great, and he was to be honored for it.

How do we apply this to our lives? Most Christians are not balanced in the practice of their faith. Some Christians spend all their time fellowshipping and hanging out with brothers and sisters in Christ, but they spend no time working to build God's kingdom and serve others. They are not willing to exert any holy sweat—any holy effort. Their work for the kingdom of God is coming to church on Sunday. As long as they have done that, they feel no responsibility to evangelize, serve, or even pray.

Some work but won't defend. They won't defend the gospel or seek to protect the church from wrong teachings. They see no point in it. They are too worried about offending someone. They often think doctrine doesn't really matter as long as one loves. However, the truth is that doctrine affects how we live. When we have lost doctrine, we have lost everything.

Many are not willing to be "apostolos"—messengers—that leave their comfort to serve and minister to others. They don't support the work of foreign missions and aren't willing to be part of it. This is true for the majority of the church in one way or another. However, we should seek to be balanced because Scripture calls us to do all of these ministries.

One of the things that made Epaphroditus a servant worthy of honor and worth imitating was his balance. He was a loving brother, a fellow worker, a fellow soldier, a messenger, and a minister—a man of great dignity for the kingdom of God. Are you a balanced Christian?

Application Question: Would you consider yourself a balanced Christian? What area that Paul mentions do you feel a need to grow in most?

Honorable Servants Are Sympathetic

> Indeed, he greatly missed all of you and was distressed because you heard that he had been ill.
> Philippians 2:26

Another characteristic of Epaphroditus is that he was sympathetic—he felt the pain of others. Look again at what Paul says: "Indeed, he greatly missed all of you and was distressed because you heard that he had been ill" (Philippians 2:26). Christ was similarly "distressed" in the Garden of Gethsemane. He said, "'My soul is deeply grieved, even to the point of death. Remain here and stay alert'" (Mark 14:34). Christ was in anguish over going to the cross, bearing the sins of the world, and being separated from God. Some versions say he was "weary unto death." This is the same way Epaphroditus felt while in Rome. However, what's strange is that he did not feel that way over his own predicament—the sickness that almost killed him—but over the pain of others. Either while making his 800 mile trek to Rome he got sick or soon after. Paul describes his healing as the mercy of God (v. 27). Again, Epaphroditus was not weary or distressed because of his own problem but because the people at Philippi heard about his sickness and were worried (v. 26).

Now, for us in the 21st century, we may not fully comprehend the scenario with Epaphroditus and the church in Philippi. Today we can simply

190

write an email, send a message on Facebook, pick up the phone, or get on Skype to communicate with someone thousands of miles away. However, in those days it would take weeks, if not months, to send a message to somebody. Somehow the Philippians heard about his situation and were worried. They might have questioned their original decision to send Epaphroditus alone for such a long trip. They were anxious and maybe felt guilty.

Epaphroditus was sympathetic, and his sympathy led to compassion. He was concerned about Paul, and so he trekked 800 miles to serve him. He was concerned about the Philippians and now he was about to trek back to encourage them. He was a sympathetic person. In fact, so was Paul. Paul said, "Therefore I am all the more eager to send him, so that when you see him again you can rejoice and I can be free from anxiety" (Phil 2:28). Why was Paul anxious? He was anxious because he also was worried about the hearts of the Philippians. They both loved this congregation dearly and therefore were sympathetic to their condition. This made them both effective servants—servants worthy of honor.

The reason sympathy is so important is because if you never feel the pain of somebody else or feel the burden of some great problem, you will never be motivated to be part of the solution. This is the problem with many in the church. We feel nobody's pain and consequently feel nobody's joy. We only feel our own pain and joy. Jesus said, "Blessed are those who mourn" (Matt 5:4). It can be translated, "Happy are the mourners." Happy are the ones who bear the pain of others. Happy are those who mourn over the effects of sin on others and on our world. These are the ones who are blessed by God.

Scripture commands us to "rejoice with those who rejoice, weep with those who weep" (Rom 12:15). We must develop the ability to be sympathetic. Those with sympathy are the only effective ministers—ministers worthy of honor. They really care and are willing to meet the needs of others.

Solomon said this: "The heart of the wise is in the house of mourning, but the heart of fools is in the house of merrymaking" (Ecclesiastes 7:4). What does this mean? It means that the wise are willing to sympathize with and to feel the pain of the sick, discouraged, and hurting. They find great value in this and therefore run to meet the needs of those hurting. However, the fool only cares about his pleasure. He lives his life primarily for his own ease and happiness. But, that is not how Epaphroditus lived. He hurt with others and rejoiced with others. His heart was in the house of mourning—he was willing to bear the pain of others in order to minister to them.

Application Question: How can one grow in sympathy for others?

I have often thought about the story of the first resurrection in Scripture in 1 Kings 17. Elijah lays his body over a dead boy three times and prays for God to heal him (v. 21-22). Why did he lay his warm body over the cold, dead

191

body of the boy three times? I believe he was seeking to empathize with him. He was seeking to feel his pain in order to more effectively and fervently pray for him. Is that not one of the reasons that Christ became a man? He became a man so he could understand our pain and empathize with us so he could more effectively pray for us as our High Priest. Hebrews 4:15-16 says,

> For we do not have a high priest incapable of sympathizing with our weaknesses, but one who has been tempted in every way just as we are, yet without sin. Therefore let us confidently approach the throne of grace to receive mercy and find grace whenever we need help.

This is exactly what many of us need to do in order to grow in sympathy. We need to be like Epaphroditus. We need to visit the person in jail and the person on his death bed. We need to touch the leper and allow his pain to change us and make us more sympathetic. Servants worth honoring are sympathetic. As they feel the pain of others, it moves them to action as displayed in the example of Epaphroditus.

Application Question: How would you rank your ability to sympathize with others from 1-10? Share a time where you were moved by the pain of another to get involved and serve.

Honorable Servants Are Willing to Take Risks for Christ

> So welcome him in the Lord with great joy, and honor people like him, since it was because of the work of Christ that he almost died. He risked his life so that he could make up for your inability to serve me. Philippians 2:29-30

Another characteristic of servants worthy of honor is that they are willing to take risks. The word "risked" that Paul used here was actually used of somebody who gambled.[84] They were voluntarily willing to risk their own welfare and be exposed to danger. This was true of Epaphroditus. He left his career, home, family, and church in order to serve Paul. He was willing to take a great risk.

Don't we see this characteristic in many men and women God used greatly? Abraham left his home and family to go to a land that he had never been to in order to follow God. Because of this risk—this gamble—God made his descendants into a great nation and brought the messiah through him. Moses also left the wealth of being a prince in Egypt to suffer shame with the people of God (Heb 11:24-26). Therefore, God exalted him and made him the leader of Israel and a type of Christ (cf. Deut 18:15). Ruth was a pagan Moabite widow who followed her mother in-law Naomi to the land of Israel so she could beg for food. She was willing to be poor because she realized that in suffering

192

with Naomi she was following the true God. This risk not only eventually led to all her needs being met, but it also brought God's blessing, as she was placed in the lineage of Christ. In addition, all the apostles gambled in following Christ. They gave up career and family to follow the messiah. Those whom God honors are willing to take risks for Christ.

Jesus said this: "And whoever has left houses or brothers or sisters or father or mother or children or fields for my sake will receive a hundred times as much and will inherit eternal life" (Matthew 19:29). Christ essentially said everybody who bets on me will receive a hundred times as much and inherit eternal life.

This is what made Epaphroditus so special. Like Abraham, Moses, Ruth, and the apostles, he was willing to risk it all in following God. Similarly, Paul said this:

> But these assets I have come to regard as liabilities because of Christ. More than that, I now regard all things as liabilities compared to the far greater value of knowing Christ Jesus my Lord, for whom I have suffered the loss of all things—indeed, I regard them as dung!—that I may gain Christ
> Philippians 3:7-8

Paul counted everything liabilities to gain Christ. He said it was a worthy gamble. Moreover, this characteristic is especially important for servants. To serve others and build the kingdom of God, one may have to leave career, home, and family. It may even cost a person his life. All the disciples, save one, lost their lives in following Christ. Many missionaries have lost their lives, contracted dangerous diseases, and suffered other pains in serving Christ and others. Paul says these are the type of people that should be honored. These are the type of people to imitate. We can be sure as Paul honors them in this letter, God was ultimately honoring them as the Author of Scripture (cf. 2 Tim 3:16). And therefore, they will be honored throughout eternity.

Application Question: In what ways has God called you to risk something for his name? Do you ever struggle with fear or apprehension about taking risks as you follow God?

Honorable Servants Will Be Rewarded

> So welcome him in the Lord with great joy, and honor people like him, since it was because of the work of Christ that he almost died. He risked his life so that he could make up for your inability to serve me.
> Philippians 2:29-30

As mentioned previously, honored servants will ultimately be rewarded. In what ways do we see these servants honored?

Observation Question: In what ways will honorable servants be rewarded as we can discern from Philippians 2:19-30 and how does this apply to our lives?

1. Honorable servants will be given greater opportunities to serve.

Timothy who had faithfully served Paul for years was being given the opportunity to serve in a greater capacity. Timothy was being sent to Philippi to fulfill what Paul could not since he was in prison. He had been faithful and God was honoring him with more. When we are faithful with little, God makes us faithful over much (cf. Mk 4:24-25, Matt 25:21). He gives us more opportunities to serve.

2. Honorable servants will be honored by men.

Paul tells the Philippians to welcome Epaphroditus (2:29). The word "welcome" refers to a favorable and glad acceptance.[85] The Philippians were to honor and welcome him for his faithful service to Paul. On this earth, many times we will be thanked and honored by those we served. Galatians 6:6 says, "Now the one who receives instruction in the word must share all good things with the one who teaches it." We should generously bless those who teach us. Many times as we serve others, we will be honored. However, it should be noted that this is not always true. For example, the very ones Paul served in Corinth became angry at him and attacked his apostleship. Second Corinthians is primarily a defense of his apostleship.

However, even though we will not always be honored on earth by those we serve, it will ultimately happen in heaven. It seems that in heaven we will have a greater clarity to evaluate those who have served us on earth. Look at what Christ taught as a motivation for generous giving to the kingdom of God in Luke 16:9: "And I tell you, make friends for yourselves by how you use worldly wealth, so that when it runs out you will be welcomed into the eternal homes." In heaven those who have given generously to build the kingdom will be welcomed by those who were blessed and saved by their ministry—they will be welcomed into eternal dwellings. Those who are faithful servants will at times be honored by those they serve on this earth and ultimately by them in heaven.

3. Honorable servants will be honored by God.

We should notice that Paul commands the Philippians to welcome him "in the Lord" (2:29). What does he mean by "in the Lord"? This means the Philippians were to honor Epaphroditus in the same way God would. This

194

implies that God will ultimately honor faithful servants in his coming kingdom. Jesus said this in Matthew 25:21: "Well done, good and faithful slave! You have been faithful in a few things. I will put you in charge of many things. Enter into the joy of your master!" One day God will not only heap praise on his servants but also rewards for their faithful service. This will include opportunities for greater service in the kingdom, riches in heaven, and crowns that represent their faithfulness and rulership in the coming kingdom (1 Cor 4:5, Matt 25:51, Matt 6:19, 1 Cor 3:12-14, Rev 4:10).

Honorable servants will be rewarded. They will be rewarded with further opportunities to serve. They will be honored by the people they have served if not here on earth, then in heaven. Their ultimate reward will come from God, as he praises them and lavishes rewards on them for their faithful service.

Application Question: Does reward for faithful service motivate you to be a more faithful servant? Why or why not?

Conclusion

What are characteristics of honorable servants—servants worth imitating? How can we become servants worth being honored and imitated (cf. 1 Cor 11:1)?

1. Honorable Servants Are Willing to Be Discipled
2. Honorable Servants Are Consumed with the Concerns of Christ and Others
3. Honorable Servants Are Sympathetic
4. Honorable Servants Are Willing to Take Risks for Christ
5. Honorable Servants Will Be Rewarded

195

How to Protect Ourselves from Spiritual Threats

> Finally, my brothers and sisters, rejoice in the Lord! To write this again is no trouble to me, and it is a safeguard for you. Beware of the dogs, beware of the evil workers, beware of those who mutilate the flesh! For we are the circumcision, the ones who worship by the Spirit of God, exult in Christ Jesus, and do not rely on human credentials
> Philippians 3:1-3 (NET)

How do we protect ourselves from spiritual threats? How do we protect the church?

When I was a child living in my parents' house, like many children, I felt that my father always repeated himself. There were always a few things he constantly repeated. He would commonly tell me to not hang around bad kids because they would get me in trouble. He also constantly reminded me to lock the door to our house so no one would break in and steal things. As a child and later a high school student, I remember always saying, "Yes, of course, Dad. I got it. I know." Moreover, I remember after college I was moving into a new apartment, as I was about to start seminary in Chicago, and my parents stayed with me for a night. As my parents were about to depart and drive back to Texas, my dad said to me, "Don't hang around any bad people and make sure you lock your doors." In my mind I thought, "I am a grown man. You don't need to tell me this." However, I just said, "Yes, Dad. Thanks for the tip."

In this text, we see Paul's fatherly care for the Philippians and like many fathers he repeats himself in order to protect the Philippians. He said, "Finally, my brothers and sisters, rejoice in the Lord! To write this again is no trouble to me, and it is a safeguard for you" (Phil 3:1).

What is he repeating? Commentators are divided on that. Some think he is talking about his exhortation to "rejoice in the Lord." Others think he is focusing on the call to beware of false teachers. Which is it? It is probably better to look at the entire section of verses 1-3 as part of Paul's holy repetition in seeking to protect the Philippians. Paul's desire is to protect the Philippians and their faith in God.

How do we protect our faith and the faith of those around us? Some things in our spiritual life should be repeated over and over again. We need to

197

repeat them to ourselves and also to others for protection. As Christians, there are many threats to our spiritual lives. We have a threat from within. We have a flesh that we must battle against at all times (Gal 5:17). We have the world system that constantly tempts and at times even persecutes us (1 John 2:15-17). We have an enemy in the devil seeking to lure us away from God and his plan for our lives (2 Tim 2:26). Also, we must not forget the general consequences of sin on this earth, as we all encounter various trials and tribulations. Life bears thorns and thistles instead of the fruit we have worked for (Gen 3:17-18). Life is hard at times and these difficulties can be threats to our faith. Because of all these realities, there is a need to protect our faith.

In this text, we will see several principles about guarding our faith and others'.

Big Question: According to Paul, what principles must we practice in order to remain safe and protect ourselves from spiritual threats?

Believers Protect Themselves by Remaining in Fellowship

> Finally, my brothers and sisters, rejoice in the Lord! To write this again is no trouble to me, and it is a safeguard for you.
> Philippians 3:1

When Paul says "finally," it is better translated "'furthermore," "so then," or "now then." It is a word of transition, not conclusion, since half of Philippians follows it.[86] Paul is marking a change in thought and focus. Paul here calls the Philippians "brothers and sisters" and then seeks to protect them by instruction. The implication of both Paul calling them "brothers and sisters" and then seeking to challenge them is that his relationship with the Philippians was part of their protection. As a loving family member, he sought to protect his spiritual brothers and sisters from various threats to their spiritual health. The Philippians had a form of protection in their fellowship with Paul and one another.

This is true for us as well. If we do not remain in healthy fellowship with believers who will hold us accountable, we are vulnerable to various attacks. The spiritual life is not meant to be walked alone. God has given us spiritual fathers, mothers, brothers, and sisters to help us grow and also to protect us from things that might draw us away from God (cf. 1 Tim 5:1-2).

Similarly, the disciples lived in a close relationship with one another and with Christ as a protection. Christ constantly warned and exhorted them as a protection. He told them to beware of the leaven of the Pharisees (Mark 8:15). He told them to not worry about what they would eat, drink, or wear (Matt 6:25). Jesus was protecting them, just like Paul was with the Philippians. His relationship with them was a form of accountability. However, it also seems as though Christ needed this fellowship as well. On the night he was betrayed, he called three of his disciples to pray with him because he was weary unto death (Matt 26:3). He needed their prayers. As a man he was dependent upon the accountability relationships with his disciples; he needed their support.

We see the need for fellowship and accountability relationships throughout Scripture. Paul also said this:

> Brothers and sisters, if a person is discovered in some sin, you who are spiritual restore such a person in a spirit of gentleness. Pay close attention to yourselves, so that you are not tempted too. Carry one another's burdens, and in this way you will fulfill the law of Christ.
> Galatians 6:1-2

Paul reminded the brothers and sisters in Galatia of their need to restore those caught in some sin. Similarly, in Matthew 18 Christ taught the need for us both individually and corporately as a church to hold people accountable as a protection from sin. Listen to what he said:

> "If your brother sins, go and show him his fault when the two of you are alone. If he listens to you, you have regained your brother. But if he does not listen, take one or two others with you, so that at the testimony of two or three witnesses every matter may be established. If he refuses to listen to them, tell it to the church. If he refuses to listen to the church, treat him like a Gentile or a tax collector.
> Matthew 18:15-17

If a person is in sin, one should go and show him his fault. If he will not listen, one should bring another person. Then, if he still does not listen, one should bring it to the church. Finally, if this person continues in sin, then the church should discipline him by treating him as a pagan or tax collector—essentially removing the person from their fellowship.

One of the ways we protect ourselves is by remaining in the fellowship. As soon as a person starts to drift away from church and Christian fellowship in general, they are on dangerous ground. Paul, as the Philippians' older brother in the Lord, sought to warn them and protect them.

Who holds you accountable? How do you respond when somebody challenges or warns you? Who do you challenge? Proverbs says, "faithful are the wounds of a friend" (Prov 27:6). Sometimes it may mean hurting somebody's feelings when you warn or challenge them, but these wounds are faithful and necessary for protection.

I think we see the importance of this in Paul's relationship with the Philippians and how he spoke to them as a loving brother. If we are going to protect ourselves, we must have healthy fellowship.

Application Question: Why are accountability relationships and genuine church fellowship so important? How do we develop these relationships? Who are your accountability partners?

Believers Protect Themselves by Guarding Their Joy

> Finally, my brothers and sisters, rejoice in the Lord! To write this again is no trouble to me, and it is a safeguard for you.
> Philippians 3:1

The next protection for the Philippians was their joy in the Lord. As their older spiritual brother, Paul calls for the Philippians to "rejoice in the Lord." Many have seen joy as the major theme of the epistle. In chapter 1, he mentioned joy several times. He says he always prays with joy because of their partnership in the gospel (Phil 1:4-5). Concerning whether he would die or live, he said he was convinced it was God's will for him to stay for their progress and joy in the faith (1:25). In Philippians 2:17-18, he declared how he rejoiced in his sacrifice for them and commands them to rejoice as well. Even though Paul was in prison, his heart was protected by his joy in the Lord, and he wanted them to be protected as well. In fact, he will repeat this call for the church to have joy in Philippians 4:4. He says, "Rejoice in the Lord always. Again I say, rejoice."

Why is the joy of the Lord so important for our faith? Why is it a protection from various spiritual threats? First of all, we should understand that this joy is not a joy in circumstances. It is a joy regardless of circumstances. A Christian can rejoice in poverty, loss, failure, heart-break, etc., because this joy is based on our relationship with the Lord. It overflows from our relationship with God. It is a fruit of the Spirit (Gal 5:22). As we are abiding in God's Spirit, he gives us joy.

Why is it a protection? Paul's command to rejoice in the Lord as a protection or a "safeguard" tells us that a loss of joy in the Lord is a sure pathway into sin and an open door for the enemy. The reality is if we lose our joy in Christ, we will try to find it somewhere outside of our relationship with him. For example, when the prodigal son was no longer content with his relationship with his father and the father's provisions, he left the father's house to find his joy and satisfaction in sin (Luke 15). If we lose our joy in Christ, we will be tempted to do the same.

This was exactly Satan's strategy in the Garden of Eden. What was Adam's and Eve's joy in the garden? It was the Lord—joy in his person, his provisions, and his blessing. Therefore, Satan's temptation was essentially an attack on their joy. He wanted them to not trust God. He wanted them to think God was actually there to keep them from having joy. Satan said, "Did God say you could not eat from 'every' tree in the garden?" He tried to make God's

200

command feel overbearing. He then attacked God's character. He said, "You will not surely die, but you will be like God."

This is Satan's attack against us. He wants us to lose our joy in the Lord. He wants us to focus on every trial, every bad situation, and every circumstance that is not ideal, because when we do that, we lose our protection. There is protection; there is power in our joy in the Lord.

Nehemiah said this in speaking to the Israelites who were mourning during the revival God brought in Israel: "Do not grieve, for the joy of the Lord is your strength" (Neh 8:10b). He said that the joy of the Lord is our strength. Therefore, to not rejoice in the Lord would be to weaken ourselves and make us vulnerable to discouragement, sin, and various other maladies of the evil one.

Application Question: How do we maintain our joy in the Lord?

1. Believers maintain their joy "in" the Lord by focusing on their relationship with God.

We learn how to maintain our joy in the Lord by noticing the small preposition "in." Our joy is "in" the Lord. We must constantly seek fellowship with Christ. We must constantly abide in his Word, fellowship, worship, etc. If we are not constantly developing our relationship with Christ, we cannot have joy. Joy is a fruit of the Spirit which comes from walking in the Spirit (Gal 5:16, 22). Therefore, if we are not walking with the Lord, we cannot have joy.

2. Believers maintain their joy in the Lord by choosing not to indulge in hazards to their relationship with God.

If focusing on our relationship with God is the positive action needed to have joy, then rejecting everything that would hinder that relationship is the negative action. It means choosing to not worry, to not be anxious, to not live in sin, to not live in discord with others, to not meditate on ungodly things which steal our joy, etc. David said, "If I had harbored sin in my heart, the Lord would not have listened" (Psalm 66:18). Sin hindered his relationship with God and therefore quenched his joy.

Personally, I have to be very careful about worry and anxiety. It can be anxiety about the future, a relationship conflict, or a task needing to be completed. Proverbs says, "Anxiety in a person's heart weighs him down" (12:25). We must zealously guard ourselves from anything that would hinder our relationship with God. Maintaining our joy is both a fruit of developing intimacy with God and also rejecting anything that would hinder that relationship.

Do you have joy in the Lord? Or have you lost it? To lose it means to be in a dangerous position spiritually.

Application Question: What are major threats to your joy in the Lord? How do you practically maintain this joy? Have you seen or experienced how a loss of joy in the Lord is a doorway to all types of sin?

Believers Protect Themselves by Living in the Word of God

> Finally, my brothers and sisters, rejoice in the Lord! To write this again is no trouble to me, and it is a safeguard for you.
> Philippians 3:1

The next principle that Paul gives for guarding the believer's spiritual life is living in the Word of God. He gives this by implication. Essentially, the Philippians would be guarded by reading the writing of the letter he sent them, the book of Philippians, and putting the truths into practice. He says "to write this again" to them was a safeguard. The letter itself was meant to help protect the Philippians.

It is the same for us; one of the primary ways we guard ourselves spiritually is by a life lived in the Word of God. It has been said that "The Word of God will keep you from sin or sin will keep you from the Word of God." You can't have both. A person who is not walking with God will not desire to read the Bible and won't desire to go to a church where the Bible is preached. However, a person growing in his relationship with God will love being in the Word of God. One's relationship with the Word of God is a spiritual thermometer. It shows where our spiritual life really is. If we are growing in the knowledge of Scripture, we will be guarded from many threats of the enemy, but if we are not growing, we are vulnerable.

Application Question: In what ways does the Word of God protect the believer from sin?

1.   The Word of God is a protection because it exposes sin.

Hebrews 4:12 says, "For the word of God is living and active and sharper than any double-edged sword, piercing even to the point of dividing soul from spirit, and joints from marrow; it is able to judge the desires and thoughts of the heart." Living in the Word of God is like having surgery. As it cuts us, it reveals wrong heart attitudes: pride, anger, unforgiveness, etc. James compares living in the Word of God to looking into a mirror (James 1:23-25). It

202

reveals all our sins and shortcomings. Some people aren't even aware of compromise in their life because they are not letting the mirror of God's Word reflect on them. The Word of God is necessary to expose sin so we can confess it and abandon it.

2. The Word of God is a protection because it enables us to stand against temptation.

David said this: "In my heart I store up your words, so I might not sin against you" (Psalm 119:11). David practiced the discipline of memorizing Scripture in order to protect him from lust, anxiety, retaliation, etc. Hiding the Word of God in our heart is a protection for us as well.

3. The Word of God is a protection because it enables us to stand against spiritual warfare.

When Jesus was tempted in the wilderness by Satan, he continually spoke the Word of God to combat the enemy's lies (Matt 4:1-10). Scripture actually teaches that the Word of God is the "sword of the Spirit" (Eph 6:17). It is the very weapon the Spirit uses to defeat the devil. We must know the Word of God thoroughly so we can win our spiritual battles.

4. The Word of God is a protection because it helps us grow into maturity.

Paul taught this in Ephesians 4:11-15:

It was he who gave some as apostles, some as prophets, some as evangelists, and some as pastors and teachers, to equip the saints for the work of ministry, that is, to build up the body of Christ, until we all attain to the unity of the faith and of the knowledge of the Son of God— a mature person, attaining to the measure of Christ's full stature. So we are no longer to be children, tossed back and forth by waves and carried about by every wind of teaching by the trickery of people who craftily carry out their deceitful schemes. But practicing the truth in love, we will in all things grow up into Christ, who is the head.

Paul said that the very reason God gave gifted teachers to the church was to help the church mature out of spiritual childhood. Spiritual children are prone to danger. They are especially prone to fall into false teaching (v. 14). However, the Word of God, as taught through spiritual leaders, helps spiritual children mature and therefore protects them from various temptations.

If we are going to stay safe, if we are going to protect ourselves from various spiritual threats, we must be people of God's Word. It exposes sin. It helps us fight against temptation and spiritual warfare, and it helps us mature in Christ.

Application Question: In what ways have you experienced the Word of God as a protection from spiritual threats? Describe your spiritual disciplines with the Word of God.

Believers Protect Themselves by Watching Out for False Teachers

> Beware of the dogs, beware of the evil workers, beware of those who mutilate the flesh!
> Philippians 3:2

Again, we see Paul using repetition to protect the Philippians. He says, "Beware of the dogs, beware of the evil workers, beware of those who mutilate the flesh!" He is using repetition for the sake of emphasis.

Most likely, Paul is referring to a group of false teachers called the Judaizers. When the gospel began to spread in the book of Acts, a group of "professing" Jewish Christians taught a need for Gentiles to practice the Mosaic Law in order to be saved. Salvation was not by faith alone. We see this conflict at the Antioch church in Acts 15:1. It says, "Now some men came down from Judea and began to teach the brothers, 'Unless you are circumcised according to the custom of Moses, you cannot be saved.'" This brought Paul and Barnabas into a sharp debate with them, and because of this, Paul and other representatives went to the Jerusalem church to seek the counsel of the apostles. The apostle James gave the final decision on this situation. He said,

> "Therefore I conclude that we should not cause extra difficulty for those among the Gentiles who are turning to God, but that we should write them a letter telling them to abstain from things defiled by idols and from sexual immorality and from what has been strangled and from blood. For Moses has had those who proclaim him in every town from ancient times, because he is read aloud in the synagogues every Sabbath."
> Acts 15:19-21

The Gentiles were not commanded to practice the Jewish law and circumcision as a means of salvation. But, they were to practice sensitivity regarding Jewish customs (meat from strangled animals, blood, etc.) in order to not offend the Jews living in various cities. Essentially, they were asked to practice the law of love (cf. Romans 14:21).

204

However, even though there was a clear ruling on this issue, it did not stop these false teachers. They essentially followed Paul everywhere he went, seeking to corrupt the churches with a false gospel. In fact, the entire letter of Galatians confronts this false teaching. Paul said this:

But even if we (or an angel from heaven) should preach a gospel contrary to the one we preached to you, let him be condemned to hell! As we have said before, and now I say again, if any one is preaching to you a gospel contrary to what you received, let him be condemned to hell!
Galatians 1:8-9

I wish those agitators would go so far as to castrate themselves!
Galatians 5:12

Paul speaks very aggressively towards them. He says anybody who preaches another gospel should be accursed. He also said he wished that those who preached the need for circumcision should go all the way and emasculate themselves.

This is very important to notice because in today's culture we have become so focused on "tolerance" and "love" that very few ever sound the alarm about false teaching. To teach that the Jehovah's Witnesses, Roman Catholics, or others teach a false gospel is considered unloving. People who hear teaching like this often become offended. However, let us be clear that this is not the way Paul felt as a good shepherd protecting his sheep. And, because these warnings are written in Scripture, we can be sure that this is not the way God feels either. Anybody that teaches a gospel other than salvation by faith through grace alone should be eternally condemned.

Now, I know this is hard to hear, but we must hear it because this is what God teaches. If we don't hear it, then we will not be heeding the serious warning that Paul gives. He essentially says beware, beware, beware. Christ taught the same thing.

"Watch out for false prophets, who come to you in sheep's clothing but inwardly are voracious wolves. You will recognize them by their fruit. Grapes are not gathered from thorns or figs from thistles, are they? In the same way, every good tree bears good fruit, but the bad tree bears bad fruit.
Matthew 7:15-17

Jesus said you will know them by their fruits. If you watch long enough, their works will manifest their inward nature. You will be able to tell who the false teachers are.

205

Observation Question: In what ways does Paul describe the false teachers? What can we learn from these characteristics?

"Beware of the dogs, beware of the evil workers, beware of those who mutilate the flesh!" (Philippians 3:2).

1.   Beware of teachers that try to steal believers from the church.

When Paul called these false teachers "dogs," he was saying they were like scavengers. This is a different word than what Christ used to refer to the Gentile woman in the gospels who asked him to heal her daughter (Matt 15:26-27). There he used the word for pet dogs.[87] Here Paul refers to dogs that ran in packs, fed on garbage, stole food, and at times even attacked humans. Therefore, they were hated and feared. Paul compared the false teachers to these scavengers. They try to steal people from God's church. Most times their converts are not unbelievers; they are those who profess Christ in the church. Jesus similarly called them wolves in sheep's clothing (Matt 7:15). This meant they would constantly come and try to steal sheep from the flock. Paul said this to Timothy about them:

> For some of these insinuate themselves into households and captivate weak women who are overwhelmed with sins and led along by various passions. Such women are always seeking instruction, yet never able to arrive at a knowledge of the truth.
> 2 Timothy 3:6-7

These teachers would go into homes while the husbands were away and seek to manipulate the women with their teachings and gain control over them. False teachers are prone to spiritual abuse—they seek to control people.

2.   Beware of teachers that exalt a particular nation or people group and demean others.

Another implication of the descriptor "dogs" is that these Judaizers taught that the Jewish race was superior to other races. The word "dog" was a common racial slur used by Jews for Gentiles. Jewish men would wake up every morning and say, "Thank you, God, that I am a man and not a woman, a Jew and not a gentile dog." There was tremendous hostility between Jews and Gentiles. Paul was using irony by calling these Judaizers dogs—the same name they used of the Gentiles.

Yes, in a sense, God called the Jews to be his special people—his kingdom of priests on the earth (Exodus 19:6). They were to be the stewards of

206

the Word of God, the temple, and the worship. But, they were meant to be servants of everybody else—missionaries and not exalted kings. They were selected based on God's electing purposes (cf. Deut 7:7-8, Rom 9:3-5), not anything special they had done.

This is a common belief among false teachers and false religions. They often exalt a particular race or people group. I remember being in undergrad and one preacher came on campus teaching how black people were the race of Shem (cf. Gen 9:26)—God's chosen people. All of a sudden, people from our Christian fellowship, specifically African Americans, began to follow this man thinking that they were very special. This teaching is very seductive because of our natural pride and desire to be exalted (cf. Gen 3:5). Certainly, we see this with the Nazi's, the KKK, other supremacist groups, and many cults. They exalt themselves and consider everybody else dogs. Beware of teachings that exalt one nation or people group over others.

3.   Beware of teachers that teach a works salvation.

Paul calls them "evil workers." Again, he seems to be using irony. These teachers taught salvation by practicing the Jewish law—a works righteousness. However, Paul confronted them by saying their works were really evil. They were evil because their works perverted the gospel, and any good works they had would never be accepted by God. Isaiah said that "all our so-called righteous acts are like a menstrual rag" before God (Isaiah 64:6).

We see works salvation taught in many groups. You can be saved by faith plus baptism. You can be saved by faith plus taking the Lord's Supper. You can be saved by faith plus other good works. Works salvation essentially is the hallmark of every religion except true Christianity. Every religion says "do this" or "do that" and you can be saved. But, Christianity says it is "all done." Everything you need to be saved has already been done by Christ. The good works you needed to be acceptable by God were completed by Jesus while on the earth (cf. Matt 3:15, 2 Cor 5:21). The punishment necessary for your sin, Jesus bore on the cross. All you need to do is accept his finished work and follow him as your Lord (cf. Rom 10:13).

We must beware of teachers that say Christ's work is not enough. They say, "You must join this church. You must do this or that, and you will be saved." No. Everything has been done. One must put his faith in Christ as sufficient for salvation and follow him as Lord. That is all one must do to be saved. Beware of teachers that preach a works salvation.

4.   Beware of teachers that practice a sinful life.

Not only was Paul's description of "evil workers" a form of irony, it also was the fruit of their lives. False teachers, like the Pharisees, often live what looks like a moral life on the outside. Christ called them "whitewashed tombs." In Matthew 23:25-28, he said this:

> "Woe to you, experts in the law and you Pharisees, hypocrites! You clean the outside of the cup and the dish, but inside they are full of greed and self-indulgence. Blind Pharisee! First clean the inside of the cup, so that the outside may become clean too! "Woe to you, experts in the law and you Pharisees, hypocrites! You are like whitewashed tombs that look beautiful on the outside but inside are full of the bones of the dead and of everything unclean. In the same way, on the outside you look righteous to people, but inside you are full of hypocrisy and lawlessness.

Often false teachers appear righteous on the outside, but on the inside, they are full of anger, pride, jealousy, selfishness, deception, and lust. And eventually, these sins will become clearly manifest. The Pharisees trumped up false witnesses against Christ and had him murdered to protect their position. Beware of teachers that preach righteousness but are full of dead men's bones. What's on the inside eventually will fully manifest. Paul said this:

> The sins of some people are obvious, going before them into judgment, but for others, they show up later. Similarly good works are also obvious, and the ones that are not cannot remain hidden.
> 1 Timothy 5:24-25

For some, their sins are obvious, but for others, it trails behind. However, it will eventually clearly manifest. Paul says this in the context of not laying hands on somebody hastily (v. 22). Essentially, he says, "Don't pick an elder too fast." Their sins or their righteousness will eventually become abundantly clear. Beware of teachers that practice a sinful life. Paul calls them "evil workers."

5. Beware of teachers that focus on rituals and traditions over God's Word.

Paul calls them "those who mutilate the flesh." Again, Paul was using irony to make a point. These false teachers taught the necessity of circumcision. Circumcision was a Jewish rite given by God to Abraham (cf. Gen 17:10). Jewish parents would circumcise their sons on the 8th day after birth. This was a sign of participation in God's covenant with Israel. If anybody was not circumcised, they were to be cut off from Israel—killed. However, this outward sign was always supposed to be a picture of an inward reality. It was to be a picture of having a changed heart before God—a heart that loved him and loved people. Jeremiah said this:

> Just as ritual circumcision cuts away the foreskin as an external symbol of dedicated covenant commitment, you must genuinely dedicate yourselves to the Lord and get rid of everything that hinders your commitment to me, people of Judah and inhabitants of Jerusalem. If you do not, my anger will blaze up like a flaming fire against you that no one will be able to extinguish. That will happen because of the evil you have done.
> Jeremiah 4:4

The Jews were to circumcise their hearts or God's wrath would break out against them. To be circumcised physically and not have a circumcised heart meant nothing before God (cf. Rom 2:25-29). It was just a ritual without the reality. This was always taught in the Old Testament. God desires obedience more than all the burnt offerings (cf. 1 Sam 15:22). To practice a ritual without the right heart is nothing before God.

It is the same for us. Our worship must be "in spirit and truth" (John 4:23). We must have the objective reality of obedience to Scripture, but if we don't have the subjective reality—the right spirit or right heart—then it is unacceptable. False teachers and false teaching often focus on the ritual over the heart. They emphasize the form—the right clothes for worship, the right outward appearances, etc. The Pharisees made a great deal out of the washing of hands to be cleansed for worship even though it was not commanded by God (cf. Mk 7:1-2). Many of their rituals were not commands of God but simply traditions of men. Jesus said this about the Pharisees:

> He said to them, "Isaiah prophesied correctly about you hypocrites, as it is written: 'This people honors me with their lips, but their heart is far from me. They worship me in vain, teaching as doctrine the commandments of men.' Having no regard for the command of God, you hold fast to human tradition."
> Mark 7:6-8

With the Judaizers, since circumcision was no longer commanded of God, it was just a ritual that was neither right nor wrong. One could be circumcised or not, and it wouldn't make them any closer to God. In the church age, it is just a tradition. Be careful of teachers that emphasize traditions and ritual, especially those not commanded in the Scripture. Traditions are an easy substitute for a right heart, which is what God is really after.

Churches that emphasize traditions and rituals often become very legalistic and judgmental. If you don't have the outside form, if the female wears pants, if this guy has long hair, if this person doesn't do this, then he or she is often judged and excluded from the fellowship. Be careful of teachers that emphasize rituals over the commands of Scripture.

The majority of the New Testament epistles contain warnings about false teachers and false teachings that attacked the early church. We also need to hear this today, especially as we near the second coming of Christ. Jesus told his disciples to "watch out" so that no one would deceive them. He said in the last days there would be many false teachers and many claiming to be Christ (Matt 24:4-5, 11). There is a new cult started essentially every day. Therefore, we must always be aware of this reality. Satan is seeking to tear people from the flock like a wild dog. In order to protect ourselves, we must beware of false teachers.

Application Question: In what ways have you been exposed to false teachers and false teaching? What are some major errors being promoted currently in the church?

Believers Protect Themselves by Developing Assurance of Salvation

> For we are the circumcision, the ones who worship by the Spirit of God, exult in Christ Jesus, and do not rely on human credentials
> Philippians 3:3

Paul teaches that one of the ways we protect ourselves is by knowing that we are truly saved. The Philippians would not become prey for the Judaizers or other false prophets if they knew that they were truly born again. And, it is the same for all Christians. Those who are not fully convinced that they are God's— that they are born again—are very susceptible to those who peddle another gospel, to spiritual warfare, and to other temptations. Paul said the Philippians should beware of them "for" or "because" (v. 4). He then gives reasons why they should beware of them. He describes them (including himself) as the circumcision—those who were truly saved. He essentially says—we are the true circumcision, true worshipers who glory in Christ, and put no confidence in the flesh.

The importance of developing assurance as a protection is taught throughout the New Testament. Peter said this: "Therefore, brothers and sisters, make every effort to be sure of your calling and election. For by doing this you will never stumble into sin" (2 Peter 1:10). Peter said to make our election sure, and if we do, we will never fall or stumble. One of the major themes of 2 Peter is warnings against false teachers (cf. 2:1-22), and Peter says assurance of salvation would help protect them from stumbling and falling into their teaching. Similarly, Paul taught the need to put on the helmet of salvation (Eph 6:17) in order to stand against spiritual warfare. What is the helmet of salvation? It is not being saved; it is assurance of salvation.

A person struggling with whether they are truly saved or not is easy prey for the enemy. Satan works overtime to comfort those who are not saved. He wants them to have a false peace so they will never truly repent of their sins and be born again. And at the same time, he works overtime to afflict those who are truly born again. He wants them to doubt their salvation, fear that they don't have it, or that they have lost it in order to keep them from being effective ministers of Christ.

Scripture everywhere teaches the necessity of knowing that we are truly born again—truly saved. In fact, Paul taught the need for assurance as the next step right after salvation. In Acts 2:20 (NIV 1984), he said, "I preached that they should repent and turn to God and prove their repentance by their deeds." Paul said repent and now prove your repentance by your works. There are necessary works in the life of a believer that prove they are saved. Believers are not saved by works, but works will be present if they are truly saved. If they are without works, then they are not truly born again (cf. James 2:17).

What works does Paul attribute to those who are truly born again?

Observation Question: What works characterize those who are truly born again in Philippians 3:3 and what can we learn from these works?

"For we are the circumcision, the ones who worship by the Spirit of God, exult in Christ Jesus, and do not rely on human credentials" (Philippians 3:3).

1. True believers will have a different relationship to sin.

Paul calls believers "the circumcision"—inferring that Christians had the true circumcision and that the Judaizers had a false one. As mentioned previously, circumcision was an outward work meant to reflect an inward reality. That inward reality was a change in their relationship to sin so that they could truly follow God. And, that is exactly what has happened to every true believer. Colossians 2:11 says this: "In him you also were circumcised—not, however, with a circumcision performed by human hands, but by the removal of the fleshly body, that is, through the circumcision done by Christ."

Paul says that those who are "in" Christ have been circumcised by putting off the sinful nature. This means that sin is no longer their master and that they are no longer controlled by sin. Romans 6:6-7 says this:

> We know that our old man was crucified with him so that the body of sin would no longer dominate us, so that we would no longer be enslaved to sin. (For someone who has died has been freed from sin.)

211

A person who is born again should continually see a decrease of sin in their life and a greater power over it. John said this:

> Everyone who has been fathered by God does not practice sin, because God's seed resides in him, and thus he is not able to sin, because he has been fathered by God. By this the children of God and the children of the devil are revealed: Everyone who does not practice righteousness—the one who does not love his fellow Christian—is not of God.
> 1 John 3:9-10

John says, no one fathered by God will practice sin. Why? It is because God's seed resides in him. This does not mean that a believer will not sin anymore, because he will. He just cannot live in it as a pattern or lifestyle anymore. The things he used to do, he can't do anymore. Sin leads to conviction and mourning because the believer is doing something contrary to his new nature. A person who lives in sin as a pattern proves that he was never circumcised by Christ (cf. Col 2:11). He is not a new creation (2 Cor 5:17). He is not born again.

Has God changed your relationship to sin? If your profession of Christ as Lord has not changed your relationship to sin, then your profession has probably not changed your eternal destiny. Paul was essentially saying, "You don't have to follow the false teachers because you are the true circumcision. At the cross, Christ severed the power of sin over your life—you are new."

What is another characteristic of somebody who is truly born again?

2.   True believers will live a life of worship by the Spirit of God.

Not only do true believers have a change in their relationship with sin but also in their relationship with God. Paul says they "worship by the Spirit of God." Because God has given believers the Holy Spirit, they now live a lifestyle of worship. The Holy Spirit enables them to worship. Romans 8:15 says, "For you did not receive the spirit of slavery leading again to fear, but you received the Spirit of adoption, by whom we cry, 'Abba, Father.'" The Holy Spirit works in believers to cry out to God. They find in themselves a desire to worship, to pray, to serve God, and to hear and study his Word. This is a work of the Holy Spirit.

In fact, the word "worship" might best be translated "'to render respectful spiritual service.' True worship goes beyond praising God, singing hymns, or participating in a worship service. The essence of worship is living a life of obedient service to God."[88] Everything the believer does can be worship because he is empowered by the Holy Spirit. Paul said this in Colossians:

"Whatever you are doing, work at it with enthusiasm, as to the Lord and not for people" (Colossians 3:23).

Some have called this worship "religious affections." Has God changed your relationship to sin and given you religious affections by the Holy Spirit? Do you desire to pray—to cry out "Abba, Father"? Do you desire to read the Word? Do you desire to share the gospel? Do you desire to serve?

This is a marvelous reality that has happened to every true believer. Where the false teachers worked in their own strength, true believers are empowered by the Holy Spirit with religious affections to serve the Lord.

3. True believers exult in Christ.

The word "exult" can be translated "boast" or "glorying." It "describes boasting with exultant joy about what a person is most proud of."[89] A true believer will boast continually in God and the things of God, whereas a person who is simply practicing religion will constantly boast in himself. Look at what Paul wrote:

> But by the grace of God I am what I am, and his grace to me has not been in vain. In fact, I worked harder than all of them—yet not I, but the grace of God with me.
> 1 Corinthians 15:10

> so that, as it is written, "Let the one who boasts, boast in the Lord."
> 1 Corinthians 1:31

True believers will constantly be glorying in Christ and boasting in their Savior. I remember reading an article about a famous basketball player who just had a string of high scoring games. The reporter asked the basketball star, "What is your secret?" He responded, "Jesus Christ." She responded, "You had nothing to do with it." He again responded, "It's all God." I read the comments section on this article and many were upset at his giving glory to God instead of boasting in all his hard work. However, this should be normative for somebody who is saved. It is not that we deny that we worked hard. Like Paul we say, "We worked harder than everybody else." But, in the same breath, we recognize it was all a grace of God (1 Cor 15:10). He gives us life, breath, and everything else. He gives us our giftings; he works in us to will and do of his good pleasure. True believers recognize their utter bankruptcy and therefore always glory in Christ. They not only need God to be saved but also for everything else. However, those who hope in their religion—their good works—will commonly boast in their works instead of God. Consider Christ's story of the Pharisee and the tax collector:

213

Jesus also told this parable to some who were confident that they were righteous and looked down on everyone else. "Two men went up to the temple to pray, one a Pharisee and the other a tax collector. The Pharisee stood and prayed about himself like this: 'God, I thank you that I am not like other people: extortionists, unrighteous people, adulterers—or even like this tax collector. I fast twice a week; I give a tenth of everything I get.' The tax collector, however, stood far off and would not even look up to heaven, but beat his breast and said, 'God, be merciful to me, sinner that I am!' I tell you that this man went down to his home justified rather than the Pharisee. For everyone who exalts himself will be humbled, but he who humbles himself will be exalted."
Luke 18:9-14

It's interesting, the Pharisee prayed "about himself" (v. 11). He boasted in his fasting and his giving and condemned others less outwardly righteous than him. However, the tax collector could only cry out for mercy from God. His hope was totally in God and not in his works.

Do you constantly give glory to Christ? This is a characteristic of a true believer.

4.   True believers do not rely on human credentials.

This can also be translated "who put no confidence in the flesh" (NIV 1984). When Paul talks about the flesh, he is referring to "man's fallen, unredeemed humanness; it pictures human ability apart from God."[90] To put no confidence in the flesh means to understand the reality that we can do nothing acceptable to God apart from his grace. Even our righteousness is as filthy rags before God (Isaiah 64:6). A true believer realizes that he can do nothing good in order to achieve salvation, but he also is growing in his understanding that there is nothing good in him apart from God. Listen to what Paul said: "For I know that nothing good lives in me, that is, in my flesh. For I want to do the good, but I cannot do it" (Romans 7:18). There was nothing good within him. In fact, he cried out at the end of Romans 7:24, "Wretched man that I am! Who will rescue me from this body of death?" Paul realized there was nothing good within him, nothing that would please God apart from grace. This doctrine is often called "Total Depravity." Jesus said this: "The Spirit is the one who gives life; human nature is of no help! The words that I have spoken to you are spirit and are life" (John 6:63).

Because of this reality, a believer, though prone to pride and boasting, will be continually growing in humility. Like the disciples, they will be growing in practicing secrecy even with their good works (Matt 6:1-8). Why? It's because they realize that it is the Spirit that gives life and that the flesh counts for nothing. They work hard at starving the flesh because it deserves no glory—only God

214

does. "Let the one who boasts, boast in the Lord" (1 Cor 1:31). The Judaizers were relying on their works—their righteousness—to be acceptable to God. However a true believer puts no confidence in his flesh and relies fully on God's work.

Are you trusting in your baptism? Are you trusting in taking the Lord's Supper? Are you trusting in church attendance? None of those count as far as salvation is concerned. Our boast is only in Christ for the flesh counts for nothing.

How do we know if we are truly saved? We are the circumcision—God has changed our relationship to sin. We can't live in sin anymore. We are the ones who worship by the Holy Spirit. The Holy Spirit has given us religious affections—a desire to pray, a desire to serve, a desire to study his Word, etc. Our boast is in Christ alone, the flesh is nothing. We glorify Christ in everything because we know the weakness of our flesh. The Spirit gives life, and the flesh counts for nothing.

Knowing that we are saved is a great protection for us. It protects us from the attacks of the devil. It will protect us from deep discouragements. It will protect us from being drawn into cults or false teachings that profess to know the way to true salvation. We must make our election sure as we grow in the faith, and if we do, it will keep us from stumbling and falling (2 Peter 1:5-11).

Application Question: How do believers grow in assurance of salvation (cf. 2 Peter 1:5-11, Matt 5:3-11, Acts 26:20, James 2:14-26)? Do you ever struggle with assurance of salvation? Why or why not?

Conclusion

How do we protect ourselves from spiritual threats and attacks? There are attacks from within through our flesh, attacks from the world, attacks from the devil, and the constant temptations that come with trials. How can we protect ourselves from stumbling and falling away from Christ?

1. Believers Protect Themselves by Remaining in Fellowship
2. Believers Protect Themselves by Guarding Their Joy
3. Believers Protect Themselves by Living in the Word of God
4. Believers Protect Themselves by Watching Out for False Teachers
5. Believers Protect Themselves by Developing Assurance of Salvation

How to Gain Christ

—though mine too are significant. If someone thinks he has good reasons to put confidence in human credentials, I have more: I was circumcised on the eighth day, from the people of Israel and the tribe of Benjamin, a Hebrew of Hebrews. I lived according to the law as a Pharisee. In my zeal for God I persecuted the church. According to the righteousness stipulated in the law I was blameless. But these assets I have come to regard as liabilities because of Christ. More than that, I now regard all things as liabilities compared to the far greater value of knowing Christ Jesus my Lord, for whom I have suffered the loss of all things—indeed, I regard them as dung!—that I may gain Christ, and be found in him, not because I have my own righteousness derived from the law, but because I have the righteousness that comes by way of Christ's faithfulness—a righteousness from God that is in fact based on Christ's faithfulness. My aim is to know him, to experience the power of his resurrection, to share in his sufferings, and to be like him in his death, and so, somehow, to attain to the resurrection from the dead.
Philippians 3:4-11 (NET)

How can we gain Christ? How can we grow in intimacy with our Lord and Savior? And for those not saved, how can they know Christ in a saving way? In this text Paul shares his testimony with the church of Philippi. False teachers in this church were teaching the need for the Philippians to follow the laws of Judaism, and specifically the rite of circumcision, in order to be saved. However, Paul combats this first by telling the Philippians to beware of these teachers, calling them dogs (Phil 3:2). He then combats it by sharing his testimony about how he also previously sought salvation through the good works in Judaism. Paul said this:

> But these assets I have come to regard as liabilities because of Christ. More than that, I now regard all things as liabilities compared to the far greater value of knowing Christ Jesus my Lord, for whom I have suffered the loss of all things—indeed, I regard them as dung!—that I may gain Christ

217

Philippians 3:7-8

Everything that Paul once considered an asset or profit, he now considered a liability or loss in order to gain Christ. Here Paul speaks in business and accounting terminology.[91] The words "asset" and "liability" are banking terms. In his salvation there was a great transaction. Like the merchant in Christ's parable who found a pearl of great price, Paul sold all he owned in order to purchase the field where the pearl was hidden (Matt 13:44-46). To Paul everything that once was his gain was a loss to gain Christ.

This text speaks to nonbelievers—those who don't know Christ. Scripture speaks of salvation as a relationship. It is not simply a belief or creed but a relationship. To those who called Christ "Lord, Lord" but practiced a lifestyle of sin, he said, "I never knew you" (Matt 7:23). This text speaks to those who don't know Christ, who are on the path of being eternally separated from God, about how to be saved.

But this text also speaks to believers. Paul speaks in the present tense when he says, "I regard them as dung!—that I may gain Christ" (v. 8). This means he still considered everything dung to gain Christ. It was his continual discipline in order to know Christ more. Paul says later in this text, "My aim is to know him, to experience the power of his resurrection, to share in his sufferings, and to be like him in his death, and so, somehow, to attain to the resurrection from the dead" (v. 10, 11). This text not only speaks about salvation but also sanctification—the believer's continual experience of seeking to know and be like Christ. For some Christians, salvation is just fire insurance, but true salvation is a continual seeking after Christ.

Here are two illustrations, one of somebody who simply has a profession of salvation and another of one who has truly been saved. A man is in the ocean swimming, and all of a sudden, he begins to drown as a great wave knocks him out. Luckily, a beautiful lifeguard rushes to his rescue and saves him. After being saved, he simply thanks her and quickly walks away. He meets the female and thanks her but never develops any real relationship with her. That is how many people's relationship with Christ is. They recognize that he died for them but, they never truly pursue him. They have a surface relationship with him. However, true salvation is like this. This man is saved by this beautiful lifeguard, and then gets down on one knee and says, "I can never truly repay what you did in saving my life. But, I want to show my gratitude by serving you and getting to know you for the rest of my life. Thank you so much." I won't fill in the rest of the details to the story, but it ends with a "happily ever after." That is true salvation, and that is a picture of Paul's salvation experience. Though he had gained Christ, he still was trying to gain more of him. He was still trying to pursue him. That is a description of true salvation, and this is what we see in Paul's testimony.

As we consider Paul's testimony, we see what it means to experience salvation but also what it means to continually seek to know Christ. How do we gain Christ—in being saved? How do we gain Christ, as a lifelong pursuit of intimacy? We will see several principles in this text.

Big Question: What principles can we learn from Paul's salvation testimony about gaining Christ both in salvation and as a lifelong pursuit in sanctification?

To Gain Christ, We Must Consider Our Achievements as Loss

—though mine too are significant. If someone thinks he has good reasons to put confidence in human credentials, I have more: I was circumcised on the eighth day, from the people of Israel and the tribe of Benjamin, a Hebrew of Hebrews. I lived according to the law as a Pharisee. In my zeal for God I persecuted the church. According to the righteousness stipulated in the law I was blameless. But these assets I have come to regard as liabilities because of Christ. More than that, I now regard all things as liabilities compared to the far greater value of knowing Christ Jesus my Lord, for whom I have suffered the loss of all things—indeed, I regard them as dung!—that I may gain Christ, Philippians 3:4-8

Again, Paul is here confronting the Judaizers who taught the need to practice Judaism for salvation—specifically through circumcision and obedience to the law (cf. Phil 3:2). Paul essentially tells the Philippians, "I have tried that route." He describes the achievements that he thought would make him acceptable to God. He says, "If somebody should be able to boast as a Jew, it is I." Paul describes his achievements by giving seven descriptors of his Jewishness. Four of them are profits that he inherited from his parents and the other three are attributed to his self-effort. Let's look at them.

Observation Question: What are the seven descriptors Paul gives of his life before Christ and how do they represent potential false hopes for salvation?

1. Paul was circumcised on the eighth day.

Literally, it says, "with respect to circumcision an eighth-dayer."[92] This means that Paul was not a Gentile convert or a late Jewish convert. No doubt, many Judaizers converted to Judaism. However, Paul says he was not. He was circumcised on the eighth day as God commanded Abraham (Gen 17:12).

However, salvation does not come by ritual. It doesn't come by baptism or the Lord's Supper. The ritual of circumcision meant nothing as far as salvation.

2. Paul was of the people of Israel.

Again, this meant that he was not a Gentile convert but someone born into the blessings of Israel. He also was not mixed. In the exile, many of the Jews started to marry Gentiles—this is how the Samaritan race formed. However, Paul had Jewish parents who stayed faithful to God's covenant, and therefore, he had pure blood. The Jews were a special people to God in that he gave them the law, the temple, and the covenants, and they were called to be God's priests to the world (cf. Rom 9:4, Ex 19:6). Indeed there were privileges to being from the nation of Israel, especially before Israel's rejection of the messiah at Christ's first coming. However, his nationality did not bring salvation. Many Jews believed they would be saved just because they were Jewish. John the Baptist rebuked the Pharisees and Sadducees saying that they should not put their hope in being a child of Abraham and that God was able to raise up children of Abraham from the rocks (cf. Matt 3:9). Salvation doesn't come from somebody's nationality.

3. Paul was of the tribe of Benjamin.

The tribe of Benjamin was a very privileged tribe that often served in the aristocracy (high social class) and the government. Among Jacob's sons only Joseph and Benjamin were from the favorite wife Rachel, and Benjamin was the only son born in the promised land (Gen 35:16-18). When the nation of Israel originally divided up the land of Canaan, Jerusalem was actually given to the Benjamites (Judges 1:21). The first king of Israel was a Benjamite named Saul (1 Sam 9:21), which was Paul's Jewish name. The tribe of Benjamin was one of only two tribes that remained faithful to King David when the kingdom split under Solomon's son and Judah was the second (1 Kings 12:21). In the exile, Mordechai who helped save all the Israelites along with his niece Esther was a Benjamite (Est 2:6).

This was a very special tribe, and Paul was proud to be part of it. However, salvation does not come by rank or nobility. It doesn't matter how privileged one is or who his parents are. It doesn't matter if he is a pastor's kid, a missionary kid, or from some other privileged spiritual or social background. Salvation doesn't come from rank. Throughout Scripture God often skipped the highest in rank to bless the lowest. God chose Jacob over his older brother Esau. God chose Ephraim over his older brother Manasseh. God chose David over all his older brothers. Rank has nothing to do with salvation.

4. Paul was a Hebrew of Hebrews.

This meant that Paul had not lost his culture. Because of the exile, many Jews lost their culture and native tongue and instead became Hellenized—speaking Greek as their common language. In fact, in the early church this was an issue as the Grecian Jewish widows were being neglected in lieu of the Hebrew widows (Acts 6:1). The Grecian Jews were often looked down upon because they had lost their Jewishness. But not Paul, he was a Hebrew of Hebrews. Paul was born in Tarsus which was a very wealthy city during those days (cf. Acts 21:39). In fact, Greek scholar Kenneth Wuest said that only wealthy families were allowed to retain their citizenship and live there, meaning that Paul probably came from a wealthy family.[93] However, even in the wealth and prosperity of Tarsus, his family still practiced their Jewish culture. In fact, Paul still spoke Hebrew (cf. Acts 21:40). Yet, we must understand that even though this was special to ancient Jews, it meant nothing to God. Salvation does not come by tradition.

5. Paul was a Pharisee.

Today when people hear the term "Pharisee," it is a negative term—a term of derision. It means a hypocrite or a judgmental person. However, that was not true in ancient times. The Pharisees were a sect of Judaism that rose up during the intertestamental period, between the time of the Old and New Testament. While the Jews were in exile, many Jews became liberal theologically. It was easy to begin to doubt God and cease to believe in the miracles of the Old Testament while the Jews were exiled and under Gentile oppression for hundreds of years. Therefore, the Pharisees arose during this period and became an elite denomination. "Pharisee means 'separated one.' The Pharisees distanced themselves from unclean persons and ate only with observant Jews."[94] They also were in disagreement with the Sadducees, the more liberal denomination in Judaism. The Pharisees, in contrast with the Sadducees, believed in every word of the Old Testament. They believed in miracles, angels, the resurrection, and the afterlife which the Sadducees—the liberals—did not. Essentially, the Pharisees were fundamentalists.

The Pharisees went astray by accepting not only the teaching of the law but the oral traditions passed down by rabbis. Jesus said this about them: "'They worship me in vain, teaching as doctrine the commandments of men.' Having no regard for the command of God, you hold fast to human tradition" (Mark 7:7-8). These traditions added to the Word of God and practically started to replace the Word of God. The Pharisees also saw their strict outward obedience to the law as a means of salvation. The historian Josephus taught that only about 6,000 people were in this elite sect of Judaism, and they were considered guardians of the law.[95] They were well respected.

We know that Paul was not only a Pharisee but a son of a Pharisee (cf. Acts 23:6). He was raised in the sect. In fact, Paul was trained by a very famous Rabbi named Gamaliel (cf. Acts 26:4-5; Galatians 1:14). If there was someone who could boast in the flesh, his own works, it was Paul. However, salvation does not come by being part of a denomination or a church. This had nothing to do with being acceptable to God, and this is true today.

6. Paul was zealous for God.

Paul was not only religious but zealous. There are two aspects of being zealous for God. There is the aspect of love for God and a desire to know him, but the other aspect of zeal is hating what God hates. With Christ, when he went to the temple and found traders cheating people, he got a whip and began to whip people and turn over tables. He declared, "It is written, 'My house will be called a house of prayer,' but you are turning it into a den of robbers" (Matt 21:13). In his zeal for God, he hated what God hated and responded with great anger towards those who dishonored God.

It was the same with Paul; he was so zealous for God that he persecuted and killed Christians. In Acts 8:1, it says that he consented to the murder of the church's first martyr, Stephen. They threw Stephen's clothes at his feet. In Acts 9, he was on his way to Damascus to imprison all Jews that professed Christ as Lord. He was zealous. Certainly, he was more zealous than any of the Judaizers who boasted in their zeal for the law and God. Again, we see Paul's impressive religious credentials. However, zeal does not make someone acceptable to God. Many are sincere and zealous, but people can be zealous and at the same time very wrong—especially if they believe in some false doctrine. Zeal will not save anyone.

7. Paul was faultless with regards to the law.

The word "blameless" can also be translated "faultless." This doesn't mean that Paul was perfect and never sinned according to the law. The law provided a means to atone for sins. In being faultless, it meant that there was no area in accordance with the law that people could accuse Paul. If he committed a sin, he offered the proper sacrifices so he could be right with God. He was meticulous in practicing the regulations of the law in order to be right with God. However, not even Paul's outward righteousness was enough to make him right before God.

Paul came to a startling conclusion when he met Christ in a vision on his way to Damascus to persecute Christians (Acts 9:3-6). There Paul met Christ in a grand vision and began to count everything he gained, both inherited privileges as a Jewish man and his earned privileges by his self-effort, a loss. He realized they were nothing. He said this: "But these assets I have come to

222

regard as liabilities because of Christ" (3:7). Jesus similarly said, "For what does it benefit a person if he gains the whole world but forfeits his life? Or what can a person give in exchange for his life?" (Matthew 16:26).

In order to gain Christ, Paul counted all his privileges and achievements as nothing for the sake of Christ. These were the very things that the Judaizers boasted in. They boasted in their righteousness, their traditions, and their Jewish culture as a means of pleasing God—a means of salvation. And this was not only true of the Judaizers, but it is also true for every religion in the world. Every religion says that in order to be saved by God, we must do certain works. We must do certain good deeds, whether that is baptism, prayer, giving, suffering, etc., in order to be saved. However, this is not true. We can do nothing on our own to be saved. Scripture says that even our good works are as "filthy rags" before God (Isaiah 64:6).

How does a person gain Christ? How does a person come to true salvation? It is through the same path that Paul walked. We must first come to the conclusion that there are no works that we can do in order to merit Christ—to merit salvation. Christ himself said that he did not come for the righteous but for the sinners (Lk 5:32). This means that he did not come for the self-righteous; he did not come for those who thought they could earn salvation based on good works. If you believe you can be saved from eternity in hell because you are a good person, because you were born into a Christian family, because you were baptized, or because you served on the mission field, then you cannot be saved. If you believe that any of your works will make you acceptable to God, you cannot be saved—you cannot have Christ.

Jesus said that anyone who enters the kingdom of heaven must become like a little child—like an infant or toddler (Matt 18:2). This simply means "dependence." The little child does not work for his food or provisions because he is unable to work. He doesn't have the physical capabilities to earn a living, to protect himself, or even to comfort himself. He needs his parents. And this is true for anybody who is truly saved. They have come to the place where they realize that they are incapable of saving themselves. They realize that even their achievements mean nothing to God. They then throw themselves upon God for his mercy in order to be saved.

Jesus also said this: "Blessed are the poor in spirit, for the kingdom of heaven belongs to them" (Matt 5:3). "The poor in spirit" means the spiritually bankrupt. It means a person realizes that he has nothing in his spiritual bank account that is acceptable to God and because of that he becomes a spiritual beggar. He throws himself at God's feet in humility because he realizes that he is unacceptable. That is what happened to Paul, and that is what must happen to anyone who will be saved—anyone who will gain Christ. In order to gain Christ, we must recognize our deep need of him and that he is the only way to heaven. If we are trusting in anything else other than Christ, we cannot be saved. Jesus said, "I am the way, and the truth, and the life. No one comes to the Father except through me" (John 14:6).

However, spiritual poverty is not only the door to salvation but also the door to our sanctification. We must grow in our spiritual poverty daily. We must constantly count our achievements as loss to know Christ. A person who is spiritually poor will continually ask for more grace to draw near Christ, through God's Word and prayer, and also for forgiveness of sin. If we are not spiritually poor, then we are spiritually satisfied, which will hinder our growth and intimacy with Christ. Do you still see your debt? Does it still draw you to the feet of Christ for more intimacy with him?

Have you thrown all your hope on Christ for salvation? That is what Paul did one day on his way to Damascus—he counted all his attainments as nothing for Christ's sake—to gain Christ.

Application Question: Some have said that all religions in comparison with Christianity can be summed up in the statement "Do versus Done." Is this a true statement? Why or why not? Please share your conversion experience.

To Gain Christ, We Must Make Christ Our Priority

> More than that, I now regard all things as liabilities compared to the far greater value of knowing Christ Jesus my Lord, for whom I have suffered the loss of all things—indeed, I regard them as dung!—that I may gain Christ
> Philippians 3:8

Next, Paul says that he not only considers his assets as liabilities or losses in order to gain Christ but "all things" (v. 7-8). To "gain Christ" is in the present tense which means that not only was this true in order to be saved but also in his sanctification. This was the continual thought process of Paul in his spiritual life. If everything was a loss to gain Christ, this meant that Christ was his priority. Everything else was a loss only because Christ was the focus of his life.

This must be true for us as well, if we are going to continually grow in our relationship with Christ. Jesus said in Matthew 5:8, "Blessed are the pure in heart, for they will see God." The pure in heart can also be translated the "single in mind." Those who focus on him above everything else will gain him.

This is the problem with many Christians. The reason we are not growing in intimacy with Christ is that everything else is not "dung to us." Many times career, family, education, entertainment, etc., are more important than Christ. It is the pure in heart—the single in mind—who see God, who experience him daily. This was Paul's pursuit and many great saints before him. David said, "I have asked the Lord for one thing—this is what I desire! I want to live in the Lord's house all the days of my life, so I can gaze at the splendor of the Lord

224

and contemplate in his temple" (Psalm 27:4). David's one thing was dwelling in the house of the Lord, gazing upon God's beauty, and seeking him in his temple. That was his pursuit in life and everything else counted for nothing.

This means that even if one must suffer or go through hard times and difficulties to know Christ more, it should be counted as a loss for the surpassing greatness of knowing Christ (v. 8). For Paul, he lost his family—the family that raised him in his Jewishness and sent him to the top schools to learn from the best rabbis. He lost his career—the one he had pursued with great zeal as a Pharisee. Basically, he lost his future—the bright one he established with his religious credentials. But, he lost more than that. He lost his comfort as he now was persecuted everywhere he went. At the moment of writing this letter, he was in prison awaiting a possible death sentence, and he even considered that small in comparison to the greatness of knowing Christ. Paul was the "single-minded" person who continually gained intimacy with Christ.

Many Christians are stagnant in their spiritual life and not growing because Christ has never become their "one thing," where everything else is a loss in comparison. Therefore, they are not growing. Not so for Paul, nothing else mattered to him. And this must also be true of good things such as ministry. Ministry can keep us from intimacy with Christ. Wasn't this Martha's problem? She was busy serving everybody else instead of sitting at the feet of Christ. Jesus said, "Martha, Martha, you are worried and troubled about many things, but one thing is needed. Mary has chosen the best part; it will not be taken away from her" (Lk 10:41-42). For many, ministry is their "one thing."

How do we gain Christ? We gain him by having a single mind, where we give up everything to pursue intimacy with him. Remember what God said through Jeremiah: "When you seek me in prayer and worship, you will find me available to you" (Jeremiah 29:13).

Application Question: What are common distractions that keep you from prioritizing Christ? How is God calling you to "count them as loss" in order to gain intimacy with Christ?

To Gain Christ, We Must Have Faith in Christ

> and be found in him, not because I have my own righteousness derived from the law, but because I have the righteousness that comes by way of Christ's faithfulness—a righteousness from God that is in fact based on Christ's faithfulness
> Philippians 3:9

Paul, again in referring to his salvation experience, said that his purpose was to be found in Christ with a righteousness that comes from God. Paul knew that the works of the law could not save him and that he needed God's righteousness. When it says, "because I have the righteousness that comes by way of Christ's faithfulness," it can also be translated "that which is through faith in Christ" (NIV 1984). Paul received this righteousness (and thus salvation) through putting his faith in Christ. Romans 3:20-22 (NIV 1984) says:

> Therefore no one will be declared righteous in his sight by observing the law; rather, through the law we become conscious of sin. But now a righteousness from God, apart from law, has been made known, to which the Law and the Prophets testify. This righteousness from God comes through faith in Jesus Christ to all who believe. There is no difference,

In salvation, a great exchange occurs. On the cross Christ became sin for us. God placed our sins upon him as he bore the wrath of God for us. And, when a person believes in the life, death, burial, and resurrection of Christ (1 Cor 15:2-4) and accepts him as Lord and Savior (Rom 10:9-10), God gives him Christ's righteousness. Second Corinthians 5:21 says, "God made the one who did not know sin to be sin for us, so that in him we would become the righteousness of God."

It has been said that Christ's death was not enough to save believers; he also needed to live a perfect life. If his death was all that was needed, Christ could have died as a baby. He didn't need to live a sinless life. We see Christ approach John the Baptist and ask to be baptized, and John responds, "I can't baptize you. I need to be baptized by you." However, Christ replies, "I must fulfill all righteousness" (Matt 3:15 paraphrase). Why did Christ need to fulfill all righteousness? It is because he needed to be the blameless perfect lamb to die for our sins. He perfectly kept the law that we could never keep so we could have his righteousness.

If Christ had only died for our sins, then we would still be in the state of the first Adam. Adam was sinless; however, he still needed to live a life of righteousness by never eating of the Tree of the Knowledge in order to be saved. He still had to secure perfect righteousness to never die. But in Christ, we not only have payment for our sins, we also have the perfect righteousness that he secured while living on the earth.

When a person recognizes their sinfulness and their need for righteousness to be right before God, when they come to the place of spiritual bankruptcy, it is only then that they can be saved. Therefore, they cry out for mercy in faith, and Christ saves them. He completes a holy transaction (Rom 10:13). He takes their sin and gives them his righteousness. Now, when we go before God, he sees the perfect righteous life of his Son. He sees the righteousness of the one who only spoke the words of his Father (John 12:49), the one who never sought his glory but only the glory of the Father (John 7:18), the one who only did what he saw the Father doing (John 5:19). He was perfect, and his perfection is applied to the account of those who have faith in him. Again, Paul said he wanted to "be found in him, not having a righteousness of my own that comes from the law, but that which is through faith in Christ—the righteousness that comes from God and is by faith" (Philippians 3:9, NIV 1984).

Interpretation Question: What does Paul mean when he says this righteousness comes by faith?

What is saving faith?

1. Saving faith means to believe in Christ and the sufficiency of his saving work.

    Consider Paul's reply to the jailor in Philippi who wanted to be saved: "Then he brought them outside and asked, 'Sirs, what must I do to be saved?' They replied, 'Believe in the Lord Jesus and you will be saved, you and your household'" (Acts 16:30).
    Similarly, Paul said this in Romans 10:9-10:

    > because if you confess with your mouth that Jesus is Lord and believe in your heart that God raised him from the dead, you will be saved. For with the heart one believes and thus has righteousness and with the mouth one confesses and thus has salvation.

2. Saving faith means to commit to following Christ as Lord of our lives.

    Jesus said, "Whoever does not carry his own cross and follow me cannot be my disciple" (Luke 14:27). Christ must be Lord of our lives in order to be Savior of our lives.
    Have you ever come to Christ in faith in order to be saved—trusting in his life, death, burial, and resurrection as sufficient for salvation? Those who put their faith in Christ as their Lord and Savior shall be saved. God will apply his righteousness to their account, and they will have eternal life.

3. Saving faith means a continual trusting in Christ for our salvation.

    Saving faith is not a moment of belief; it is a continual trusting in Christ as sufficient for our ultimate salvation. Those who do not continually follow Christ prove that they never had true saving faith. Paul said this about saving faith in Colossians 1:22-23:

    > but now he has reconciled you by his physical body through death to present you holy, without blemish, and blameless before him— if indeed you remain in the faith, established and firm, without shifting

227

from the hope of the gospel that you heard. This gospel has also been preached in all creation under heaven, and I, Paul, have become its servant.

Christ has reconciled you (saved you), if you continue in your faith. When Paul said he was seeking a righteousness that comes through faith, he was not just looking backwards to the moment he accepted Christ on that Damascus road. He was speaking of his continual experience. He was still trusting in Christ through faith. This is true for every real believer.

Are you still putting your full trust in Christ for salvation? Are you still recognizing your utter sinfulness and need for a savior? Paul sought to gain Christ—to know him—by continuing to have faith in Christ.

Application Question: In this section we talked about saving faith including not only belief but Lordship and continuing in the faith. Some people believe that saving faith needs to only be intellectual, not necessarily including Lordship or perseverance. Some believe people can even lose their salvation. What do you believe about these issues? How would you support your belief with Scripture (cf. Matthew 16:25-26, Luke 14:26-33, John 6:38-40, 10:27-30)?

To Gain Christ, We Must Continually Cultivate Our Desire for Him

My aim is to know him, to experience the power of his resurrection, to share in his sufferings, and to be like him in his death, and so, somehow, to attain to the resurrection from the dead.
Philippians 3:10-11

Paul next said, "My 'aim' is to know him." In order to gain Christ, we must continually cultivate our desire for him. The real reason many are not growing in intimacy with Christ—growing in relationship with him—is because of a lack of desire. We don't really desire him. Look at how David described his desire to know God: "As a deer longs for streams of water, so I long for you, O God! I thirst for God, for the living God. I say, "When will I be able to go and appear in God's presence?" (Psalm 42:1-2).

David described his desire to know God as similar to a deer panting for streams of water. He was desperate to know God. Moses, even though God already spoke to him face to face, said this, "Show me your glory" (Ex 33:18). He was desperate to know God. This type of desire is uncommon among Christians. We are often desperate for many things in life other than God. This is the type of desire each of us must cultivate. Jesus said this in the Beatitudes: "Blessed are those who hunger and thirst for righteousness, for they will be

228

satisfied" (Matt 5:6). The most righteous thing you can desire in life is to know God more, and he promises that if this is your desire, he will fill it. He will bless this craving. He doesn't promise to always give you physical healing or wealth, but he does promise righteousness—more of him.

Interpretation Question: How do we cultivate a desire to know Christ?

1.   We cultivate our desire for Christ by being with Christ.

The more you are with Christ—in his presence through the Word of God, prayer, and fellowship with saints—the more you will desire him. However, the more you neglect him, the less you will desire him. Mark 4:25 says, "For whoever has will be given more, but whoever does not have, even what he has will be taken from him." The person enjoying the revelation of Christ will be given more, but the person who is not, even what he has will be taken away—he will lose his desire for Christ. Being with Christ is a practical way to cultivate one's desire.

2.   We cultivate our desire for Christ by being around believers who desire God.

Proverbs 13:20 says, "The one who associates with the wise grows wise, but a companion of fools suffers harm."
The wisest thing a person can do is desire to know God (cf. Psalm 14:1). Therefore, by being around people who are wisely seeking God, you will become wiser as well—your desire for God will increase. "As iron sharpens iron, so a person sharpens his friend" (Prov 27:17). We cultivate this desire by being around those who similarly are cultivating it.

3.   We cultivate our desire for Christ by persevering through trials.

Romans 5:3-5 says, "Not only this, but we also rejoice in sufferings, knowing that suffering produces endurance, and endurance, character, and character, hope. And hope does not disappoint, because the love of God has been poured out in our hearts through the Holy Spirit who was given to us." Paul says trials lead to endurance, endurance leads to character, and character leads to hope. What does it mean to hope? It means to hope in God. The more we persevere through suffering and pain on this earth, the more it helps us cultivate a hope in God—a desire for him.
We see this often in Christians with a terminal illness. They have been in pain for months or years, and now they no longer are "hoping" to stay but hoping to go home to God. It is amazing to see so much peace in darkness. Their hope—their desire for God has increased through persevering. This is one

229

of the reasons God graces us with pain. He allows us to go through pain to wean us off the temporary joys of this life and to create a genuine hope, a genuine desire for him. In fact, it is for this reason Scripture calls us to rejoice in trials and tribulation (cf. Rom 3:4-5, James 1:3). Our desire for him and holiness is more important than our comfort.

In order to gain intimacy with Christ, Paul cultivated his desire. He wanted to know Christ. In the same way, in order for us to gain Christ, we must desire him as well. Are you cultivating your desire?

Application Question: In what ways have you experienced pain or trials that have increased your desire for God? How are you cultivating your desire for God?

To Gain Christ, We Must Continually Experience Christ

> My aim is to know him, to experience the power of his resurrection, to share in his sufferings, and to be like him in his death, and so, somehow, to attain to the resurrection from the dead.
> Philippians 3:10

The word "know" is more than intellectual knowledge—it means an experiential knowledge. In the Septuagint, the ancient Greek translation of the Old Testament, the word ginosko was used to refer to the intimacy of sex. Genesis 4:1 (KJV) says, "Adam knew his wife and she conceived." Paul used this word which described experiential knowledge to share how deeply he wanted to grow in intimacy with Christ. One of the ways Paul wanted to know Christ was through experiencing the very things Christ experienced. He implied that he would know Christ more deeply through the experience of his power, his sufferings, his death, and his resurrection.

Interpretation Question: What does Paul mean by the power of the resurrection, fellowship with his sufferings, being conformed to Christ's death, and being resurrected like Christ? How do we get to know Christ more through these experiences?

1. Paul desired to know Christ through the power of the resurrection.

For Paul it was not enough to follow Christ, he wanted Christ's power in his life—the power of the resurrection. He wanted to have power to serve God, to pray for people, to persevere through trials, etc. To follow Christ and not have power seemed like a paradox to Paul, and it should be to us as well. We follow a God that healed the sick, raised the dead, and multiplied food and drink. How can a Christian not have power in his life?

230

Consider what Paul prayed for the Ephesian church in Ephesians 1:18-20:

—since the eyes of your heart have been enlightened—so that you may know what is the hope of his calling, what is the wealth of his glorious inheritance in the saints, and what is the incomparable greatness of his power toward us who believe, as displayed in the exercise of his immense strength. This power he exercised in Christ when he raised him from the dead and seated him at his right hand in the heavenly realms,

Paul prayed for them to know (experientially) the incomparable power that is in the life of a believer. It is the same power that raised Christ from dead. We must know this power as well. We must know it to break habitual sins in our life. We must know it to be a healing agent in the lives of others. We must know it to persevere in the midst of trials. It is available and working in all who are truly born again.

It is paradoxical that Paul implied he would know Christ more by experiencing this power in his life because the very way for us to experience this power is to know Christ more. Christ said this: "Abide in me and you will produce much fruit, apart from me you can do nothing" (John 15:5 paraphrase). Power to live the spiritual life, to develop the fruits of the Spirit, to serve others all comes through intimacy with Christ.

This must be our desire as well. We must desire to leave powerless Christianity behind by knowing Christ and therefore daily experiencing his power. However, Paul hoped for even more than this.

2. Paul desired to know Christ through sharing in his sufferings.

It is one thing to want Christ's power. Who doesn't want that? But, Paul also wanted to have fellowship with Christ's sufferings. He didn't want the crown without the suffering. This is one of the problems with prosperity gospel teaching. They want the power and the reward, but they don't want the cross. To follow Christ in this world means to suffer just like him (cf. Lk 14:27). For many followers of Christ, it meant imprisonment, having their wealth confiscated, and physical suffering. Jacob limped for the rest of his life. Timothy was constantly sick. Epaphroditus had a sickness that almost killed him. Many in the church have been martyred. Paul followed Christ knowing and welcoming both the crown and the cross—the power and the suffering.

In fact, it must be known that many times God brings great power through suffering. We see this with Paul and his struggle with a thorn in his flesh. God said to him, "My grace is enough for you, for my power is made perfect in weakness" (2 Cor 12:9). And certainly, we see this throughout the rest of the Scriptures. Christ after fasting for forty days and being tempted by Satan in the wilderness left full of power in the Holy Spirit (Luke 4:14). Many of those God used greatly were first allowed to go through suffering and pain. This suffering and pain drew them closer to God in order that he might more powerfully work through their lives. Joseph spent around fifteen years as a slave and in prison. Moses went into the wilderness for forty years before God could mightily work in his life.

Paul was willing to take on the sufferings of Christ, and Christ calls us to do the same as well. He calls us to take up the very cross he bore, which is a great privilege. Paul said this to the Philippians: "For it has been granted to you not only to believe in Christ but also to suffer for him" (Phil 1:29). "Granted" comes from the word "grace." Paul taught that suffering for Christ is a tremendous grace that each true believer has received in some measure or another. Paul wanted not only the power but the suffering, and through these, he would know Christ more.

3.   Paul desired to know Christ through dying like him.

He said that he wanted to become like Christ in his death. Literally, he wanted to "conform" to his death. He wanted to die in the same way Christ died in order to know him more. This sounds masochistic; however, it is really not. Paul earlier said, "For to me, living is Christ and dying is gain" (Phil 1:21). Death was the door way to know Christ even more intimately. Death meant unhindered fellowship with Christ.

4.   Paul desired to know Christ through experiencing the resurrection.

Finally, Paul desired to experience the resurrection of the dead as well. When Paul says, "and so, somehow, to attain to the resurrection from the dead" (v. 11), it is not an expression of doubt but of his humility.[96] His humility never left him. He considered himself least of the apostles (1 Cor 15:9), least of all God's people (Eph 3:8), and the chief of sinners (1 Tim 1:15). Paul had no doubt that he would be resurrected.

"The phrase the resurrection from the dead is unique in Scripture. It literally reads 'the out resurrection from among the corpses.'"[97] The implication is that believers will one day be resurrected while other corpses are still in the grave. This certainly is in line with the rest of Scripture. It teaches that believers will be resurrected from amongst the dead at the rapture and that dead unbelievers will not be resurrected until the end of the millennium to be judged by Christ (cf. 1 Thess 4:15-17, 1 Cor 15:51-53, Rev 20:13).

Why was it important to experience the resurrection of the dead to know Christ more? If death brought Paul into the very presence of Christ, why was the resurrection so important in order to know Christ? It was probably because after the resurrection of saints, the church will then be fully united to Christ in marriage. It seems that the marriage of the bride and Christ waits for the time of the resurrection (Rev. 19:7-8). It is then that we will know Christ in an even more intimate way that will continue throughout eternity. Revelation 19:7-8 says this:

> Let us rejoice and exult and give him glory, because the wedding celebration of the Lamb has come, and his bride has made herself ready. She was permitted to be dressed in bright, clean, fine linen" (for the fine linen is the righteous deeds of the saints).

Application Question: What are your thoughts about Paul's earnest desire to know Christ through the power of the resurrection, suffering, death, and the resurrection of his body? In what ways did this challenge you? How can you apply these truths to your life?

Conclusion

How do we gain Christ? How does a nonbeliever become saved, and how does a believer grow in intimacy with Christ? Through Paul's testimony we learn a great deal about how to gain Christ—both in salvation and sanctification.

1. To Gain Christ, We Must Consider Our Achievements as Loss
2. To Gain Christ, We Must Make Christ Our Priority
3. To Gain Christ, We Must Have Faith in Christ
4. To Gain Christ, We Must Continually Cultivate Our Desire for Him
5. To Gain Christ, We Must Continually Experience Christ

Pursuing Spiritual Maturity

Not that I have already attained this—that is, I have not already been perfected—but I strive to lay hold of that for which Christ Jesus also laid hold of me. Brothers and sisters, I do not consider myself to have attained this. Instead I am single-minded: Forgetting the things that are behind and reaching out for the things that are ahead, with this goal in mind, I strive toward the prize of the upward call of God in Christ Jesus. Therefore let those of us who are "perfect" embrace this point of view. If you think otherwise, God will reveal to you the error of your ways. Nevertheless, let us live up to the standard that we have already attained.
Philippians 3:12-16 (NET)

How should we pursue spiritual maturity—growth into the image of Christ?

One of the things I really love about Paul's writing is his tendency to use athletic illustrations. It's a common feature in his letters. In Ephesians 6:12, he uses a wrestling metaphor; he says, "For our struggle is not against flesh and blood, but against the rulers, against the powers, against the world rulers of this darkness, against the spiritual forces of evil in the heavens." In 1 Corinthians 9:24, he uses a running metaphor; he says, "Do you not know that all the runners in a stadium compete, but only one receives the prize? So run to win." Later in the same passage, he uses a boxing metaphor; he says, "So I do not run uncertainly or box like one who hits only air" (v. 26). I would imagine that if I met Paul in person that not only would we have great theological conversations but also great conversations about sports. However, the reason he commonly used these sporting illustrations was because he saw many similarities between a competitive athlete and our spiritual lives. Christians should work at their spiritual life like a competitive athlete works at his craft.

This text is no different. Paul compares his pursuit of becoming more like Christ to a person running a foot race. In verse 3:12 he says, "I strive to lay hold of that for which Christ Jesus also laid hold of me." The word "strive" can be translated "'to run' or 'follow after.' It speaks of 'an aggressive, energetic endeavor.'"[98] Paul saw himself in pursuit of being like Christ in every way. What was it that Paul was running after? It was what he previously mentioned in Philippians 3:10-11. He said,

My aim is to know him, to experience the power of his resurrection, to share in his sufferings, and to be like him in his death, and so, somehow, to attain to the resurrection from the dead.

Paul did not just want to know Christ intimately; he wanted to be just like him in every way. He wanted to have the power of the resurrection in his life, share in Christ's suffering, die like him, and be resurrected like him. That was the reason that Christ "laid hold" of him while he was traveling to persecute Christians in Damascus (v. 12). Christ grabbed Paul so that he could make him into his very image.

This reality of being called by God to look like Christ is true for each of us. Romans 8:29 says, "because those whom he foreknew he also predestined to be conformed to the image of his Son, that his Son would be the firstborn among many brothers and sisters." Even before birth, this process of God taking hold of us began. It began in the counsel of God before the creation of the earth. Like a soon to be mother or father planning to have a child, each Christian was not an accident. He chose and predestined us to be conformed to the image of Christ.

How do we pursue this reality? How do we grow into the very image of Christ? How do we grow into maturity? In verse 15, he speaks to the mature and says, "Therefore let those of us who are 'perfect' embrace this point of view." "Perfect" refers to maturity—not perfection. Paul essentially speaks to the Philippians and says, "Those of you who are mature in Christ should think the same way. You should pursue Christ in the same way I am." Next, he speaks to those who may think differently and says, "If you think otherwise, God will reveal to you the error of your ways" (v. 15b). He says if you don't agree, God will reveal this to you.

How do we pursue maturity in Christ? How do we implement the disciplines of a competitive athlete into our lives so we can look more like Christ? We do it by modeling Paul's disciplines. In fact, he will later explicitly call the Philippians, and therefore us, to model him in the next section. He says, "Be imitators of me, brothers and sisters" (3:17). In this text, we will study Paul's pursuit of spiritual maturity—knowing Christ—so that we can implement his disciplines into our own lives.

Big Question: What principles can we learn from Philippians 3:12-16 about pursuing maturity in Christ?

In Order to Pursue Spiritual Maturity, We Must Have the Right Attitude—a Holy Discontent

> Not that I have already attained this—that is, I have not already been
> perfected—but I strive to lay hold of that for which Christ Jesus also
> laid hold of me
> Philippians 3:12

What is the right attitude we must have in order to pursue maturity? Paul says, "Not that I have already attained this—that is, I have not already been perfected." Paul said, "I am not there yet." Paul had a holy discontent. This is a very important attitude to develop if we are going to reach maturity.

Application Question: Why is it important to have the right attitude—a holy discontent—in order to pursue spiritual maturity?

1. Having the right attitude is important to spur growth.

    Paul was probably the greatest Christian to ever live—he wrote almost half of the New Testament. His ministry led to the Gentile world being reached, and yet, he saw himself having not fully attained Christlikeness. This disposition is true of every great athlete. They are never content with their successes. And therefore, they continue to work hard to become better and to win more championships. Be careful of spiritual contentment. Many Christians are not growing because they are content with their attainments. They feel that they know the Bible enough, pray enough, serve enough, and therefore, they have ceased to progress spiritually. Spiritual contentment is the antithesis of spiritual growth; while a holy discontent is the catalyst for spiritual growth.
    Are you content with your spiritual life?

2. Having the right attitude is important to deliver us from depression and discouragement when we fail.

    Personally I struggle with perfectionism; meaning, I have an overriding feeling that I must always do things as perfect as possible. And when I have failed God, especially as a young Christian, this would often lead to bouts of discouragement and depression. Satan would at times attack me with great condemnation over my failures and even make me feel like I shouldn't read my Bible or go to church. However, when a great athlete fails, it makes him work even harder. Michael Jordan would have a bad game where he only scored ten points, and then, the next game he would score fifty. Failures make great athletes work even harder. Similarly, Paul said, "Not that I have already become perfect, but I strive (or press)." His imperfection inspired him to seek to know God even more, instead of causing him to quit or give up. It should be that way in our spiritual life as well. Let your spiritual failures make you pursue Christ

237

even more, instead of allowing them to encourage you to quit or settle for less than Christlikeness.

3. Having the right attitude is important to not be led astray into false teachings that emphasize "perfectionism".

Some scholars believe Paul was indirectly attacking the belief of the Judaizers when he said that he had not been "perfected." It was common in those days for pious Jews to believe they could perfectly keep the law. When the rich man approached Christ about how to gain eternal life, Christ told him to keep the law. The rich man replied that he had kept it since his youth (Matt 19:16-20). Christ told him that perfectly keeping the law was enough for salvation so he could see that he had not kept the law and that he needed a savior. However, the rich man believed he had kept the law as many pious Jews did. Maybe, the Judaizers thought that combining law-keeping with faith in Christ could take them to an even higher spiritual plane. If they could keep the law without him, how much more could they attain perfection with him? Kent Hughes said this, "Paul's enemies claimed to have reached a state of perfection that made them possessors of all the blessings of salvation, in effect the arrival of Heaven itself. Heavenly perfection was theirs now, they argued."[99] However, perfection is not attainable on this side of heaven. It must be our continual pursuit, our continual endeavor, but we will not reach it until the second coming of Christ. Listen to what John the apostle said: "We know that whenever it is revealed we will be like him, because we will see him just as he is" (1 John 3:2b). We will never reach perfection on this side of heaven.

With that said, this belief in perfectionism has at times appeared throughout church history. Groups of Christians often from a Wesleyan background have taught that if they achieved a second work of the Holy Spirit after salvation, then instantaneously they could achieve holiness or perfection. Some even believe in the eradication of the sin nature. However, that was not Paul's perspective. He said he had not achieved perfection. He also said in Romans 7 that the things he wanted to do, he didn't do. He cried out, "Who will rescue me from this body of death" (v. 15-25). Also, perfectionism contradicts the rest of Scripture. John the apostle said this, "If we say we do not bear the guilt of sin, we are deceiving ourselves and the truth is not in us" (1 John 1:8).

When John said, "If we say we do not bear the guilt of sin, we are deceiving ourselves and the truth is not in us," he was not just denying perfectionism; he also was probably referring to a person being deceived about one's salvation. The very theme of the book is assurance of salvation. He says in 1 John 5:13, "I have written these things to you who believe in the name of the Son of God so that you may know that you have eternal life." Since meeting God in Scripture always is shown to create an awareness of sin, a person that thinks they have achieved perfection is probably deluded about his salvation.

Isaiah saw God and cried out, "Too bad for me! I am destroyed, for my lips are contaminated by sin, and I live among people whose lips are contaminated by sin. My eyes have seen the king, the Lord who commands armies" (Isaiah 6:5). This man saw how grave his sin was when he met God. Peter, when convinced that Jesus was the messiah, said, "Go away from me, Lord, for I am a sinful man" (Lk 5:8). Paul the apostle calls himself the chief of sinners (1 Tim 1:15). To truly know God means to keenly know one's own sin. Therefore, to claim perfection is very dangerous; it might actually prove that one has never truly met God at all. Scripture vehemently denies the possibility of being perfect here on earth.

As mentioned, perfectionism is the antithesis of spiritual growth. If a person thinks they have attained perfection, then there is no reason to continue to grow and seek Christ. We must be aware of this teaching, and we must also be careful of living this out implicitly by being satisfied with our spiritual attainments.

Application Question: In what ways does Paul's statement about not having achieved perfection yet encourage or challenge you in your spiritual life?

In Order to Pursue Spiritual Maturity, We Must Have the Right Effort

> Not that I have already attained this—that is, I have not already been perfected—but I strive to lay hold of that for which Christ Jesus also laid hold of me.
> Philippians 3:12

One wrestler asked his coach if he could wrestle without working so hard in practice. The constant running, weight lifting, and dieting had taken its toll on him. The coach replied, "Why, yes, you can. However, you can't wrestle and win without working hard." Another aspect of pursuing spiritual maturity we must develop is having the right effort. The word "strive" means "'to run' or 'follow after' and speaks of 'an aggressive, energetic endeavor.'"[100] The word in ancient Greek was used of a hunter eagerly pursuing his prey.[101] If we are going to grow into spiritual maturity, we must give maximum effort. We must work hard in order to be like Christ just like a competitive athlete.

Look at what Paul said in 1 Corinthians 15:10: "But by the grace of God I am what I am, and his grace to me has not been in vain. In fact, I worked harder than all of them—yet not I, but the grace of God with me." When Paul described his effort as an apostle he said, "I worked harder than all of them." This doesn't seem to be boasting but a realistic evaluation of his effort in serving Christ. Unlike most of the apostles, Paul chose to forgo pleasures like marriage in order to have more time to serve Christ. At times, he also forewent pay from churches and earned his money by building tents. He worked hard in accordance with the grace God gave him to become like Christ.

Why are so many Christians not growing in maturity? For many of them, they are not willing to "strive." They are not willing to work hard to take hold of that for which Christ Jesus took hold of them. If we were really honest in our evaluation of one another in the church, many people work hard but at things other than their spiritual lives. They work hard, even at times forgoing sleep, to get a project done for school or work. They get up early to go to a job interview, but many never do that for the kingdom of God. That was Paul's continuous labor; he worked hard—he pressed to become like Christ.

In the Parable of the Sowers in Matthew 13, four different soils hear the Word of God—the wayside, the stony ground, the thorny ground, and the good ground. I believe that only the person who hears the Word and bears fruit is really saved—the good ground. However, listen to how Christ describes the fruitfulness of the good ground: "But other seeds fell on good soil and produced grain, some a hundred times as much, some sixty, and some thirty" (Matt 13:8). Some people who are truly born again produce a 100 fold, some 60 and some 30. What makes the difference? Is it the fact that God gives some people more grace? I don't believe so. We each receive grace from God; however, some people work harder than others with it. Some people do what Paul did: "his grace to me has not been in vain. In fact, I worked harder than all of them—yet not I, but the grace of God with me" (1 Cor 15:10). Paul essentially said, "I used the grace God gave me to serve. I strove in my spiritual life to become more like Christ and complete the works that he called for me to accomplish."

This must be true for us as well; we must have the right effort. Some people will never reach maturity because they don't give any real effort to their spiritual life. Everything else in their life gets maximum effort other than their relationship and service to God. Paul said this to Timothy, "train yourself for godliness" (1 Tim 4:7). It can also be translated "exercise." We must work to be godly.

Remember the discipline that Christ put his disciples through right before going to the cross. He called three disciples to pray with him for one hour. However, when they fell asleep, he didn't say, "Oh it's OK. I understand that you are tired. Go back to sleep." He said, "Pray another hour." They fell asleep again and he said, "Pray another hour" (Matt 26:38-45). He disciplined them. I think really what we see in the Garden of Gethsemane is something of the discipline Christ implemented in their lives throughout the three previous years. He made them exercise themselves unto godliness. Remember they were following a Savior that prior to starting his ministry fasted from food for forty days (Matt 4:2). Christ disciplined himself unto godliness. He woke up early in the morning throughout his ministry and went to the mountain to pray (Mark 1:35). He was disciplined, and he trained his disciples to be disciplined.

240

I have never been a great reader other than reading the Bible and books that explain the Bible. (I am still working out my sanctification.) However, when I have gotten the chance to read biographies of men and women that God used greatly, I often am left astounded at their great discipline—their great effort in pursuing Christ. Martin Luther had a thriving prayer life, where he would at times pray for two hours or more. I have read of other ministers who constantly finished the Bible several times a month. These people were willing to "strive." Their lives were energetic endeavors of pursuing Christlikeness and serving others. If we are going to grow in maturity, we must similarly "strive" to take hold of that for which Christ took hold of us.

Application Question: In what ways is God challenging you to be more disciplined in your spiritual life—to put more effort into pursuing Christ?

In Order to Pursue Spiritual Maturity, We Must Have the Right Focus

> Brothers and sisters, I do not consider myself to have attained this. Instead I am single-minded: Forgetting the things that are behind and reaching out for the things that are ahead, with this goal in mind, I strive toward the prize of the upward call of God in Christ Jesus.
> Philippians 3:13-14

Another aspect of pursuing maturity is having the right focus. Paul said, "Instead I am single-minded." It can also be translated, "But one thing I do." This is the very reason many Christians are not growing; they have too many things they are focusing on. But for Paul, he had one thing that was above all other things and that was to know Christ and be like him. That was his one thing.

This is true of most people who became great at something in their lives; they learned the discipline of focus. Very few people are great at more than one thing. The great businessman, the great musician, the great athlete, the great scholar, the majority of them became great because of their focus. I remember, after my junior year in high school, my mom approached my varsity basketball coach and asked, "What does Greg have to do in order to get a basketball scholarship?" My coach replied, "Greg is going to have to live basketball. He must eat it, drink it, and sleep it. It must consume him if he is going to get a scholarship." I remember taking those words to heart. I would sleep with my basketball and my Bible every night. I would bring my basketball and Bible in my backpack to school every day. It consumed me. This must be true of us as spiritual athletes as well. Christ must become our one thing before every other endeavor.

241

What makes this so difficult is the fact that the enemy of the best thing—knowing and being like Christ—is often not the bad but the good. We see this in the story of Mary and Martha (Luke 10:38-42). Christ visited their house, and he was in the living room teaching everybody with Mary sitting at his feet listening. However, in the kitchen, Martha was working hard to serve everybody by being a good host. She became upset at the fact that Mary, her sister, was not doing anything except sitting at the feet of Jesus. She approached Christ about this, and he replied, "Martha, Martha, you are worried and troubled about many things, but one thing is needed. Mary has chosen the best part; it will not be taken away from her" (v. 41-42).

Martha was doing good things. She was serving everybody in the house, including her Lord, Jesus Christ. However, Mary chose the better thing which was sitting at the feet of Jesus. Christ was her one thing, even before ministry. This is very common for people who serve. We often get busy with many good things and neglect our one thing. This was what enabled Paul to be effective at ministry. His ministry flowed out of this one thing—an abiding relationship with Christ. Remember what Christ said in John 15:5: "I am the vine; you are the branches. The one who remains in me—and I in him—bears much fruit, because apart from me you can accomplish nothing." This "one thing"—abiding in Christ—will actually enable us to do everything better.

Application Question: What are some of scriptural benefits of living a life focused on Christ?

1. Seeing God is a benefit of focusing on Christ.

Matthew 5:8 says, "Blessed are the pure in heart, for they will see God." The "pure in heart" means "the single-minded." Jesus taught that the single-minded—those who are focused on God and the things of God—will see God everywhere. In the midst of a trial, when others only see problems and difficulties, the pure in heart see God and his abundant grace.

2. Fulfilling God's purpose in our lives is a benefit of focusing on Christ.

Jeremiah 29:11-14 in the KJV says this:

For I know the plans I have for you," declares the LORD, "plans to prosper you and not to harm you, plans to give you hope and a future. Then you will call upon me and come and pray to me, and I will listen to you. You will seek me and find me when you seek me with all your heart. I will be found by you," declares the LORD, "and will bring you back from captivity.

242

We often quote this passage written to the Israelites who were exiled in Babylon. God said he had plans for them to give them a hope and a future. However, we must ask, "How would Israel go from being under God's judgment in Babylon to fulfilling God's plans?" Here is the answer: when they would seek him with all their heart, God would not only reveal himself to them but deliver them from exile.

The very reason they were under judgment was for neglecting God, but when they sought God with all their heart, God would reveal himself and deliver them from exile in order to fulfill his promises to them. I wonder how many people are going through trials in their life, even right now, and all God is saying is, "Seek me. Just seek me. Make me your priority, and I will deliver you and fulfill my plans for you."

3. God meeting our needs is a benefit of focusing on Christ.

Matthew 6:33 says this: "But above all pursue his kingdom and righteousness, and all these things will be given to you as well." In the context, Christ told the disciples to not worry about what they would eat, drink, or wear. God would provide if they would put God's kingdom first in their lives. Many Christians go through lack because Christ and his kingdom are not their priority. In fact, often they put other things first before God in order to make sure their provisions are met. However, when they put school, work, friends, and family before God, he often allows them to suffer lack until he becomes their priority. Jesus said if we make God our priority, he will meet all our needs.

4. God answering our prayers is a benefit of focusing on Christ.

James 1:5-8 says,

> But if anyone is deficient in wisdom, he should ask God, who gives to all generously and without reprimand, and it will be given to him. But he must ask in faith without doubting, for the one who doubts is like a wave of the sea, blown and tossed around by the wind. For that person must not suppose that he will receive anything from the Lord, since he is a double-minded individual, unstable in all his ways.

James, in the context of teaching about trials, said that if we lack wisdom we should ask God, for he gives liberally. However, he said that we should ask in faith because a double-minded man will receive nothing. What is a double-minded man? A double-minded man is a person who is trying to live for God and live for the world (cf. James 4:3-4). He is not a focused man. God is not his priority. This person will receive nothing from God. God answers the prayers of those who make him their priority and live a life of faith.

5. God using us greatly is a benefit of focusing on Christ.

Second Chronicles 16:9 in the KJV says, "For the eyes of the LORD run to and fro throughout the whole earth, to shew himself strong in the behalf of them whose heart is perfect toward him." The chronicler said that the eyes of the Lord are always looking for someone whose heart is perfect towards him. What does "perfect" mean in this verse? It seems to be referring to someone who is focusing on God—seeking him first with their lives. For those who do this, God shows his strength in their lives. Why did God use a youth named David mightily for his name? Why did God call a junior high girl named Mary to birth the Messiah? He saw they had hearts that were perfect towards him. He was their focus and God blessed them.

Making Christ our focus comes with many benefits. However, when we neglect him, we will find ourselves deprived. Christ must be our "one thing." How do we keep the right focus?

Maintaining the Right Focus

"...Instead I am single-minded: Forgetting the things that are behind and reaching out for the things that are ahead, with this goal in mind, I strive toward the prize of the upward call of God in Christ Jesus" (Phil 3:13b-14).

After declaring his focus (But one thing I do), Paul described how he maintained a focus on Christ. Again, Paul is using a running metaphor. The focus of the runner is to win the prize and for Paul that was primarily intimacy with Christ and being like him. He describes disciplines that we all must practice in order to do this. How do we keep the right focus?

Observation Question: How did Paul keep a right focus on Christ in Philippians 3:13, and how can we apply this to our lives?

1. We maintain a focus on becoming like Christ by forgetting the things that are behind.

Interpretation Question: What does Paul mean by forgetting the things that are behind?

•   When Paul says forgetting the things that are behind, he is probably referring to all his achievements (Phil 3:4-9).

As mentioned in the previous passage, Paul was proud of his Jewish heritage and his accomplishments as a Pharisee. He was from the tribe of

244

Benjamin, a tribe which produced many nobles. He was a Hebrew of Hebrews meaning that he never lost his Jewish culture. He was a Pharisee. However, when he found Christ, he counted his previous successes as a loss in order to gain salvation through Christ. Now it should be noted, Paul didn't mean that he literally forgot his previous successes. "Forgetting the things that are behind" simply means that his past no longer had power over him. When God says in Hebrews 10:17, "Their sins and their lawless deeds I will remember no longer," he doesn't mean that he forgets. It is impossible for God to forget, it simply means that he no longer holds our failures against us.

In continuing the athletic metaphor, this is true of any great athlete. Michael Jordan, who was one of the most successful NBA basketball players of all time, could have been really content with one NBA championship. However, it did not make him content; it just increased his hunger. He wanted to be even more successful, and he eventually won six NBA championships. In a sense, this must be true for us as Christians as well. We must always have a holy hunger. We must never be satisfied with previous successes in Christ. Moses had a more intimate relationship with God than all the prophets during his time— God spoke to him face to face. However, the fact that he was more intimate with God than others did not make Moses content. He said to God, "Show me your glory" (Ex 33:18). He wanted more of God—more intimacy with him. This must be the same for us as well. Even though Paul had started many churches for God, he wasn't content with his spiritual success. He forgot his successes in order to continue to pursue Christ and his calling. This enabled him to stay focused on the goal of Christ.

- When Paul says forgetting the things that are behind, he is also probably referring to his failures and the failure of others.

In mentioning his achievements in Judaism, Paul also mentioned how he previously was so zealous for Judaism that he persecuted the church (Phil 3:6). This no doubt was a big stain in Paul's memory that may have taken many years to purge. Paul consented to the killing of the church's first martyr, Stephen. After he was stoned, the Jews threw his clothes at the feet of Paul (Acts 8:1). All the Christians were afraid of him. No doubt, during his ministry he met the families of those he persecuted or even had a hand in their children's murder. This blot was enough to destroy anybody's ministry. Again, Paul could never truly forget his failures, but he could change the way he thought about them. Look at what Paul said about his past failure in persecuting the church:

> Even though I was formerly a blasphemer and a persecutor, and an arrogant man. But I was treated with mercy because I acted ignorantly in unbelief, and our Lord's grace was abundant, bringing faith and love in Christ Jesus

245

1 Timothy 1:13-14

When Paul remembered his previous failures, being a violent man and a persecutor of the church, he only saw God's mercy and grace. It reminded him of how God poured out faith and love in his life through Christ Jesus. Where, no doubt, Satan tried to condemn him and keep him from doing ministry, Paul saw the mercy and grace of God on his life. No, he never forgot his past, but he allowed God to change the meaning of it in his life.

This is the problem with many Christians. They remember how they failed God or how someone hurt them, and these sins keep them from ever fully serving God. For some, it even keeps them from attending church or reading their Bible. If we are going to stay focused on Christ, we must exercise a holy forgetting in order to keep the right focus. We must take God at his Word and allow him to change the way we think about things that happened in our past. He works all things to the good of those who love the Lord (Rom 8:28). We must let our past failures and the failures of others draw us even closer to Christ.

We see how God wants to change the power of the past in the story of Joseph. Consider how Joseph responded to his brothers who previously sold him into slavery. He said this: "As for you, you meant to harm me, but God intended it for a good purpose, so he could preserve the lives of many people, as you can see this day" (Genesis 50:20). Joseph said their sending him into slavery was a grace of God to save many. Believe it or not, God wants to use our failures and the failures of others as well in order to help save many. It has been said that one's misery often becomes his/her ministry.

Have you learned how to forget the past? Have you learned how to see God's hand and grace even over your failures and the failure of others? Again, Scripture says, "And we know that all things work together for good for those who love God, who are called according to his purpose" (Rom 8:28). One of the things we must do if we are going to learn how to focus on Christ is develop a holy forgetting.

2.   Christians maintain a focus on Christ by looking towards the prize.

"...Instead I am single-minded: Forgetting the things that are behind and reaching out for the things that are ahead, with this goal in mind, I strive toward the prize of the upward call of God in Christ Jesus" (Phil 3:13b-14).

Again, in using the running illustration, a successful runner never looks back, to the side, or at himself while running. He constantly looks ahead towards the goal. The phrase reaching out "describes stretching a muscle to its limit, and pictures a runner straining every muscle to reach the finish line."[102] Paul was reaching towards the goal of the prize for which God called him heavenward.

246

Many Christians cannot grow spiritually because instead of looking forward they are always looking at others or at themselves, and it either discourages them or makes them prideful. They get discouraged because they are not as spiritually mature as others or as successful. Or they get prideful because they are more mature than others. Both hinder their spiritual growth. Competitive runners keep their eyes on the goal—not on themselves or others around them. It's the same with Christians who are maturing in Christ.

Interpretation Question: What goal or prize was Paul straining and pressing towards?

It was the goal of knowing and being just like Christ (Phil 3:9-10), but it also seems to refer to him being approved and rewarded by him at the judgment seat of Christ. Paul said this:

> So then whether we are alive or away, we make it our ambition to please him. For we must all appear before the judgment seat of Christ, so that each one may be paid back according to what he has done while in the body, whether good or evil.
> 2 Corinthians 5:9-10

Paul aimed to please Christ because he realized that one day he would appear before the judgment seat of Christ. We see the athletic metaphor in this judgment as well. The word "judgment seat" used here is not the judgment seat of a court case but one from an athletic competition. It is the word "bema" which was a raised platform where the judge would give a reward for winning an athletic competition.

That was Paul's goal; he wanted to look like Christ and be approved by him. This approval would ultimately come when Christ said, "Well done, good and faithful servant" (Matt 25:21, ESV).

There is a story about a great pianist who had just finished a concert and the crowd stood and gave him a raving applause. However, the renowned pianist did not seem satisfied. Only when a man in the rafters stood and began to clap did the pianist smile and bow before the audience. The man in the stands was his teacher. Only the approval of his teacher mattered, and this should be true of us as Christians as well. We press to receive the approval of our Master.

In seeking the approval of the Master, Paul also wanted to be rewarded by him—possibly the ultimate form of approval. Listen to what Paul said in 1 Corinthians 9:24-27:

> Do you not know that all the runners in a stadium compete, but only one receives the prize? So run to win. Each competitor must exercise self-control in everything. They do it to receive a perishable crown, but

we an imperishable one. So I do not run uncertainly or box like one who hits only air. Instead I subdue my body and make it my slave, so that after preaching to others I myself will not be disqualified.

Paul did not want to be disqualified from the prize—the approval of Christ and the rewards that came with it. This was always on his mind. In fact, look at what Paul said at the end of his life:

I have competed well; I have finished the race; I have kept the faith! Finally the crown of righteousness is reserved for me. The Lord, the righteous Judge, will award it to me in that day—and not to me only, but also to all who have set their affection on his appearing.
2 Timothy 4:7-8

Paul, like a competitive runner, kept his eyes focused on the prize. For him, the prize was knowing Christ, looking like him, and being approved by him.

If we are going to stay focused on Christ in a secular world, we must be motivated by heavenly things. We must be motivated by the approval of Christ and his reward. Jesus said this: "Look! I am coming soon, and my reward is with me to pay each one according to what he has done" (Revelation 22:12).

Practicing these truths will help us stay focused. We must forget what is behind, including past successes and failures. We must continue to look forward at our goal in the future, which is Christ.

Application Question: In what ways is God training you to practice a holy forgetting so you can progress in your spiritual life? What distractions—achievements or failures—commonly keep you from pressing forward to know Christ more?

In Order to Pursue Spiritual Maturity, We Must Have the Right Practice

Therefore let those of us who are "perfect" embrace this point of view. If you think otherwise, God will reveal to you the error of your ways. Nevertheless, let us live up to the standard that we have already attained.
Philippians 3:15-16

A great athlete never neglects his basic disciplines. The basketball player practices dribbling, shooting, passing, and defense over and over again. The runner focuses on the swing of his arms, the distance of his stride, breathing, and pacing himself. All athletes are faithful in practicing the basics which

248

eventually makes them successful in competition. It's the same with a spiritual athlete pursuing maturity in Christ. In order to pursue spiritual maturity we must have the right practice.

In verses 15 and 16, Paul calls for those who were mature in the congregation to practice the same disciplines as him in pursuing Christ and Christlikeness. However, he recognized some in the congregation might not agree with him. Maybe, they believed that sanctification was a process that God did all on his own without the believer's help. This is at times taught today. "Let go and let God," some say. But Paul taught spiritual maturity was attained, at least in part, by our rigorous effort. He said to those who disagreed with him that God would make it clear to them, but they had to live up to the standard they had already attained (v. 16). The ESV translates verse 16 this way, "Only let us hold true to what we have attained." In order for God to correct them, they had to be faithful with what he had already taught them. What they had already attained may have seemed liked basics, but they needed to continue to practice them in order to receive further revelation.

This is true for each one of us. If we are faithful with what God has already revealed to us, he will give us more. We will know Christ more and grow in Christlikeness. We see this principle taught in other parts of Scripture. Christ said this to the disciples:

> "Take care about what you hear. The measure you use will be the measure you receive, and more will be added to you. For whoever has will be given more, but whoever does not have, even what he has will be taken from him."
> Mark 4:24-25

Christ told the disciples that the measure they used what God had already revealed to them, it would be given back and even more. Those who were faithful in practicing the truths that God had already taught them, would be given more, but those who did not, even what they had would be taken away.

When you look at any person who is growing in the Lord, you can be sure this principle is working in their lives. God has taught them truths, and they are applying it to their lives. They are faithfully practicing it and sharing it, and therefore God is giving them more. However, instead of growing, many are going backwards based on the same principle. God taught them to delight in and meditate on the Word of God day and night (Psalm 1:2), but they choose to delight in other things. God taught them to let no corrupt communication come out of their mouths (Eph 4:29), but they instead talk much like the world. God taught them to forgive so they will be forgiven (Matt 6:14), but instead they harden their hearts against others. Therefore, God takes away.

If the Philippians who did not agree with Paul's assessment of following Christ and growing in maturity were faithful to all God had already taught them, then eventually he would correct their wrong theology. When we are faithful, God by his grace enables us to progress into the image of Christ. However, when we rebel, there is a taking away, a hardening of a person's heart (Matt 13:12-15).

Are you living up to what you have already attained? If so, God will give you more. If not, God will take away. Great athletes never stop practicing the basics, and it's the same with mature Christians.

Application Question: In what ways have you seen the principle in Mark 4:23-24 happen in your life or others? Are there any areas where God is especially calling you to live up to what he has already taught you, so you can grow in maturity?

Conclusion

How do we pursue spiritual maturity in Christ?

1. In Order to Pursue Spiritual Maturity, We Must Have the Right Attitude—a Holy Discontent
2. In Order to Pursue Spiritual Maturity, We Must Have the Right Effort
3. In Order to Pursue Spiritual Maturity, We Must Have the Right Focus
4. In Order to Pursue Spiritual Maturity, We Must Have the Right Practice

Pursuing Spiritual Maturity—Part Two

> Be imitators of me, brothers and sisters, and watch carefully those who are living this way, just as you have us as an example. For many live, about whom I have often told you, and now, with tears, I tell you that they are the enemies of the cross of Christ. Their end is destruction, their god is the belly, they exult in their shame, and they think about earthly things. But our citizenship is in heaven—and we also eagerly await a savior from there, the Lord Jesus Christ, who will transform these humble bodies of ours into the likeness of his glorious body by means of that power by which he is able to subject all things to himself.
> Philippians 3:17-21 (NET)

How should we pursue Christ? How should we pursue spiritual maturity? In this text Paul calls for the Philippians to follow his example (Phil 3:17). In the context, he has just shared his testimony with the Philippians. He was a Hebrew of Hebrews, from the tribe of Benjamin. He was zealous for the law, and yet when he found Christ, he counted everything a loss in order to gain Christ (v. 4-9). He gave up his religion, culture, career, and family to gain Christ and to be found with a righteousness that comes only from God. Paul spoke as an accountant—everything else was a liability or a loss in order to gain Christ (v. 8). But Paul's pursuit of Christ did not stop at salvation. For many Christians, salvation is just a profession of their belief in Christ, but that was not true for Paul. Paul said this:

> My aim is to know him, to experience the power of his resurrection, to share in his sufferings, and to be like him in his death, and so, somehow, to attain to the resurrection from the dead.
> Philippians 3:10-11

Paul was utterly consumed with knowing Christ. The word "know" is not a word used simply for head knowledge but an experiential knowledge. The Greek word was used in the Septuagint to refer to marital relations between a husband and a wife. Genesis 4:1 (KJV) said, "Adam knew Eve and she conceived." Paul wanted to continue to grow in intimacy with Christ for the rest of his life. He then left the accounting terminology and used athletic terminology

251

in Philippians 3:12-16. He said, "I strive [or run] to take hold of that for which Christ Jesus took hold of me" (v. 12 paraphrase). Paul saw himself running a race, giving all his energy, in order to know Christ and be like him.

Here in this text, he calls for the Philippians, and us, to follow his example (v. 17). He calls us to pursue Christ in the same way that he did. Christianity is not only the profession of a creed, "I believe that Jesus Christ is God, and he died for my sins." No, it is more than that. Christianity is a relationship with Christ that will be ever deepening for the rest of our lives. When Christ spoke about those who "professed" to know him in Matthew 7:21-23, they called him, "Lord, Lord," however he responded to them, "I never knew you." Christianity is a relationship. These people had doctrine, but they had never experienced what Paul had—a desire to be a disciple, to be just like the Master in every way. That is what true Christianity is.

In this text, we will continue with the theme from Philippians 3:12-16, the pursuit of spiritual maturity. How do we grow in spiritual maturity?

Big Question: How should we pursue spiritual maturity according to Philippians 3:17-21?

In Order to Pursue Spiritual Maturity, We Must Focus on Godly Models

> Be imitators of me, brothers and sisters, and watch carefully those who are living this way, just as you have us as an example.
> Philippians 3:17

Paul commands the Philippians to follow his example in pursuing Christ. This is not the first time Paul has taught this. He said in 1 Corinthians 11:1, "Be imitators of me, as I am of Christ" (ESV). Now this may sound strange to many people. Is Paul trying to say he is perfect and that is why we should model him? Absolutely not! He already said that he wasn't perfect in Philippians 3:12. He said, "Not that I have already attained this—that is, I have not already been perfected." Paul called himself the chief of sinners (1 Tim 1:15), least of the apostles (1 Cor 15:9), and less than least of all God's people (Eph 3:8). Paul was imperfect, and he would be the first to say that. However, it is his imperfections that make him a perfect model of how to pursue Christ. Consider what John MacArthur said about imitating Paul:

> Had he been perfect, Paul would not have been an example believers could follow. We need to follow someone who is not perfect so we can see how to overcome our imperfections; someone who can show us how to handle the struggles of life, its disappointments, and its trials;

252

someone who can show us how to handle pride, resist temptation, and put sin to death. Christ is the perfect standard, model, and pattern for believers to emulate. But Christ never pursued perfection; He has always been perfect.[103]

Listen, we need to follow somebody imperfect so we can learn how to overcome imperfections. That's what makes Paul such a great model. We need to learn from somebody who struggles with pride, anger, lust, and insecurity. We need to see somebody else's path to spiritual maturity. Christ is our perfect standard and model, but he never had to pursue perfection because he was always perfect. We need to study people who are pursuing that perfect standard and being successful. What do I do when I fail and make a mistake? In one sense, I can't learn that from Christ's example in the Scripture because he never had to get back up after falling to lust or anger. He was always perfect and therefore is our model to pursue. But, we also need to pattern our lives after people who are imperfect and yet pursuing perfection to look like Christ.

When Paul said to follow him as a model, he did not point to himself alone. He says, "and watch carefully those who are living this way, just as you have us as an example." "Watch" can also be translated "observe" or "fix your gaze on."[104] We need to fix our gaze on people that are demonstrating the same apostolic pattern of pursuing Christ. They are pressing—working with all their energy to pursue Christ. They are single minded—saying this "one thing" I do. They are not double-minded in their pursuit of Christ and Christlikeness. When he says watch those who live this way, just as you have "us" as an example, he is probably referring not only to himself but to Timothy and Epaphroditus who were mentioned in chapter 2. He said of Timothy that he had no one else like him who cared about the interests of Christ (v.20-21). He said of Epaphroditus to honor men like him for he almost died for the work of Christ (v. 30). But, also some commentators believe that he may be referring to the elders and deacons in the church of Philippi who the letter was originally addressed to (Phil 1:1).[105] These people were put into spiritual leadership positions not only to lead but to be examples to the flock. Listen to what Peter said to the elders in 1 Peter 5:2-3:

> Give a shepherd's care to God's flock among you, exercising oversight not merely as a duty but willingly under God's direction, not for shameful profit but eagerly. And do not lord it over those entrusted to you, but be examples to the flock.

These leaders were selected by the Holy Spirit to be examples to the flock. They were to be examples in how they led their families, handled money and conflict, cared for others, etc. Paul taught this in 1 Timothy 3 when he gave the qualifications of elders and deacons. Therefore, these leaders should be people worth modeling.

This is important to hear not only so we can fix our "gaze on them" in our churches, but also because in many church models we might have a part in the selection of these people. It also should be a large consideration when selecting a new church to serve in the future. Are the leaders in the church handling themselves in a way worth modeling? How do they handle their own imperfection? Are they like Paul in being transparent and humble in their own failures? Do they handle their own families well? Are they people of the Word and prayer?

Moreover, these potential models go much farther than our pastors and deacons. They refer to anybody demonstrating a Christian walk worth imitating. Paul says we should fix our gaze on these people; we should observe them in order to grow.

Certainly, this method of growth is true in any field. A child observes his parents in order to learn how to walk and talk. When a person gets hired at a job, many times he has to shadow the person being replaced in order to learn how to do the job. Many of us read books and articles about people we want to model in some endeavor whether that be sports, business, art, or even cooking. Modeling is a necessary part of growing.

With that said, we learn the very reason that many people are not growing. They are not modeling anybody. They have no true models for their spiritual growth. As we consider this principle, we should ask ourselves, "Who am I observing?" "Who are the people that God placed around me that I should fix my gaze on?"

Application Question: How can we practice the discipline of modeling in order to grow spiritually?

1. We must find people who are good models.

Obviously, in order to practice modeling we must find people to observe and fix our gaze on. Since this is one of the ways God commanded us to pursue spiritual growth, we can assume that he has already placed people around us to model. It may be an elder, a deacon, a small group leader, an older man, an older woman, etc. We must find these people and get around them so we can learn. Now we should be aware that these people are not perfect; they are people who are zealous in seeking to get rid of their imperfections and are being successful in that pursuit. They are people for whom Christ is their "one thing," and they are pressing to be like him.

2. We must be humble and teachable to learn from someone spiritually mature.

254

For many people, pride keeps them from being able to learn from others. Mankind has a competitive spirit. The apostle John called this the "pride of life" (1 John 2:16 ESV). This pride many times keeps us from seeking or being able to learn from the examples God has surrounded us with. To learn from somebody is a humbling experience. It requires accepting that we don't know everything and others know better than us. The pride of life is a work of the flesh and a hindrance to spiritual growth. God opposes the proud but gives grace to the humble (James 4:6). Those who humble themselves and follow somebody else's model will receive God's grace to grow.

Are you humble and willing to be taught?

3. We must be willing to develop intimate relationships with people who are spiritually mature.

The fact that we are called to "watch" does not mean that all we need to do is look. To really have a focused look, the implication is that you need to get close to these models. You need to develop intimate relationships with them so you can learn how they deal with their imperfections and pursue maturity in Christ. You may also need to confess some issues or problems that you have in order to get help. "Watching" is an intimate endeavor. The Philippians had an intimate relationship with Paul. That is why he could say, "watch carefully those who are living this way, just as you have us as an example" (v. 17). They knew Paul's lifestyle intimately and therefore would be able to recognize those who modeled it. If you are not willing to be intimate, then you will probably stay stagnant in your growth.

Are you willing to develop intimate relationships with those who are spiritually mature?

4. We must be ready to change in order to follow somebody spiritually mature.

If you are not ready to change, if you are not ready to get rid of sin, then you will not develop intimate relationships with spiritually mature people in order to grow. This is what Christ said:

"For everyone who does evil deeds hates the light and does not come to the light, so that their deeds will not be exposed. But the one who practices the truth comes to the light, so that it may be plainly evident that his deeds have been done in God."
John 3:20-21

When Christ was talking about "the light" in this context, he was referring to himself. However, this reality is true with others who are spiritually mature as well. If you are not ready to get rid of sin in your life, then you won't develop intimate relationships with those living in the light for fear that it will expose your sin. Personally, I remember when I was in high school, even though I was a Christian, I didn't hang around Christians who were too sold out for God. I needed to be around people who had a little bit of compromise in their life, because I was compromised. The light would expose too much of what I was not yet willing to give up. John also said this in his epistle: "But if we walk in the light as he himself is in the light, we have fellowship with one another and the blood of Jesus his Son cleanses us from all sin" (1 John 1:7). If we walk in the light we have fellowship with one another. Because I wasn't always walking in the light, it hindered my fellowship with those in the light. I didn't want the light shining on my life.

If you are going to walk in intimate relationships with those who are mature, you must be willing to change. Otherwise, you will not come to the light for fear that your sinful deeds will be exposed.

5. We must be willing to be models.

Another application we can take from Paul's call to imitate him and others who are mature is being willing to be models ourselves. I remember when I was in high school, a Nike commercial came out with a very famous professional basketball player named Charles Barkley. In the commercial Charles exclaimed, "I am not a role model!" He essentially was saying that he should not be expected to live at a higher standard simply because he played professional sports. Similarly, this is how many Christians live their lives. They think that just because they are a Christian, it doesn't mean that they should be role models for others to follow. However, that is not true. For Charles Barkley, just because he played professional sports and was in the spotlight, people were going to see him and model him, especially children. Therefore, he was accountable. This is also true for Christians. Because you profess Christ, people are always watching you. And your life will either push people towards Christ or push people away. There is no in between. Christ said, "Whoever is not with me is against me, and whoever does not gather with me scatters" (Matt 12:30).

You are either gathering or scattering. Essentially, he says that if you profess Christ and yet scatter by your lifestyle, then you are against him. You are either his disciple—imitating him and seeking to be an example to others—or you are not. It's very simple. Are you willing to be a model? This is something we can gain from Paul's challenge to imitate other godly models. We are called to be godly models as well. This means asking such questions as: "Could what I am doing (even though it may not be sin) cause another brother or sister to stumble?" Paul said, "It is good not to eat meat or drink wine or to do anything that causes your brother to stumble" (Romans 14:21). This is the type of question we must be willing to ask ourselves if we are going to be the models God called us to be.

If we are going to pursue Christ, we must have the right models.

Application Question: What Christian models outside of Scripture have had the most effect on you and in what ways? In what ways is God calling you to be a model for others?

In Order to Pursue Spiritual Maturity, We Must Recognize and Stay Away from Wrong Models

> For many live, about whom I have often told you, and now, with tears, I tell you that they are the enemies of the cross of Christ. Their end is destruction, their god is the belly, they exult in their shame, and they think about earthly things.
> Philippians 3:18-19

The next thing we must do in order to pursue spiritual maturity is to recognize and stay away from wrong models. This text is very interesting. It is the only time Paul ever mentions his tears in the present tense.[106] This means he was crying even as he wrote the passage. Essentially, he says watch out for those who are enemies of the cross of Christ. The implication is that these people are not outside of the church but inside it. They are those who profess faith in Christ but are not truly born again. Their witness and lifestyle actually lead people away from the Lord they profess. They are dangers to one's spiritual growth.

We see this reality taught throughout Scripture. Jesus taught in Matthew 13 that there are tares and wheat in the church (v. 24-30, 36-44). They may look very similar to true believers on the outside but their internal make up is very different. If somebody mistakenly ate a tare thinking it was wheat, they would get very sick. Again, they may look similar but their chemical makeup is different; a tare was not created to be eaten.

In fact, in the parable Christ taught that an enemy came and planted tares among the wheat. This was a common practice in ancient times. There was actually a Roman law against it. If somebody was angry with his neighbor or a competitor, he would plant tares among that person's wheat. The purpose of doing this was to negatively affect the harvest—to stop it from being productive. If the owner tried to pluck the tares out before the harvest, they would lose the wheat as well.

Similarly, in the church Satan has planted tares among the wheat. In the church there are good examples and bad examples. If you model somebody who is a tare, the consequences could be drastic. Listen to what Paul told Timothy about God's household in 2 Timothy 2:20-21 (NIV 1984):

> In a large house there are articles not only of gold and silver, but also of wood and clay; some are for noble purposes and some for ignoble. If a man cleanses himself from the latter, he will be an instrument for noble purposes, made holy, useful to the Master and prepared to do any good work.

Paul says in a large house there are objects used for noble purposes and also for ignoble. Certain objects are honored like a pearl necklace or a person's framed graduation certificate. We treat these objects with great honor, but other objects are not honored such as the trash can and the toilet. This house metaphor is a picture of God's house. Paul tells Timothy that both exist in God's house, and if he cleansed himself from the objects of dishonor, he would be a noble vessel, useful to the Master and prepared to do any good work. What are the objects of dishonor that we must rid ourselves of if we are going to be objects prepared for any good work—mature servants of Christ? Listen to the context:

> But avoid profane chatter, because those occupied with it will stray further and further into ungodliness, and their message will spread its infection like gangrene. Hymenaeus and Philetus are in this group. They have strayed from the truth by saying that the resurrection has already occurred, and they are undermining some people's faith.
> 2 Timothy 2:16-18

In 2 Timothy 2:16-18, he talked about those who have profane chatter and consequently become more ungodly. He names two false teachers who wandered from the faith and were destroying the faith of some. Paul told Timothy to stay away from these types of people—these vessels of dishonor. Their talk is ungodly, and consequently, they become more and more ungodly. Their teachings spread like gangrene, destroying the faith of some. They are tares among the wheat. They were planted by the enemy to destroy the harvest of God. It is these types of ungodly models that Paul is talking about in Philippians 3:18.

Some commentators think Paul is again referring to the Judaizers who had infiltrated the church. Paul previously warned the church of them in Philippians 3:2. He called them dogs, evil workers, and mutilators of the flesh. They taught the need for Gentiles to follow the Jewish law in order to be saved. However, it doesn't seem that Paul is only referring to these teachers. The Judaizers focused on a legalistic righteousness and taught strict adherence to the law. They were more like the Pharisees—legalists. However, the group Paul addressed here seemed to be people that were following no law at all. They would say, "Since Christ is my Savior and he paid for my sins, I can live any way I want." That's why Paul said their god is their belly (v. 19).

We must be aware that ungodly models are in the church. There are those that should not be followed. Like Paul said to Timothy, if we cleanse ourselves from such, we will be vessels of honor suitable for every good work. God can't use some Christians for every good work because they have areas of compromise in their lives. Many times this compromise is compounded by their relationships with those who are not truly following Christ. This is a hard and difficult teaching, but we must be aware of it.

Paul describes these professed believers so we can recognize them and have nothing to do with them in the sense of following and partnering with them. Paul said this to the Corinthians: "Do not be deceived: 'Bad company corrupts good morals'" (1 Cor 15:33).

Observation Question: In what ways does Paul describe these wrong models—these false professors—and what do these descriptors mean practically?

> For many live, about whom I have often told you, and now, with tears, I tell you that they are the enemies of the cross of Christ. Their end is destruction, their god is the belly, they exult in their shame, and they think about earthly things.
> Philippians 3:18-19

1.   They are enemies of the cross of Christ.

Paul calls them enemies of the cross of Christ. What does he mean by this?

Interpretation Question: What does Paul mean by enemies of the cross?

John MacArthur said, "The term cross is not limited to the actual wooden instrument of death (1 Cor. 1:17–18, 23; 2:2; Gal. 3:1; 6:14; Eph. 2:16; Col. 1:20; 2:14; 1 Peter 2:24), but signifies Christ's atoning death in all its aspects."[107] It, therefore, could have many meanings since Christ's atoning death has many aspects to it.

- "Enemies of the cross" could mean that they deny the need for us to take up our cross daily and live sacrificial lives for Christ.

Christ taught that we must take up our cross to follow him (Luke 14:27); however, many would deny our need to take up the cross. Some deny it by teaching that believers should always be prosperous. They would say Christ

259

died so we would not have to suffer. Christ died so we could be free of problems and have healthy and wealthy lives. However, taking up our cross is not just spiritual, it meant literally being willing to suffer and die for Christ. Others deny it by teaching that there is no need to take up one's cross in order to be saved. Some believe that at salvation one takes Christ as Savior and then later takes him as Lord—meaning to take up our cross. They see discipleship as secondary to salvation, instead of necessary for it (cf. Lk 14:26-33). Dietrich Bonhoeffer called this type of theology "cheap grace." Others deny the cross not necessarily by their teaching, but by their lives. They will not sacrifice for him or others; they will not put to death sin. There is no cross in their lives. Christ is often viewed as a virtual genie who supplies all our wants and desires, and all we have to do is claim it. In these congregations, the necessity of the cross has affectively been removed. Maybe Paul was referring to this when he warned the Philippians of those who were enemies of the cross.

What else could enemies of the cross mean?

- "Enemies of the cross" could mean that by their lives they deny the power that comes through the cross of Christ.

Christ's death on the cross did not just pay the penalty for our sins; it also broke the power of sin over our lives. It delivered us from being slaves of sin to slaves of righteousness. Christ said, "So if the son sets you free, you will be really free" (John 8:36). Paul taught this specifically about Christ's death:

> We know that our old man was crucified with him so that the body of sin would no longer dominate us, so that we would no longer be enslaved to sin. (For someone who has died has been freed from sin.). Romans 6:6-7

Paul said our old self, our sin nature, was crucified with him on the cross and that we have been freed from sin. This doesn't mean that we won't sin as believers. It just means that sin is no longer our master. It no longer should control us. These "professed" believers denied the power of the cross through their lifestyle and possibly their teaching. They claimed the cross for salvation but denied its power to change their lives.

Paul talked about this elsewhere also. He told Timothy that in the last days there would be "difficult times" in the church (2 Tim 3:1). In describing the character of the people, he said they would be "treacherous, reckless, conceited, loving pleasure rather than loving God. They will maintain the outward appearance of religion but will have repudiated its power. So avoid people like these" (2 Tim 3:4-5). These people would only have the "outward appearance of religion." They would come to church and say the right things, but there was no power in their lives. Their living effectively denied the power of the cross as they chose to indulge in sin and worldliness. However, Scripture says, "So then, if anyone is in Christ, he is a new creation; what is old has passed away—look, what is new has come" (2 Cor 5:17). True believers are new creations because of the cross, not in spite of it.

Paul said to Timothy, "So avoid people like these" (2 Tim 3:5). He says the same thing to the Philippians. With tears in his eyes, he says, "There are some people among you that you must not model." Jesus Christ taught us that in the church there would be tares and wheat, true and false. You will be able to tell them apart by their fruit (Matt 5:20).

What else could this mean?

- "Enemies of the cross" could mean that they deny the sufficiency of the cross.

This was true of both those Judaizers and the Gnostics—two early cults who attacked the early church. The Judaizers said the cross was not enough for salvation. One needed to practice the law and circumcision to be saved. The Gnostics said that in order for a person to be saved they needed some lofty experience of knowledge where one became closer to the deity. They both said the cross was not enough. The cross was not sufficient. And, many today teach the same thing. You need baptism, the Lord's Supper, church membership, etc., in order to be saved, they say. However, those who teach such things are enemies of the cross. They deny its power by teaching the need for something else. There is no other way for people to be saved other than the cross. The cross is enough. Christ's death was enough. He provided a way for us to the Father. Let no one teach you anything different. Paul wrote this with tears dripping on the page. They dripped because of his concern for the Philippians and also us. We must be careful of bad examples who are enemies of the cross.

How else does Paul describe these believers?

2. Their end is destruction.

The word "destruction" can be translated "waste." It was translated waste in Mark 14:4 when the woman with the alabaster box poured the expensive perfume on Christ's head. The people said, "Why this waste...?" These professors in the church lived a wasted life on earth, and they will live a wasted eternity.[108] The word "destruction" does not mean annihilation— that these people will cease to exist—as some would teach. No, the Bible teaches something much different than that. God made each person in the image of God, and because of that, each person will live eternally in one of two places. Some will spend eternity in heaven and others will spend eternity suffering in a burning fire in hell (Matt 5:29-30, Matt 25:41). Matthew 25:41 describes people

261

being sent into an "eternal fire" prepared for the devil and his angels. If it were simply annihilation—simply ceasing to exist—that would be much more bearable. No, the clear teaching of Scripture is that this will be an eternal punishment. That is the destiny of these believers who professed Christ but truly did not live for him. In fact, Scripture teaches that there will be varying degrees of reward and punishment in eternity. Listen to what Christ said in Luke 12:47-48:

> "That servant who knew his master's will but did not get ready or do what his master asked will receive a severe beating. But the one who did not know his master's will and did things worthy of punishment will receive a light beating. From everyone who has been given much, much will be required, and from the one who has been entrusted with much, even more will be asked."

This is the lot for these professed believers. They will be severely beaten throughout eternity. Their torment will be greater than others because they knew the Word of God and thus were more accountable for it. Their life was a waste and their eternity will be one as well. Saints, be careful of those you partner with and model in the church.

3.   Their god is their belly.

As mentioned previously, these professed believers are not legalists; they are antinomian—meaning they believe Christ has given us a license to sin. When Paul says, "their god is their belly," he is saying that they live to feed every carnal desire. Even though Christ taught to not store up riches on this earth (Matt 6:19), they instead are consumed with the pursuit of wealth and the comforts of this life. When Paul said he buffeted his body and made it a slave (1 Cor 9:27), they instead live to give their bodies whatever it desires, even when it is outside the teaching of Scripture. Like the hypocrites Christ spoke of, the righteous deeds they practice are done for the applause of people instead of the applause of heaven (Matt 6:1-7). They are earthly instead of heavenly. Be aware of those who profess Christ and yet live for their belly. One commentator said this about these teachers: "There is no chapel in their life. It is all kitchen."[109] Their life is not about worship; it is about the fulfilling of their desires. They live for self and not for Christ. Beloved, beware of Christians like this. They are not to be modeled.

4.   They exult in their shame.

What does Paul mean by "they exult in their shame"? This simply means that they boast in the very things they should be ashamed of. We get a

262

clear picture of this in the Corinthian church. In 1 Corinthians 5, a man in the church was having sex with his father's wife—his step mom. However, instead of disciplining this man, the church was boasting in his sin. Listen to what Paul said:

> "It is actually reported that sexual immorality exists among you, the kind of immorality that is not permitted even among the Gentiles, so that someone is cohabiting with his father's wife. And you are proud! Shouldn't you have been deeply sorrowful instead and removed the one who did this from among you?... Your boasting is not good. Don't you know that a little yeast affects the whole batch of dough?"
> 1 Corinthians 5:1-2, 6

This was the advertisement for their church, "We accept everybody. It doesn't matter how you live. Christ has paid for our sins, and therefore, we can live however we want." I remember studying at a coffee shop one day while visiting the States. A group of ladies were having a conversation at the table next to me, and it sounded like one of the ladies was looking for a church to attend. Another lady excitedly shared the name and denomination of her church and then added, "We accept homosexuality!" She boasted in the very thing that she should have been ashamed of. In addition, I remember preaching a series on purity at a university chapel, and after the service, an older gentleman from the audience approached me and shared that he was introduced to pornography at a church retreat. The church he grew up in was very liberal, and when he entered the retreat, there was a nude poster for all to see. At the retreat they taught that sex was great, and that it was a gift from God to be explored and enjoyed in various ways. That was his first exposure to pornography as a child. This is the characteristic of these bad models. They boast in the very things they should be ashamed of. They boast in their drunkenness, sexual immorality, greed, and deceit, and yet profess Christ. Beloved, we must be aware that this is in the church. There are many bad models.

5.   Their mind is on earthly things.

Scripture teaches that the mind of the unregenerate is very different from a believer. Their minds are set on totally different things. Look at how Romans describes the mind of both the believer and the unbeliever.

> For those who live according to the flesh have their outlook shaped by the things of the flesh, but those who live according to the Spirit have their outlook shaped by the things of the Spirit. For the outlook of the flesh is death, but the outlook of the Spirit is life and peace, because

> the outlook of the flesh is hostile to God, for it does not submit to the
> law of God, nor is it able to do so.
> Romans 8:5-7

The mind of the unbeliever is set on what the flesh desires. It is consumed with temporary things, earthly things—things that only pertain to this life. But those who are truly born again desire what the Spirit desires. They desire to know God more, to spread his Word, and to bring glory to God. Their mind is set on heavenly things. The unbeliever's mind is death—meaning they are separated from the life of God. Their thoughts are without genuine consideration of God and his will. The believer's mind is life—knowing God (John 17:3)—and knowing God brings peace.

For this reason, the unbeliever will constantly misjudge the believer because he can't understand him. He cannot understand the believer's thinking. It's foolishness to him. This will bring constant conflict in the church. Sadly, this will often happen even between family members when one person is not truly born again. There will be conflicts between church leaders and parishioners and conflicts between the leaders themselves. The conflicts will be based on having different minds—one earthly and one spiritual. The "professed believer" in the church will constantly be in conflict with the thoughts and plans of the redeemed. If a believer is truly being led by the Spirit, then this will be met with animosity from those who are earthly. Paul said, "The unbeliever does not receive the things of the Spirit of God, for they are foolishness to him. And he cannot understand them, because they are spiritually discerned" (1 Cor 2:14). We must be aware of this reality in the church. There are those who are earthly and only consumed with earthly things within the church.

Christ taught this throughout the Scripture. There will be wolves in sheep's clothing and tares amongst the wheat. If we are going to protect ourselves, we must be aware of the characteristics of bad models. They are enemies of the cross. Their belly is their god. Their destiny is destruction. Their boast is their shame, and their mind is set on earthly things. Beloved, beware.

Application Question: What are your thoughts about the dramatic imagery and description Paul gives of these bad models in the church? How have you seen this type of Christianity in the church?

In Order to Pursue Spiritual Maturity, We Must Maintain a Heavenly Focus

> But our citizenship is in heaven—and we also eagerly await a savior
> from there, the Lord Jesus Christ, who will transform these humble

bodies of ours into the likeness of his glorious body by means of that power by which he is able to subject all things to himself.
Philippians 3:20-21

Observation Question: What are characteristics of citizens of heaven as stated or implied from the text (Phil 3:20-21)?

Finally, Paul says the last thing we must do if we are going to pursue spiritual maturity is maintain a heavenly focus. In comparing us to the "professing Christians" whose destiny is destruction, he says, "But our citizenship is in heaven." This is the factor that should make us different than them and also affect the trajectory of our lives. It is all about citizenship—where our home is. The professors live like the world because the world is their home. In the same way, citizens of heaven live differently because heaven is their home. Paul spoke as an accountant as he counted everything loss to gain Christ (3:8). He spoke as an athlete, as he pressed to pursue a deeper relationship with him (3:12). Now he speaks as an alien, someone in a foreign land waiting to go home. This must be true of us as well.

The word "citizenship" Paul used here "refers to the place where one has official status, the commonwealth where one's name is recorded on the register of citizens."[110] The word is related to the same word he used in Philippians 1:27. The New Living Translation says, "Above all, you must live as citizens of heaven, conducting yourselves in a manner worthy of the Good News about Christ." This would have struck a chord with the Philippian church. They understood the reality of being a citizen of another country while living abroad. Philippi was a Roman colony. They wore Roman clothes; their leaders had Roman titles, and they spoke Latin. Their Roman citizenship was coveted and opened many doors for them. However, as Christians they had an even greater citizenship, and therefore, a greater responsibility to uphold it.

As citizens of heaven, we should have a different language than everybody else. Paul said, "You must let no unwholesome word come out of your mouth, but only what is beneficial for the building up of the one in need, that it may give grace to those who hear" (Eph 4:29). As citizens of heaven, we should have different values and a different thinking than those around us—a mind focused on what the Spirit desires instead of the flesh (Rom 8:5). As citizens of heaven, we should have different clothing. Paul commanded the women in Ephesus to dress modestly—to avoid the extremes (1 Tim 2:9). He said, "Likewise the women are to dress in suitable apparel, with modesty and self-control. Their adornment must not be with braided hair and gold or pearls or expensive clothing." He challenges them to not be consumed with expensive clothes like worldly women. It also would be a challenge to stay away from the provocative dress, so common in Roman culture, as it flaunted the beauty of the naked body.

265

As citizens of heaven, we must be different. We must always seek to keep our identity and not conform to the world. To the Romans, he said, "Do not be conformed to this present world, but be transformed by the renewing of your mind, so that you may test and approve what is the will of God—what is good and well-pleasing and perfect" (Rom 12:2). We must keep ourselves from being pressed into conformity by the world system. That is how citizens of heaven should live on this earth.

Observation Question: How does Paul describe the focus of a heavenly citizen?

> But our citizenship is in heaven—and we also eagerly await a savior from there, the Lord Jesus Christ, who will transform these humble bodies of ours into the likeness of his glorious body by means of that power by which he is able to subject all things to himself.
> Philippians 3:20-21

Heavenly citizens should be focused on their coming King. Paul says that as citizens of heaven we should eagerly await our Savior's coming. The phrase "eagerly wait for is strong language (in the original) to express the earnest expectation of something believed to be imminent. It means literally to thrust forward the head and neck as in anxious expectation of hearing or seeing something."[111] This should be our daily passion and our daily prayer, ushering in the second coming of Christ. Paul wrote this to Titus:

> For the grace of God has appeared, bringing salvation to all people. It trains us to reject godless ways and worldly desires and to live self-controlled, upright, and godly lives in the present age, as we wait for the happy fulfillment of our hope in the glorious appearing of our great God and Savior, Jesus Christ.
> Titus 2:11-13

Paul says, "we wait for the happy fulfillment of our hope in the glorious appearing of our great God and Savior, Jesus Christ." He said something similar in 1 Corinthians 1:7: "so that you do not lack any spiritual gift as you wait for the revelation of our Lord Jesus Christ." As citizens of heaven, we eagerly wait for our Lord Jesus Christ to be revealed.

One commentator said this about citizens waiting to see their sovereign:

> "The greatest event in any country on earth is a visit from its chief emperor. History records the most elaborate preparations and memorials for such an event. Special coins have been minted, commemorative stamps issued, and highways built. Looking forward

to the Coming of our Lord Jesus Christ is the highlight of Christian expectation. We should be dwelling daily in this thought of His return....Imagine how the residents in your neighborhood would feel if the President of the United States had announced that he was making a personal appearance in your community. I feel certain there would be some special preparations for his coming."[112]

I remember working as a Reserve chaplain in a Navy Hospital in Bethesda, Maryland. One day at work, the President of the United States visited the hospital to talk to our injured veterans. Before he came, there was a buzz around the hospital as people awaited his arrival. At his arrival, everything shut down. People couldn't leave the building; people couldn't come in. Everything stopped because the POTUS came. There should be something of this in the lives of every believer. We should have an eager expectation for our Lord. Our heads should be pressed forward looking up awaiting his imminent return. It is the event that we should anxiously await and continually seek as citizens of heaven.

If we are honest, many of us lack an eager expectation for our coming Savior. How do we develop it and maintain it?

Application Question: How do we develop and maintain this eager expectation for the coming of Christ?

1. We develop and maintain an eager expectation for the second coming by practicing daily obedience to his commands.

A servant who is not obedient doesn't want the master to return because of fear of judgment. It is the same with us. If we are not practicing holiness, we will not have an eager expectation for Christ to come. Worldliness will dampen the fires of our expectation.

2. We develop and maintain an eager expectation for the second coming by praying for it.

The Lord's Prayer contains a petition for the coming of Christ. When we pray, "may your kingdom come, may your will be done on earth as it is in heaven," essentially, we are praying for Christ's coming (Matt 6:10). It is at Christ's second coming that his kingdom will fully come to the earth. Therefore, we should literally pray this daily. We should pray for our Savior to come. In fact, many believe the prayer at the end of the book of Revelation is a petition for Christ to come. It says, "And the Spirit and the bride say, 'Come!' And let the one who hears say: 'Come!'" (Rev 22:17). Finally, Christ replies, "Yes, I am coming soon," and John, a citizen of heaven living on earth, said, "Amen! Come,

Lord Jesus" (Rev 22:20). This should be our daily prayer as well. The Spirit says come, the church says come, and the individual citizen says, "Come, Lord Jesus."

Are you praying for the coming of our Lord? Through prayer we develop an eager expectation.

3. We develop and maintain an eager expectation for the second coming by practicing the Lord's Supper.

Often we take the Lord's Supper and only think of Christ's death on the cross, but it is also meant to help us have an expectation of his second coming. Look at what Paul said: "For every time you eat this bread and drink the cup, you proclaim the Lord's death until he comes" (1 Corinthians 11:26). As we eat the bread and drink the cup, we are not only looking back at his death, but we are also looking forward to his coming. It is meant to help us say, "Come, Lord, come!"

4. We develop and maintain an eager expectation for the second coming by focusing on the benefits of his coming.

Paul describes two of these benefits in this passage. He says,

But our citizenship is in heaven—and we also eagerly await a savior from there, the Lord Jesus Christ, who will transform these humble bodies of ours into the likeness of his glorious body by means of that power by which he is able to subject all things to himself.
Philippians 3:20-21

Observation Question: What are two benefits of the second coming of Christ as mentioned in Philippians 3:21?

• When Christ comes, he will bring everything under his control.

The phrase "subject all things" means "to arrange in ranks."[113] It is military terminology. This is the very problem with society. Christ is not first. There is corruption in our governments, the education system, the health care system, and even in the church. However, at his coming, everything will ultimately submit to the authority of Christ. He will arrange everything into ranks—everything will submit to him and his Lordship. He will remove the curse from all creation. There will be no earthquakes and no tsunamis. There will be peace between animals and men. Those who do not profess Christ now will ultimately be made to submit to him. Paul said this in Philippians 2:9-11:

268

As a result God highly exalted him and gave him the name that is above every name, so that at the name of Jesus every knee will bow —in heaven and on earth and under the earth— and every tongue confess that Jesus Christ is Lord to the glory of God the Father.

Paul said that every knee would bow and every tongue confess that Jesus Christ is Lord to the glory of God. Everything in the universe, everything that is currently in a state of confusion and rebellion will arrange into ranks to give glory to Christ. When this happens, Christ will ultimately give all glory to the Father. First Corinthians 15:28 says, "And when all things are subjected to him, then the Son himself will be subjected to the one who subjected everything to him, so that God may be all in all." The Father exalts the Son to the highest place and the Son in return exalts the Father so that he may be "all in all." Amen.

As we focus on this reality, it should create an eager expectation in us. We should desire for Christ to be exalted throughout the earth and ultimately for God to be "all in all." Lord, let it be so.

- When Christ comes, he will make our lowly bodies like his glorious body.

It is at the second coming that Christ will transform our lowly bodies— our bodies of weakness, sickness, and infirmity— into a perfect resurrected body. We do not fully comprehend what this means or what this will look like. We do know that we will be without sickness, without sin, and that these bodies will be glorious. Paul gives us some understanding of the nature of our glorified bodies in 1 Corinthians 15. He says,

> But someone will say, "How are the dead raised? With what kind of body will they come?" Fool! What you sow will not come to life unless it dies. And what you sow is not the body that is to be, but a bare seed—perhaps of wheat or something else... It is the same with the resurrection of the dead. What is sown is perishable, what is raised is imperishable. It is sown in dishonor, it is raised in glory; it is sown in weakness, it is raised in power; it is sown a natural body, it is raised a spiritual body. If there is a natural body, there is also a spiritual body.
> 1 Corinthians 15:35-37, 42-44

He essentially describes it as a seed that is put into the ground and grows into a large, beautiful tree. He says that is the difference between our current lowly body and our future glorious body. They are comparable to the difference between a seed and a tree. They are sown perishable and raised imperishable. They are sown in dishonor and raised in glory. They are sown a natural body and raised a spiritual body. They will be glorious.

269

It has been my experience that as I continue through the aging process that I yearn more and more for the second coming and my new body. I handle many of my aches and pains by comforting myself with the fact that one day I will have a new body. One day I will not have knee problems, foot problems, back problems, etc. As we focus on the benefits of our King's coming—which are many—it helps create an eager expectation in us. We begin to say, "Lord, come. Lord, come."

Application Question: At what times have you most desired or had an eager expectation for the second coming of Christ? What are the benefits of maintaining this expectation?

Conclusion

How should we pursue spiritual maturity in Christ?

1. In Order to Pursue Spiritual Maturity, We Must Focus on Godly Models
2. In Order to Pursue Spiritual Maturity, We Must Recognize and Stay Away from Wrong Models
3. In Order to Pursue Spiritual Maturity, We Must Maintain a Heavenly Focus

Developing Spiritual Stability

So then, my brothers and sisters, dear friends whom I long to see, my joy and crown, stand in the Lord in this way, my dear friends! I appeal to Euodia and to Syntyche to agree in the Lord. Yes, I say also to you, true companion, help them. They have struggled together in the gospel ministry along with me and Clement and my other coworkers, whose names are in the book of life. Rejoice in the Lord always. Again I say, rejoice! Let everyone see your gentleness. The Lord is near!
Philippians 4:1-5 (NET)

How do we stand firm in the Lord? How do we develop spiritual stability? The lives of many believers are fraught with ups and downs. They are tossed here and there by the various trials and difficulties. Scripture describes spiritual infants and the double-minded as being tossed like the waves of the sea in Ephesians 4:14 and James 1:6. They are spiritually unstable. However, our faith in Christ should enable us to stand firm.

Paul in this text encourages the Philippians to "stand in the Lord," also translated "stand firm in the Lord" (Phil 4:1). This is not the first time Paul encouraged this church to stand. He said the same thing in chapter 1. He said,

Only conduct yourselves in a manner worthy of the gospel of Christ so that—whether I come and see you or whether I remain absent—I should hear that you are standing firm in one spirit, with one mind, by contending side by side for the faith of the gospel,
Philippians 1:27

Paul said whatever happens, they should stand firm in one spirit. Trials attacking the Philippians could cause them to give up ground to the enemy. They were being persecuted for their faith (Phil 1:29), people in the church were arguing and complaining (Phil 2:14), and false teachers were attacking the congregation (Phil 3:2). These difficulties could shake their faith in Christ. Still, Paul encourages them to stand firm. The word stand firm means to persist or preserve. "It is a picture of a soldier standing fast against the onslaught of an enemy."[114]

Scripture continually uses the metaphor of war for the Christian life. Peter said, "Dear friends, I urge you as foreigners and exiles to keep away from fleshly desires that do battle against the soul" (1 Peter 2:11). Peter described the believer as warring with his soul or flesh. Paul said in Romans 7, the things I would do, I don't do, and the things I wouldn't do, I do. Who can save me from this body of sin? Christians are in a war with the flesh—in a fight to be holy.

Christians are also in a war with the world. James said, "So whoever decides to be the world's friend makes himself God's enemy" (James 4:4). John said, "Do not love the world or the things in the world. If anyone loves the world, the love of the Father is not in him" (1 John 2:15). Paul said, "Do not be conformed to this present world, but be transformed by the renewing of your mind" (Romans 12:2). There is an enmity between the world and the people of God (cf. 1 John 3:13, Matt 10:22). There is a war of viewpoints, and at times there is persecution towards believers over these viewpoints and the lifestyle that comes from them. The world persecuted and killed Christ, and since then it has persecuted his followers.

However, our battle is not just in our flesh and with the world; it is also in the spiritual realm. Paul called for the Ephesian church to stand firm against the devil and his schemes. He said, "Clothe yourselves with the full armor of God so that you may be able to stand against the schemes of the devil" (Ephesians 6:11). The believer needs to stand firm because he is always under the attack of the enemy. He attacks one's mind, one's body, and one's family. Many things could cause the believer to become discouraged, to retreat, or to even give up on following Christ altogether.

As Paul closes the letter and says, "stand in the Lord in this way," he is reaffirming their need to stand firm amongst various attacks, and he shows them how to do so.

How can we stand firm? How can we hold our ground and not be tossed to and fro by the various hardships and difficulties of life. In Philippians 4:1-5, we will study principles about spiritual stability.

Big Question: What principles can we learn from Philippians 4:1-5 about standing firm in the Lord?

Spiritual Stability Is Developed by Pursuing Intimacy with Christ and Christlikeness

So then, my brothers and sisters, dear friends whom I long to see, my joy and crown, stand in the Lord in this way, my dear friends!
Philippians 4:1

272

Interpretation Question: What does it mean to stand firm in the Lord and how do we develop this in our lives?

The "so then" in this text points back to Philippians 3:10-21 as one of the ways that we stand firm in the Lord. There Paul described his desire to know Christ and the power of the resurrection, to have fellowship with his suffering, die like him, and one day be resurrected like him (v. 10-11). He described himself as "pressing" to take hold of that for which Christ took hold of him, and he called this his "one thing" in life (v. 12-13 NIV 1984). Paul saw himself in an athletic endeavor to know Christ and be just like him. Then in 3:17 Paul calls for the church to follow his example in pursuing Christ. Now in Philippians 4:1 he says this is how we should stand firm in the Lord.

Spiritual stability comes from a continual pursuit of knowing Christ. The Christian life has often been compared to walking up stream. If at some point you stop walking forward against the current of water, you will by necessity go backwards. The power of the current is too strong; it is impossible to stay in the same place. One will either go forwards or backwards. In order to stand firm, one must press against the current. It's the same spiritually; we must always press to know Christ more, like Paul. Knowing and being like him must be our one thing if we are going to develop spiritual stability in our lives. Otherwise, we will always be tossed to and fro like the waves of the sea, up and down in our spiritual lives.

We must stand firm "in the Lord." Proverbs 18:10 says, "The name of the Lord is like a strong tower; the righteous person runs to it and is set safely on high." Name in the Hebrew culture referred to somebody's characteristics or person. Essentially, the writer of the Proverb is saying that those who know the Lord and his person are safe. They are protected because of their knowledge of God. They are not tossed to and fro by the difficulties of life. The righteous understand that and therefore are always pursuing the knowledge of the Lord. They want to know and understand his name.

We can only be spiritually stable if we are growing in the knowledge of him. It is at the point when we are not growing that we are vulnerable. It is when we are not in the Word of God. It is when we are inconsistent in the fellowship of the church (where God is present), and it is when we are no longer growing into his image that we become spiritually unstable and more susceptible to the attacks of the enemy.

It is the sheep that are not close to the Shepherd that are most susceptible to the attacks of an enemy. It is the son who has left the protection of the Father's household—left the intimacy of the Father's hand—that is most prone to stumble and fall. Paul says this is how you stand firm in the Lord. If you are not growing and pursuing growth as your one thing, it is then that you are most prone to be taken captive by the enemy.

Paul describes POW's (prisoners of war) in 2 Timothy 2:24-26. He says,

> But be kind toward all, an apt teacher, patient, correcting opponents with gentleness. Perhaps God will grant them repentance and then knowledge of the truth and they will come to their senses and escape the devil's trap where they are held captive to do his will.

He describes them as not thinking correctly (come to their senses), trapped by the devil, and doing his will. Christians who find themselves in captivity, bound to their lusts, their pride, and other habitual sins are typically Christians who were not growing and Christ wasn't their one thing. This created a spiritual apathy and a lack of sensitivity to their conscience and the Holy Spirit which led them into the stronghold of the devil.

Spiritual growth is necessary to stand firm. Are you still growing in the Lord and in Christlikeness? If not, you are vulnerable to the enemy's attacks.

Application Question: In what ways have you experienced spiritual stability when growing in Christ? In what ways have you experienced being tossed to and fro with the trials of life when not growing?

Spiritual Stability Is Developed by Fostering Harmony in the Body of Christ

> I appeal to Euodia and to Syntyche to agree in the Lord. Yes, I say also to you, true companion, help them. They have struggled together in the gospel ministry along with me and Clement and my other coworkers, whose names are in the book of life.
> Philippians 4:2-3

The next thing needed for us to develop spiritual stability is to foster harmony in the body of Christ. In continuing the warfare metaphor associated with "stand firm," Satan is always trying to bring conflict in a marriage, a friendship, and a church. Jesus said, "no town or house divided against itself will stand" (cf. Matt 12:25), and Satan realizes that. He always seeks to bring division in the house of God so that it will fall. In fact, division gives him an open door to attack and speed up the destruction process. Ephesians 4:26-27 says, "Be angry and do not sin; do not let the sun go down on the cause of your anger. Do not give the devil an opportunity." Unresolved conflicts give the enemy an opportunity to attack a church—an opportunity to defeat and destroy it. This was happening in the church of Philippi with two women specifically.

274

Paul challenged two women, Euodia and Syntyche, to stand firm by agreeing with each other in the Lord. We are not sure exactly what the nature of their conflict was. However, it seemed to be of a personal nature instead of a doctrinal conflict. If it was doctrinal, Paul would have just explained the doctrine and said who was right. Something personal divided these two women.

Most likely, the conflict was affecting everybody in the church, and they may have separated into factions because of it. Throughout the letter Paul hinted at potential problems. He called for them to stand "firm in one spirit, with one mind, by contending side by side for the faith of the gospel" (1:27). This implies they were not contending side by side. In Philippians 2:2 he again encouraged them to be "united in spirit" and to have "one purpose." Finally, in Philippians 2:14 he called for the church to do all things without "grumbling or arguing." Again, the implication was that they were complaining and arguing and maybe the conflict between Euodia and Syntyche was the primary source of that tension.

Who were these women? All we know is that they were prominent women in this church. They were probably there when Paul started the church in Philippi (cf. Acts 16). Paul said these women had "contended at his side," as translated in the NIV 1984, for the cause of the gospel. "Contended at my side" is a gladiatorial term. It literally can be translated "fought side by side with me."[115] He also says that their names were written in the Book of Life. The Book of Life is where all the names of the redeemed are listed (cf. Daniel 12:1, Luke 10:20, Revelation 3:5). This means that these women weren't some carnal Christians causing problems in the church. They were warriors for Christ. While Paul was in Philippi, they faithfully fought by his side to present the gospel and possibly start the church there.

It is good for us to hear this because sometimes even well-meaning and devoted Christians have conflicts. Paul and Barnabas fought over the inclusion of Mark on a missionary journey (cf. Acts 15:36-39). It actually led them to split and go different ways. Sometimes our spiritual warriors, the spiritual elite, if we can call them that, fight amongst one another. This actually makes sense because it is the devoted Christians that really care. Caring about the lost, ministering to the poor, and discipling the saints is really important to them, and it is this passion that at times causes conflict. Sometimes their methods are different. Sometimes their personalities are very different. Sometimes their doctrine is different, and these differences can cause conflict among passionate people. People who really don't care aren't usually the ones who fight. This is more of a danger for passionate Christians.

Observation Question: How can we foster harmony in the church, especially amidst personal conflict as seen in Philippians 4:2-3?

1.   Believers foster harmony in the church by thinking like Christ.

Paul said, "I appeal to Euodia and to Syntyche to agree in the Lord." "To agree in the Lord" literally can be translated "think the same thing in the Lord"[116] or "to be of the same mind."[117]

What does he mean by this? This seems to point back to what he taught in Philippians 2:3-5. These women needed to develop the mind of Christ. If they thought the same way as Christ, then they could work out their conflict. Listen to what Paul said previously:

> Instead of being motivated by selfish ambition or vanity, each of you should, in humility, be moved to treat one another as more important than yourself. Each of you should be concerned not only about your own interests, but about the interests of others as well. You should have the same attitude toward one another that Christ Jesus had
> Philippians 2:3-5

The very thing that often causes conflict in our lives is "selfish ambition." It is the desire for our own way and for things to be done the way we think is best. However, the mind of Christ considers others first. Christ cared about the interests of God and others before his own. If we adopt the same mind, a servant's attitude (cf. Phil 2:7), then we can have harmony and unity in the church even amidst our various differences.

Do we consider others and their interest over our own? This is the secret to harmony and unity in the church. We must have the mind of Christ.

2. Believers foster harmony in the church by fixing their relationship with Christ.

"To agree in the Lord" also may infer that they needed to fix their relationship with Christ in order to agree with one another. John MacArthur said, "Paul knew that if they both got right with the Lord, they would be right with each other."[118] He calls them to "agree in the Lord."

This is the reality of most relational conflict. Relational conflict, and how we respond to it, is a picture of where our relationship with Christ is. The conflict shows us our selfishness. It shows us our lack of patience and our lack of love for others. Our relationship with others is a picture of our relationship with God. If our horizontal relationships are off then so is our vertical relationship. John said,

> If anyone says "I love God" and yet hates his fellow Christian, he is a liar, because the one who does not love his fellow Christian whom he has seen cannot love God whom he has not seen. And the

276

commandment we have from him is this: that the one who loves God should love his fellow Christian too.
1 John 4:20-21

John said it is impossible to love God and hate our fellow Christians. It is impossible to love God whom we have not seen, if we don't love Christians whom we see every day. He says emphatically that whoever loves God must also love his fellow Christian. The implication is that if one is in discord with another believer or hates him or her, one's relationship with God is not right. In the context of 1 John, hate and love are actually pictures of truly being saved or not according to 1 John 5:13. The very reason John wrote the book was to give assurance to those who believed in Christ. However, the principle is the same. Our earthly relationships reflect our heavenly relationship. Jesus said if we don't forgive others, God won't forgive us (Matt 6:15). To fix our heavenly relationship is therefore the key to fixing our earthly relationships and vice versa.

The way that we mend relationships is by first going into the secret place and meeting with Christ. He cares about the unity and harmony of his body, and it is from that relationship that we gain what is needed to agree in the Lord.

Often when I am sharp or impatient with my wife or daughter, it is very clear to me that I am not living in the Lord as I should. I don't have the peace, the patience, or the love that comes from abiding in him. The way for me to fix these relationships is to be with Christ (cf. John 15:5).

3. Believers foster harmony in the body of Christ by carrying the burdens of others.

Paul calls for a man named "companion" or "yokefellow" to help these two women agree in the Lord. We do not know who this man is, but since he was addressed in the letter, he obviously was known by the congregation. He must have been a prominent man and maybe one of the elders mentioned in Philippians 1:1.[119] The name in the Greek is actually "Suzugos." It is a word picture of two oxen yoked together carrying the same burden. Many commentators believe that the name should remain untranslated. Paul was using a play on his name. He calls him "true" or "loyal" yokefellow meaning that his character fit his birth name. In the same way that this man's name meant yokefellow, he should help these women resolve their conflict. The yoke was an instrument fitted around the neck of two oxen that attached to the plow. The yoke enabled the oxen to pull together and get the work done more quickly.[120] As Suzugos worked with these women, it would enable them to resolve their conflict speedily.

This is the same thing we should do as believers in order to have harmony in the church. Conflict in a congregation creates spiritual instability. It

277

opens the door for Satan's attacks; it affects everybody. Since we are the body of Christ, the problems of others affect us as well. If one part of the body is sick, the whole body is sick. Therefore, we have a responsibility to lovingly get involved with people in conflict so the body of Christ can remain stable and healthy. Paul said this in Galatians 6:2: "Carry one another's burdens, and in this way you will fulfill the law of Christ."

We must willingly take on the burdens of others in order to work for unity. This means praying for a couple struggling in their marriage—getting involved and showing the love of Christ. It means encouraging those who are down. Sometimes it even means getting other spiritual leaders involved so they can help carry the load. We are the body of Christ.

In the West, we have a very independent culture that often doesn't want to get involved in anybody else's life. However, this is not a biblical culture. Christ said, "Just as I have loved you, you also are to love one another" (John 13:34). This does not only mean that we need to be sacrificial in how we love. It means that we must teach the Word of God to one another as Christ did. That is one of the ways he loved us (cf. Eph 5:26). It means sometimes there is a need for admonishment. It means to carry one another's burdens and problems as Christ carries ours. That is what Paul called for this yokefellow to do. He called him to love these two women by helping them work through their conflict as Christ would.

If we are going to be spiritually stable, we must maintain harmony in the church. A soldier who fights by himself will not stand. We must work together if we are going to stand, and for that reason Satan always seeks to bring discord among congregations. We must stand by walking in harmony with the church.

Application Question: In what ways have you seen or experienced the enemy's attempts to destroy the church through conflict? In what ways is God calling you to work for harmony in a relationship or to be a yokefellow to others?

Spiritual Stability Is Developed by Maintaining Our Joy in the Lord

> Rejoice in the Lord always. Again I say, rejoice!
> Philippians 4:4

What else is needed to develop spiritual stability? Paul commands them to "Rejoice in the Lord always." In fact, he repeats the command for emphasis, "Again I say, rejoice!" (Phil 4:4). The repetition shows its importance. Satan is always seeking to attack our joy. He knows that a discouraged Christian is a vulnerable Christian. A discouraged Christian is a Christian that typically will not be active in serving Christ and others. They typically are too self-consumed.

278

Therefore, he works hard to bring discouragement and take away our joy. Nehemiah said, "the joy of the Lord is your strength" (Neh 8:10), and therefore, to not have joy means to be weak and vulnerable. In order for us to stand firm in the Lord, we must rejoice in him.

Some may find it strange to command an emotion. Many people look at an emotion as something that comes and goes as it pleases. They say things like, "I just fell in love. I couldn't help it." or "I really don't like that person, and I don't know why." But Scripture doesn't treat our emotions in the same way others do. They are treated as an act of the will, and that is why they are commanded. We are commanded to love our enemies, to be anxious for nothing, and here, we are commanded to rejoice.

How is it possible to rejoice always, especially when things are difficult?

It is good for us to remember the context of this letter. Christians were being persecuted throughout the Roman Empire, and Paul himself was in prison for the faith. He was awaiting a possible death sentence, and yet throughout the letter, he talks about his own joy despite his present circumstances. In Philippians 1:4, he says, "I always pray with joy in my every prayer for all of you." He experienced joy while praying for the Philippians. He said in Philippians 2:17-18, "But even if I am being poured out like a drink offering on the sacrifice and service of your faith, I am glad and rejoice together with all of you. And in the same way you also should be glad and rejoice together with me."

Many believe Paul was talking about his potential death when he referred to being poured out like a drink offering. Even if he died and his imprisonment was the end of his sacrifice for God, he said, "I am glad and rejoice with all of you." Doesn't that sound crazy? How can one have joy at the prospect of death?

Moreover, Paul commanded the Philippians to have this joy, despite their circumstances. They similarly were being persecuted for the faith. Paul said in Philippians 1:29 that it had been granted them by God to not only believe in Christ but also to suffer for him. At the founding of the Philippian church in Acts 16, Paul was imprisoned for serving Christ, and no doubt, some had suffered the same fate as him. Despite all that, he calls for the Philippians to rejoice.

How is it possible to always have joy regardless of our circumstances? It is only possible if our joy is in the Lord. For many their joy is based on circumstances. If life is good, they are joyful, but when life is bad, they lose their joy. Instead of being Christians that stand firm, they are up and down with every event in life. If we are going to stand firm, we must develop a joy that is constant, regardless of trial or persecution.

Application Question: How can we develop a joy in the Lord regardless of our circumstances?

1. We can have joy in the Lord as we get to know his person more.

Many Christians cannot have joy "in the Lord" because they don't know Christ well enough. Knowing God is much like any other relationship in the sense that we must develop it and foster it through intimacy. When you know God's characteristics, when you know his perfections, and you constantly think about them, it creates joy. But again, this is a problem for most Christians. We don't know God very well, and therefore, we don't think about him often. Remember how Job responded in the midst of his trials which included losing his wealth, his sons, and many other difficulties? He said,

"Naked I came from my mother's womb, and naked I will return there. The Lord gives, and the Lord takes away. May the name of the Lord be blessed!" In all this Job did not sin, nor did he charge God with moral impropriety.
Job 1:21-22

Job saw God as in control of everything that happened in life including bad things. He said the Lord gave and took away, and he praised him for it. He also never charged God with wrong. See, Job understood two major doctrines about God. He understood God's sovereignty and God's goodness. Scripture says that God works all things according to the counsel of his will (Eph 1:11). There is not one event God isn't in control of and that includes evil committed by men and Satan. However, Job also knew another characteristic of God and that is the fact that the Lord is good. James 1:17 says that every good and perfect gift comes from God. The Psalmist simply declares, "For the Lord is good. His loyal love endures, and he is faithful through all generations" (Psalm 100:5). God is good. In fact, he is the definition of good. That is why Job did not sin by charging God with wrongdoing. He saw no conflict in God being in control of the bad things that happened to him and God's goodness. For him, he must have thought, "In some way or another, even the bad things must work for the good."

See, some Christians, who don't know God well and don't understand his characteristics, become angry at God. They think he didn't do what was best, and unlike Job, they charge him with wrongdoing. They do this because they don't understand his goodness. They don't know his character. Others don't see God at all. All they see is the difficult boss, the corrupt government, or Satan, and therefore, they can't praise God. They have no comprehension of the sovereignty of God and his goodness in all things.

When you see God in control of all things—the job you have, the food you eat, the friends he gave you, and the trial that he allowed—then everything in life will make you look up. When you realize that the character of God is good

280

in everything, then not only will you know to look to God but also to worship, praise, and rejoice. David in Psalm 13:1 cried out, "How long, Lord, will you continue to ignore me? How long will you pay no attention to me?" However, in verse 5 he responded this way, "But I trust in your faithfulness. May I rejoice because of your deliverance." He could rejoice even in the waiting season because he knew God was eventually going to deliver and save him. He knew the character of God, and it caused him to rejoice.

Therefore, in order to rejoice in God, we must simply know him more. We should give great attention to studying his characteristics, his perfections, and his works throughout biblical history, and this will enable us to begin to have joy in every situation. We can have joy because we know the one who holds our past, our present, and our future. We can have joy because we know him.

2.   We can have joy in the Lord as a fruit of the Spirit.

One of the wonderful things about God's commands is that what he commands, he empowers us to do. Paul taught in Galatians 5:22 that the fruit of the Spirit is joy. He teaches us in Galatians 5:16 how to bear this fruit. He says, "But I say, live by the Spirit and you will not carry out the desires of the flesh." When we live in the Spirit or it can be translated "abide" in the Spirit, we will not gratify our sinful nature because of the fruit that is born in our life. When I obey the commands of the Spirit through the Word of God, when I am worshiping God through the work of the Holy Spirit, then the fruit of the Spirit is born in my life and one of them is joy.

This reality is very important for me as one who often struggled with depression in the past. I have to remember that the fruit of the Spirit is joy, and that the way I bear this fruit is by living in the Spirit. It is a reminder to me that as a believer my depression and discouragement is not a product of my circumstances, it is a product of me not making my home in the Spirit of God. I am not negating precipitating factors such as environment or physical issues, but Scripture promises this fruit regardless of our situation. When I first got married and I would start to get depressed, I would tell my wife that I needed to go "take a pill." What that meant was that I needed to go spend time in the Word of God, prayer, and worship so I could have joy. In order for us to rejoice in the Lord, we must make our home in his person. We must live in this relationship because as we abide, he gives us joy. He equips us to rejoice.

3.   We can have joy in the Lord as an act of obedience.

Again, "rejoice in the Lord" is a command. This means that God calls us to choose to rejoice no matter our circumstances. When a trial comes, somebody harms us, or something unpleasant happens, we have a decision to make. We can choose to be angry or to be depressed, or we can choose to respond to God in obedience. Joy is a choice. We can choose to reflect on God's sovereignty, God's goodness, and his wisdom, or we can choose to reflect on the storm, the person who hurt us, or the unknown. We make this choice every day. Focusing on God will bring joy. Focusing on the difficulties will bring worry, discouragement, anger, and depression. We must choose just like Paul did while in prison. He could have joy while on death row, and he called the Philippians, who also were suffering persecution, to do the same. He called them to make a choice to focus on God and trust him. We have the same choice. What will you choose?

Many Christians cannot stand firm because their joy is based on circumstances instead of their relationship with God. Circumstances are constantly changing, and therefore, it affords them no stability. Our joy must be based on a person that is unchanging. God's unchangeableness, or his immutability as theologians call it, is something that should give us joy (cf. James 1:17). He is not like us; we constantly change. However, God never changes, and therefore, as we know him and seek him, we can have joy. Are you rejoicing in the Lord? Are you living in intimacy with him? This relationship will keep us from being up and down like the waves of the sea. This relationship will enable us to stand firm.

Application Question: What are some things that constantly take away your joy? How is God calling you to develop joy in him despite your circumstances?

Spiritual Stability Is Developed by Practicing Gentleness to All

> Let everyone see your gentleness.
> Philippians 4:5a

Another thing we must do in order to stand firm in the storms and trials of life is develop the characteristic of "gentleness." Paul says, "Let everyone see your gentleness." This is one of the hardest words in the Greek to translate. In fact, there is no one English word that can fully express what this word means. One might even say that it is untranslatable. We can see this by the various words used to translate it. It has been translated "sweet reasonableness, generosity, goodwill, friendliness, magnanimity, charity toward the faults of others, mercy toward the failures of others, indulgence of the failures of others, leniency, bigheartedness, moderation, forbearance, and gentleness are some of the attempts to capture the rich meaning."[121] John MacArthur believes the best way to translate the word is "graciousness." [122] However, most commentators tend to agree that "either forbearance or gentleness is the better translation."[123]

Application Question: How do we let our gentleness be made known to everyone and how will this help us stand firm?

1. "Let everyone see your gentleness" means that we must be merciful towards others' faults.

A person that is vengeful and vindictive when harmed will never stand firm. Proverbs 25:28 describes an angry person as a "city that is broken down and without a wall." In ancient times, a city without walls was not only open for attack but ultimately for destruction. In the same way, a person that is constantly angry at people who hurt him or treat him badly will not stand. Their anger will ultimately lead to destruction.

Jesus was the ultimate gentle one (cf. Matt 11:29). When his enemies crucified him, he said, "Father, forgive them, for they don't know what they are doing" (Lk 23:34). He is also gentle in his response to our failures. He continually washes us with his blood so we can be in a right relationship with the Father (cf. 1 John 1:7, 9). He taught his followers to turn the other cheek instead of responding in wrath to wrong doings (cf. Matt 5:39). His gentleness allowed him to stand amidst constant attacks and also the failures of those he loved.

How do you respond when people hurt or mistreat you? Scripture says that instead of being harsh, you should let your gentleness—your forbearance—be made known to all. This will enable you to stand. Anger is destructive not only to those who are recipients of it but also for the person who harbors it.

2. "Let everyone see your gentleness" means that we must graciously serve others, especially those who hurt us.

Not only must we be gentle in response to those who hurt us, but we should also respond with graciousness and kindness. In America, we have something called a gentleman. He opens the door for those behind him so they can enter a building first. He pulls out a chair so a lady can sit down first. He serves others before he serves himself. He is a gentleman. In the same way, as Christians, everybody should be able to see our gentleness, especially those who harm and persecute us. Again, all this is given in the context of Euodia and Syntyche's conflict. Instead of holding a grudge toward one another, they should forgive and serve one another. This is what we should do as well. Listen to what Paul said in Romans 12:20-21:

> Rather, if your enemy is hungry, feed him; if he is thirsty, give him a drink; for in doing this you will be heaping burning coals on his head. Do not be overcome by evil, but overcome evil with good.

283

We must be gentle to all but especially to those who hurt us. We should feed them when they are hungry and give them something to drink when they are thirsty. We should overcome evil with good.

One of the ways we stand firm is not by fighting for our rights but giving up our rights and serving others. Jesus said, "Blessed are the meek, for they will inherit the earth" (Matt 5:5).

This is very relevant as persecution towards believers is growing rapidly throughout the world, and one day, according to Christ, we will be hated by all nations because of him (Matt 24:9). How can we stand? We stand by responding gently to those who hurt us and returning good for evil.

Application Question: How do you typically respond when mistreated? Why is gentleness important for spiritual stability? How is God calling you to develop gentleness?

Spiritual Stability Is Developed by Maintaining a Constant Awareness of the Lord

> The Lord is near!
> Philippians 4:5b

Next, Paul seems to give motivation or encouragement for being gentle to all and also for not being "anxious about anything" in the next verse (4:6). He says the Lord is near. However, this is not just a motivation for gentleness, but it is also necessary for us to foster if we are going to stand firm. We must develop a constant awareness of the Lord.

Interpretation Question: What does Paul mean by "the Lord is near" and how is that meant to encourage us to be gentle towards others, especially those who mistreat us?

1. "The Lord is near" could mean that the Lord is near in space.

This would encourage people suffering or being persecuted in several ways. Scripture says, "The Lord is near the brokenhearted; he delivers those who are discouraged" (Psalm 34:18). (a) God is near to comfort those who are hurting. (b) In addition, the Lord is near to empower them to serve those around them. Paul said this:

> But the Lord stood by me and strengthened me, so that through me the message would be fully proclaimed for all the Gentiles to hear. And so I was delivered from the lion's mouth!

284

2 Timothy 4:17

(c) It also could mean that he is present to defend and judge those who hurt them. Listen to what Paul said in Romans 12:18-19: "If possible, so far as it depends on you, live peaceably with all people. Do not avenge yourselves, dear friends, but give place to God's wrath, for it is written, 'Vengeance is mine, I will repay,' says the Lord."

Live at peace with everyone. God will fight your battles. He is near to fight for you. Your job is to be gracious and serve people (v. 12: 20-21). (d) Finally, it also could be a form of accountability. God is near to discipline us if we are not gentle and gracious to others. James uses God's presence as a form of accountability for the Hebrew Christians in the book of James. He said, "Do not grumble against one another, brothers and sisters, so that you may not be judged. See, the judge stands before the gates!" (James 5:9). If we grumble and complain in the midst of conflict and injustice, it could bring the discipline of God (cf. 1 Cor 10:10).

Certainly, God's nearness in space means all these things. We should be gentle to all because he is near to comfort us when we suffer, to empower us, to defend us, and even to judge us if we do wrong.

We must develop this awareness by practicing his presence. How is this done? Living in a state of prayer and thanksgiving is necessary for developing a sense of the Lord's presence and also thinking on the right things (Phil 4:6-9). This will help us be stable in life and not up and down with various events. Do you seek to live in a constant awareness of the Lord's presence?

2.   "The Lord is near" could mean that God is near in time.

This would be an encouragement by the fact that the second coming is near. When he comes, he will make all things right. In addition, we will be held accountable when our Master comes. Reward and loss of reward will occur based on our faithfulness (cf. Lk 12:42-48). Jesus gave this parable about his coming:

> The Lord replied, "Who then is the faithful and wise manager, whom the master puts in charge of his household servants, to give them their allowance of food at the proper time? Blessed is that slave whom his master finds at work when he returns. I tell you the truth, the master will put him in charge of all his possessions.
> Luke 12:42-44

Scholars who believe "the Lord is near" refers to the second coming, point to Philippians 3:20-21 in the previous chapter. Paul said:

But our citizenship is in heaven—and we also eagerly await a savior from there, the Lord Jesus Christ, who will transform these humble bodies of ours into the likeness of his glorious body by means of that power by which he is able to subject all things to himself.

However, since the text is ambiguous, it probably refers to both. The Lord is near both in space as his presence is always with us and in time as he is coming soon.[124] We must develop an awareness of Christ's presence if we are going to stand firm amidst the trials of life, and we must develop a sense of his immanency—our Lord could come at any moment.

Application Question: How do we develop or practice an awareness of Christ's presence throughout the day? How should this help us stand firm? In addition, how do we develop and maintain a sense of Christ's immanency—that he could come at any moment? How should that comfort and enable us to stand firm, regardless of our circumstances?

Conclusion

How do we stand firm amidst the various trials and temptations in life? Paul in this text calls for believers to stand firm.

1.   Spiritual Stability Is Developed by Pursuing Intimacy with Christ and Christlikeness
2.   Spiritual Stability Is Developed by Fostering Harmony in the Body of Christ
3.   Spiritual Stability Is Developed by Maintaining Our Joy in the Lord
4.   Spiritual Stability Is Developed by Practicing Gentleness
5.   Spiritual Stability Is Developed by Maintaining a Constant Awareness of the Lord

Developing Spiritual Stability Part Two

Do not be anxious about anything. Instead, in every situation, through prayer and petition with thanksgiving, tell your requests to God. And the peace of God that surpasses all understanding will guard your hearts and minds in Christ Jesus. Finally, brothers and sisters, whatever is true, whatever is worthy of respect, whatever is just, whatever is pure, whatever is lovely, whatever is commendable, if something is excellent or praiseworthy, think about these things. And what you learned and received and heard and saw in me, do these things. And the God of peace will be with you.
Philippians 4:6-9 (NET)

How do we stand firm in the Lord? How do we develop spiritual stability? Scripture describes the immature in Christ as being tossed back and forth like the waves of the sea and blown here and there like the wind (Eph 4:14, James 1:6). The enemy of our souls is always trying to discourage us, make us quit, and make us fall away from God. The spiritual life is a continual war (cf. Eph 6:11-12, 1 Peter 2:11, 1 John 3:13). How do we stand firm? At the end of Paul's epistle to the Philippians, he challenges them to stand firm and shows them how to. He says, "So then, my brothers and sisters, dear friends whom I long to see, my joy and crown, stand in the Lord in this way, my dear friends!" (Phil 4:1).

In Philippians 4:1-9, Paul teaches principles about spiritual stability. The first principles we looked at in Philippians 4:1-5 were:

1. Spiritual Stability Is Developed by Pursuing Intimacy with Christ and Christlikeness
2. Spiritual Stability Is Developed by Fostering Harmony in the Body of Christ
3. Spiritual Stability Is Developed by Maintaining Our Joy in the Lord
4. Spiritual Stability Is Developed by Practicing Gentleness
5. Spiritual Stability is Developed by Maintaining a Constant Awareness of the Lord

287

In Philippians 4:6-9, we will consider several more principles about spiritual stability in the believer's life.

Big Question: What principles about spiritual stability can be taken from Philippians 4:6-9 and how can they be applied practically?

Spiritual Stability Is Developed by Rejecting Anxious Thoughts

Do not be anxious about anything
Philippians 4:6

One of the ways we develop spiritual stability is by rejecting anxiety. The word "anxious" in the Greek means to be "drawn in opposite directions; divided into parts."[125] When we are anxious, our mind is divided. This is one of Satan's tactics that will keep us from standing firm in the Lord (Phil 4:1). We cannot stand firm in the Lord if we are divided. A house divided against itself will not stand and neither will a mind divided against itself. Satan uses anxiety to take our focus off Christ—our foundation (Eph 2:20). He aims to take our focus off Christ so that we cannot be effective in serving him or progressing in our spiritual lives.

Isn't this what we saw in the story of Peter walking on the water (Matt 14:22-33)? While Peter was focused on Christ, he walked on the water in the midst of a great storm. However, when he turned his eyes away from Christ to focus on the storm and the water, he began to sink. The text doesn't say that he became anxious, but we can be sure that's exactly what happened. He had a divided mind; the storm and his precarious predicament took his focus off Christ causing him to sink.

This happens to us daily. Trials, sickness, discord, and difficult circumstances at work or with family, all vie for our attention and focus. Satan wants us to play these scenarios over and over again in our mind so that we will be divided and therefore not stand in Christ. It's one of his secrets to defeat the Christian. If he can take his focus off Christ, then the Christian is vulnerable.

Application Question: Why is Satan so diligent in working to bring anxiety in the hearts of Christians? How does anxiety negatively affect our lives?

1. An anxious heart cannot worship God.

The Psalmist prayed, "give me an undivided heart, that I may fear your name" (Psalm 86:11, NIV 1984). Satan realizes a divided mind cannot worship. Many times I come into worship or prayer and I can't focus on God. My mind keeps drifting to the problems and anxieties of the day. We must have a unified heart to worship God, which is our greatest call in life. We are called to "love God with all our heart, mind, and soul."

2. An anxious heart will be ineffective in prayer.

James talked about the man who prays without faith. He said this:

But he must ask in faith without doubting, for the one who doubts is like a wave of the sea, blown and tossed around by the wind. For that person must not suppose that he will receive anything from the Lord, since he is a double-minded individual, unstable in all his ways.
James 1:6-8

This person cannot pray effectively because he is worrying—he is doubting God's faithfulness and care for him. This person is double-minded and therefore unstable like the waves of the sea. He should expect nothing from God. To worry is to essentially say, "God I don't trust you. You do not know what is best." Satan realizes if he can divide our mind and make us not trust God, it will limit the effectiveness of our prayers.

3. An anxious heart will make the Word of God ineffective in our lives.

Christ described the seed upon thorny ground as a person in whom the "worldly cares and the seductiveness of wealth choke the word, so it produces nothing" (Matt 13:22). The worrier cannot effectively receive the Word of God. The worries of this life choke the Word and make it unfruitful. Many read the Word of God and listen to sermons all day long, and yet, it is unproductive in their lives. It is unproductive because it is not received in faith. Instead of trusting God, they are consumed with the worries and the anxieties of life. It renders Scripture unfruitful and ineffective.

4. An anxious heart limits the work of God's power in our lives.

If anxiety severely affects our prayer and reception of the Word of God, then it goes without saying that it renders much of the power of God ineffective in our lives as well. As mentioned previously, it was when Peter started to worry while walking on the water—as he focused on the wind and the storms of life— that he began to sink. The very power that was operating in his life was rendered useless. It is the same with us. Worry saps us spiritually. It hinders our faith. A worrier will many times limit the display of God's power in his life.

5. An anxious heart will commonly cause physical ailments.

Doctors and psychologists would agree that anxiety actually causes the body to turn on itself. It is the cause of various sicknesses and ailments. Scripture would seem to support this. Proverbs 17:22 says, "A cheerful heart brings good healing, but a crushed spirit dries up the bones." If a cheerful and joyful disposition aids in the healing processes, then it just makes sense that a negative disposition, an anxious disposition, will increase or prolong sickness.

6. An anxious heart will lead us into sin.

If an anxious heart limits the ability for us to take part in God's grace, then it only makes sense that anxiety will lead us into many sins.

Application question: What types of sin will anxiety bring in the life of a believer?

*   Anxiety brings depression.

"Anxiety in a person's heart weighs him down, but an encouraging word brings him joy" (Proverbs 12:25).

*   Anxiety will cause us to make bad decisions.

When Abraham became anxious about having the child of promise, when he became tired of waiting on God, he took his calling into his own hands. He married his wife's slave girl, Hagar, which brought conflict into his family (Gen 16:3). If you will not trust and wait on God, anxiety will often lead you into hasty or wrong decisions that could have long term consequences. The son of the flesh, Ishmael, persecuted the son of the Spirit, Isaac (Gal 4:29). In fact, these people groups have been warring ever since as seen in the conflict between the Arabs and the Jews throughout history.

Similarly, many single people get into unhealthy dating relationships or marriages because they are not willing to wait on God. Their anxiousness leads them into bad decisions. Sometimes these anxious decisions have long term consequences.

Are you a worrier? Are you prone to anxiety?

Proverbs 3:5-6 says, "Trust in the Lord with all your heart, and do not rely on your own understanding. Acknowledge him in all your ways, and he will make your paths straight." We must learn how to trust him no matter what our circumstances, our heart, or others are saying. As long as we put him first, he will direct our paths. He will guide us. Christ told the disciples who were worrying about their future to "But above all pursue his kingdom and righteousness, and all these things will be given to you as well" (Matt 6:33). As long as we put him first, God will take care of all our needs. We don't have to worry. Isaiah 40:31

says that those who wait upon the Lord will renew their strength. If we are going to stand firm, we must reject anxiety and choose to trust God.

Application Question: What anxieties do you commonly struggle with? How is God calling you to reject the anxieties of life so that you can stand firm?

Spiritual Stability Is Developed by Constant Prayer

> Do not be anxious about anything. Instead, in every situation, through prayer and petition with thanksgiving, tell your requests to God. And the peace of God that surpasses all understanding will guard your hearts and minds in Christ Jesus.
> Philippians 4:6-7

How else do we develop spiritual stability? Paul teaches the Philippians who are suffering persecution for the faith (Phil 1:29), have false teachers in the church (3:2), and are also having a major conflict between two women (4:2) that they must learn to pray in everything. He says, "Instead, in every situation, through prayer and petition with thanksgiving, tell your requests to God."

The very reason many of us are constantly shaken by the various events that happen in our lives is because we are not constant in prayer. For many of us, it is the hardships of life that draw us into prayer, but when things are going well, we are prayerless. Paul said this to the Thessalonian church: "constantly pray, in everything give thanks. For this is God's will for you in Christ Jesus" (1 Thess 5:17-18).

It is those who have learned the discipline of constant prayer who will be able to stand in the midst of trials. In fact, after teaching the Ephesians to put on the armor of God in order to stand against the attacks of Satan, Paul said, "With every prayer and petition, pray at all times in the Spirit, and to this end be alert, with all perseverance and requests for all the saints" (Eph 6:18). He said if we are going to stand firm against the attacks of Satan, we must pray "at all times… with all perseverance and requests for all the saints." Spiritual warfare is done in the atmosphere of prayer.

Have you developed the discipline of constant prayer? It is necessary in order to stand firm.

Observation Question: What are the three types of prayer that Paul mentions and what do they represent?

1. Paul says that in every situation we should have "prayer."

The word "prayer" in verse 6 is a general word for prayer. However, in this context it probably means more than that since it is listed beside other types of prayer. It seems to refer to "special times of prayer that we share in periods of devotion and worship."[126] We must constantly adore and worship God throughout the day, talk to him, and share our innermost secrets with him. To pray means to live in a sense of awe and worship of God throughout the day.

2. Paul says that in every situation we should have "petition."

Petition, or it can be translated "supplication," means to have "an earnest sharing of our needs and problems"[127] with God. Peter said to cast all our cares [anxieties] before the Lord because he cares for us (1 Peter 5:7 paraphrase). Many times Christians only feel the need to bring their big problems before God and not their small ones. Paul says we should have supplication in everything. God wants to know our anxieties, our worries, our doubts, our joys, and the things that excite us. He wants us to lay them all down before him. Jesus taught us in the Lord's Prayer to ask for "our daily bread" (Matt 6:11). He wants us to bring our daily needs before him. Our God cares that much for us. In everything we must bring our petitions before the Lord.

James said that we do not have because we do not ask (4:2). Many cannot stand because they don't constantly bring their petitions before God. They feel sufficient in themselves for certain tasks and therefore do not feel the need to bother God. But it is this independence that actually weakens them. They may consider their independence a strength, but in fact, it is their weakness. Christ said this to the church of Laodicea as a rebuke: "Because you say, 'I am rich and have acquired great wealth, and need nothing,' but do not realize that you are wretched, pitiful, poor, blind, and naked" (Revelation 3:17). Their lack of dependence upon God was their weakness. They thought that they needed nothing from him, or at least they lived that way practically. However, it is when we recognize our weakness and dependency that God's strength is truly displayed. Paul said this:

> But he said to me, "My grace is enough for you, for my power is made perfect in weakness." So then, I will boast most gladly about my weaknesses, so that the power of Christ may reside in me. Therefore I am content with weaknesses, with insults, with troubles, with persecutions and difficulties for the sake of Christ, for whenever I am weak, then I am strong.
> 2 Corinthians 12:9-10

Are you constantly bringing your needs and cares before the Lord? Or are you independent—virtually living as though you don't need him? It is those who depend upon God who will stand. The independent will not stand in the trials of life. They rely too much on their strength. We must constantly bring our petitions before the Lord.

3. Paul says that in every situation we should give "thanksgiving."

This may be the hardest aspect of prayer—thanksgiving. We must give thanks in everything. Christ told the story of ten lepers who wanted healing. He sent them to show themselves to the priest. While on the way, they all were miraculously healed. However, only one of them, a Samaritan, came back to tell Christ, "Thank you" (Luke 17:11-19). Many times we are just like the lepers. God saved us and daily provides for us, but we often forget to say, "Thank you." Personally, I am constantly convicted of this. I will pray for grace for a sermon, an important meeting, or something dealing with my future, and when God answers my prayer, I forget to thank him. Many of us are just like the nine lepers. We fail to give God thanks for his continual blessings.

This is a secret to standing firm. We must develop a spirit of thanksgiving. This is not only true for when God blesses us but also for the trials of life. Again, Paul said "in every situation." We must learn how to give thanks even in the midst of the storm. This is exactly what we saw in the story of Job. After he lost his family and his career, he cried out, "The Lord gives, and the Lord takes away. May the name of the Lord be blessed" (Job 1:21). Job gave thanks in every situation and that allowed him to stand amidst the attacks of Satan and the trials of life.

How often do you give God thanks? Do you give him thanks every day and in every situation? This is a necessary discipline that will help us stand firm in the Lord. On the reverse, a grumbler and complainer will not stand. In fact, grumbling and complaining will only bring the discipline of God in our lives and make our situation worse. Listen to what Paul said to the Corinthians:

> And let us not put Christ to the test, as some of them did, and were destroyed by snakes. And do not complain, as some of them did, and were killed by the destroying angel. These things happened to them as examples and were written for our instruction, on whom the ends of the ages have come.
> 1 Corinthians 10:9-11

If we are going to stand, we cannot grumble and complain. We must instead be full of thanksgiving. It is in thanksgiving that God's grace becomes available to us. His grace is upon the thankful believer, and his discipline is upon the grumbler and complainer.

In order to live in prayer, we must start to see God's hand in every situation and his hand must prompt us to prayer—adoration and praise. It must draw us to petition for our needs and the needs of others, and ultimately it must draw us to thanksgiving.

Observation Question: What is the result of a lifestyle that rejects anxiety and instead lives in prayer (Phil 4:6-7)?

Philippians 4:7 says, "And the peace of God that surpasses all understanding will guard your hearts and minds in Christ Jesus."

Paul promises that the peace of God that transcends all understanding will guard our hearts and minds in Christ Jesus. John MacArthur said this about the phrase "will guard":

> Phroureō (will guard) is a military term used of soldiers on guard duty. The picture would have been familiar to the Philippians, since the Romans stationed troops in Philippi to protect their interests in that part of the world. Just as soldiers guard and protect a city, so God's peace guards and protects believers who confidently trust in Him.[128]

Interpretation Question: What does Paul mean by the peace that transcends all understanding?

What is the peace of God? Scripture says that when we accept Christ as our Savior, we have "peace with God." Romans 5:1 says, "Therefore, since we have been declared righteous by faith, we have peace with God through our Lord Jesus Christ." We were once enemies of God because of our sin and rebellion, but now because of Christ, we have a right relationship with him. We are no longer enemies but friends and sons of God. We have the Spirit of God in us, and he makes us cry "Abba, Father" (Rom 8:15).

However, not only has our relationship with Christ given us peace with God, Christ has also given us the ability to have the "peace of God." This is an inward peace of heart and mind regardless of the storms of life. Jesus said in John 14:27, "Peace I leave with you; my peace I give to you; I do not give it to you as the world does. Do not let your hearts be distressed or lacking in courage." One of the inheritances of every believer that Christ left us is the very peace he had while on the earth. This was the peace that allowed him to sleep while a storm threatened to destroy the boat he and the disciples were sailing in (Lk 8:23-25). This was the peace that enabled him to go to the cross and endure the suffering. He had a settled peace and confidence in God. He knew that God was ultimately in control. He cried out, "Then Jesus, calling out with a loud voice, said, 'Father, into your hands I commit my spirit!' And after he said this he breathed his last" (Lk 23:46). He invested his life and death into the hands of God, and this gave him peace. This is the very peace we can always have, no matter our circumstances. In fact, we are called to let this peace rule in our hearts. Colossians 3:15 says, "Let the peace of Christ be in control in your heart (for you were in fact called as one body to this peace), and be thankful." Again, this peace comes as we refuse to be anxious and live in constant prayer. When we do this, the peace that passes all understanding will guard our hearts and minds.

What does Paul mean when he says this peace passes all understanding? This means that the peace God gives does not make any sense, and it is beyond human understanding. How could Paul, who was in prison and on death row, write a letter about joy to the Philippians? How could he say in the opening of the letter that he always prays with joy when he thinks about the Philippians (1:4)? Any normal person would be full of anxiety while on death row. The only reason this was possible is because he had the peace of God that passes all understanding. Others will not understand it, and when we have it and are letting it rule in our lives, sometimes we won't understand it. We will say to ourselves, "Why am I not angry about this situation? Why am I not worrying?" The reason is because we put ourselves in an atmosphere where God's peace could rule our hearts. We rejected anxiety and lived in prayer. It is there where God sends this supernatural soldier named "Peace" to guard our hearts. And it is in this peace that we are commanded to stay. We must let it rule in our hearts at all times. We should always check our hearts by asking ourselves, "Do I have peace? If not, why not? What is God calling me to do in order to live in his peace and let it rule?"

Is peace ruling your heart (emotions) and your mind (thoughts)? Peace is a promise to those who choose not to be anxious and instead choose to live in prayer.

Application Question: Have you ever experienced the peace that surpasses all understanding? When did you experience the most peace of God in your life? How is God calling you to cultivate this peace and let it rule in your life?

Spiritual Stability Is Developed by Right Thinking

> Finally, brothers and sisters, whatever is true, whatever is worthy of respect, whatever is just, whatever is pure, whatever is lovely, whatever is commendable, if something is excellent or praiseworthy, think about these things. And what you learned and received and heard and saw in me, do these things. And the God of peace will be with you
> Philippians 4:8-9

Next, Paul teaches that we must have right thinking if we are going to stand firm in the Lord. "The word finally indicates that Paul has arrived at the climax of his teaching on spiritual stability. The principle that he is about to relate is both the summation of all the others and the key to implementing them."[129]

Satan's primary place of attack is the mind—the thoughts of a believer. At times he attacks the body and other times he works through other circumstances, but even in these attacks, he always prioritizes the mind. He does so because the mind affects the feet—how one lives. Proverbs 23:7 in the NASB says, "For as he thinks in himself so he is." Scripture says that whatever we continually think on is what we are or what we will become. We become what we think on, and Satan realizes this. If we continually meditate on music or TV shows that teach sexual immorality, rebellion towards authorities, the pursuit of money and power, anger, or murder, then we will become like these things. This is scary considering the fact that most Christians watch the same TV shows, the same movies, and listen to the same music that the world listens to. No wonder most Christians look no different from the world. When they think on the same content the world does, it creates a lifestyle that is sub-Christian. These believers will virtually become just like the world. Therefore, the enemy continually seeks to bombard the mind of each believer with ungodly thoughts that will affect how they live and who they will become.

With these things in mind, Paul calls believers to continually think on right things. He gives a list of qualities that should dominate the thought life of every believer if they are to stand firm. The word "think" is the word "Logizomai." "It means 'to evaluate,' 'to consider,' or 'to calculate.'"[130] It is the word "from which we get the mathematical word logarithm. Paul commands the same deliberate, prolonged contemplation of these virtues that it takes to weigh a mathematical problem."[131] The believer is not called to passive thinking but to active thinking, where he is not only testing each thought but rejecting bad thoughts. This is how a person becomes anxious for nothing. Like one calculating a math problem, they know that worry, anger, insecurity, or depressive thoughts are not the right answer, and therefore, they reject them. But they also reject many other thoughts. Paul says in 2 Corinthians 10:5 that in our warfare, the battle of the mind, we must "take every thought captive to make it obey Christ."

Interpretation Question: What does Paul mean by thinking on, "Finally, brothers and sisters, whatever is true, whatever is worthy of respect, whatever is just, whatever is pure, whatever is lovely, whatever is commendable, if something is excellent or praiseworthy"?

Sometimes the best way to understand something is to ask the question, "What is the opposite of it?"

1. To think on what is true means to reject what is false. If it does not align with the teaching of Scripture which is truth (John 17:17), if it does not align with the person of Christ who is the truth (John 14:6), then we should not meditate on it.

296

2. To think on whatever is worthy of respect, or it can be translated honorable, means to reject what is dishonorable. If it dishonors God or others, then we should not think on it.

3. To think on what is just means to reject what is unjust or wrong. The word "just" can also be translated "righteous." If it propagates sin and ungodliness, then we should not meditate on it.

4. To think on what is pure means to reject anything that is mixed. In 1 Timothy 5:22 (NASB), the same word is translated "free from sin."[132] A lot of what we are exposed to is a mixed bag of evil and good. That is how Satan works. He puts enough truth in a lie that many believers will welcome it into their homes and eventually into their hearts.

5. To think on what is lovely means to reject what is unlovely or unattractive. A lot of what our minds focus on is full of the ugliness of the world instead of what reflects the beauty of God.

6. To think on what is commendable means to reject what is not commendable or admirable. This means if we wouldn't brag about it or recommend it to others, or rather if God wouldn't brag about it or recommend it (cf. Job 1:8), then we shouldn't think on it. We should always ask ourselves, "Would God recommend this?"

As a summary of these six qualities, Paul says, "if something is excellent or praiseworthy, think about these things." Believers should only think on what is best for them and others spiritually.

Therefore, believers must continually guard their hearts (Prov 4:23). How many Christians have been destroyed in part because of the music they listened to? They may have been unaware of it, but it was part of the process of leading them into sexual immorality. It was part of the process of changing their language. It was part of the process of leading them into depression or away from God and his Word. How many have been detrimentally affected by the movies they watch, the books they read, and the conversations they entertain? If we are going to stand firm, we must guard our minds.

David said this in Psalm 1:1, "How blessed is the one who does not follow the advice of the wicked, or stand in the pathway with sinners, or sit in the assembly of scoffers." David essentially says the beginning of losing the blessing of God begins with what we are listening to—the advice of the wicked. For many of us we need to be violent in the removal of what is ungodly in our lives. Christ said this: "If your right eye causes you to sin, tear it out and throw it away! It is better to lose one of your members than to have your whole body thrown into hell" (Matthew 5:29). The eye is the doorway to the mind. Christ said if your eye causes you to sin pluck it out. Get rid of the TV, throw away CD's and the DVD's, turn off the Wi-Fi, stop hanging around certain people, do whatever it takes to keep a pure mind. Are you willing to be violent in order to be holy and have the blessing of God on your life? As we will see later, the blessing of God for a godly mind is his very presence (Phil 4:9).

What do you continually think on? Are you thinking on what is godly or ungodly? There are consequences to our thinking.

Observation Question: How do we think on things that have the godly virtues that Paul mentioned so that we can stand firm in the Lord?

"And what you learned and received and heard and saw in me..." (Philippians 4:9).

1.   We think on right things by thinking on God's Word.

Paul says, "what you learned and received and heard and saw in me" (v. 9). This undoubtedly is referring to what they learned from his teachings in person and specifically the letter to the Philippians. If we are going to have right thinking, it must be thinking saturated with the Word of God. We should listen to it, study it, memorize it, and teach it. When Christ was tempted by Satan in the wilderness, he confronted every lie with the Word of God (Matt 4:1-11). David said, "In my heart I store up your words, so I might not sin against you" (Psalm 119:11). In the same way, we will not be able to stand if God's Word is not hidden in our hearts. If we are not memorizing and meditating on it, we will not stand.

David described the man who meditates on the Word of God day and night like a tree planted by the river. Its leaves are evergreen, and it produces fruit in its season (Psalm 1:2-3). The leaves do not fade because of the constant nourishment and strength that comes from the nearby water system. During a storm, the tree will stand because of its deep roots. Trees can live for hundreds of years. They stand through the storms, and that is a picture of people who live in the Word of God. They stand and produce fruit, even in the storms of life.

2.   We think on right things by thinking on the godly examples God has given us.

Paul says whatever you have "seen in me." The Philippians saw Paul personally when he started the church in Acts 16, but they also saw his example through the letter (Phil 3:17). He was a man who rejoiced even while in prison (cf. Phil 1:4, 2:17-18). He was a man consumed with knowing Christ and being like him (Phil 4:10-12). Christ was his one thing (Phil 3:10-16). In fact, he called for the Philippians to follow his example (Phil 3:17).

298

By walking with and keeping our eyes on godly Christians, we will find that those relationships enable us to stand firm in the Lord. "As iron sharpens iron, so a person sharpens his friend" (Prov 27:17). We stand firm by focusing on godly examples.

But it also must be said that bad examples will keep us from standing (Prov 13:20). Paul said, "Bad company corrupts good morals" (1 Cor 15:33). The enemy is aware of this as well. Therefore, he ardently seeks to destroy generations through the bad models he propagates in the media. The media frequently promotes movie stars, rock stars, or professional athletes who are committing adultery or getting a divorce. They are continually shown partying, getting drunk, or using drugs, and these are the examples daily promoted in our societies. Many of them have their own reality TV shows. Satan knows that if he can fill people's minds with these ungodly examples, he can lead people to destruction. Therefore, as Christians, we must reject bad examples and focus on godly ones.

What godly examples are you keeping your eyes on? The writer of Hebrews said this about the godly examples in Scripture:

> Therefore, since we are surrounded by such a great cloud of witnesses, we must get rid of every weight and the sin that clings so closely, and run with endurance the race set out for us.
> Hebrews 12:1

The great cloud of witnesses refers to the many great men and women of faith in Hebrews chapter 11. By looking at their lives, by continually thinking on Abraham, Moses, Joseph, and others, we will find the ability to persevere in the race marked out before us and also get rid of everything that holds us back. We must consider and think on godly examples if we are going to stand firm.

Application Question: In what ways is God calling you to change your thinking in order to think on godly things and godly models? What makes this discipline of godly thinking so difficult? Who are the godly models God is calling you to think on?

Spiritual Stability Is Developed by Right Practice

> And what you learned and received and heard and saw in me, do these things. And the God of peace will be with you.
> Philippians 4:9

After calling the believers to think on godly things, he commanded them to put the godly truths or principles into practice. It is not enough to simply think on or listen to right things; we must practice them if we are going to stand. Christ taught the same thing. At the end of the Sermon on the Mount, he described a person who listened and obeyed his teachings and another who only listened. He described the person who heard and practiced his teachings as the one who built his house on the rock, and when the storms came, the house stood. However, he described the one who simply listened as building his house on the sand, and when the storm came, the destruction was great (Matt 7:24-27). In order to stand in the storms of life, we must practice holiness. We must be doers of God's Word and not hearers only deceiving ourselves (James 1:22). Are you building on the rock of Christ's Word?

Paul calls for the believers to put into practice the righteous virtues they should be thinking on. Paul had given them a model of right thinking in his teachings and his living. The word "do" can also be translated "practice." It "refers to repetition or continuous action. The English word 'practice' can have the same connotation. We speak of a lawyer or a doctor as having a practice because their profession maintains a normal routine. Christians are to make it their practice to lead godly, obedient lives."[133]

The believer is not only to have orthodoxy but orthopraxy—right thinking and right practice. This must be his daily endeavor. They must develop a consistent walk of righteousness in order to stand. This is important because Satan always looks for little compromises in the believer's life in order to destroy him. This is why in Ephesians 6:14 Paul calls for believers to put on the breastplate of righteousness in order to stand against the attacks of the enemy. Compromise in the life of a believer can ultimately lead to his destruction. We protect ourselves by daily practicing righteousness and opening no doors for sin.

In fact, Paul says that righteous thinking and righteous living will lead to the very presence of God. He says the "God of peace" will be with us when we practice right thinking and right practice. God's manifest presence will not be with those who continually think on ungodly things—those whose thinking is worldly. God's presence will not be with those who continually practice sin. However, his manifest presence is with those who both think on and practice righteousness. His presence is there to strengthen and encourage them. Listen to what Paul shared about his experience of God's presence in the midst of his trial.

> At my first defense no one appeared in my support; instead they all deserted me—may they not be held accountable for it. But the Lord stood by me and strengthened me, so that through me the message would be fully proclaimed for all the Gentiles to hear. And so I was delivered from the lion's mouth.
> 2 Timothy 4:16-17

When everybody else had left him while imprisoned in Rome, God's presence was with him to stand firm and preach for Christ. That was Paul's desire for the Philippians. If they were going to stand firm amidst the persecution they were encountering (Phil 1:29), the false teaching that had entered the church (3:2), and the discord threatening to divide them (4:2), they needed God's manifest presence to strengthen them. This presence only comes to those who practice right thinking and right living.

Beloved, this is how we stand firm in the Lord. Are you living a faithful Christian life? Are you putting your faith into practice? If not, you will not be able to stand.

Application Question: How would you describe your experience with the "presence" of God? Are there times when you have felt nearer or farther away from him? What seems to affect those seasons?

Conclusion

How can Christians faithfully stand in the Lord? How can we stand against the attacks of the enemy and no longer be tossed to and fro like the waves of the sea? In Philippians 4:1-9, Paul teaches us truths about spiritual stability.

1. Spiritual Stability Is Developed by Pursuing Intimacy with Christ and Christlikeness
2. Spiritual Stability Is Developed by Fostering Harmony in the Body of Christ
3. Spiritual Stability Is Developed by Maintaining Our Joy in the Lord
4. Spiritual Stability Is Developed by Practicing Gentleness
5. Spiritual Stability is Developed by Maintaining a Constant Awareness of the Lord
6. Spiritual Stability Is Developed by Rejecting Anxious Thoughts
7. Spiritual Stability Is Developed by Constant Prayer
8. Spiritual Stability Is Developed by Right Thinking
9. Spiritual Stability Is Developed by Right Practice

The Right Perspective on Supporting Missions

I have great joy in the Lord because now at last you have again expressed your concern for me. (Now I know you were concerned before but had no opportunity to do anything.) I am not saying this because I am in need, for I have learned to be content in any circumstance. I have experienced times of need and times of abundance. In any and every circumstance I have learned the secret of contentment, whether I go satisfied or hungry, have plenty or nothing. I am able to do all things through the one who strengthens me. Nevertheless, you did well to share with me in my trouble. And as you Philippians know, at the beginning of my gospel ministry, when I left Macedonia, no church shared with me in this matter of giving and receiving except you alone. For even in Thessalonica on more than one occasion you sent something for my need. I do not say this because I am seeking a gift. Rather, I seek the credit that abounds to your account. For I have received everything, and I have plenty. I have all I need because I received from Epaphroditus what you sent—a fragrant offering, an acceptable sacrifice, very pleasing to God. And my God will supply your every need according to his glorious riches in Christ Jesus. May glory be given to God our Father forever and ever. Amen. Give greetings to all the saints in Christ Jesus. The brothers with me here send greetings. All the saints greet you, especially those who belong to Caesar's household. The grace of the Lord Jesus Christ be with your spirit.
Philippians 4:10-23 (NET)

What is the right perspective to have in supporting missions?

Scripture teaches that we are all called to be missionaries whether we serve in missions at home or abroad. We all are called to go throughout the world and make disciples (Matt 28:19). However, many of us have wrong perspectives on supporting missions. Some may feel like they are not called to support missions. Some feel like giving to missions is a burden. Some feel ashamed about raising funds for missions, and some will not consider going simply because they lack finances. All of these are wrong perspectives on missions that hinder God's great work. As we look at Paul's final words to the Philippians, we learn a great deal about a proper perspective on supporting missions as he speaks about how they supported him in the past and also while imprisoned in Rome.

It is good for us to remember that God has chosen to do the work of missions through the financial support of faithful saints. When God sent his Son to do the work of missions on the earth, he chose to provide for him through the faithful financial support of others. Luke 8:3 says this: "and Joanna the wife of Cuza (Herod's household manager), Susanna, and many others who provided for them out of their own resources."

Christ was provided for through the faithful support of others and specifically through women, who had a low standing in that society. Similarly, when God sent Elijah to Sidon, he commanded a widow to provide for him there (1 Kings 17:9). When God called for Nehemiah to rebuild the walls around Jerusalem, God gave him favor with the Persian king to pay for it (Nehemiah 2). Even here in this text, Paul was being supported by the Philippians who were extremely poor as seen in 2 Corinthians 8:1-2.

> Now we make known to you, brothers and sisters, the grace of God given to the churches of Macedonia, that during a severe ordeal of suffering, their abundant joy and their extreme poverty have overflowed in the wealth of their generosity.

What is a proper perspective on supporting missions? How can we have the right heart and mindset in supporting others? How can we have the right heart in seeking support? God may be calling many people to missions, but they will not go simply because of finances. God is bigger than our finances. God owns the cattle on a thousand hills (Psalm 50:10). The main thing we must discern is if God has called us to go.

In this text, we see the end of Paul's letter to the Philippians, and also, Paul's great joy in their support of him while in prison. As we look at this text, we learn principles about what a right perspective is on supporting missions. As we go through this, we must ask ourselves, "Do I have a right perspective on supporting missions?" And, if not, "How can I have a more biblical perspective and practice on giving or receiving support for missions?"

Big Question: What principles can we learn about giving to missions in Philippians 4:10-21?

Our Giving to Missions Must Continually Be Renewed

> I have great joy in the Lord because now at last you have again expressed your concern for me. (Now I know you were concerned before but had no opportunity to do anything.).
> Philippians 4:10

Paul said that he rejoiced greatly in the Lord because of the Philippians' renewal of concern and support for him. While Paul was in Rome under house arrest, the Philippians sent Epaphroditus who supplied Paul with basic living subsistence, as the prison system did not provide food, clothing, or money. The phrase "again expressed," or it can be translated "renewed" (NIV 1984), is horticultural terminology used of a flower or tree budding or blossoming.[134] It seems that the Philippians had not supported him for some extended time period; some believe it had been nearly ten years. [135] They were concerned for him but had no opportunity to show it. Maybe it was because of the extreme poverty they were suffering (cf. 2 Cor 8:1-2), Paul's great distance, or their lack of understanding what his needs were. Either way, they had ceased to support him in the work of ministry for some amount of time, and they had just renewed it. For this reason, Paul greatly rejoiced.

Similar to the Philippians, our giving should continually be renewed like a flower in blossom as well. For many Christians, they give their monthly tithe and feel no need to blossom, no need to excel in the work of giving. However, this is a wrong understanding of giving. In fact, the New Testament never commands the tithe and continually states how we are no longer under the law (cf. Gal 3:24-25, Rom 6:14). Paul actually teaches in 1 Corinthians 16:1-2 about how to give weekly. There he says it should be given in keeping with our income or as God prospers us (v. 2). Look at what he said:

> Now concerning the collection for the saints: as I directed the churches of Galatia, so you also are to do. On the first day of every week, each of you is to put something aside and store it up, as he may prosper, so that there will be no collecting when I come. (ESV)

In contrast to simply giving our tithe every week, New Testament giving must continually be renewed. In fact, we are commanded to excel in it. Consider what Paul said in 2 Corinthians 8:7: "But as you excel in everything—in faith, in speech, in knowledge, and in all eagerness and in the love from us that is in you—make sure that you excel in this act of kindness too."

Paul says we must seek to excel in giving in the same way we seek to excel in faith, speech, knowledge (of God and Scripture), and love. Our giving must continually be renewed before the Lord, especially as the Lord prospers us or we encounter the needs of others.

We serve a God that gave all he had. He gave his only begotten Son, and his Son, Jesus Christ, gave his life for the sins of the world. If we are growing more into his image, then there will be great feats of sacrificial giving happening in our lives as well. Paul rejoiced at their renewal of giving.

Is your giving blossoming as well?

Application Question: What is the difference between the concept of the tithe and New Testament grace giving (cf. 2 Cor 8:7)? Do you believe Christians are still under the tithe? Why or why not? In what ways has God been challenging you to grow in being a giver? What makes giving difficult?

Our Giving to Missions Should be a Ministry of Great Joy

> I have great joy in the Lord because now at last you have again expressed your concern for me. (Now I know you were concerned before but had no opportunity to do anything.).
> Philippians 4:10

We must also notice Paul's great joy in their giving. Now some might say his joy makes perfect sense. Of course he is joyful; the Philippians are helping him out. However, in the next verse he makes it clear that he is not joyful because they met his need. He says, "I am not saying this because I am in need" (v. 11).

Paul was not rejoicing because they provided for him, but he rejoiced at the grace that God would give them because of their support and how it honored God. He later says this:

> I do not say this because I am seeking a gift. Rather, I seek the credit that abounds to your account. For I have received everything, and I have plenty. I have all I need because I received from Epaphroditus what you sent—a fragrant offering, an acceptable sacrifice, very pleasing to God.
> Philippians 4:17-18

The gifts they gave were an offering to God that would be rewarded. Therefore, Paul rejoices greatly in their giving because it brought glory to God, and it would lead to God's blessing. Similarly, this should be our mindset as well in the ministry of giving. It is something that we should rejoice greatly in as well, not only because it helps people, but because it brings glory to God. It's a sacrifice that honors God.

In fact, Paul taught this about giving: he said it must always be accompanied with joy in order for it even to be acceptable to God. Second Corinthians 9:7 says this: "Each one of you should give just as he has decided in his heart, not reluctantly or under compulsion, because God loves a cheerful giver."

Paul says if our giving is reluctant or under compulsion, "I must give because God told me so" or "I feel like I must," then we should not give. Giving to the ministry of the Lord is something that we should rejoice greatly in as Paul did. It's a ministry that brings honor to God.

Certainly, we see something of this great joy in Israel's building of the tabernacle. They were commanded to bring gold, silver, and special offerings to build the tabernacle, but eventually the people had to be "restrained" in their giving because they gave so much (Ex 36:6). When something is truly a joy, you typically have to practice some amount of wise restraint. However, we can never out give God (Mal 3:10). We must have great joy in our giving to the work of missions. Joyful giving is the only type of giving that is acceptable to God.

Application Question: What do you think about Paul's teaching on how reluctant giving or giving under compulsion is not acceptable to God (2 Cor 9:7)? Do you consistently experience great joy in your giving? Why or why not?

Our Giving to Missions Is Needed but Not Necessary

> I am not saying this because I am in need, for I have learned to be content in any circumstance. I have experienced times of need and times of abundance. In any and every circumstance I have learned the secret of contentment, whether I go satisfied or hungry, have plenty or nothing. I am able to do all things through the one who strengthens me.
> Philippians 4:11-13

Paul did not want the Philippians to think that he was rejoicing greatly at their gift because they met his need. He says, "I am not saying this because I am in need" (v.11). No, he wanted them to know that he had learned contentment in every circumstance whether in plenty or in want. The word "learned" means to learn by experience.[136] Paul had been shipwrecked, beaten, imprisoned, and he also experienced times of prosperity. No doubt, on some of his missionary journeys the churches would support him and take good care of him. Some churches were wealthy as seen with Laodicea (Rev 3:17). While with other churches, he lived in extreme poverty and under severe persecution. Some might think being content in poverty would be the hardest task; however, being content in wealth is even greater. It is often the extremely wealthy who are the most discontent in life and also tend to commit suicide the most.

Paul said he learned the "secret of being content" in any and every circumstance. The word "secret" can be translated "initiated into the secret." It was used of being initiated into a pagan religion and their inner secrets.[137] Paul said that he had been initiated into the secret of contentment that very few find.

Even though contentment is commanded of Christians, very few learn this discipline. First Timothy 6:6-8 says this: "Now godliness combined with contentment brings great profit. For we have brought nothing into this world and so we cannot take a single thing out either. But if we have food and shelter, we will be satisfied with that." Hebrews 13:5 says this: "Your conduct must be free from the love of money and you must be content with what you have, for he has said, 'I will never leave you and I will never abandon you.'"

The word "content" means to be self-sufficient. It was a word used by stoic philosophers who sought to avoid emotions and to learn indifference to things not under one's control. In ancient Greek the word was used of a city that provided for all its goods without any need for imports. [138] It was self-sufficient. However, Paul changed the word to mean essentially "Christ-sufficient." He could always be content because Christ would give him strength and meet all his needs.

Even though Scripture continually commands contentment, most Christians never learn this discipline. The media and the culture seek to bring discontentment in every way. We must look like this, dress like that, have this type of job, have that type of phone, this type of computer, etc. Most Christians run around like the world after every new gadget, every new thing that comes on the market. Because they are discontent, they, like everybody else, complain about their family, their in-laws, their job, their home, their car, their clothes, their church, etc. Most know nothing about contentment. How do we learn contentment? What was Paul's secret?

Observation Question: How could Paul be content in every situation?

He said the secret was that he could do all things through him who gives him strength (v. 13). "I am able to do" "means 'to be strong,' 'to have power,' or 'to have resources.'"[139] Paul was glad the Philippians provided for him, but he also knew that God would provide his resources in some way or another. Their offering was needed but not necessary because of the grace of God.

The word "through" can also be translated "in."[140] He could do all things "in" the one who strengthened him. In Paul's relationship to Christ, the one whom Paul counted everything rubbish to gain (cf. Phil 3:8), the one he was pressing to know and be like in every way (Phil 3:12), he found sufficiency for every task, difficulty, and need. We see these promises throughout the Scripture. Matthew 6:33 says, "But above all pursue his kingdom and righteousness, and all these things will be given to you as well."

Paul said that he wasn't speaking in regard to need because he had learned this truth in his life. God was always going to meet his needs as long as he was building God's kingdom. He knew that his relationship with the Lord was sufficient for the tasks God called him to accomplish. He had no need to beg or become anxious. God knew his needs and would provide for them in one way or another. Therefore, he could be content in his all-sufficient Lord.

Remember what Christ said to the disciples, "So then, don't worry saying, 'What will we eat?' or 'What will we drink?' or 'What will we wear?' For the unconverted pursue these things, and your heavenly Father knows that you need them" (Mat 6:31). We should be content because we know the faithfulness of our Father. He will always meet our needs.

Not only would God meet Paul's need, but Paul had learned by experience that when he was weak, God's power was the strongest in him. Second Corinthians 12:8 says this: "'My grace is enough for you, for my power is made perfect in weakness.' So then, I will boast most gladly about my weaknesses, so that the power of Christ may reside in me." When Paul was at the end of his resources, when he was weak, God's power was made perfect in his weakness. It was sufficient for him to persevere through severe trial or weakness. Paul learned this through experience, and this made him content. God would meet his needs by providing strength or material resources.

Now, this brings us back to our main point. God is winning the world to himself through the work of missions, and he will always provide for his ministers. He will meet their needs. The Psalmist said this: "I was once young, now I am old. I have never seen a godly man abandoned, or his children forced to search for food" (Psalm 37:25). The question is not, "Will God provide?" The question really is, "Will we get involved? Will we be one of the hands used as part of his provision?" Our giving is needed, but it is not necessary because God will provide for his people.

Paul knew that if the Philippians did not help, God was very capable of sending manna from heaven or ravens with meat every day. He could command a widow or Caesar himself to meet his needs. Or God could simply empower him to persevere. Whatever way, God was going to meet his needs, and he had learned contentment in Christ's sufficiency. Paul needed help, but if the Philippians didn't help, God would have provided in some other way. Remember what Mordecai said to Queen Esther in challenging her to help the Jews who were about to be exterminated by their enemies in Persia? He said this:

> If you keep quiet at this time, liberation and protection for the Jews will appear from another source, while you and your father's household perish. It may very well be that you have achieved royal status for such a time as this!"
> Esther 4:14

Mordecai knew that help and deliverance would come for God's people from some place. The question was whether Esther would be part of God's deliverance. Are you willing to be part of the process of God helping and delivering his ministers? Because Esther helped she was blessed. The book of Esther is about the salvation that came through her, even as the book of Philippians is in part a thanksgiving for the Philippians' faithful help. God honored them for their faithfulness.

Our help is needed but not necessary. God will provide for his ministers. This should be a great comfort to each believer who is seeking first the kingdom of God—God will meet their needs. They should also learn to be content as they wait on the Lord. "But those who wait for the Lord's help find renewed strength; they rise up as if they had eagles' wings, they run without growing weary, they walk without getting tired" (Is 40:31). But, it also should encourage us to get more involved with God's work. God will honor those who do.

Application Question: In what ways do you struggle with contentment? How is God calling you to learn sufficiency in him? What do you think about the concept of "our missions support is needed but not necessary"?

Our Giving to Missions Should Be Intentional

> Nevertheless, you did well to share with me in my trouble. And as you Philippians know, at the beginning of my gospel ministry, when I left Macedonia, no church shared with me in this matter of giving and receiving except you alone. For even in Thessalonica on more than one occasion you sent something for my need.
> Philippians 4:14-16

Another principle that we can take from Paul's final words to the Philippians is that our giving to missions should be "intentional." Consider how Paul describes their giving. He says, "Nevertheless, you did well to share with me in my trouble" (v. 14). "For even in Thessalonica on more than one occasion you sent something for my need" (v. 16). The Philippians continually met the needs of Paul. The circumstances and needs of Paul fueled and directed their giving.

John the apostle said this:

> But whoever has the world's possessions and sees his fellow Christian in need and shuts off his compassion against him, how can the love of God reside in such a person? Little children, let us not love with word or with tongue but in deed and truth.
> 1 John 3:17-18

John said that helping the needs of our brothers is an act that proves the love of God dwells in us—that we are truly saved (cf. 1 John 5:13). God saw the needs of the world, and he responded. The love of God swelled up in

310

generosity as God offered his Son. If God lives in us, we similarly should be drawn to meet the needs of others as well.

Certainly, we still have our regular giving to the church (cf. 1 Cor 16:1-2, 1 Tim 5:17), but we also should be prepared to help the urgent needs of others and especially those serving on the mission field. Ephesians 4:28 says, "The one who steals must steal no longer; rather he must labor, doing good with his own hands, so that he may have something to share with the one who has need." Paul essentially commands the Ephesians to prepare to share with those who had needs. When a need arises in the church or on the mission field, many Christians have nothing to give. Paul told the Ephesians to intentionally prepare to give to those who had needs. This seems to be beyond the regular support given to the church.

Are you preparing to give to those who are in need? Galatians 6:2 says, "Carry one another's burdens, and in this way you will fulfill the law of Christ." This is intentional giving—meeting the needs of others. What needs has God already placed around you that he is calling you to meet? Many times someone's need is God's signal for us to give or to get involved.

With that said, we also should diligently make sure that this ministry, organization, or person truly has a legitimate need. Our funds can be misused and at times further handicap people. Paul gave instructions to Timothy about how to care for widows in the church. He commanded him to make sure the widows were "truly in need," following God, and not living for pleasure (1 Tim 5:5-6). We also must make sure that our giving is best used to honor God, benefit his people, and his work.

Application Question: How do we prepare to be someone who carries others' burdens and meets the needs of others? How do we discern if a person or ministry is "really in need"? What does that discernment process look like?

Our Giving to Missions Is Honored by God

> I do not say this because I am seeking a gift. Rather, I seek the credit that abounds to your account. For I have received everything, and I have plenty. I have all I need because I received from Epaphroditus what you sent—a fragrant offering, an acceptable sacrifice, very pleasing to God. And my God will supply your every need according to his glorious riches in Christ Jesus. May glory be given to God our Father forever and ever. Amen.
> Philippians 4:17-20

Paul said that the gifts sent by the Philippians through Epaphroditus were honored by God. He describes the honor these gifts received in verses 17-20.

Observation Question: In what ways were the Philippians' gifts honored by God and how is this honor reflected in our giving?

1. Our gifts are honored by God through reward in heaven.

Again, Paul was not rejoicing because his need was met, but because the Philippians would receive credit to their account (v. 17). The word "credit" is business terminology. God was keeping a record of their gifts, and they would be rewarded for them. Christ said something similar to the rich man. He said, "go sell your possessions and give the money to the poor, and you will have treasure in heaven" (Matt 19:21). Our giving is recorded and rewarded in heaven. In addition, Christ taught us to not store up riches on earth, but to store them up in heaven (Matt 6:19). One of the ways we store our riches in heaven is by giving them to the Lord.

It has been said that everything we earn will one day be left on the earth when we die. However, what we give to the Lord will follow us to heaven. God honors our giving by crediting it to our account and rewarding us in heaven.

2. Our gifts are honored by God through becoming acceptable, sweet smelling sacrifices to him.

Paul said that the gifts the Philippians sent were a fragrant offering, an acceptable sacrifice, pleasing to God (v. 18). Maybe, the Philippians thought they were just giving to Paul; however, they were really giving to God. Through an angel, God said something similar to Cornelius about his giving. Listen to the account in the book of Acts:

> About three o'clock one afternoon he saw clearly in a vision an angel of God who came in and said to him, "Cornelius." Staring at him and becoming greatly afraid, Cornelius replied, "What is it, Lord?" The angel said to him, "Your prayers and your acts of charity have gone up as a memorial before God.
> Acts 10:3-4

In addition, Christ said this in his discourse with the righteous at his second coming in Matthew 25:

> Then the righteous will answer him, 'Lord, when did we see you hungry and feed you, or thirsty and give you something to drink? When did we see you a stranger and invite you in, or naked and clothe you? When did we see you sick or in prison and visit you?' And the king will answer them, 'I tell you the truth, just as you did it for one of the least of these brothers or sisters of mine, you did it for me.'

312

Matthew 25:37-40

Whatever we give, even to the least of Christ's brothers, is essentially given to God. They are sweet smelling sacrifices that bring pleasure to God. The writer of Hebrews said, "And do not neglect to do good and to share what you have, for God is pleased with such sacrifices" (Heb 13:16).

3. Our gifts are honored by God through reward on earth.

Paul said, "And my God will supply your every need according to his glorious riches in Christ Jesus" (4:19). He essentially says, "You met my need. Therefore, God will meet 'all' your needs." This means that not only would God meet their financial needs but also their emotional, physical, social, and spiritual needs. Everything that they gave would come back in abundance.

This truth is taught throughout Scripture. In Luke 6:38 Christ said, "Give, and it will be given to you: A good measure, pressed down, shaken together, running over, will be poured into your lap. For the measure you use will be the measure you receive." Christ said that God would abundantly give back to the giver.

Similarly, Paul said this to the Corinthians, "And God is able to make all grace overflow to you so that because you have enough of everything in every way at all times, you will overflow in every good work" (2 Corinthians 9:8). The promise for giving was that all grace would abound in the givers' lives. This grace would meet their needs at all times, and also they would abound in every good work. Giving would affect their ability to understand the Bible, to lead people to Christ, to disciple others, to be a good husband or wife, and to be a good parent or employee. Their faithful giving would open the door for abundant grace in every good work. Grace will overflow into the life of a giver. This then is the very reason many are in lack. They are not giving, and therefore, they find a lack of grace for every need or good work in their lives.

In addition, Paul says that God would meet their need "according to his glorious riches in Christ Jesus" (v. 19). It has often been noted that this text does not say "out of his riches." A rich man could donate a dollar out of his riches. But to give "according" to his riches means that he might give millions of dollars. That is in accordance with his riches and not simply out of them. God's supply for the giver is abundantly given according to his riches.

4. Our gifts are honored by God by bringing glory to the Father eternally.

Paul says in verse 20, "May glory be given to God our Father forever and ever." The word "glory" has to do with the "weight" of something. When we give, we demonstrate how much God really matters to us. We demonstrate something of what is intrinsic to his nature, his glory. When the early church

313

sold all they had and gave to the poor (Acts 2:45), it brought glory to God. It showed how much God really meant to them. It showed his importance in their lives. It's the same for us. As we faithfully and sacrificially give, we bring glory to God eternally through the gift. This is the ultimate honor we receive from God. We receive the honor of glorifying him. The Westminster Catechism says man's very purpose is "to glorify God and enjoy him forever."

Application Question: What stood out or challenged you most about the honor that God bestows upon us for giving?

Conclusion

What is the right perspective on giving to missions?

1. Our Giving to Missions Must Continually Be Renewed
2. Our Giving to Missions Should Be a Ministry of Great Joy
3. Our Giving to Missions Is Needed but Not Necessary
4. Our Giving to Missions Should Be Intentional
5. Our Giving to Missions Is Honored by God

Study Group Tips

Leading a small group using the Bible Teacher's Guide can be done in various ways. One format for leading a small group is the "study group" model, where each member prepares and shares in the teaching. This appendix will cover tips for facilitating a weekly study group.

1. Each week the members of the study group will read through a select chapter of the guide, answer the reflection questions (see Appendix 2), and come prepared to share in the group.

2. Prior to each meeting, a different member can be selected to lead the group and share Question 1 of the reflection questions, which is to give a short summary of the chapter read. This section of the gathering could last from five to fifteen minutes. This way, each member can develop their gift of teaching. It also will make them study harder during the week. Or, each week the same person could share the summary.

3. After the summary has been given, the leader for that week will facilitate discussions through the rest of the reflection questions and ask select review questions from the chapter.

4. After discussion, the group will share prayer requests and pray for one another.

The strength of the study group is that the members will be required to prepare their responses before the meeting, which will allow for easier discussion. In addition, each member will be given the opportunity to teach, which will further equip their ministry skills. The study group model has distinct advantages.

Reflection Questions

Writing is one of the best ways to learn. In class, we take notes and write papers, and all these methods are used to help us learn and retain the material. The same is true with the Word of God. Obviously, all of the authors of Scripture were writers. This helped them better learn the Scriptures and also enabled them to more effectively teach it. In studying God's Word with the Bible Teacher's Guide, take time to write so you can similarly grow both in your learning and teaching.

1. How would you summarize the main points of the text/chapter? Write a brief summary.

2. What stood out to you most in the reading? Did any of the contents trigger any memories or experiences? If so, please share them.

3. What follow–up questions did you have about the reading? What parts did you not fully agree with?

4. What applications did you take from the reading, and how do you plan to implement them into your life?

5. Write several commitment statements: As a result of my time studying God's Word, I will . . .

6. What are some practical ways to pray as a result of studying the text? Spend some time ministering to the Lord through prayer.

Walking the Romans Road

How can a person be saved? From what is he saved? How can someone have eternal life? Scripture teaches that after death each person will spend eternity either in heaven or hell. How can a person go to heaven?

Paul said this to Timothy:

> You, however, must continue in the things you have learned and are confident about. You know who taught you and how from infancy you have known the holy writings, which are able to give you wisdom for salvation through faith in Christ Jesus.
> 2 Timothy 3:14-15

One of the reasons God gave us Scripture is to make us wise for salvation. This means that without it nobody can know how to be saved.

Well then, how can a people be saved and what are they being saved from? A common method of sharing the good news of salvation is through the Romans Road. One of the great themes, not only of the Bible, but specifically of the book of Romans is salvation. In Romans, the author, Paul, clearly details the steps we must take in order to be saved.

How can we be saved? What steps must we take?

Step One: We Must Accept that We Are Sinners

Romans 3:23 says, "For all have sinned and fall short of the glory of God." What does it mean to sin? The word sin means "to miss the mark." The mark we missed is looking like God. When God created mankind in the Genesis narrative, he created man in the "image of God" (1:27). The "image of God" means many things, but probably, most importantly it means we were made to be holy just as he is holy. Man was made moral. We were meant to reflect God's holiness in every way: the way we think, the way we talk, and the way we act. And any time we miss the mark in these areas, we commit sin.

Furthermore, we do not only sin when we commit a sinful act such as: lying, stealing, or cheating. Again, we sin anytime we have a wrong heart motive. The greatest commandments in Scripture are to "Love the Lord your

319

God with all your heart and to love your neighbor as yourself" (Matt 22:36-40, paraphrase). Whenever we don't love God supremely and love others as ourselves, we sin and fall short of the glory of God. For this reason, man is always in a state of sinning. Sadly, even if our actions are good, our heart is bad. I have never loved God with my whole heart, mind, and soul and neither has anybody else. Therefore, we have all sinned and fall short of the glory of God (Rom 3:23). We have all missed the mark of God's holiness and we must accept this.

What's the next step?

Step Two: We Must Understand We Are Under the Judgment of God

Why are we under the judgment of God? It is because of our sins. Scripture teaches God is not only a loving God, but he is a just God. And his justice requires judgment for each of our sins. Romans 6:23 says, "For the payoff of sin is death."

A wage is something we earn. Every time we sin, we earn the wage of death. What is death? Death really means separation. In physical death, the body is separated from the spirit, but in spiritual death, man is separated from God. Man currently lives in a state of spiritual death (cf. Eph 2:1-3). We do not love God, obey him, or know him as we should. Therefore, man is in a state of death.

Moreover, one day at our physical death, if we have not been saved, we will spend eternity separated from God in a very real hell. In hell, we will pay the wage for each of our sins. Therefore, in hell people will experience various degrees of punishment (cf. Lk 12:47-48). This places man in a very dangerous predicament—unholy and therefore under the judgment of God.

How should we respond to this? This leads us to our third step.

Step Three: We Must Recognize God Has Invited All to Accept His Free Gift of Salvation

Romans 6:23 does not stop at the wages of sin being death. It says, "For the payoff of sin is death, but the gift of God is eternal life in Christ Jesus our Lord." Because God loved everybody on the earth, he offered the free gift of eternal life, which anyone can receive through Jesus Christ.

Because it is a gift, it cannot be earned. We cannot work for it. Ephesians 2:8-9 says, "For by grace you are saved through faith, and this is not from yourselves, it is the gift of God; it is not from works, so that no one can boast."

320

Going to church, being baptized, giving to the poor, or doing any other righteous work does not save. Salvation is a gift that must be received from God. It is a gift that has been prepared by his effort alone.

How do we receive this free gift?

Step Four: We Must Believe Jesus Christ Died for Our Sins and Rose from the Dead

If we are going to receive this free gift, we must believe in God's Son, Jesus Christ. Because God loved us, cared for us, and didn't want us to be separated from him eternally, he sent his Son to die for our sins. Romans 5:8 says, "But God demonstrates his own love for us, in that while we were still sinners, Christ died for us." Similarly, John 3:16 says, "For this is the way God loved the world: He gave his one and only Son, so that everyone who believes in him will not perish but have eternal life." God so loved us that he gave his only Son for our sins.

Jesus Christ was a real, historical person who lived 2,000 years ago. He was born of a virgin. He lived a perfect life. He was put to death by the Romans and the Jews. And he rose again on the third day. In his death, he took our sins and God's wrath for them and gave us his perfect righteousness so we could be accepted by God. Second Corinthians 5:21 says, "God made the one who did not know sin to be sin for us, so that in him we would become the righteousness of God." God did all this so we could be saved from his wrath.

Christ's death satisfied the just anger of God over our sins. When God saw Jesus on the cross, he saw us and our sins and therefore judged Jesus. And now, when God sees those who are saved, he sees his righteous Son and accepts us. In salvation, we have become the righteousness of God.

If we are going to be saved, if we are going to receive this free gift of salvation, we must believe in Christ's death, burial, and resurrection for our sins (cf. 1 Cor 15:3-5, Rom 10:9-10). Do you believe?

Step Five: We Must Confess Christ as Lord of Our Lives

Romans 10:9-10 says,

> Because if you confess with your mouth that Jesus is Lord and believe in your heart that God raised him from the dead, you will be saved. For with the heart one believes and thus has righteousness and with the mouth one confesses and thus has salvation.

Not only must we believe, but we must confess Christ as Lord of our lives. It is one thing to believe in Christ but another to follow Christ. Simple belief does not save. Christ must be our Lord. James said this: "...Even the demons believe that – and tremble with fear" (James 2:19), but the demons are not saved—Christ is not their Lord.

Another aspect of making Christ Lord is repentance. Repentance really means a change of mind that leads to a change of direction. Before we met Christ, we were living our own life and following our own sinful desires. But when we get saved, our mind and direction change. We start to follow Christ as Lord.

How do we make this commitment to the lordship of Christ so we can be saved? Paul said we must confess with our mouth "Jesus is Lord" as we believe in him. Romans 10:13 says, "For everyone who calls on the name of the Lord will be saved."

If you admit that you are a sinner and understand you are under God's wrath because of them; if you believe Jesus Christ is the Son of God, that he died on the cross for your sins, and rose from the dead for your salvation; if you are ready to turn from your sin and cling to Christ as Lord, you can be saved.

If this is your heart, then you can pray this prayer and commit to following Christ as your Lord.

> *Dear heavenly Father, I confess I am a sinner and have fallen short of your glory, what you made me for. I believe Jesus Christ died on the cross to pay the penalty for my sins and rose from the dead so I can have eternal life. I am turning away from my sin and accepting you as my Lord and Savior. Come into my life and change me. Thank you for your gift of salvation.*

Scripture teaches that if you truly accepted Christ as your Lord, then you are a new creation. Second Corinthians 5:17 says, "So then, if anyone is in Christ, he is a new creation; what is old has passed away – look, what is new has come!" God has forgiven your sins (1 John 1:9), he has given you his Holy Spirit (Rom 8:15), and he is going to disciple you and make you into the image of his Son (cf. Rom 8:29). He will never leave you nor forsake you (Heb 13:5), and he will complete the work he has begun in your life (Phil 1:6). In heaven, angels and saints are rejoicing because of your commitment to Christ (Lk 15:7).

Praise God for his great salvation! May God keep you in his hand, empower you through the Holy Spirit, train you through mature believers, and use you to build his kingdom! "He who calls you is trustworthy, and he will in fact do this" (1 Thess 5:24). God bless you!

About the Author

Greg Brown earned his MA in religion and MA in teaching from Trinity International University, a MRE from Liberty University, and a PhD in Theology from Louisiana Baptist University. He has served for over fourteen years in pastoral ministry, and currently serves as chaplain and professor at Handong Global University, teaching pastor at Handong International Congregation, and as a Navy Reserve chaplain.

Greg married his lovely wife, Tara Jayne, in 2006 and they have one daughter, Saiyah Grace. He enjoys going on dates with his wife, playing with his daughter, reading, writing, studying in coffee shops, working out, and following the NBA and UFC. His pursuit in life simply put is "to know God and to be found faithful by Him."

To connect with Greg, please follow at http://www.pgregbrown.com/

Coming Soon to the BTG Series

Praise the Lord for your interest in studying and teaching God's Word. If God has blessed you through the BTG series, please partner with us in petitioning God to greatly use this series to encourage and build his Church. Also, please consider leaving an Amazon review and signing up for free book promotions. By doing this, you help spread the "Word." Thanks for your partnership in the gospel from the first day until now (Phil 1:4-5).

Available:
First Peter
Theology Proper
Building Foundations for a Godly Marriage
Colossians
God's Battle Plan for Purity
Nehemiah
Philippians
The Perfections of God
The Armor of God
Ephesians
Abraham
Finding a Godly Mate
1 Timothy
The Beatitudes
Equipping Small Group Leaders
2 Timothy
Jacob

Coming Soon:
The Sermon on the Mount

Notes

[1] MacDonald, W. (1995). *Believer's Bible Commentary: Old and New Testaments*. (A. Farstad, Ed.) (p. 1957). Nashville: Thomas Nelson.
[2] MacDonald, W. (1995). *Believer's Bible Commentary: Old and New Testaments*. (A. Farstad, Ed.) (p. 1958). Nashville: Thomas Nelson.
[3] MacDonald, W. (1995). *Believer's Bible Commentary: Old and New Testaments*. (A. Farstad, Ed.) (p. 1957). Nashville: Thomas Nelson.
[4] MacArthur, John (2003-08-19). The MacArthur Bible Handbook (Kindle Location 9913). Thomas Nelson. Kindle Edition.
[5] MacDonald, W. (1995). *Believer's Bible Commentary: Old and New Testaments*. (A. Farstad, Ed.) (p. 1958). Nashville: Thomas Nelson.
[6] MacArthur, John (2003-08-19). The MacArthur Bible Handbook (Kindle Locations 9932-9934). Thomas Nelson. Kindle Edition.
[7] MacArthur, John (2003-08-19). The MacArthur Bible Handbook (Kindle Locations 9932-9934). Thomas Nelson. Kindle Edition.
[8] MacArthur, John (2003-08-19). The MacArthur Bible Handbook (Kindle Locations 9916-9921). Thomas Nelson. Kindle Edition.
[9] MacDonald, W. (1995). *Believer's Bible Commentary: Old and New Testaments*. (A. Farstad, Ed.) (p. 1957). Nashville: Thomas Nelson.
[10] Motyer, J. A. (1984). *The message of Philippians* (p. 15). Downers Grove, IL: InterVarsity Press.
[11] Martin, R. P. (1987). *Philippians: An Introduction and Commentary* (Vol. 11, p. 18). Downers Grove, IL: InterVarsity Press.
[12] MacArthur, John (2003-08-19). The MacArthur Bible Handbook (Kindle Locations 9938-9941). Thomas Nelson. Kindle Edition.
[13] Motyer, J. A. (1984). *The message of Philippians* (p. 15). Downers Grove, IL: InterVarsity Press.
[14] MacArthur, John (2003-08-19). The MacArthur Bible Handbook (Kindle Locations 9941-9944). Thomas Nelson. Kindle Edition.
[15] Motyer, J. A. (1984). *The message of Philippians* (p. 15). Downers Grove, IL: InterVarsity Press.
[16] MacArthur, John (2003-08-19). The MacArthur Bible Handbook (Kindle Locations 9941-9944). Thomas Nelson. Kindle Edition.

[17] Motyer, J. A. (1984). *The message of Philippians* (p. 15). Downers Grove, IL: InterVarsity Press.

[18] MacDonald, W. (1995). *Believer's Bible Commentary: Old and New Testaments.* (A. Farstad, Ed.) (p. 1957). Nashville: Thomas Nelson.

[19] Motyer, J. A. (1984). *The message of Philippians* (p. 21). Downers Grove, IL: InterVarsity Press.

[20] Wiersbe, W. W. (1996). *The Bible exposition commentary* (Vol. 2, p. 65). Wheaton, IL: Victor Books.

[21] Motyer, J. A. (1984). *The message of Philippians* (p. 55). Downers Grove, IL: InterVarsity Press.

[22] Hendriksen, W., & Kistemaker, S. J. (1953–2001). *Exposition of Philippians* (Vol. 5, p. 60). Grand Rapids: Baker Book House.

[23] MacArthur, J. F., Jr. (2001). *Philippians* (p. 47). Chicago: Moody Press.

[24] Hughes, R. K. (2007). *Philippians: the fellowship of the gospel* (p. 43). Wheaton, IL: Crossway Books.

[25] MacArthur, J. F., Jr. (2001). *Philippians* (pp. 49–50). Chicago: Moody Press.

[26] MacArthur, J. F., Jr. (2001). *Philippians* (p. 51). Chicago: Moody Press.

[27] MacArthur, J. F., Jr. (2001). *Philippians* (p. 53). Chicago: Moody Press.

[28] Hughes, R. K. (2007). *Philippians: the fellowship of the gospel* (p. 44). Wheaton, IL: Crossway Books.

[29] Wiersbe, W. W. (1996). *The Bible exposition commentary* (Vol. 2, p. 67). Wheaton, IL: Victor Books.

[30] MacArthur, J. F., Jr. (2001). *Philippians* (p. 61). Chicago: Moody Press.

[31] Teacher's Outline and Study Bible - Commentary - Teacher's Outline and Study Bible – Philippians: The Teacher's Outline and Study Bible.

[32] MacArthur, J. F., Jr. (2001). *Philippians* (pp. 59–60). Chicago: Moody Press.

[33] Accessed 7/1/15 http://www.christianpost.com/news/pastor-rick-warren-shares-story-of-fathers-final-dying-words-reach-one-more-for-jesus-126720/

[34] Hughes, R. K. (2007). *Philippians: the fellowship of the gospel* (pp. 51–52). Wheaton, IL: Crossway Books.

[35] Wiersbe, W. W. (1996). *The Bible exposition commentary* (Vol. 2, p. 70). Wheaton, IL: Victor Books.

[36] Motyer, J. A. (1984). *The message of Philippians* (p. 85). Downers Grove, IL: InterVarsity Press.

[37] Motyer, J. A. (1984). *The message of Philippians* (pp. 85–86). Downers Grove, IL: InterVarsity Press.

[38] Motyer, J. A. (1984). *The message of Philippians* (p. 86). Downers Grove, IL: InterVarsity Press.

[39] Barclay, W. (2003). *The Letters to Philippians, Colossians, and Thessalonians* (3rd ed. fully rev. and updated., p. 31). Louisville, KY; London: Westminster John Knox Press.

[40] Wiersbe, W. W. (1996). *The Bible exposition commentary* (Vol. 2, p. 67). Wheaton, IL: Victor Books.

[41] MacArthur, J. F., Jr. (1986). *Ephesians* (p. 119). Chicago: Moody Press.

[42] MacArthur, J. F., Jr. (2001). *Philippians* (p. 84). Chicago: Moody Press.

[43] The Teacher's Outline and Study Bible – Philippians

[44] MacArthur, J. F., Jr. (2001). *Philippians* (p. 91). Chicago: Moody Press.

[45] Hughes, R. K. (2007). *Philippians: the fellowship of the gospel* (p. 68). Wheaton, IL: Crossway Books.

[46] Hughes, R. K. (2007). *Philippians: the fellowship of the gospel* (p. 69). Wheaton, IL: Crossway Books.

[47] Hughes, R. K. (2007). *Philippians: the fellowship of the gospel* (p. 70). Wheaton, IL: Crossway Books.

[48] *The Letters to the Philippians, Colossians, and Thessalonians*. Rev. ed., [Louisville, Ky.: Westminster, 1975], 31

[49] MacArthur, J. F., Jr. (2001). *Philippians* (p. 104). Chicago: Moody Press.

[50] Vine, W. E., Unger, M. F., & White, W., Jr. (1996). *Vine's Complete Expository Dictionary of Old and New Testament Words*. Nashville, TN: T. Nelson.

[51] MacArthur, J. F., Jr. (2001). *Philippians* (p. 106). Chicago: Moody Press.

[52] MacArthur, J. F., Jr. (2001). *Philippians* (p. 108). Chicago: Moody Press.

[53] Hughes, R. K. (2007). *Philippians: the fellowship of the gospel* (p. 76). Wheaton, IL: Crossway Books.

[54] MacArthur, J. F., Jr. (2001). *Philippians* (p. 110). Chicago: Moody Press.

[55] MacArthur, J. F., Jr. (2001). *Philippians* (p. 110). Chicago: Moody Press.

[56] MacArthur, J. F., Jr. (2001). *Philippians* (p. 110). Chicago: Moody Press.

[57] MacArthur, J. F., Jr. (2001). *Philippians* (p. 111). Chicago: Moody Press.

[58] MacArthur, J. F., Jr. (2001). *Philippians* (p. 112). Chicago: Moody Press.

[59] MacArthur, J. F., Jr. (2001). *Philippians* (p. 113). Chicago: Moody Press.

[60] Barclay, W. (2003). *The Letters to Philippians, Colossians, and Thessalonians* (3rd ed. fully rev. and updated., p. 42). Louisville, KY; London: Westminster John Knox Press.

[61] MacArthur, J. F., Jr. (2001). *Philippians* (p. 129). Chicago: Moody Press.

[62] Barclay, W. (2003). *The Letters to Philippians, Colossians, and Thessalonians* (3rd ed. fully rev. and updated., p. 42). Louisville, KY; London: Westminster John Knox Press.

[63] Wiersbe, W. W. (1996). *The Bible exposition commentary* (Vol. 2, p. 75). Wheaton, IL: Victor Books.

[64] MacArthur, J. F., Jr. (2001). *Philippians* (p. 129). Chicago: Moody Press.

[65] MacArthur, J. F., Jr. (2001). *Philippians* (p. 161). Chicago: Moody Press.

[66] MacArthur, J. F., Jr. (2004). *1 Peter* (p. 100). Chicago: Moody Publishers.

[67] MacArthur, J. F., Jr. (2001). *Philippians* (p. 161). Chicago: Moody Press.

[68] MacArthur, J. F., Jr. (2001). *Philippians* (p. 160). Chicago: Moody Press.

[69] MacArthur, J. F., Jr. (2001). *Philippians* (p. 172). Chicago: Moody Press.

[70] Hughes, R. K. (2007). *Philippians: the fellowship of the gospel* (p. 99). Wheaton, IL: Crossway Books.

[71] Barclay, W. (2003). *The Letters to Philippians, Colossians, and Thessalonians* (3rd ed. fully rev. and updated., p. 51). Louisville, KY; London: Westminster John Knox Press.

[72] MacArthur, J. F., Jr. (2001). *Philippians* (p. 180). Chicago: Moody Press.

[73] MacArthur, J. F., Jr. (2001). *Philippians* (p. 182). Chicago: Moody Press.

[74] Teacher's Outline and Study Bible - Commentary - Teacher's Outline and Study Bible – Philippians: The Teacher's Outline and Study Bible.

[75] MacArthur, J. F., Jr. (2001). *Philippians* (p. 202). Chicago: Moody Press.

[76] Hughes, R. K. (2007). *Philippians: the fellowship of the gospel* (p. 113). Wheaton, IL: Crossway Books.

[77] MacArthur, J. F., Jr. (2001). *Philippians* (p. 197). Chicago: Moody Press.

[78] MacArthur, J. F., Jr. (2001). *Philippians* (p. 198). Chicago: Moody Press.

[79] Wiersbe, W. W. (1996). *The Bible exposition commentary* (Vol. 2, pp. 81–82). Wheaton, IL: Victor Books.

[80] Hughes, R. K. (2007). *Philippians: the fellowship of the gospel* (p. 108). Wheaton, IL: Crossway Books.

[81] Hughes, R. K. (2007). *Philippians: the fellowship of the gospel* (p. 109). Wheaton, IL: Crossway Books.

[82] Wiersbe, W. W. (1996). *The Bible exposition commentary* (Vol. 2, p. 82). Wheaton, IL: Victor Books.

[83] Teacher's Outline and Study Bible - Commentary - Teacher's Outline and Study Bible – Philippians: The Teacher's Outline and Study Bible.

[84] MacArthur, J. F., Jr. (2001). *Philippians* (p. 207). Chicago: Moody Press.

[85] MacArthur, J. F., Jr. (2001). *Philippians* (p. 206). Chicago: Moody Press.

[86] MacArthur, J. F., Jr. (2001). *Philippians* (p. 215). Chicago: Moody Press.

[87] MacArthur, J. F., Jr. (2001). *Philippians* (p. 217). Chicago: Moody Press.

[88] MacArthur, J. F., Jr. (2001). *Philippians* (p. 221). Chicago: Moody Press.

[89] MacArthur, J. F., Jr. (2001). *Philippians* (p. 222). Chicago: Moody Press.

[90] MacArthur, J. F., Jr. (2001). *Philippians* (p. 223). Chicago: Moody Press.

[91] MacArthur, J. F., Jr. (2001). *Philippians* (p. 226). Chicago: Moody Press.

[92] MacArthur, J. F., Jr. (2001). *Philippians* (p. 228). Chicago: Moody Press.

[93] Teacher's Outline and Study Bible - Commentary - Teacher's Outline and Study Bible – Philippians: The Teacher's Outline and Study Bible.

[94] Hughes, R. K. (2007). *Philippians: the fellowship of the gospel* (p. 131). Wheaton, IL: Crossway Books.

[95] Hughes, R. K. (2007). *Philippians: the fellowship of the gospel* (p. 131). Wheaton, IL: Crossway Books.

[96] MacArthur, J. F., Jr. (2001). *Philippians* (p. 240). Chicago: Moody Press.

[97] MacArthur, J. F., Jr. (2001). *Philippians* (p. 240). Chicago: Moody Press.

[98] MacArthur, J. F., Jr. (2001). *Philippians* (p. 245). Chicago: Moody Press.

[99] Hughes, R. K. (2007). *Philippians: the fellowship of the gospel* (p. 146). Wheaton, IL: Crossway Books.

[100] MacArthur, J. F., Jr. (2001). *Philippians* (p. 246). Chicago: Moody Press.

[101] Wiersbe, W. W. (1996). *The Bible exposition commentary* (Vol. 2, p. 90). Wheaton, IL: Victor Books.

[102] MacArthur, J. F., Jr. (2001). *Philippians* (p. 247). Chicago: Moody Press.

[103] MacArthur, J. F., Jr. (2001). *Philippians* (pp. 254–255). Chicago: Moody Press.

[104] MacArthur, J. F., Jr. (2001). *Philippians* (p. 255). Chicago: Moody Press.

[105] MacArthur, J. F., Jr. (2001). *Philippians* (p. 255). Chicago: Moody Press.

[106] MacArthur, J. F., Jr. (2001). *Philippians* (p. 257). Chicago: Moody Press.

[107] MacArthur, J. F., Jr. (2001). *Philippians* (p. 257). Chicago: Moody Press.

[108] Wiersbe, W. W. (1996). *The Bible exposition commentary* (Vol. 2, p. 93). Wheaton, IL: Victor Books.

[109] MacDonald, W. (1995). *Believer's Bible Commentary: Old and New Testaments*. (A. Farstad, Ed.) (p. 1976). Nashville: Thomas Nelson.

[110] MacArthur, J. F., Jr. (2001). *Philippians* (pp. 260–261). Chicago: Moody Press.

[111] MacDonald, W. (1995). *Believer's Bible Commentary: Old and New Testaments*. (A. Farstad, Ed.) (p. 1977). Nashville: Thomas Nelson.

[112] Teacher's Outline and Study Bible - Commentary - Teacher's Outline and Study Bible – Philippians: The Teacher's Outline and Study Bible.

[113] Wiersbe, W. W. (1996). *The Bible exposition commentary* (Vol. 2, p. 94). Wheaton, IL: Victor Books.

[114] Teacher's Outline and Study Bible - Commentary - Teacher's Outline and Study Bible – Philippians: The Teacher's Outline and Study Bible.

[115] Hughes, R. K. (2007). *Philippians: the fellowship of the gospel* (p. 163). Wheaton, IL: Crossway Books.

[116] Hughes, R. K. (2007). *Philippians: the fellowship of the gospel* (p. 164). Wheaton, IL: Crossway Books.

[117] MacArthur, J. F., Jr. (2001). *Philippians* (p. 271). Chicago: Moody Press.

[118] MacArthur, J. F., Jr. (2001). *Philippians* (p. 271). Chicago: Moody Press.

[119] MacArthur, J. F., Jr. (2001). *Philippians* (p. 272). Chicago: Moody Press.

[120] Teacher's Outline and Study Bible - Commentary - Teacher's Outline and Study Bible – Philippians: The Teacher's Outline and Study Bible.

[121] MacArthur, J. F., Jr. (2001). *Philippians* (p. 276). Chicago: Moody Press.

[122] MacArthur, J. F., Jr. (2001). *Philippians* (p. 276). Chicago: Moody Press.

[123] Teacher's Outline and Study Bible - Commentary - Teacher's Outline and Study Bible – Philippians: The Teacher's Outline and Study Bible.

[124] Hughes, R. K. (2007). *Philippians: the fellowship of the gospel* (p. 168). Wheaton, IL: Crossway Books.

[125] http://biblehub.com/greek/3309.htm

[126] Teacher's Outline and Study Bible - Commentary - Teacher's Outline and Study Bible – Philippians: The Teacher's Outline and Study Bible.

[127] Wiersbe, W. W. (1996). *The Bible exposition commentary* (Vol. 2, pp. 94–95). Wheaton, IL: Victor Books.

[128] MacArthur, J. F., Jr. (2001). *Philippians* (p. 284). Chicago: Moody Press.

[129] MacArthur, J. F., Jr. (2001). *Philippians* (pp. 284–285). Chicago: Moody Press.

[130] MacArthur, J. F., Jr. (2001). *Philippians* (pp. 284–285). Chicago: Moody Press.

[131] Hughes, R. K. (2007). *Philippians: the fellowship of the gospel* (p. 177). Wheaton, IL: Crossway Books.

[132] MacArthur, J. F., Jr. (2001). *Philippians* (pp. 289–290). Chicago: Moody Press.

[133] MacArthur, J. F., Jr. (2001). *Philippians* (p. 291). Chicago: Moody Press.

[134] Wiersbe, W. W. (1996). *The Bible exposition commentary* (Vol. 2, p. 98). Wheaton, IL: Victor Books.

[135] MacArthur, J. F., Jr. (2001). *Philippians* (pp. 297–298). Chicago: Moody Press.

[136] Wiersbe, W. W. (1996). *The Bible exposition commentary* (Vol. 2, p. 97). Wheaton, IL: Victor Books.

[137] Wiersbe, W. W. (1996). *The Bible exposition commentary* (Vol. 2, pp. 97–98). Wheaton, IL: Victor Books.

[138] Hughes, R. K. (2007). *Philippians: the fellowship of the gospel* (p. 186). Wheaton, IL: Crossway Books.

[139] MacArthur, J. F., Jr. (2001). *Philippians* (p. 303). Chicago: Moody Press.

[140] Hughes, R. K. (2007). *Philippians: the fellowship of the gospel* (p. 186). Wheaton, IL: Crossway Books.

www.ingramcontent.com/pod-product-compliance
Lightning Source LLC
Chambersburg PA
CBHW072338090426
42741CB00012B/2829